Mrs Thatcher's Casebook

Mrs. Thatcher's Casebook

non-partisan studies in Conservative policy in the Eighties

Terry Garrison

**Reader in Business at
Buckinghamshire College of Higher Education**

Published in the UK by Elm Publications,
Seaton House, Kings Ripton, Cambs PE17 2NJ.

Printed in Great Britain by
St Edmundsbury Press, Bury St Edmunds, Suffolk

 British Library Cataloguing in Publication Data

Garrison, Terry
  Mrs Thatcher's casebook.
  1. Policy sciences   2. Great Britain ——
  Politics and government —— 1979-
  I. Title
  354.4107'2   JN318

  ISBN 0-946139-86-5
  ISBN 0-946139-41-5 Spiral

CONTENTS

Introduction

To my sons,
Alistair and Christopher

INTRODUCTION

This is a book about the 'how' and 'why' of power politics in Britain in the '80s.

It was not designed as a text about Mrs. Thatcher personally, as Conservative Prime Minister or party leader, or about the nature of her Government's management of the nation or about the range and viability of the often radical policies pursued by them, reviled or admired according to one's political persuasion. Taken collectively, however, the case studies in *Mrs. Thatcher's Casebook* do shed a considerable, but not of course exhaustive, light on Conservative Government thinking on matters economic, social and industrial during this period. They also reveal, very starkly, the changes that were taking place in the nationalised industry sector as it reacted to the imposition of a previously inexperienced financial discipline.

The book is, in fact, intended as a record of some of the biggest, most controversial and intractable problems that confronted the two administrations led by Mrs. Thatcher over the period 1981-6. Here are problems — strategic, tactical and administrative. National and international. Simple and complex. Problems arising from the Conservatives' own policies and inescapable dilemmas thrown up by the outside world. Here are GCHQ, De Lorean, British Leyland, the Falklands War . . .

Presented as case studies rather than case histories, these problems invite analysis by the reader without any 'leading' by or bias from the author. Sufficient detail is given to bring the problems vividly to life and allow perceptive judgement on cause and effect, the soundness of the power-plays made by involved parties and the plausibility of the rationales they advance for their actions.

Many people have helped in the creation of this case book, particularly successive groups of Public Policy students at Slough College and my erstwhile colleagues, Roger Martin-Fagg, Jack Moore and Brian Watts. To them I owe much.

To my wife, Ann, and my sons, Christopher (proof reader extraordinaire) and Alistair, my thanks not only for invaluable aid but also for immeasurable fortitude and forbearance.

Terry Garrison.

A BASIC FRAMEWORK FOR
PUBLIC POLICY STUDIES

The study of U.K. public policy in the 1980's provides the student with an exceptionally rich field for exploration. Highly significant new forces were at work shaping the ways in which decisions were being taken in this sector (*policy-making processes*) and the means-end relationships involved in the decisions and ensuing actions themselves (*policies*).

The impact of such new forces threw into more prominent relief than previously the paradoxical position of public utilities (coal, gas, electricity, transport) and state-owned manufacturing corporations (steel, cars, shipbuilding) as:

(a) actual (or potential) profit earners subject to the canons of economic productivity and

(b) real-life examples of the degree of application to the work-place of such ideological tenets as 'full employment', 'industrial democracy' and 'social justice' and

(c) strategic buttresses supporting the remainder of U.K. manufacturing industry, which was predominantly in private ownership (pharmaceuticals, engineering, computing, etc.).

With a dogmatic Conservative Government firmly holding the reins of power, it was a time of novel difficulties. These included privatisation moves, high control of industry financing and a 'backdoor' public industry pay policy through the simultaneous application of free collective bargaining and the establishment of pay increase 'norms' for managers and unionised workforces in nationalised industry.

Whereas previous Administrations had accepted nationalised industry as the bedrock of U.K. industry and 'the commanding heights of the economy', the Conservative Government which came to power in 1979 was enamoured neither of the concept of public ownership *per se* nor of the results of its *modus operandi*. It differed from its forbears in its limited tolerance of a 'middle of the road' political ideology and especially disliked for example:

■ The degree of oligopolistic bargaining power which public industry unions had acquired, partly as a result of past governmental full-employment stances and partly because of what it

FIG.1   THE EXTENT OF ORGANISATIONAL INTERDEPENDENCE

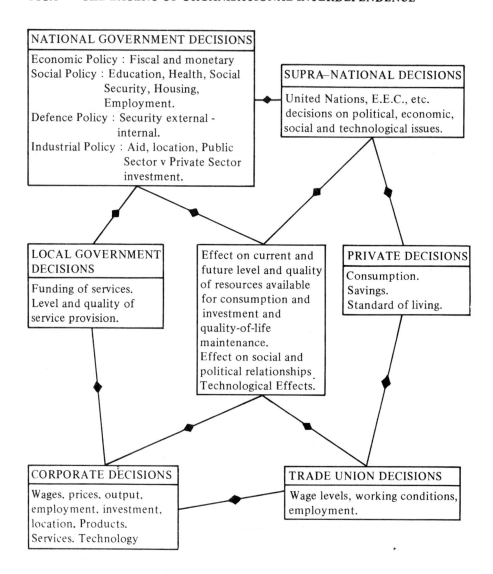

NATIONAL GOVERNMENT DECISIONS
Economic Policy : Fiscal and monetary
Social Policy : Education, Health, Social
              Security, Housing,
              Employment.
Defence Policy : Security external -
              internal.
Industrial Policy : Aid, location, Public
              Sector v Private Sector
              investment.

SUPRA–NATIONAL DECISIONS
United Nations, E.E.C., etc.
decisions on political, economic,
social and technological issues.

LOCAL GOVERNMENT DECISIONS
Funding of services.
Level and quality of
service provision.

Effect on current and
future level and quality
of resources available
for consumption and
investment and
quality-of-life
maintenance.
Effect on social and
political relationships.
Technological Effects.

PRIVATE DECISIONS
Consumption.
Savings.
Standard of living.

CORPORATE DECISIONS
Wages, prices, output,
employment, investment,
location, Products.
Services. Technology

TRADE UNION DECISIONS
Wage levels, working conditions,
employment.

2

saw as the inability of governments to fully 'stand up' to the Trade Unions.

This power and its knock-on effects were seen by Government Ministers to have been a major promoter of cost-push inflation and as an inhibitor of changes in the resource-allocation patterns which were deemed to be necessary for our future competitive capabilities as a trading nation.

- The extent to which some state industries were obliged to borrow (to make up for revenue deficits and for capital expenditure) rather than being able to rely on internal generation of funds. This was attributed by Ministers to inadequate economic productivity, the absence of an appropriate sense of financial discipline, excessive labour costs and lack of managerial control.

- The scale to which the financial demands of some nationalised industries represented not only an economic burden, which forced the Government's hand on its fiscal (direct and indirect taxation, excise duties) and monetary (interest rate, control of the money supply, Public Sector Borrowing Requirement) policies. But also, given the Cabinet's doctrinal attitude to the superiority of private as opposed to public ownership, as a major political nuisance.

- The perceived power imbalance between management and unions, on the one hand, and between owners (the Government and taxpayers) and state industry employees, on the other. In particular, they saw the Trade Unions as having exceeded their 'proper' role and as having acquired the form and status of a political 'Workplace Party', whilst avoiding full acceptance of the criteria of manifest democracy in their internal workings.

The ideological pressures produced by the Conservatives' commitment to their 'value-for-money' model also led to turmoil in Local Government. Several notable 'Town Hall Revolts' resulted from the unremitting application of a consistent financial strategy aimed at restricting Local Authorities' capacity to levy rates and spend income. The legislation making up this strategy symbolised the Government's drive to achieve its primary aim, the curbing of the growth in public expenditure. Nor were directly-administered services such as the DHSS and

NHS isolated from the Government's economy-efficiency-effectiveness thrust. 'Managerialism' became the new watchword in these departments.

Significantly, the key purpose of the Government appeared to be a restoration of the personal economic freedom of the citizen on the grounds that:

(1) the post-war blend of cradle-to-grave Welfare State provision (Education, Health, Social Security, Personal Social Services) plus the doctrinaire industrial interventionism/'lame duck' approach of previous governments had sapped the individual's sense of personal responsibility for his own destiny and

(2) only through the renaissance of such an individual competitive spirit could the collectivised, economic decadence-tolerating mood of the nation be altered and a new sense of realism be created and

(3) only this new 'sense of realism' could engender the entrepreneurial momentum necessary to move the U.K. towards some new technology-intensive *sunrise* industries and away from some outdated, labour-intensive *smoke-stack* industries.

A harsher wind was blowing on managers and trade unionists. It had a cutting edge. Out had gone the fundamental political commitment to full employment which had made it easier for unions to press for higher wages. In had come the new discipline of Monetarism and the profitability ethic. Whereas, under the previous Socialist Government, it had been a breeze, now it was a culture-shock gale. Vanished also the degree of permissiveness and liberalism that had guided Central Government's past relationships with Local Government and other agencies. Now members and officers alike had to square up to an apparently inexorable trend towards tighter and more visible centralist control.

The public policy case studies in this book have been chosen to give a graphic and factual picture of life in the public sector during the 1980's and, in particular, of the Conservative Government's approach to some of the key policy issues.

This section aims at developing a greater understanding of some of the ways and means in which underlying policy issues may be investigated.

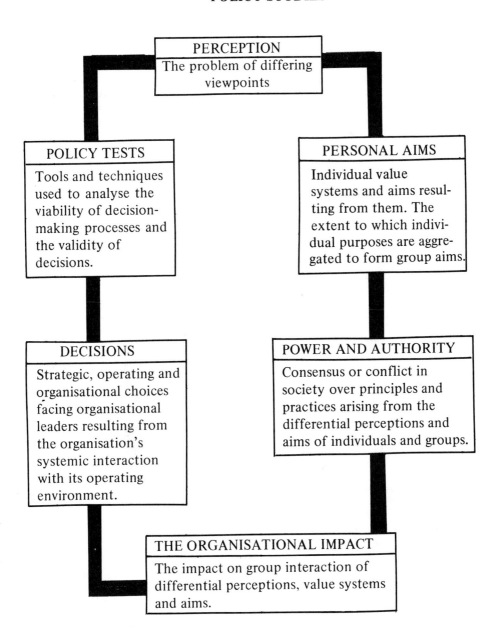

FIG.2 :   **A BASIC FRAMEWORK FOR PUBLIC POLICY STUDIES**

PERCEPTION
The problem of differing viewpoints

POLICY TESTS
Tools and techniques used to analyse the viability of decision-making processes and the validity of decisions.

PERSONAL AIMS
Individual value systems and aims resulting from them. The extent to which individual purposes are aggregated to form group aims.

DECISIONS
Strategic, operating and organisational choices facing organisational leaders resulting from the organisation's systemic interaction with its operating environment.

POWER AND AUTHORITY
Consensus or conflict in society over principles and practices arising from the differential perceptions and aims of individuals and groups.

THE ORGANISATIONAL IMPACT
The impact on group interaction of differential perceptions, value systems and aims.

FIG. 3:   KEY ELEMENTS IN THE LEGISLATIVE FRAMEWORK

MAIN TYPES OF BILLS

Public Bills affect the whole of the nation and stem mostly from the Party's electoral programme (manifesto), immediate crises (emergency legislation), the administrative needs of Government departments or from the findings of official inquiries eg. Select Committees, Royal Commissions, etc. Some Bills eg. Finance (tax gathering) and Consolidated Fund (spending) have to be introduced every session.

Private Bills affect only a section of the community. They can be promoted by the Central or Local Government or a private Member of Parliament.

DEBATES

1) The Monarch's Speech. This is given at the start of each Parliamentary session and contains the Government's legislative programme for the session. Followed by 5-6 days of debate.

2) General Debates: 15 or so days in a normal session are given over to general debate on Government-chosen topics. Some 26 days is set aside for topics selected by the Opposition.

3) Censure Motions

4) Standing Order No. 9. Motions proposed after Question Time, having the Speaker's agreement and the support of 40 members, are allowed. Topics must be specific, important and urgent.

5) Adjournment Debates. The basis for this daily debate is the historic principle that the House should not rise without debating outstanding grievances. Speakers are chosen partly by ballot and partly by the Speaker. It often provides a means of querying Governmental policy more effectively than is possible at Question Time.

6) Debates on Select Committee Reports eg. Public Accounts, Expenditure, Nationalised Industries.

HANDLING BILLS

1) Drafting by Parliamentary Counsel in the light of Government requirements. Examination of Bills by Cabinet Committee, Government Departments, etc.

2) First Reading: Introduction of the title of the Bill in the Commons.

3) Printing.

4) Debate on the Second Reading taken on the floor of the house or in a Standing Committee. Allows discussion of the principles of the Bill.

5) Committee Stage. The Bill is considered clause-by-clause by a Committee of MPs.

6) Report Stage. The amendments made in Committee are considered and sometimes adopted.

7) Third Reading. Another debate. Passage to the Lords for a repetition of the procedure (or, if the Bill has been introduced first in the Lords, to the Commons).

8) Royal Assent given either by the the Monarch or the Lords Commissioners.

9) Statutory Instruments issued as part of the Act.

STATEMENTS OF INTEREST

Discussion Document – what do you think?

Green Paper – what do you think about what we think?

White Paper – what do you think of what we intend to do?

Legislation – please do what we want you to do. It's the law.

FIG. 4: KEY ELEMENTS IN PUBLIC AGENCIES' POLICY FORMULATION

GOVERNMENT'S MACRO-POLICY FRAMEWORK?

The Government's authoritative framework of economic, social, industrial and security policies. These are based on the legacy of the past, ideological drive, reality perception, risk-return attitudes, Parliamentary Majority and length of term to run.

AGENCY'S APPRECIATION OF ITS CURRENT/POTENTIAL POSITION?

Based on analysis of power play within Government and between Government Departments and the Agency. Consideration of strengths and weaknesses relative to threats and opportunities in the operating environment. Evaluation of resource base, performance levels, constraints. Effect of micro-political dissensus within the Agency itself.

EXTERNAL ENVIRONMENTAL CHANGE?

Political, legal, economic social and technological change - national and international - affecting the Agency's actual and potential performance.

ATTITUDE TO PERFORMANCE?

Cabinet, Government, Opposition, Civil Service, consumers, Management, workforce, unions, media the voting public.

ADEQUACY OF PERFORMANCE?

Politically, financially/economically (R.O.C.E.), socially (welfare), technologically. Based on the viability of decisions with explicit recognition of risks. Based on expertise in the Agency's policy formulation and execution system: planning, budgeting, execution and control.

GOVERNMENT DEPARTMENT'S MICRO-POLICY APPROACH?

Technocracy/Ideology-based action guidelines for the Agency. Involve Acts of Parliament, general guidelines, a plan approval system, etc. Specified level of Governmental intervention, operating constraints e.g. finance.

AGENCY AND MANAGEMENT'S APPROACH IN THE LIGHT OF DEPARTMENTAL MICRO-POLICY?

Changes in long-term aims and strategy; operating tactics; management style; organisation structure. Resource acquisition and deployment. Conflicts between Agency and Department. Conflicts over execution of Departmental guidelines. Search for efficiency and effectiveness in task execution.

Note: "Agency" is taken to mean all organisations charged legislatively with executing Government policy, e.g. Local Government, Nationalised Industry, etc.

EYES, EARS AND MENTAL SETS

To understand how policies - organisational decisions about appropriate courses of action to achieve desired results - are determined, it is vital to grasp two elementary (but all-too-easily disregarded) notions:

(1) All decisions are man-made. There is nowhere in existence a physical mechanism which 'decides'. When we speak of Government policy (say, on immigration), we mean that the leaders of Government have proposed, and gained acceptance from their followers for, a certain line of action.

(2) All decisions are based on a mixture of logic (cold rationalisation) and emotion. We do not, as members of organisations charged with decision-making, divest ourselves of our hopes, fears, loves, hates, aspirations and disinclinations, when we carry out our tasks. Our pessimism/optimism, risk-seeking/risk-aversion attitudes are rooted in our feelings as well as in our reasoning.

The study of past decisions (as a student) and involvement in current ones (either as a policy adviser or a member of a decision-making team) inevitably involves a comprehension of what makes us 'tick' and not just some algorithmic (machine-like) system called 'policy determination'. We are inescapably concerned with:

(a) how organisational members view their relationships with their colleagues (superiors and subordinates) and the relationship between their organisation and the world to which it relates and

(b) what they wish and seek to achieve for themselves personally and for the organisation as a network of human beings with - to a certain extent - shared interests and concerns and a common focus.

Perception is the term given to the manner in which we, through our sense organs and our minds, interpret the physical and social environment in which we find ourselves. Our decisions and actions proceed from the process of this interpretation and the results of it.

On some matters, say physical laws - like the temperatures at which, and conditions under which, we know water freezes - there are only a few possible interpretations. Provided of course that, in this example, we are all familiar with the current concepts of freezing, water pressure and can accept the validity of empirical demonstration and scientific truths. On other matters, such as economic 'laws', moral 'codes', social 'conventions', there are enormous variations in our perceptions, depending on such factors as education, age, wealth-status, culture and so on. Consider, for instance, the different personal views which exist on such propositions - accepted by some as 'facts of life' - as:

- "Pay rises, unaccompanied by productivity improvements, are the main engine for inflation"

- "The State has a comprehensive duty of care towards the unemployed since unemployment is not a product of personal failing on their part"

- "The use of nuclear weapons is immoral and their use, from UK bases, is intolerable"

It is noteworthy, that none of these is an objective, provable scientific truth, however strongly protagonists may try to argue its validity. We are dealing with 'social facts', normative statements, 'oughts' and 'shoulds' rather than 'is' and 'are'.

The reasons for our particular, individualised viewpoints - which we would like to feel give us a true picture of the world and which are *not* seen by us as biases, prejudices and preconceptions - are, clearly, the product of our own knowledge and experience of life. But, whilst we may be all different, there seems to be a significant pressure on us for group thought-conformity, induced, perhaps through the pleasure derived from belonging to a group or the psychological anxiety produced by non-acceptance by, or alienation from, groups to which one wishes to belong. Groups and organisations spring into being and continue to exist, not only because of the communality of interests of members, but also because of perceptions which are relatively common to all members.

The sum total of our past knowledge and experience provides us with an individual cognitive structure which processes received stimuli and interprets for us those stimuli in terms of a personalised theory of 'how the world works'. It tells us what to do.

TABLE 1

POLAR PRINCIPLES OF UK POLITICAL IDEOLOGY

The way in which committed political party members perceive issues of resource ownership, usage and control stems from relatively fixed views on:

The desirability of less social and economic inequality in our society.	The need to preserve individuality and individual freedoms - economic and social.
The need for comprehensive Welfare State provision of social services.	The need for individuals to shoulder personal responsibility for their own destinies.
The extent to which Governmental policy should be based on welfare principles.	The extent to which, in a Trading Nation, Governmental policy should be based on a thrust towards economic productivity.
The desirability of State intervention in industry and a degree of centralised planning.	The desirability of free enterprise and competition
Rejection of 'laws of the jungle' even if it means living in something more reminiscent of a "zoo".	Acceptance of the 'laws of the jungle' as a guide to decision-making since a UK 'zoo' is not economically viable.
PRIMARY TENETS OF SOCIALISM	PRIMARY TENETS OF CONSERVATISM

In theory, our cognitive structures should be continuously updated and expanded as we meet with new experiences. In practice, it is often difficult to "teach an old dog new tricks". Whatever new knowledge or experiences we receive, some of our attitudes, opinions and beliefs - rooted in some past seminal influence that affected us greatly - do not change. We thus, on occasion:

- actively reject such new information which seems to contradict views we hold dear,

- try to falsify new data so that it does fit in with the *a priori* preconceptions of our assumptive world,

- contend that our version of reality is still superior — despite evidence to the contrary - and fight a rear-guard action,

- reject new ideas, not on grounds of their validity, but because of our attitude towards those who propound them.

Such an effort towards perceptual constancy is especially marked in politicians. Or, at least, in terms of their public performance. Indeed, it may be the case that:

- perceptual constancy — giving the politician a feeling of psychological security and a sense of doctrinal purity - is innate to the politician's self-image

- membership of a political party may depend on full acceptance of party dogma, since without this the Party has limited cohesion and its power is restricted

- expedient deviance from 'the party line' is punishable by labelling - "trimmer", "time-server", "juke-box politician", "traitor to the cause" - or by dismissal.

Not that 'remaining true to one's ideals' is somehow, of itself, reprehensible. The key question is the extent to which total unswerving allegiance to past principles may inhibit a realistic view of the changing environment - political, economic, social and technological - and its decision-inducing difficulties; the extent to which perceived facts count less than ingrained values, reality less than rhetoric and pragmatism less than principle.

TABLE 2: SELECTED CONCEPTS FROM MOTIVATION THEORY STUDIES

SOURCE	CONCEPT	EXPLANATION	REF.
A. Wayne & R. Leys	Values	Values such as survival, happiness, harmony, loyalty, integrity and lawfulness are seen as the basis for aims and goals and as creating norms for conduct.	1
W. Guth & R. Tagiuri	Typology of Man	Analysis of the range of human values indicates five types of man - theoretical, economic, aesthetic, political and religious - according to the particular values espoused by the individual.	2
H. Simon	Typology of Man	Classifies 'Organisation Man' into 3 types : psychological (beset by insecurities and emotional needs), rational (sensible and aware : alert in plans to pursue his own interests) and administrative (his own private goals and rationality are subordinated to those of the organisation).	3
A. Maslow	Needs Hierarchy	Postulates that human needs range in ascending order of priority, from physiological (food, shelter), through security and love/belongingness to self-esteem and self-actualisation (personal autonomy). Once basic needs are satisfied, they cease to have the same degree of significance.	4
F. Herzberg	Organisational Motivation	Research indicated the difference, in personnel motivation, between motivators (direct determinants of job satisfaction) and 'hygiene' factors (elements relating to psychological satisfactions).	5
F. Taylor	"Man as Machine"	Pioneer of 'time-motion studies' aimed at improving productivity by mechanising man.	6

TABLE 2 :   **SELECTED CONCEPTS FROM MOTIVATION THEORY STUDIES (2)**

SOURCE	CONCEPT	EXPLANATION	REF.
F. Roethlisberger & W. Dickson	"Hawthorne Study"	Research indicated that work performance was heavily influenced by environmental and control factors. The 'man as machine' conception was erroneous.	7
R. Bales	Interaction Analysis	Examined the processes of behavioural interaction among group members (active : passive, aggressive : conciliatory, positive : negative).	8
A. Gouldner	Locals and Cosmopolitans	Analysis of the relative influence, power and authority exercised within organisations by locals (with comprehensive local knowledge and credibility through proven performance) and cosmopolitans (outsiders with professional credentials and a wider frame of reference).	9
W. Whyte	Organisation Man	An organisational automaton whose only purpose is to serve the rigid bureaucracy in which he works.	10
W. Bennis	Typology of Man	Classifies mankind (in what he sees as a post-bureaucratic world) into : militants (who wish to mutilate/destroy the existing system), apocalyptics (who, "with verbal ferocity, burn everything in sight"), regressors ("fruitless exercises in nostalgia"), retreators (those who hope the problem will go away), technocrats ("full steam ahead") and liberals.	11
D. Macgregor	"Cosmology"	The particular way in which each of us construes the "reality" around us. We each have our own personal "cosmology" - picture of the outside world.	12

Our physical and emotional make-up also plays a role in the perceptual process. The older we are, the more we tend to cling to habits, mental sets, likes and dislikes. We wish that the world would conform to our view of it and are disappointed when it does not. We tend to try to apply old solutions, which have worked for us in the past, to new problems. We have a vested, emotional commitment to what has been.

Consider, for instance, the degree of individual and collectivised conditioning of the Jehovah's Witness, the Kamikaze pilot, the Red Brigade terrorist.

Our intellectual competence deeply affects our ability to perceive and the way in which the perception process is executed. Judgmental capacity - the ability to assimilate new knowledge and ideas, to weigh them against ingrained conceptions, to ponder and meditate on what should be done in given circumstances - is a function of intellect. The more ignorant we are, i.e. bereft of knowledge/data/experience and of judgmental capacity, the more likely we are to try to mitigate the effects of cognitive dissonance by:

- wishing problems away by pretending they don't exist — the 'head in the sand' syndrome

- transforming very large, open-ended difficulties into smaller, closed-ended problems which we then find manageable - the 'pick a problem your own size' syndrome

- short-cutting the thinking process and its needs for intense perceptual activity (reading, listening, debating, etc.) by basing our opinions and beliefs on:

  - those 'authorities' whom we consider reliable

  - the inferred views of the majority

  Both these approaches involve logical fallacies

- transferring attention from the difficulty to be faced, (e.g. unemployment) to those who are perceived to be the instigators of the difficulty and attacking them, (by impugning their motives - the logical fallacy of the Subject-Motive Shift) or their characters.

- avoiding searching out the real causes of our anxiety and simply blaming it on what happened before — the 'after this and, therefore, because of this' approach.

It should be well noted that, however intellectually-competent, emotionally-balanced and perceptionally-rational we might claim to be, all future decisions and actions are bound to be based, to some degree, on misperceptions, because the future is never a replica of the past.

WHAT'S IN IT FOR ME?

The human being is a purposive creature; the continued existence of the species depends on feeding, finding shelter and breeding. Considerations of an aesthetic or moral nature, however dominant or seemingly so, are supplements to what must be basically biology-driven behaviour.

Man is also, however, a gifted animal; gifted in his reasoning capacity for evaluating his requirements and the variety of ways in which they can be most expeditiously met. He needs to be driven by purposes if for no other reason than:

- the onward march of time and the ultimate arrival of an old age in which powers, mental and physical, to achieve personal security are heavily reduced

---

Gross National Product (volume, value, make-up, trends)
Imports and Exports (visibles, invisibles: surplus or deficit: trends)
Fiscal Policy (direct and indirect tax, duties)
Monetary Policy (money supply, base rate)
Sterling Value. State of the Stock Market
Employment — Unemployment (job category, region, industry)
Budget Size (sectoral spending, surplus or deficit)
Public Sector Borrowing Requirement
Exchange Controls. Import Controls
Wage and Salary Levels. House prices. Inflation levels

TABLE 3:   **SALIENT ECONOMIC FACTORS**

- the hostility of the natural elements (fire, flood, tempest)

- the unequal global distribution of resources, e.g. food, raw materials, scenery among the 'haves' and 'have nots'

- the intrinsically-competitive struggle among nations as measured, for example, in terms of territory, security, food supply, standard of living, etc.

Our existence, under such inescapable conditions, dictates primary purposes, aims, goals and targets. It may also dictate conflict, if and when individual purposes cannot be achieved by group consensus.

In the developed countries of the world, where material living standards are relatively high, the sheer problem of survival has little relevance. Instead, interest centres on such issues as the pluralist-elitist form/scope of government, equality of wealth and life-chance distribution, the reward system for producers/non-producers and inter-governmental relations. Within each country such factors are debated (politically) or fought over (outside the political system, by force) and impermanent results achieved. Each individual - as a society member, producer/non-producer, citizen - is affected by these results, however apolitical or politically indifferent he/she may seem to be. Our level of incomes, freedoms (speech, movement, wealth accumulation and transfer, behaviour and thought) and life-styles are all determined by an incessant process of political discussion and power play.

This is not to suggest, of course, that macro-politics dominates either our behaviour or our thoughts. In highly-developed democratic societies such as the UK, a tacit assumption seems to exist that:

- there is a fundamental agreement among politicians of all shades as to the basics of civilised democratic life

- political discord concerns marginal shifts in ends and means which leave most people relatively unaffected.

For most of the population, political action occurs at intervals with voting at national elections and (to a much lesser extent) local elections. We do not give the impression of being a highly politicised nation.

So what are our individual concerns and purposes? They vary, as do perceptions, from individual to individual. Some have thought long and hard about what they want from· life for themselves and their families; others less so. Some are materialistic, placing a high value on money (income, wealth) and possessions; others have a more philosophical or aesthetic disposition. Some are vitally concerned with a 'good' future and prepared to make present sacrifices; others with the instant gratification of the hedonist. Among us there are the naive, uncalculating and easily-satisfied, as well as the calculating, Machiavellian high-achievers: the moral, the amoral and the immoral.

At the heart of our aims and ambitions, hopes and desires, aversions and hates are the values we hold dear. The bundle of personal values - strong attitudes (positive/negative) towards ideas, things, people - self help to preselect and predispose us to certain aims/targets and means of their attainment. We value "a good job" both as an end in itself and as an instrument in the attainment of other aims, e.g. a good living standard, high social status, pride and satisfaction.

Disentangling instrumental values and aims from ultimate values and aims is often as difficult as it is unrewarding. A further complication is that people's overt, publicly-stated aims often vary from their concealed covert targets. Another is the fact that aims and targets cannot, for the individual, always be precisely laid down. By "a good standard of living" or "a high degree of personal security" we are not meaning a certain level of income or the value of a property so much as a feeling that a person has reached what he or we would regard as a "good position" or "a happy situation".

So we march (or stagger, as the case may be) along the high road of life from one 'position' to the next, hopeful for improvements (according to the value set we espouse at different times of our lives) and anxious that each successive 'position' reached will be a good springboard for the next.

POWER AND AUTHORITY

The capacity of an individual - whether as a social animal, worker or citizen - to achieve his own ends and purposes is bound up with the extent of his power. Over the forces of nature, certainly, but especially in his relationships with his fellow men. We tend, though, to shy

TABLE 4 :   **SELECTED CONCEPTS FROM POWER THEORY STUDIES**

SOURCE	CONCEPT	EXPLANATION	REF.
T. Hobbes	Power Urge	Power is needed and sought not necessarily for an improvement in living standards but for preservation of the standards already reached.	13
N. Machiavelli	Statecraft	Believed that the art of Government largely depends on an appropriate blend of force and craft (guile), and that the ruler should be morally indifferent to the means used for political purposes so long as they are successful in their main object - the maintenance and, if possible, extension of political power itself. Key elements in this blend are pragmatism, expediency, manipulation and coercion.	14
M. Weber	Authority	Postulated three main sources of authority (the claimed 'right' to act in a certain way or to control others) : tradition (the status quo sanctified by the past), : the rational-legal system (the country's legislative arrangements conferring power and authority on organisational personnel) : charisma (the highly personal qualities of a 'leader').	15
R. Blake & J. Mouton	Power Spectrum	Power acquisition is seen as a key factor in human relationships. The spectrum ranges from powerlessness through collaboration (power sharing) to competition (battle over who dominates). A '1/0 power ratio' signifies that the manager has total work control of the subordinate.	16
A. Etzioni & D. Selznick	Leadership Types	Distinguished among 'officials' (who control because of their hierarchical position), 'informal leaders' (who possess charismatic qualities) and 'formal leaders' (who should possess both).	17

18

TABLE 4 :   **SELECTED CONCEPTS FROM POWER THEORY STUDIES (2)**

SOURCE	CONCEPT	EXPLANATION	REF.
A. Etzioni	Sources of Power	Contrasts three forms of power : coercive ("stick"), utilitarian ("money or advancement reward") and normative ("symbolic" as in use of appeals to patriotism, sense of duty, etc.).	18
J. Carroll	Neotic Authority	The power and authoritative influence that comes from the individual's possession of important knowledge that is not widely available and is badly needed.	19
K. Lewin	"Gatekeeping"	Power achieved by persons in an organisation as a function of their position in a communication channel ('gates' manned by 'gatekeepers').	20
P. Bachrach & M. Baratz	"Agenda Setting"	The process whereby power is exercised within, or between, groups to achieve the suppression of the discussion of (and decision-making about) issues which powerful elements do not want raised.	21
C. Wright Mills	Power Elite	Analyses the extent to which organisations and policy making are dominated by 'power elites' (cliques, cabals, gangs) who have decisive control over resources, the operating system or rewards.	22
R. Dahl	Polyarchy	Our system of 'democratic' decision-making is not pluralistic (allowing access by all concerned parties) but polyarchical (dominated by powerful groups who are in competition).	23
E. Latham	Policy & Power Relationships	Policies are seen as the outcome of the resultant power balance arising from the competition among groups with conflicting interests, aims and objectives.	24

away from the use of the word 'power' in the interpersonal context since it carries implications of unacceptable manipulation and coercion of others. Thomas Hobbes was no mincer of words, however, when he wrote in his *Leviathan*:

> "I put it for a general inclination of all mankind, a perpetual and restless desire after power that ceaseth only in death. And the cause of this is not always that a man hopes for a more intensive delight than he has already attained to, or that he cannot be content with a more moderate power; but because he cannot assure the power and means to live, which he hath at present, without the acquisition of more".

Clearly, we are not all in the grip of a megalomaniac power urge, spending all our time in the pursuit of our own advancement and self-interest. Some, indeed, opt out of what is organisationally labelled "the rat race" or adopt "live and let live", "do unto others as you yourself would be done by", "keep your head down", "don't stick your neck out" postures. Others, by contrast, seek to out-do Hobbes and dominate others. They seek to impose their will on others, socially and organisationally, through the use of weapons which include:

- their physical and mental capacity, their access to resources and the strength of their convictions

- guile, craft, manipulation, stage-management and orchestration

- the threatened or actual use of sanctions or force and the distribution of actual or potential rewards

- propaganda, indoctrination and blackmail.

It is self-evident that such power seekers will go to elaborate lengths to disguise their aims and methods (strategies and tactics) from those they seek to control. On the other hand, there are those who - having analysed the available options in a power struggle - pursue their own self-interest by becoming committed 'followers'. They 'hitch their waggon to a star', perhaps finding deep psychological satisfaction in the act of obedience or a structured world in which tricky decisions are made by others. Additionally, if 'followership' means rewards (money, prestige, titles) the leader may not be short of supporters.

Power Base Element	Some of the mix of factors determining the extent of Personal Power.
Personal Attributes	Appearance, stature, physique, face, voice, speech, gestures, mannerisms, dress. Charismatic presence. Demonstrated will-power. Apparent honesty, directness, simplicity. Intellect and education, easily carried. Powers of argument. Life experience. Ability to shape arguments to the listeners' needs.
Ideological Stance	Principles - moral/religious/political/military etc. - and the strength, skill, courage and pertinacity with which they are advocated and followed.
Material Resources	Degree of access to all forms of required resources - money, information, media, authority, technology, manpower, knowledge, organisational status - relative to others.
Personal Position	Influence derived from family, friends; position in employing organisation, professional organisation, political party. Ability to distribute rewards and impose sanctions, actually or as perceived by those involved.

TABLE 5 :   POSSIBLE SOURCES OF PERSONAL POWER

Authority is another source of power and conveys a notion that obedience is not just a matter of reward/sanction, but also of duty. The power source which acts with authority is deemed by the subordinate to have the right to issue orders.

In the UK, Parliament (The House of Commons) possesses sovereign authority since it is the highest organ of government and it is democratically elected and invested by the electorate with the right to rule. There are, however, other claimed bases for authority which greatly affect power play among public bodies, for example:

- the rights of workingmen, as advocated by the TUC and individual Unions

- the right to live, as proclaimed by the Nuclear Disarmament Movement.

Disputes have arisen between the Government and the TUC (over Trade Union Rights and the Government's Labour Relations legislation) and between the Government and the CND (over the deployment of Cruise Missiles) based on groups' perceptions over whose authority is most valid.

What is clearly at stake is a power struggle based on principles, held with equal conviction by the various parties. So it was in English history with the "Divine Right of Kings" conflicting with the "Sovereign Rights of the People" (Vox Populi, Vox Dei) prior to the death of Charles I.

It is often a complex matter to isolate those members of a group who pursue principles as principles for their own sake and those who advocate principles simply as an expedient to the acquisition of power, which is then used for other purposes. Similarly, it is often difficult for a "man of principle" to wage his battle for what he believes in without soiling his hands with power politics. Religious wars have claimed countless victims.

WHAT DOES THIS MEAN, ORGANISATIONALLY?

Organisations are collections of individuals. They may be associations (free assemblies of people united for a common purpose) or employment systems (hierarchic systems in which the output of brain or manual work is exchanged for money) or representative bodies (attended by those chosen from particular populations to represent the population). Whichever the form, organisations have leaders and followers, those with power and those without, those with authority and those who are subordinate to those with it. In all forms of collective bodies, hierarchies exist with orders and instructions flowing from the decision-maker ("what is to be done" and "how it should be done") to the work-doer. What is interesting is that actual power and authority does not always square with the power and authority distribution represented by the role or job titles held. So the power hierarchy on paper may start with the Managing Director or the Prime Minister or the Committee Chairman, for instance, but in practice the epicentre of influence - the key power-source decision maker - may be located elsewhere.

This poses very interesting problems in highly-unionised organisations. Here two parallel hierarchies co-exist; the one, the employing hierarchy, processing instructions from the apex to the base of the organisational triangle, potentially (if not actually) opposed to the other, the trade union membership hierarchy with its managers (representatives, stewards, convenors). The real power is not necessarily in the hands of the Managing Director or in the Trade Union convenor's.

In such situations there are, potentially at least, abundant reasons for power struggles between management and unions over such matters as the level of employment, wages and working conditions. Their interests may diverge on the salient question of the extent to which the owners are profit - and productivity - minded rather than interested in the fortunes of the workforce that they employ. It is noteworthy that each trade union is in fact in business, selling its members' labour at the highest obtainable price, and is faced by managements who:

- may not be able physically for competitive reasons, to pay the price asked

- may have the choice, using microprocessor technology or robots for example, of getting the same work done more cheaply or perhaps more dependably

The power struggles of the past resulted in the creation of union "rights" (e.g. closed shop arrangements and picketing), whereby the employer was often confronted with a labour-selling monopoly whose strike threats or strikes he was ill-equipped to withstand.

The perceptions and purposes of unionised workforces tend to differ significantly from those of owners (whether Government or private capital) and managers. Managers in executive positions in the employment hierarchy, charged with responsibility for the work of others and authority over them, are rewarded for:

- deciding what is correct to do in given circumstances

- ensuring the cost-effective pragmatic and technocratic execution of the tasks involved

- the achievement of results which are deemed appropriate to the owners or themselves, or both.

"White-collar" work is, necessarily, more conceptual than physical (and gets more so, the nearer to the organisational apex one gets) and carries status connotations (job titles, office size, perks) as well as appropriate financial rewards. The workforce carry out the instructions they receive and perform predominantly discretion-free work, (more physical, the nearer to the organisational base) for salary/wage.

What is a question of pay rates to the Personnel Director is a matter of bread, butter and holidays to the British Leyland car assembler. What is to the Managing Director a question of redundancy pay, is to the redundant worker a matter of at best, a gratefully-accepted retirement or, at worst, a livelihood destroyed.

Optimally - at least from an organisational harmony viewpoint - the situation within the organisation should be one of total agreement with decisions on what to aim for and the methods to use (plans, technology, work and administrative procedures). In practice, of course - disregarding the management-union issue - there is always the possible disagreement among individual departmental managers and even between the directors and owners. Thus the Government could find itself at odds with the management of a particular nationalised industry: a Minister could see substantial differences in what he wants and what his Civil Service Department thinks is realistic. Why?

- Because the problem is being looked at differently by the parties involved.

- Because there are differences in the aims and objectives of the parties involved.

- Because the parties involved see in the problem, not just a technical decision to be faced up to, but also a forum for power politics (winning/losing : elitism/pluralism) and a stage for debate on matters of political principles as opposed to what is seen as pragmatism.

If this be regarded as problematic, just consider the dissensus that existed between Central Government and some Local Authorities over the Conservative Government's legislation on council house sales.

PROFITABILITY

The subject of profitability is one such key factor which divides the Conservative and Labour Parties, management and unions. It is a simple business concept, namely that:

$$\begin{array}{l} \text{Return on Capital} \\ \text{Employed} \end{array} = \begin{array}{c} \text{Profit on Sales} \\ \text{(Margin)} \end{array} \times \begin{array}{c} \text{Asset Turnover} \\ \text{(Activity)} \end{array}$$

$$\frac{\text{Profit}}{\text{Capital Employed}} = \frac{\text{Profit}}{\text{Sales}} \times \frac{\text{Sales Value}}{\text{Assets Value}}$$

$$10\% = \frac{50}{1000} \times \frac{1000}{500}$$

and its role in cost-benefit analysis decision-making is elemental since:

- resources are scarce relative to the uses to which they can be put ("money doesn't grow on trees") and

- it makes sense to put the resources (i.e. capital) into the uses which offer the best pay-back (i.e. profit) and avoid those which offer the worst (backing 'winners') . . . at least in economic terms.

- the relationship between the pay-back and the resources may be objectively measured in financial terms as % Return on Capital Employed ("how much is it worth?"). Note, however, that the pay-back need not necessarily be financial, but can be psychological satisfaction or political power.

- It disciplines the decision-maker into thinking through the economic implications of choices, even where 'shadow pricing' – the imputation of a *fabricated price* for a social service which has no *market price* – is used.

The application of the concept of profitability to some fields of Government policy-making (particularly social and industrial) has, however, caused enormous dissension, since it involves questions of:

- the extent to which 'scarce' resources should be pumped into, say, the NHS on the basis of assumed need or whether tests of value-for-money should be applied to say, heart operations, laundry services, etc.

- pit closures on the grounds of financial losses made, despite social dislocation that would be created and the political furore aroused

- running the Rail transport system as an Economic Enterprise rather than as a heavily subsidised social service (*See Fig.5*)

- the effect of policy decisions on voting patterns in marginal constituencies.

Socialists find the concepts of "value for money" and "social accounting" somewhat demeaning, insofar as they reduce the human being to an entry on a profit and loss account and fly in the face of the social needs of the non-producers in our society. Conservatives see the concepts as elementary common sense for a nation that needs to improve its competitiveness. The unions see them as a direct threat to the livelihoods of their members in those "smoke-stack" industries which were once the pride of Great Britain and which are now commercially suspect. Managements see them as one of the key rules for decision-making. Or, since we can never know for certain what people think, we assume that they tend to.

And then there's the issue of the extent to which the parties involved in the economic productivity debate are:

- so ideologically-committed to a vision of the political future they would like us to share, that minor importance is attached to some matters of "fact" or practicality

- so technocratic is their orientation (concerned with efficiency, effectiveness and operating technicalities in, for example, Planning-Programming-Budgeting or Zero-based Budgeting systems) that values are seen as unwarranted impositions.

A good example of this trade-off can be seen in the 1984 Coal Miners' strike. The NUM, value-driven in terms of its perceptions of the social need to maintain employment in mining (and increase wages): the Government, value-driven in its desire to see greater democracy in trade union management and in reducing union power. How to cope with workforce intractability, on the one hand, and the Government's demands for improved economic productivity, on the other, was the NCB's prime concern. The strike itself was the cockpit in which the drama of political dissension was played.

"NO MAN IS AN ISLAND"

Every human being co-exists with others; every organisation - being a collection of human beings - co-exists similarly with others. To varying degrees, depending on the inter-dependence in the relationship, they:

- influence and are influenced
- depend on and are depended upon.

The actions taken by the members of one organisation (The World Bank, the United Nations, the EEC Commission, the UK Treasury, the Boards of Directors of Nationalised Industries, Local Authorities, etc.) can significantly affect the action-options of other such public organisations – directly or indirectly – and ultimately "the man in the street".

Thus organisational leaders find themselves surrounded by an operating environment in which other organisations exert political, economic, social and technological 'pulls' and 'pushes' at the same time as having to meet the demands of those who:

(a) give the organisation its purposes (the Government, Private Owners)

(b) those who pay for the product or service produced by the organisation and help maintain it in existence, (the Taxpayer, the Customer buying the product).

The organisation's 'life-space' and freedom for manoeuvre is, unless it has some degree of monopoly power, threatened by environmental pressures and constraints applied by its owners and customers. It will seek power to influence things in its favour, if it can, to 'optimise its match with the environment'.

It's a difficult matter. Organisation leaders have to simultaneously manage:

- the internal coalition of employees (or, in the case of associations, members), the work systems used to produce products/ services and the organisation structure within which the coalition of employees (members) is deployed

- the relationships between the organisation and its environment, owners and product/service users.

FIG.5 :   **THE DEMAND - NEEDS CURVE**

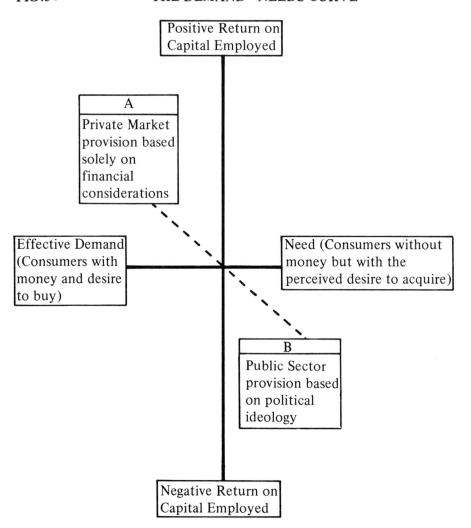

Success further depends on the sound management of the internal and interface systems over time and under circumstances which change little ("placid") or much ("turbulent"). A military analogy is not inappropriate since:

- current "battles" need to be won to ensure that the organisation has a good chance of fighting future "battles"

- fighting current "battles" should not be allowed to detract attention from the facts that winning the "war" is more important and that the final "battle" may be the most significant.

Hence the army needs to be well-equipped, trained and led for present success but also have created for it the platform on which future long-term success can be built.

The imagery is justified also by the actual/potential existence of antagonisms or adverserial relationships between individuals, within internal groups, between the leaders of internal groups (section v section, department v department), and between organisations and external bodies, over:

- the aims to be pursued

- the means by which the aims shall be achieved.

Of particular relevance in the public sector is the relative status of the:

- aims of nationalised industry (greater operating freedom, technological rejuvenation, ample supply of funds, etc.)

- aims of Government (degree to which nationalised industries work within the confines of economic policy generally and cash limits specifically)

- aims of Local Government in terms of, say, rate-raising independence

- aims of Trade Unions (maximum employment and employee protection, guarantee of traditional trade union rights, "appropriate" wage levels, etc.).

Just as there are possible conflicts over means and ends, so there are thrusts towards alliance-building among involved organisations. The National Union of Miners soliciting aid from the Steel and Rail Unions, the Militant Tendency leadership of Liverpool Council urging mainline Socialist buttressing of their 1985 rate-revolt stance, for example.

Private-sector industrial firms can find themselves in a similar position.

TABLE 6 :   **SELECTED CONCEPTS FROM BUREAUCRACY THEORY STUDIES**

SOURCE	CONCEPT	EXPLANATION	REF.
L. Gulick & L. Urwick	Administration Activities	Administration seen as being composed of planning, organising, staffing, directing, co-ordinating, reporting, budgeting.	25
J. Mooney & A. Reilley	Organisation Principles	Outlined principles governing organisation structures as : co-ordinative (span of control), scalar (hierarchy), functional (division of labour) and staff/line.	26
T. Burns & G. M. Stalker	Models of Organisations	Organisation structure and management style seen as dependent on the nature of work done and the degree of environmental stability. The model is "closed" (formal) when the environment is stable and the work routine; "open" (informal) when the environment is turbulent and the work innovative.	27
H. Wilensky	Culture impact	Attitudes, values, goals of participants and the work system itself are heavily affected by the socio-political culture of the nation.	28
E. Goffman	Total Institutions	Researched the depersonalising effects of rule-bound "closed community" organisations.	29
R. Merton	Indoctrination	Traced the extent to which the training/development/ socialisation of a bureaucratic administrator can amount to a pathological indoctrination.	30
I. Jarvis	Groupthink	Concurrence-seeking behaviour becomes so dominant in a cohesive in-group that it can over-ride rational considerations of actions. Members can back stupid ideas out of fear of ostracism; the greater the group tyranny, the greater the amount of "group think".	31

TABLE 6 :   **SELECTED CONCEPTS FROM BUREAUCRACY THEORY STUDIES (2)**

SOURCE	CONCEPT	EXPLANATION	REF.
R. Cyert & J. March	Theory of the Firm	Organisations don't have objectives; people do. The "organisation's objectives" are a negotiated concensus (at a given time) of the aims of influential participants. When an organisation becomes stabilised (external/internal change decreases), goals become 'displaced'. Sub-optimisation occurs. Means rather than ends are emphasised. Organisation drift occurs, by contrast, in unstable conditions.	32
G. Tullock	Bureaucracy as Feudalism	Visualises bureaucracy as a medieval society with the reference politician interacting with spectators, allies, peers, courtiers, barons and the sovereign.	33
A. Downs	Personality Types	Divided administrators in bureaucracies into climbers, conservers, zealots, advocates and (the decision-making level) statesmen.	34
G. Tullock	Hierarchical Distortion	The possibility of communicating 'noise-free' information varies according to the size of the organisation and the levels of hierarchy.	35
F. E. Emery & E. L. Trist	Strategies and Environments	Researched the degree to which the strategies adopted by an organisation - competition, bargaining, coalition - are a function of their operating environment - placid, dynamic, turbulent.	36
D. Macgregor	Theories 'X' and 'Y'	The employee has relatively little interest in his work and even less involvement, "carrots and sticks" are the main weapon for achieving results (Theory 'X'). Theory 'Y', suggests, to the contrary, that such crudity will not work.	37

"Do we achieve a higher level of long-run profitability through competition, or through industrial agreement (cartels, official or unofficial) or by mergers with, or take-overs of, our competitors?" would be a salient question facing not a few Boards of Directors.

The ever-changing relationship between organisations (Associations with members, Employers with employees) and the environment in which they exist means that those who do not consistently update and change their -

- internal management system (work processing technology), management style, organisational structure) and

- interface capability (access to appropriate resources — labour, funds, technology; producing products/services which are valued by customers; politically managing relationships with other involved organisations; maintaining demand for their output),

will fail. They will cease to have importance, relevance, power. The higher the degree of constraint placed on them and the lower the level of their countervailing power, the speedier their demise. Past glorious achievements lie in the past; the problem is always how to cope with the future. And that means choices.

DECISIONS, DECISIONS

Decisions, which ought to be faced up to but are sometimes avoided either through fear or ignorance, are manifold. They vary, in size, complexity and impact; in the scale of activity/passivity they engender.

Some are of crucial significance (but not always recognised as such by organisational leaders), others less so (but misperceived as crucial) : some have long-term relevance, some relate predominantly to the short-term. They may appear to arrive singly in a "one-off" fashion, whereas in fact, all the organisational decisions taken today have their roots in decisions taken in the past and today's choices determine those to be taken in the future.

Work procedures are easily dealt with on the basis of practicability

TABLE 7 :   METAPHORICAL POLICY MOVES

FRONTAL ATTACK	Aimed at capturing the "commanding heights" or the "centre of the stage". All resources are committed. No holds barred.
PRE-EMPTIVE STRIKE	You hit your opponent before he can hit you. A "fait accompli". Use of surprise/shocks. Mastery in the use of time.
DIVERSIONARY RAIDS	You make your opponent fight on a variety of fronts, whilst perhaps disguising from him where your main attack will occur.
A WAR OF ATTRITION	Grinding the opponent down by allowing him no breathing space and cutting off his supply of resources. A "scorched earth" policy is a variant of this. Allies vital.
PROPAGANDA	Use all methods of propaganda — making grandiose claims/threats, using smear tactics to frighten your opponent. Actually or artificially "upping the ante", raising the temperature. Personal attacks/innuendo. Fabricatio Falsi v. Suppressio Veri.
PINPRICKS	Goad your opponent into making mistakes by continual pressure skilfully administered. Engineer a collapse from within, through stimulating internal conflict. Divide and rule.
STONEWALLING	The rejection of the opponent's viewpoint and a complete unwillingness to compromise with much emotional bluster. Procrastinate. Play for time.
BLUFFING	Pretending that you have greater resources than you have. Hyperbole and exaggeration are used to enlarge your apparent power relative to your opponent and affect his perceptions of the costs and benefits of action alternatives. Playacting.
YIELDING	Recognising "no-win" situations. Parleying; going to arbitration (eg. ACAS). Selling defeats as "victories for common sense", etc. Giving in gracefully. Damage limitation.
LINE OF LEAST RESISTANCE	Keep your head down. Adopt a low profile. Hope the problem will go away. Do just enough to show you are still in the fight. Going through the motions.

and the regularity of occurrence of the problem/issue. They involve low-level programmed responses. Difficulties can arise, however, over the technology which is used to do the work (labour-intensive/machine-intensive) and decisions on the organisation structure within which the work is executed. Quite apart from possible conflict arising over the technocratic aspect of decisions i.e. the best aims/methods based on the purely managerial criteria of efficiency/effectiveness, there may be also micro-political difficulties (organisational "winners" and "losers") to be overcome. They are certainly less easy to reverse — given the inertia of bureaucratic systems — than they might at first appear. Similarly with the internal style of management (autocratic/permissive, hierarchic/collegiate) employed by organisational leaders.

Such decisions are important but not so crucial to the organisation's future vitality and success as those of an interface nature. In the Nationalised Industries sector resource-acquisition in the form of political patronage as well as funding, if the Corporation is unprofitable and cannot draw its income wholly from its customers, is vital. The availability and price of raw materials purchased is critical, as is the tractability and cost of labour. Unsound choices of actions, which affect the nature of a corporation's relationships with suppliers adversely, impact immediately and over the longer run on performance.

The same is true of the actions which link Nationalised Corporations with their customers, i.e.

strategic actions : those which are aimed at establishing a viable platform for long-term success, aimed at "winning the war", for example, the quality/quantity/price of the product/service provided, the consumer group at whom the product/service is aimed, the technology used and access to resources,

tactical actions : those which aim at "winning the current battle", e.g. Marketing, Production.

It should be noted that, in the public sector, strategic and tactical actions are not simply related to services/products but are very much concerned with inter-organisational political power relationships and the management of time (*See Table 7*). Instances include:

FIG .6 : **RISK-RETURN ORIENTATIONS**

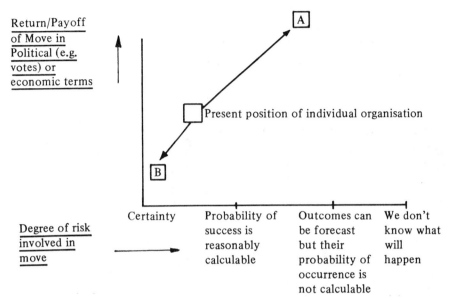

A = A highly risky, speculative move aimed at improving
the current pay-off achieved.

B = A low-risk, high-safety move which is sure to succeed
but will not improve the current pay-off.

- the range of strategic/tactical decision issues facing the Government and the TUC over trade union membership at the GCHQ Cheltenham

- the "power politics" involved in Government's elimination of the Greater London Council from the Local Government map

- the Conservative's privatisation policy (British Telecom, British Gas, etc.)

- the strategic and tactical postures of the Government, the NCB and the NUM over the 1984 coal strike and the critical nature of the timing of moves and counter-moves.

TABLE 8 : SELECTED CONTRIBUTIONS IN THE FIELD OF PUBLIC POLICY ANALYSIS

Limitations on a Rational Approach to Policy Making

Herbert Simon

The simple model of classical economic man (all-knowing and with ample technocratic skills) is inadequate as a basis for understanding the decision-making processes involved in complex policy problems. Here 'goals and values' may be simple or complex, consistent or inconsistent; the facts may be real or supposed; the inferences may be valid or spurious. (38)

Whilst a logical approach to making the decision may be followed (procedural rationality), it does not follow that the decision output is logical (substantive rationality) since all such decision participants suffer from 'bounded rationality' (perceptual and cognition variations, data and computational limitations). (39)

Hence organisational decisions are concerned with 'satisficing' (satisfy and suffice) rather than with maximising (the ideal solution). (40)

Charles Lindblom

In public policy matters there is almost always controversy over what the problem is, let alone the solution. Such controversy puts 'a limit on analytic policy making' and provides an entry point for politics and other 'irrationalities'. (41)

As a comprehensive and wholly reliable knowledge of means-ends relationships is unattainable, a completely 'rational-deductive' approach to policy making is impossible. (42)

In fact, pragmatism, expediency and disjointed incrementalism ('muddling through') are the real hallmarks of policy making in the public sector where opportunity for 'search' - for alternatives - is limited, goals are not clear cut and where the wide acceptibility of policies depends on a 'satisficing' solution. (43)

'Muddling Through' is not enough

Aaron Wildavsky
Amitai Etzioni
Yehezkel Dror

These three writers strongly resist the elemental defeatism inherent in the 'muddling through' approach diagnosed by Lindblom.

Aaron Wildavsky, for example, advocates the need for in-depth 'strategic' analysis of policy situations as a key factor to avoid the simplistic use of tools such as Planning-Programming - Budgeting and Zero-Based Budgeting. (44)

Amitai Etzioni's 'Mixed Scanning' approach has such a purpose, namely to ensure the isolation of a range of policy options (and their inputs and outputs) rather than just a few. He highlights the differences that should be seen to exist between fundamental and incremental decisions. (45)

Yehezkel Dror, in a similar vein, stresses the need for 'selective rationalism' (i.e. as much rationality and comprehensiveness as possible), as well as a structured approach (termed 'metapolicy') to policy making. (46) For him, the process should not be simply about 'Partisan Mutual Adjustment' (43) - compromises among groups involved in a policy-struggle.

Thus the aims of public bodies such as Nationalised Industries cannot be reduced to that which is assumed to be the common denominator for private enterprise ; Return on Capital Employed and Return on Shareholders' Equity. British Rail, as one example among many, has a set of potentially divergent aims based on:

- economic results (making profits/cutting losses)
- welfare provision (maintain routes that can never pay their way)
- organisational power maintenance (defence of BR's life space") in the political arena.

POLICY TESTS

'Policy' is the catch-all name given to the host of decisions made by organisations. Usually greater precision is given by labelling decisions as strategic, tactical/operational, administrative/procedural and organisational. But, whilst clarity of view on the level of importance to be given to a particular decision is desirable, it is not always attainable. Not all the members of the organisation or their leaders, whether "nominal" or "extant", will agree on what is crucial, important, interesting but not significant, and fascinating but trivial. Some are not even bothered. Also, what is a grave matter for one organisational part (miners in a doomed pit) may be a minor issue for another. Furthermore, it is always the case that one decision leads to another . . .

For those who aspire to a decision-making or decision-advising role in an organisation, the ability to analyse policy decisions of a wide variety of types in a wide variety of organisations is a must. But the arts of the policy analyst are hard to pin down. The disciplines useful to policy analysis - Economics, Sociology, Psychology, Politics - and the very form of the analysis - a step-by-step examination of the problem and the ensuing decisions - cannot be prescribed in detail in advance. Indeed, such is the nature of human decision-making, that the final product of policy studies is not the ability to make necessarily better decisions more often (though that is the hope) but the ability to avoid crass stupidity.

TABLE 9 :   **THINKING ABOUT THINKING**

Source	Types of Thinking	Ref.
J. D. Steinbrunner	"Grooved" thinking occurs in organisations which are well-established and have a regular-patterned work load. There is in such organisations a "highly stable pattern of reaction", a "short-time frame" and a "low level of abstraction". There is a tendency for members to "break a particular short-range component out of a complex policy problem and make decisions solely in that context", or perhaps, to become pathologically obsessive about low-level tasks, e.g. administrative tidiness, systematic procedures. "Theoretical thinking", by contrast, is the product of extensive belief patterns and a generalised, highly deductive belief system. It involves the ability to think in abstract terms.	47
Elliott Jacques	Bureaucracies are seen as having five different work strata, each characterised by the mixture of conceptual (thinking) and practical (doing) work performed. They are: 1. Perceptual Motor Concrete 2. Imaginal concrete 3. Imaginal scanning 4. Conceptual modelling 5. Intuitive theory The work done at stratum 1 level is routine 'hewing of wood and drawing of water'. The stratum 5 level demands little by way of concrete motor skills but requires high conceptual ability. The time horizon may be distant and the issue one of principles rather than practices.	48

This is not so much a counsel of despair, as a "word to the wise".

To study policy "situations" we use whatever forensic tools seem appropriate. The following entry points are of value:

(1) The nature of the policy-making process.

Is the forum in which the policy is being decided upon

- collegiate?   all those affected by the decision are party to the discussion on what should be done, the final outcome being wholly representative of their announced standpoints,

- democratic?   those affected by the decision are represented by elected individuals. The degree of representativeness may be limited, (e.g. the election mechanism may be 'first past the post' rather than proportional representation) and the extent of the mandate placed on the elected representative may be low,

- hierarchic?   decisions are made by those with power and authority without representation in the process of those affected. Ideas are given and orders obeyed.

- a mixture?   decisions are made in a hierarchic fashion but token gestures to democracy are made by having some degree of representation of those affected.

Is the policy decision the result of a due process? Of

- an in-depth size-up of internal strengths and weaknesses, external opportunities and threats?
- a lengthy deliberation of the risks and returns, pros and cons of alternatives in the light of ideological and technocratic criteria?
- a systematic appraisal of ends and means?

- a consideration of "externalities" which may affect the policy.

or is it more the result of snap judgments, mere whim or preconceived notions?

To what extent do certain individuals, groups or bodies play a disproportionate elite role — through their exercise of power play — in:

■ managing the agenda?	: precluding certain policy options from discussion or being acted upon,
■ information management?	: suppressing certain significant items of information which could affect the policy outcome,
■ time management?	: putting pressure on for speedy decisions which again short-cut option choice,
■ force, guile?	: e.g. excluding certain decision-makers from the process,
■ indoctrination?	: making sure that "the party line" is well and truly toed,
■ bargaining?	: "fixing" particular decisions by working out with opponents beforehand the price of acquiescence.

(2)   The logic of the policy-making process

Do the parties involved in the policy situation give the impression that they have thought clearly about the aims they are wanting to pursue and the strategy/tactics employed? Are they realistic and feasible? Or are they based on bias, prejudice or political dogma to a degree which makes them seem unrelated to the real world? Can we assume that what is said to be the aim is really so? This is often a difficult problem insofar as the organisations involved may be pursuing multiple aims (political, economic, social and technological) rather than single ones and as what might, to the analyst, appear as an individual tactic may be, in fact, part and parcel of a deep-laid strategy.

We anticipate that policy makers will go out of their way to acquire as much information as they can to assist them in forecasting:

TABLE 10 :   **SYSTEMS CONCEPTS**

Source	Contribution	Ref.
L. V. Bertalanffy	Produced a basic model of the working of "ecosystems" in the natural world. These are characterised by a state of equilibrium among their constituent parts and are known as 'open systems'. Disturbances of the equilibrium set up forces which lead to the restoration of a changed equilibrium.	49
F. E. Emery & E. L. Trist	See the organisation as operating within a "socio-technical system", influencing and being influenced by the environment. "The primary task of managing an enterprise as a whole is to relate the total system to its environment and not internal regulation per se".	50
S. Beer	Described the elements characterising systems as : boundaries, interacting and mutually interdependent parts, feedback and equilibrium.	51
N. Wiener	Analysed cybernetics, the science of communication and control which deals with the phenomena of information feedback systems which are part of living organisms and their work activities.	52

(1)   Future "states of nature" — the nature of the operating environment facing the organisation in five or ten years time, say.

(2)   The likely results — "scenarios" of the actions to be taken.

(3)   The probability that successful results will be achieved.

This is a fair assumption in as much as they will try to move as far along the continuum of ignorance—knowledge as possible, in order to predict what might happen and the probability of its occurring.

But the acquisition of data, however valuable, has a cost in time and money, as Table 12 (p.46) shows. What, however, of the situation in which the policy-makers do not know about how to get more data or can't afford it if they could? What of the situation in which an urgent decision is deferred by one of the parties involved (to gain advantage) through the tactic of stating "We need more information?" And what of the situation in which the decision-maker will not search for more data because it might invalidate what he has already 'made up his mind' about?

Further reference to Table 12 will reveal another interesting facet of policy making : the decision-maker's attitude to risk. Some decision-makers will, however preposterous it may seem, prefer in this example Option B to Option A. Why? Because the pay-off for a win is approximately four times that of a win for Option A. If they are, for one reason or another, desperate for a win (and £100/110 will not be enough) then they might be tempted. This risk-seeking behaviour - (almost involving wilful ignorance of the probability of, and penalty for, a loss) is called MAXIMAX – MAXIMISING THE MAXIMUM POSSIBLE GAIN. It is the decision rule of the super-optimist and the 'do or die' terrorist.

Option A is, by contrast, the safe and sure one. You don't gain much, but if it fails you don't lose much either. Some decision-makers are, by virtue of a prudent, cautious, risk-averse personality, more concerned with what they might lose by doing the 'wrong' thing (or the 'right' thing in the 'wrong' way) than by what they might gain if they were winning. This is the hallmark of the MINIMAX operator - MINIMISING THE MAXIMUM POSSIBLE LOSS IF ALL TURNS OUT BADLY. The pessimist's decision rules.

It is the task of the policy analyst or adviser to evaluate the risk orientation of parties to the policy decision. Have they an awareness of the risks they are running? Are the implications of a failure, given the prior assessment of risks and returns, clearly understood? What is their individual fall back position in the event of lack of success? Will their action cope adequately with the "worst case scenario"?

Risk appraisal is one of the key elements in three specific policy analysis tools - Decision Mapping, Matrix Analysis and Decision Trees.

TABLE 11 :   **DECISION TYPES**

Source	Decision Types	Ref.
Herbert Simon	Programmed (repetitive and routine dealt with by proven methods) v non-programmed ("novel, unstructured and consequential" with no cut and dried solutions) where there is no possibility of algorithmic (machine-like processing) handling.	53
W. Mackenzie	Decision, indecision (a decision not to make up your mind just yet), non-decision (a decision not to decide), a decision by default (a decision made without your participation, wilful or otherwise).	54
Igor Ansoff	Strategic (long-term crucial interface decisions) v operating (short term, 2nd Order functional activity decisions) v administrative (internal procedures and organisation structure).	55

The first of these links together, as if in a road map, those who are deciding, affected by the decision and can affect the issues. It states what are seen as the value premises, rationales and aims of each and their risk orientation. The 'roads' which link them are the actions and reactions to moves which are possible/likely together with an assessment of probabilities. The purpose of the map is to try to ascertain the cause and effect relationships involved in these actions/reactions.

Matrix Analysis is another basic technique which helps one organisation involved in a "battle" with another — political, economic, social — to map out in advance of a decision:

(a) the options open to it

(b) the counter-strikes open to its opposition

(c) the effect of each combination.

An example of the use of this technique is given in Table 13.

EXAMPLE OF USE OF DECISION TREE ANALYSIS IN PUBLIC INDUSTRY POLICY MAKING

STAGE I   STAGE II   STAGE III

A

Major union action

Government proceeds with
legislation but with no offer
of compensation to
workforce.

Minor union action

B

Political furore results.
Utility unions seek to
whip up support from
other unions

Government proceeds with
legislation and offers
compensation to workforce

C

Yes

Utility unions set
the price for their
compliance and
prepare to
negotiate

Unions accept
Governmental
terms which
they consider
favourable

No

Unions dislike the terms but
are obliged to accept because
of perceived weakness relative
to the Government's position

Will the Government
proceed with 'vital
services' legislation
removing the right to
strike from key utility
workers?

D

Notes :

☐ = Decision Node   ◯ = Event Node

A,B,C,D : Results of Outcomes in cost-benefit terms both economic and political.
The outcomes are reviewed in terms of the probability of occurrence.

TABLE 12 : THE CONCEPT OF EXPECTED VALUE

Pay-offs and Chances	Option A		Option B	
	Forecast Result based on 60% information	Forecase Result based on 70% information	Forecast Result based on 60% information	Forecast Result based on 70% information
a. Results of policy if it works £	100	110	500	550
b. Chances of success	.7	.75	.3	.2
c. Results of policy if it fails £	- 50	- 55	- 250	- 280
d. Chances of failure	.3	.25	.7	.8
e. Expected Value of Option ((a x b) - (c x d))	55	68.75	- 25	- 134

Explanation: The policy makers have 2 options, A or B. If it is successful, B will produce a much better result than A, but conversely its chances of success are much less. It is more risky. The expected value — the average result (which never happens!) — indicates that A is much more viable than B. In fact with B, the chances are you'll lose money. It can be seen that improving the knowledge on which the decision is based has demonstrated that B is even less viable than it was first thought and that A is more attractive. In fact, as a gambler, you would be prepared to consider paying up to £13.75 (£68.75 – £55) for the extra information on option A since by obtaining it you have improved the pay-off.

Note the possibility of applying Sensitivity Analysis (how much of a difference would it make to the decision is probabilities were out by a factor of 20%?) in this situation.

TABLE 13 : **MATRIX ANALYSIS**

Action Option ⟶ Open to ↓ Organisation B		Organisation A		Result for Organisation B
		Option 1	Option 2	
	Option 1	- 4	+3	- 1
	Option 2	+2	- 4	- 2
Result for Organisation A		+2	+1	0

Explanation: The figures given in the *central* boxes represent gains or losses to Organisation B. So - 4 = a loss by B and commensurately a gain of 4 by A. If Organisation B pursues Option 1 it will lose 4, if Organisation A follows Option 1, and gain 3 if it goes for Option 2, etc. On the basis of assumed *Maximum Pursuit of Self-Interest (M.P.S.I.)*, A will follow Option 1 rather than Option 2. Whichever option it follows, B will lose. It should choose Option 1. Naturally, if we add to this the probabilities of success or failure (as in Table 12), the final choice might be different.

The third tool is the Decision Tree, whose value lies in permitting decisions which have sequential effects to be structured and analysed before final choices are made. Consider the example given in Figure 7 and note that:

■ At each stage in the Policy implementation there are pay-offs for success or failure.

■ Neither the financial aspects of these, nor the probabilities, are included in the diagram here, but they could be used to work out precisely the expected value pay-offs. "Rolling back" from the end result of Stage III could, for example, indicate that it was feasible to introduce Policy A and go for the first two stages, but not the third. Of course, a full-scale Tree diagram would illustrate all the potential Expected Values for proceeding with Policy A (or not) in all 3 stages. Its potential as a diagnostic device is immediately apparent.

A Fault Tree procedure — one which lists all the pathways to failure in a particular policy dilemma — is a variant of this approach.

CONCLUSION

'Deciding to do' is one thing; achieving required results is another. Whilst the first can be difficult, the second can be an equally fraught process as it deals with the leadership - motivation - planning - task execution - control spectrum of activity. Here our concern is, evidently, with the former.

This section has sought to deal with some highly interesting aspects of public decision-making which taken collectively constitute a Framework for Policy Studies. Such a framework can be applied to a wide variety of policy problems to elucidate cause and effect, to enquire into issues of organisational psychology and sociology and to validate the mechanisms of decision-taking. Its use can be a highly rewarding exercise in laying bare so many of the fundamental mainsprings of the nation's political and economic life.

References:

1. A. Wayne, R. Leys, 'The Value Frame-work of Decision Making' in Concepts and Issues in Administrative Behaviour, S. Manilick and E. Van Ness, Prentice Hall, Englewood-Cliffs, 1962.

2. William Guth and Renato Tagiuri, 'Personal Values and Corporate Strategy', *Harvard Business Review*, September-October 1965.

3. Herbert Simon, *Administrative Behaviour : A Study of Decision-Making Processes in Administrative Organisation*, Free Press, New York, 1947.

4. Abraham Maslow, *Motivation and Personality*, Harper and Brothers, New York, 1954.

5. Frederick Herzberg, *Work and the Nature of Man*, World Publishing Co. Cleveland, 1965.

6. Frederick Taylor, *Principles of Scientific Management*, Harper and Row, New York, 1911 (Reprint 1949)

7. Fritz   Roethlisberger and William Dickson, *Management and the Workers*, Harvard University Press, 1939.

8. Robert Bales, *Interaction Process Analysis*, Addison Wesley Press, Cambridge (Mass.), 1950.

9. Alvin Gouldner, "Cosmopolitans and Locals. Towards an analysis of Latent Social Roles". *Admin. Science Quarterly*, December 1957 and March 1958.

10. William Whyte, *The Organisation Man*, Simon and Schuster, 1956.

11. Warren Bennis, "A Funny Thing happened on the way to the Future", *American Psychologist* 1970, Vol.25, No.7.

12. Douglas Macgregor, *The Professional Manager*, McGraw Hill, New York, 1967

13. Thomas Hobbes, *Leviathan*.

14. Niccolo Machiavelli, *The Prince*.

15. Max Weber, *The Theory of Social and Economic Organisation*, Oxford Univ. Press, 1947 (First published in German in 1922).

16. Robert Balke and Jane Mouton, *Group Dynamics - Key to Decision Making*, Gulf Publishing Co., Houston, 1961.

17. Amitai Etzioni and David Selznick (Eds.), *Complex Organisations - A Sociological Reader*, Holt Rhinehart Wilson, New York, 1961.

18, as 17.

19. James Carroll, "Neotic Authority", *Public Admin. Review* 29, 1969.

20. Kurt Lewin in *Readings in Social Psychology*, E. Maccoby, T. Newcomb and E. Hartley (Eds.), Holt Rhinehart Wilson, New York, 1958.

21, Peter Bachrach and Morton Baratz, *Power and Poverty*, Oxford Univ. Press, New York, 1979.

22. C. Wright Mills, *The Power Elite*, Oxford Univ. Press, New York, 1957.

23. Robert Dahl, *Polyarchy*, Yale Univ. Press, Newhaven, 1971.

24. Earl Latham in *The Group Basis of Politics in Political Behaviour*, Heinz Eylau, Samuel Eldesveld and Morris Janowitz (Eds.), Free Press, New York, 1956.

25. Luther Gulick and Lyndall Urwick, *Papers on the Science of Administration*, Institute of Public Administration, New York, 1937.

26. James Mooney and Alan Reilley, *The Principle of Organisation*, Harper and Bros., New York, 1939.

27. Tom Burns and G. M. Stalker, *The Management of Innovation*, Tavistock, London, 1961.

28. Harold Wilensky, *Organisational Intelligence*, Basic Books, New York, 1967.

29. Erving Gottman, "The Characteristics of Total Institutions", Walter Reed (Ed.), *Institute of Research Symposium on Preventive and Social Psychiatry*, US Govt. Printing Office, 1957.

30. Robert Merton, 'Bureaucratic Structure and Personality', *Social Forces* 18, 1940.

31. Irving Jarvis, *Psychology Today*, Ziff Davis, New York, 1971.

32. Richard Cyert and James March, *A Behavioural Theory of the Firm*, Prentice Hall, Englewood Cliffs, 1967.

33. Gordon Tullock, *Politics of Bureaucracy*, Public Affairs Press, Washington, 1965.

34. Anthony Downs, *'Inside Bureaucracy'*, Little Brown, Boston, 1967.

35. as 33.

36. F. E. Emery and E. L. Trist, 'The Causal Texture of Organisational Environments' in Walter Hill and Douglas Egan (Eds.), *Readings in Organisation Theory : A Behavioural Approach*, Allyn and Baron, Boston, 1966.

37. Douglas Macgregor, *The Human Side of Enterprise*, McGraw Hill, 1961.

38. Herbert Simon, "Theories of Decision Making in Economics and Behavioural Science, *American Economic Review* 49, No.3.

39. Herbert Simon, "Theories of Bounded Rationality" in C. B. McGuire and R. Rander (Eds.), *Decisions and Organisations*, New Holland, Amsterdam, 1972.

40. Herbert Simon, "A Behavioural Model of Rational Choice", *Quarterly Journal of Economics*, 1955.

41. Charles Lindblom, *The Policy Making Process*, Prentice Hall, New York, 1968

42. David Braybrooks and Charles Lindblom, *A Strategy of Decisions*, Free Press, New York, 1963.

43. Charles Lindblom, "The Science of Muddling Through", *Public Admin. Review*, 1959 and "Still Muddling, not yet through", *Public Admin. Review*, Vol.29, No.6, 1979.

44. Aaron Wildavsky and Arthur Hammond, "Comprehensive v Incremental Budgeting in the Dept. of Agriculture", *Admin. Science Quarterly*, 10, December 1965.

45. Amitori Etzioni, "Mixed Scanning : A 'Third' Approach to Decision Making", *Public Admin. Review*, Vol.28.

46. Yehezkel Dror, *Public Policy Making Re-examined*, Chandler, New York, 1968.

47. J. D. Steinbrunner, *The Cybernetic Theory of Decision*, Princeton Univ. Press 1974.

48. E. Jacques, *A General Theory of Bureaucracy*, Heinemann, 1976.

49. L. V. Bertalanffy, "The Theory of Open Systems in Physics and Biology", *Science*, Vol.III, 1950.

50. "Socio-technical systems", *10th International Meeting of the Institute of Management Sciences*, Paris, September 1959.

51. Stafford Beer, *Cybernetics and Management*, John Wiley and Sons, 1964.

52. Norbert Wiener, *Cybernetics*, John Wiley and Sons, 1948.

53. Herbert Simon, *'The New Science of Management Decision'*, Harper and Row 1960.

54. W. Mackenzie, *'Power, Violence and Decision'*, Peregrine Books, 1975.

55. Igor Ansoff, *'Corporate Strategy'*, Penguin, 1968.

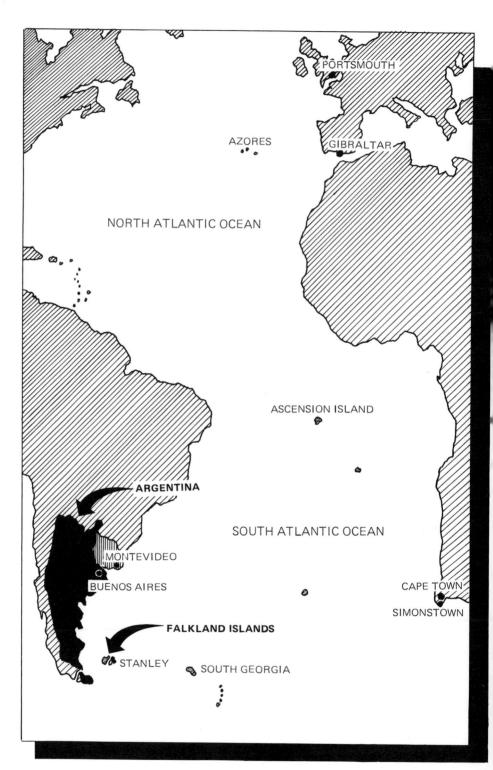

PORTSMOUTH

AZORES

GIBRALTAR

NORTH ATLANTIC OCEAN

ASCENSION ISLAND

ARGENTINA

SOUTH ATLANTIC OCEAN

MONTEVIDEO

BUENOS AIRES

CAPE TOWN

SIMONSTOWN

FALKLAND ISLANDS

STANLEY

SOUTH GEORGIA

CASE NO. 1

THE FALKLAND ISLANDS BUSINESS

Wars and Rumours Thereof

On Thursday, 8 April 1982 Britain announced that any Argentinian vessel found within a 200-mile "Maritime Exclusion Zone" around the Falkland Islands would be sunk. This move, immediately denounced by the Argentine Ambassador to the United Nations, Eduardo Roca, as an "act of war", was a significant escalation of the long-standing, tangled, and increasingly frenetic territorial dispute between the two nations.

The latest round in the disagreement over who should have sovereignty over the Falkland Islands had begun in bizarre fashion on 19 March. On this date Dr Stephen Martin, Commander of the British Antarctic Survey Expedition, reported to London that a party of Argentinians had landed, without immigration clearance, on South Georgia. When he had requested them to obtain proper authorisation to stay, he said, the ship and 50 men had sailed, leaving behind 10 of their companions and a hoisted Argentine flag. The reason for their presence on the island was, they claimed, the demolition of a whaling station, disused since the 1960s, for which purpose they had been hired by a Greek businessman.

The British Government saw this as "an apparently minor problem" and dealt with it accordingly. Nor was the Government unduly perturbed by the information received on 25 March which led it to conclude that a large number of ships — including an aircraft carrier, destroyers and landing craft — were heading for Port Stanley in the Falkland Islands. These activities were classified by Defence Secretary, John Nott, as "substantial Argentine naval exercises". (1)

By 1 April, however, the true nature of these "exercises" began to be fully appreciated. On this day Britain called for an urgent meeting of the U.N. Security Council to discuss what it saw as a menacing situation. Sir Anthony Parsons, Britain's U.N. Ambassador, explained:

> "My Government has received information which leads them to believe that an armed attack on the Falkland Islands may be imminent. My Government is a serious Government. We don't make a practice of imagining totally groundless threats." (2)

He was supported by his deputy, who argued that the urgency was necessary:

> "because the information that we have strongly suggests that if we had left it until tomorrow morning (i.e. 2 April) it might have been too late." (3)

In fact it was already too late, as the Falklands Governor, Rex Masterman Hunt, was only too aware. At 8.15 pm. he went on the Islands' radio to announce "emergency measures" in view of the "mounting evidence" to hand that Argentine armed forces were preparing to invade. He spoke on the radio again at 00.30 am. on the 2 April to inform the islanders of the outcome of the Security Council Meeting — a routine call to both Britain and Argentina to "refrain from the use of force".

The atmosphere on the 1 April in the Argentine capital had been electric. The Foreign Minister, Senor Nicanor Costa Mendez found himself on the receiving end of strenuous representations from the British and American Ambassadors. The U.S. Commander of Naval Operations, Admiral Thomas Heywood, was reported to have paid a visit to President Galtieri, head of Argentina's 3-man military junta Government. The junta itself — Admiral Jorge Isaac Anaya (Navy C-in-C), Brigadier-General Basilio Lami Dozo (Air Force C-in-C) and President Galtieri (also, as General, C-in-C of the Army) — met in almost permanent session.

There were heavy hints of what was to come. Later in the day, against a background of reports of large-scale movements of transport aircraft, the Argentine Defence Minister, Amadeo Frugoli, declared on TV that a 2-day visit to Puerto Belgrano, Argentina's key naval base, had indicated that "the state of preparation and operational capability of the navy is excellent." (4) To this he added the portentous statement that the navy was fully prepared to defend the nation's frontiers, national sovereignty and dignity.

U.S. President Reagan sought, reportedly, to dissuade the Argentine President from precipitate action in a pre-dawn 'phone call on 2 April. He knew what was coming. So did Rex Hunt. In the small hours he convened a meeting of chief officials and the commanders of the military forces on the islands. Only a garrison of a company of Royal Marines and a detachment of "irregulars" (Falkland Islands Defence Force and Settlement Volunteers) was on hand to repel the imminent invasion.

In December 1980 Nicholas Ridley, Minister of State at the Foreign and Commonwealth Office, presented the Falkland Islands Legislative Council with three policy options and asked for their preference. The Council voted for a 25-year "freeze" on the sovereignty issue and rejected the other choices of British administration/Argentine sovereignty or joint British—Argentine administration. This decision was denounced in February 1981 by the Argentines who offered, as a counter, to make the Falklands their "most favoured region".

EXHIBIT 1 : PICK WHERE YOU LIKE

They came at dawn in OPERATION BLUE. Two thousand picked troops to start with and another ten thousand later. A ferocious gun battle ended when the Governor ordered the Marine's commander, Major Gareth Noot, to surrender. Simultaneously the 22 Marines on South Georgia, led by Lt. Keith Mills, were fiercely resisting an Argentine landing at Grytviken and, in the process, damaging a Puma helicopter and a corvette. By mid-morning the invasion was over: the Falkland Islands had become "Las Malvinas" and Port Stanley renamed "Puerto Rivera".

Because of the confused situation and the lack of direct contact between the Falklands Government and the Foreign Office since the start of the invasion, it was not until the afternoon of 2 April that final confirmation of the Argentine action was given in Parliament.

At the abortive U.N. Security Council Meeting the day before, Senor Roca had protested about the "150 years of British aggression against my country". (5) Now the boot was clearly on the other foot!

One Man's Meat . . .

> "Twenty eight million Argentines have realised a dream. Every Argentine is breast-fed on the belief that Britain stole the islands from Argentina and can never be weaned from that idea. After lactation, indoctrination in the perfidy of "los Ingleses" continues at school. Every village in the country has at least one street named after Las Malvinas. The Argentines have always been deadly serious about their claim of sovereignty over the islands and have always said they would never give up until the Argentine flag was flying over Port Stanley." (6)

Thus Robert Cox, editor of the *Buenos Aires Herald* until 1979 when he was forced to flee. Nevertheless, the fascinating history of the Falklands and the dependencies (South Georgia, the South Sandwich, Shag and Clerke rocks) did not, in British eyes, bear out the Argentine claim.

First seen and landed on by the British (Captains Davies and Strong in 1592 and 1690, respectively), the islands were not settled, in fact, until 1764 and then by the French — at Port Louis in East Falkland! It is their name for the islands — Les Maloines, signifying the settlers' origins in St Malo — which became in Spanish "Las Malvinas". The British Captain Strong named them, by contrast, after the Navy Treasurer of his time, Viscount Falkland. In 1765 the British, apparently ignorant of the French presence, settled Port Egmont on Saunders' Island in the West Falklands. One year later France sold its interest in the islands to Spain and, in 1774, after a struggle between the Spanish and the British, the latter withdrew their settlement but not their claim to sovereignty. In 1812 the Spanish left, too.

"War" proclaimed Pope John Paul II in a speech during his U.K. visit in May 1982, "should belong to the tragic past, to history". It was a theme he continued to stress during his trip to Argentina a few weeks later. Here he condemned "the absurd and always unjust spectacle of war". Interestingly, during the visit and as "a symbol of peace", the Argentine military junta freed 128 "political" prisoners on 8 June. Some of these were thought to have been among the thousands of "disappeared ones" (desparicidos), Argentine citizens arrested by the military and whose whereabouts were unknown.

EXHIBIT 2 : THE PAPAL VIEW

The United Provinces of La Plata (later to become Argentina), having gained their independence from Spain in 1816, sent a frigate to take formal possession of the islands in 1820 and revived, under Governor Louis Vernet, the old Spanish settlement. In 1829 the British revived their claim also.

A mercantile dispute, in which Governor Vernet seized 3 American sealing schooners, led to the sacking of the Argenine settlement by an American squadron in 1831. In 1832 a British squadron removed the remaining Argentines and left control in the hands of the "senior" British resident.

Violent wrangles among the islanders brought the Royal Navy back in

1833 and order was maintained until 1841 under naval officer "Superintendants of the Islands". In this year the first civilian Governor was appointed and, since then, both inhabitants and islands have been regarded by Westminster as wholly British.

Ever since 1832 Argentina, on the other hand, had resisted Britain's claim and had repeatedly raised the subject at the United Nations, notably in 1946, 1965, 1976. The most recent in a series of talks between the two nations had taken place in February 1982 in New York, where the Argentine purpose had been bluntly spelled out as "achieving recognition of Argentine sovereignty over Las Malvinas". (7)

Not surprisingly, the successful regaining of the islands unleashed a patriotic furore. The British, having been unable to succeed in an attempt to invade Argentina in 1806 and having failed to impose a trade blockade in 1845, had again suffered a defeat. And a humiliating one at that!

By the afternoon of invasion day, a vast Buenos Aires crowd was in the Plaza de Mayo shouting support. Flags flew, horns hooted, lights flashed. The country's main trade union — the General Confederation of Labour — even went so far as to say that it was delaying plans for a general strike, a somewhat dramatic reversal of policy given the mauling its rally in the capital on 30 March had received at the hands of the authorities.

There was no end to the jubilation. President Galtieri spoke for the nation when he said on TV:

> "We have recovered the Southern Islands which, by legitimate right, are part of the national patrimony — with firmness but without rancour. Argentina had no choice but to use force because of an interminable succession of delays and evasions by Britain in perpetuating its rule ... The important step which we have just taken was made without taking any political calculation into account. It was taken in the name of each and every Argentinian citizen without sectional or factional interest." (8)

He had come to power with the promise of restoring the islands to Argentina, he said, and he had succeeded.

In another speech, on 10 April, he revealed the extent of the Argentine will to resist any attempt at restoring the *status quo ante bellum*. A chanting crowd of 100,000 in the Plaza de Mayo heard President

Galtieri declaim from the balcony of the Presidential Palace:

> "If they want to come, let them come! We will do battle . . . Our nation must be prepared to extend its hand in peace in a gentlemanly and honourable way. But the dignity and honour of Argentina is not negotiable." (9) "Our flag must fly." (10)

In this he echoed the "No Retreat!" speech of his Foreign Minister at the United Nations on 3 April. This justification for the Argentinian action had ended with the viewpoint that:

> "One of the last vestiges of colonialism ended yesterday in Latin American territory. The Republic of Argentina is threatening nobody . . . is not carrying out acts of aggression against anyone. It is of no interest to us to have an armed confrontation with anybody. We are willing to negotiate through channels of diplomacy anything but the sovereignty of our land. This is not open to negotiation." (11)

A War of Words

Nicanor Costa Mendez's speech was only one of a whole series in which both sides sought to mobilise support for their respective positions. It was a reply to Britain's demand on the day of the invasion for a speedy denunciation by the U.N. Security Council of Argentina's aggression. A heavily-pressed Sir Anthony Parsons successfully moved a resolution calling for an end to hostilities based on the immediate withdrawal of all Argentine forces. This was supported 10 - 1, with the U.S.S.R., Poland, Spain and China abstaining. Panama, hostile to the British position, proposed an abortive counter-resolution of its own. This called upon Britain:

> "to cease its hostile conduct, refrain from any threat or use of force and co-operate with the Argentine Republic in the de-colonisation of the Malvinas." (12)

In its preamble to Security Council Resolution 502, the Council recalled that Argentina had ignored its call to refrain from the use of force. The resolution itself gave Britain right to use force in self-defence under Article 51 of the United Nations Charter.

Support for the British position was evident from the reaction of the Commonwealth and the EEC. The latter had no hesitation in imposing trade sanctions. Japan's Prime Minister, Zenko Suzuki, affirmed that his country too backed Britain, provided it did not use force.

The Americans? That was seemingly a different story. British Ambassador, Sir Nicholas Henderson, straight from a meeting with U.S. Secretary of State Haig, sounded to have had an unsympathetic hearing,
judging by a subsequent press conference remark he made:

> "You Americans were concerned when you had 52 hostages in Iran.
> We have 1800 down there. These usurpers should leave that territory
> to live in the kind of democratic society to which it has belonged for
> 150 years . . . This is not something the U.S.A. can possibly tolerate
> or condone . . . It is not just a British problem but a problem of law
> and order in the American hemisphere." (13)

But the U.S.A. was not to be drawn. President Reagan's concern was
with mediation. "Because they are both our friends" he commented
"I have offered our help in an effort to bring the two countries together". (14)

Argentina, for its part, sought support from the Organisation of
American States at a meeting called on 5 April. Its 28 members had
previously shown themselves favourable to Argentina's stance on the
Falklands. Indeed, in 1976 its Inter-American Juridicial Committee
had issued a Falkland Islands Resolution stating that Argentina had
"an unassailable right to sovereignty" over the territory. In addition to
seeking support for his country's position, Foreign Minister Costa
Mendez also stated that, if necessary, his country might consider in-
voking the 1947 Rio Treaty, a Mutual-Assistance Defence Pact of the
South American nations.

The Soviety Union's U.N. Ambassador, Oleg Troyanovsky, simply denounced Britain's attitude and reproved it for "stubbornly opposing
the de-colonisation of the islands".

Matters Economic

Argentina, and the three-month old anti-Communist Galtieri junta,
was in early 1982 in deep economic trouble. Despite the appointment
of the respected Roberto Aleman as Economy Minister with a brief to
pursue free-market monetarist measures, facing up to the problems
was bound to be exceedingly difficult. Not least because of the opposition of the trade union movement.

The country had, on the other hand, substantial natural resources and
a well-developed economic infrastructure. Since the stopping of U.S.
grain exports to the Soviet Union as a reaction to the latter's invasion

of Afghanistan in 1979, Argentina had capitalised on Russia's requirements to the melodious tune of approximately £1.8 billion per annum.

There was also the question of oil. Much international excitement was generated in 1977 by an authoritative American report on the oil potential of the Falklands area and Esso, Shell and Total are known to have prospected in Argentine waters. To date, however, no large finds had been disclosed.

But such vistas were overshadowed by Argentina's economic illness — a mixture of incipient "slumpflation" and massive international indebtedness. Not only had the peso suffered a decline in its $ parity from 1300 in 1979 to over 11,000 in early 1982, but the nation had somehow to meet a repayment of £4 billion (capital and interest) on its total foreign debt of over £19 billion by the end of 1982. In the view of one disconsolate commentator, Argentina had a banking problem equal to that of "10 Polands", Poland being proverbial for its intractability as a debt rescheduling conundrum. Of Argentina's total foreign debt almost £6 billion was owed to American banks and almost £1 billion to U.K. finance houses. No matter. As from midnight on 6 April, Britain imposed a trade embargo on all Argentine goods and froze all the country's British assets. It suspended ECGD cover on British exports to Argentina and, by 10 April, had obtained the agreement of its EEC partners to an EEC trade boycott.

Whatever the impact of such moves militarily, it was quite clear that they would damage President Galtieri's economic recovery programme. This was based on denationalisation and deregulation of, and control of wages in, a public sector which accounted for 60% of the nation's GDP. It was also plain that the moves would have adverse consequences for Britain and its EEC partners since:

- British assets in Argentina were worth £250m and it was Britain's third largest customer in Latin America, taking (1980) £173m of our exports in return for £114m imports.

- Argentina's exports to the EEC made up about one fifth of its total exports. Italy, heavily dependent on Argentine leather was, after West Germany, the country's biggest EEC trading partner.

There were considerable worries in the City about the effect that a trade blockage would have on those firms — like Lloyds Bank, ICI, Pilkington's and BAT — who had Argentine subsidiaries and those who enjoyed substantial trading links (eg. Brooke Bond, Black & Decker, EMI). Especial anxiety was felt with regard to the potential spin-off effects on Britain's lucrative arms trade with Argentina, in the hands of such companies as Marconi, Plessey and Rolls Royce.

The biggest victim of all? Some thought that this might be the Falkland Islands Company itself. Whilst something of a commercial anachronism — it was one of the last remaining "Victorian Royal Charter" companies — the FIC dominated the Islands trade in its chief (and only) product: pure wool. It owned 43% of the land, 40% of the sheep and employed just under 50% of the economically-active population of "Kelpers", as the inhabitants of the Falklands called themselves. It controlled the only supermarket, the jetty, the supply ship and the bank. And strange to relate, it was itself owned by the smokeless fuel manufacturer, Coalite PLC, based in Bolsover, Derbyshire.

Call up the Guns

On Saturday, 3 April, the House of Commons met in Emergency Session to discuss the most recent developments. MPs listened intently as Prime Minister Margaret Thatcher announced that a large Task Force would be leaving shortly with the express intention of restoring British sovereignty to the Falklands. As soon as Argentine purposes had been correctly devined, the Royal Navy had, it was said, been put on immediate operational alert and all necessary preparations set in train for the Task Force's departure. The hunter-killer submarine, *Superb*, had already left port along with two of the largest fleet auxiliaries. It was estimated that it would take 3 weeks for Task Force vessels sailing from Britain to cover the journey to the Islands. Fortuitously a flotilla of RN ships was, at the time, engaged in a NATO exercise code-named SPRINGTRAIN off Gibraltar. They could reach the Falklands within 2 weeks.

To service the quarter of a million ton expedition would be, it was evident, an immense logistics undertaking. Supplies in excess of those carried by the Task Force would all have to be ferried by RAF Hercules transports via Ascension Island, a remote British-owned outcrop in the mid-Atlantic whose airbase was leased to the U.S.A. Even this was still 3300 nautical miles away from the Falklands and any flights would necessarily involve mid-air refuelling. What a contrast with the flight time for Argentine jets from their bases on the mainland! They were literally minutes away from the islands.

ARGENTINA

Airforce

Seven missile-armed fighter-bomber squadrons — Skyhawks, Mirages and Super-Etendards.

Navy

One ex-British aircraft carrier — the *25 de Mayo*. The cruiser *General Belgrano*, a Pearl Harbour survivor bought from the U.S.A. Two destroyers — *Hercules* and *Santissima Trinidad*.

Army

12,000 troops, a mixture of professionals and conscripts.

BRITAIN

Navy

Two aircraft carriers (*Invincible* and *Hermes*), six destroyers, one assault ship, seven frigates.

Airforce

Sea Harrier jets and Wessex helicopters, heavily armed with a diverse range of missiles — Seacat, Seaslug, Seaskua, Seadart and Exocet.

Army

6000 professionals drawn chiefly from 2nd and 3rd battalions of the Parachute Regiment, the Royal Marines, the Guards and the Ghurkas.

EXHIBIT 3 : FIRST TEAM LINE-UP

A Close-run Thing?

The carriers *Invincible* and *Hermes* sailed on 5 April. On that day considerations of military logistics loomed less large for the Government than the need to present an image of tight-lipped political resolution. And yet there were worries . . .

The Conservative Government's Defence policy was hinged on the replacement of its ageing Polaris nuclear ballistic missile system with the up-to-date Trident II system. Arguably this would provide a relatively low cost nuclear "shield" per person, but it was still a major expenditure — a cool £7.5 billion payable to the U.S.A. in installments — and one which impacted on the Government's ability to simultaneously fund an extensive conventional naval force.

The need for reduced public expenditure, the central plank in the Government's platform, also affected the size of the cake which had to be divided among the military. Particularly so, in the light of the launch of the new "cash limits" regime which was applied to the defence expenditure laid down for 1982/3. There was to be absolutely no spending in excess of the cash budget laid down.

Had the Argentines waited until 1984 and until the Government's 1981/2 plans had been effected, they would have found that:

- the carrier *Invincible* had been sold to the Australians and that *Hermes* had been retired from service.

- the ice-patrol ship *Endurance*, which performed sterling work during the Falklands crisis on station off South Georgia, had also been paid off.

- the naval dockyard at Gibraltar had been closed. Notably, its personnel worked desperately hard to transform the *SS Uganda* from a cruise ship into a floating Task Force hospital.

- four hundred of the workers at Portsmouth Naval Dockyard had lost their jobs through redundancy. Indeed 200 of these had already received their notices when the invasion took place. They were recalled to prepare *Hermes* and *Invincible* for sailing.

Defence cuts had already meant the paying-off in 1981, 6 months earlier than the date originally planned, of the Navy's last proper "Commando Ship", the 27,000-ton *HMS Bulwark*. Indeed *HMS Fearless*, the assault ship used in the Task Force, had already been condemned in the defence review of Summer 1981 but was later reprieved.

The Conservative Government's approach on defence spending was well summarised in a speech to businessmen made by Leon Brittan, Chief Secretary to the Treasury, in Oxford on 15 April. Without referring to the vociferous opposition of the Labour Party to the purchase of the American nuclear missile Trident II system (and their commitment to cancelling it on gaining office), he declared that:

"Far from cutting defence spending, we have actually increased it from a level of £7.5 billion which we inherited (from Labour) in 1978/9 to over £14 billion today. This cash increase of over 8% represents a real increase of about 11%. This financial year we will be spending more in real terms on conventional naval forces than was spent in the year before we came to office. As to the future, we will be spending more on the conventional navy, even when expenditure on modernising the strategic deterrent is at its peak, than in 1978/9. The navy still enjoys as high a proportion of the defence budget — 28% — as it did in that year.

Some critics have complained of the forthcoming loss to the fleet of the carriers *Invincible* and *Hermes*. This criticism is simply ludicrous because it ignores the crucial fact that two carriers will continue to be kept in service. *Illustrious*, which is to replace *Invincible*, will join the fleet late this year and the construction of *Ark Royal*, to replace *Hermes*, is proceeding satisfactorily.

The significant feature of our defence policy today is that the current programme of modernisation and rebuilding will actually leave us with more major ships and submarines operational in 1985 than there are today." (15)

The Falkland Islands: The Lessons

This White Paper was published on 14 December 1982. Its coverage was wide and embraced topics ranging from communications to public relations. Its central conclusion was that a sizeable garrison would have to be maintained in the Falklands for the foreseeable future.

Falkland Islands Review

This report, by a committee of Privy Counsellors under the chairmanship of Lord Franks, was published on 18 January 1983. It exonerated Mrs Thatcher and her governmental colleagues from any blame for the Argentine invasion. Heavy criticism was, however, aimed at the intelligence processing system.

The Future Defence of the Falklands

Published on 14 June 1983, this report advocated inter alia the building of a strategic airfield on the Falklands since failure to do so might be interpreted by the Argentines as a sign of weakness. The Government accepted this suggestion and announced its plan for a £215m facility — to be completed by 1986 — on 27 June 1983. This expenditure was additional to the already-agreed 6-year £31m economic development programme for the Islands which had been recommended in the up-dated Shackleton Report published on 13 September 1982. This latter was itself a revision of Lord Shackleton's 1976 *Economic Survey of the Falklands*. In this he had pointed out that, unless the Islands received more aid, they would suffer an economic collapse within 5 years.

EXHIBIT 4 : DRAWING CONCLUSIONS

Interestingly, the anti-nuclear defence stance of the Labour Party was to broaden much later into a 1986 Party Conference decision to get rid of all American "nuclear strike capability" bases in Britain. The Liberals echoed this viewpoint in their Conference of that year, much to the dismay of the leaders of the Liberal Party-Social Democratic Party Alliance (David Steel and Dr. David Owen). They were keen to maintain a nuclear deterrent — but of a predominantly European, rather than American, nature. Such considerations were anathema to the Conservatives. They were as committed in 1986 as they had been in 1982 to the maintenance of the nuclear defence partnership with the USA. It is noteworthy that some Conservative political strategists saw Labour's anti-American nuclear weapons stance as their opponents' Achilles Heel in the 1979 and 1983 elections. And they had no hesitation in kicking them in it. The same view was held in 1986 when Foreign Secretary Sir Geoffrey Howe vitriolically attacked a Labour Conference speech by the Labour leader:

> "Last week Mr. Kinnock said that he would not let his country die for him. The danger is that it could die because of him." (16)

However high the cost of sending the conventionally-armed Task Force to the Falklands — one well-informed estimate was £50 m plus £1 m per day to keep it on station without fighting — it was clear that the Government was prepared to pay it. Mrs. Thatcher's view was straightforward:

> "If the argument of "No Force At Any Price" were to be adopted at this stage, it would serve only to perpetuate the occupation of those very territories which have themselves been seized by force. The cost now . . . must be set against the costs we would one day have to pay if this principle went by default." (17)

And where could such costs arise? Consider the potential for trouble in Guyana (the erstwhile British Guiana) whose 160,000 sq. km. Essequibo region was claimed by Venezuela. Or Belize, another former British colony claimed by a territorial neighbour, in this case, Guatemala. Here the dispute was made more complicated by virtue of the agreement made in December 1981 for the maintenance of a British defence presence. This deal was made after Belize became independent in September 1981 and after acceptance of a British £6 billion independence grant. Or Gibraltar, which Spain has always claimed we seized illegally through the Treaty of Utrecht in 1713, and which one Spanish Prime Minister called "the pebble in Spain's shoes". Or Hong Kong . . .

THE FALKLANDS FIASCO?   Source: *Guardian*, 6 April, 1982.

All Those in Favour

An Emergency Debate followed the Prime Minister's announcement of the Task Force's departure. Mrs. Thatcher opened it with a ringing declaration of intent:

> "This House meets . . . to respond to a situation of great gravity. We are here because, for the first time for many years, a British sovereign territory has been invaded by a foreign power. I am sure the whole House will join me in condemning totally this unprovoked aggression . . . It has not a shred of justification and not a scrap of legality . . . It is the Government's objective to see that the Islands are freed from occupation and are returned to British administration at the earliest possible moment . . . The people of the Falkland Islands, like the people of the United Kingdom, are an island race. Their way of life is British, their allegiance is to the Crown. The people are few in number but have a right to live in peace and determine their own allegiance." (18)

Mrs. Thatcher's stance was strongly supported by the Leader of the Opposition, Michael Foot. He denounced the Argentines' "foul and brutal aggression" and stressed the dangers for "this dangerous planet" that would arise if such aggression were seen to succeed. He placed no trust in any guarantee given by invading forces from a country in which "thousands of people fighting for their political rights have been imprisoned". (19)

Two members in particular took the strongest possible line. One, Enoch Powell (Ulster Unionist), stated unequivocally:

> "There is only one reaction which is fit to meet the unprovoked aggression upon one's own sovereign territory. That is direct, unqualified, immediate willingness . . . to use force." (20)

Reminding Mrs. Thatcher of her reputation as the "Iron Lady" of British politics, he commented:

> "In the next week or two the nation, and Mrs. Thatcher herself, will find out what metal she is made of."

Another was Conservative Patrick Cormack. For him there was simply no alternative:

> "Our united resolve must be to utilize the unanimity expressed in this debate and to know that we will not shrink, however distasteful the use of force may be, in trying to free these prisoners and restoring our sovereignty to these bleak and barren lands. If the Government fails

along that line there may be many of us who would have to question our position on these benches." (21)

The threat made by Patrick Cormack was also in the minds of others. Sir Bernard Braine, for instance. His "normal Englishman's blood" was boiling at the thought that 1800 of "our people" should be left in the hands of "these criminals". Firm action from the Government, he said, or his support couldn't be relied upon.

TABLE 1 :   **ELECTION RESULTS (1979 and 1983)**

| | GENERAL ELECTION IN | | | | | |
| | 1983 | | | 1979 | | |
	Cons.	Lab.	Lib-SDP All.	Cons.	Lab.	Lib-SDP All.
Seats	397	209	23	332	238	42
% of Seats	61	31.2	3.5	52.2	37.4	6.6
Votes Cast ('000)	13012	8456	7793	13697	11509	4313
% of Votes	44.4	28.8	26.6	46.4	38.9	14.6
Turnout (%)	73			76		
% Change in Seats (increase/decrease on 1979)	19.5	(12.1)	(45.2)			
% Change in Vote	(5.0)	(26.5)	80.6			
Votes needed to elect 1 Member of Parliament ('000)	32.7	40.4	338.8	41.2	48.3	102.7

Notes : 1979 Seats as at dissolution in 1983.
: 1979 Votes cast for "Lib-SDP Alliance" is for Liberal Party only.

Not all were of such a mind. George Foulkes posed the agonising dilemma:

"Can anyone tell me how we retake the Falkland Islands without loss of life to the men and women we are interested in protecting? My gut reaction is to use force. Our country has been humiliated but we must be sure that we are not going to kill thousands of people in using that force." (22)

Others were averse to the use of force in support of what they clearly saw as an outdated imperialist posture. Alex Lyon (Lab., York) delivered his broadside in the debate on 14 April:

> "I would not say that they (the Falklanders) have the right to determine whether we shall expend in pursuance of their right of self-determination not only money, not only ships or aircraft, but people's lives in order to ensure that the 1800 are entitled to maintain the way of life they already have. I do not care whether it brings down a Government. What I care about is whether human lives are going to be lost — whether Argentine or British — so we can preserve an illusion about the power of the British Empire." (23)

Tam Dalyell (Lab., West Lothian) — a major critic of what he called the "operation to recover Mrs. Thatcher's face" — put a different gloss on the use of force. In a Commons speech on the day the aircraft carriers sailed, he said:

> "Would you advise the Foreign Secretary and the Defence Secretary that as soon as the first shot is fired they will be taking on the right, left and centre of the entire Spanish-speaking world." (24)

By far the strongest opponent of the Government's approach, however, was MP Tony Benn. In a speech at Salisbury on 6 April he warned the Labour Party to have nothing to do with Mrs. Thatcher's "military adventure" which he forecast would cost £500m. (25) This estimate was revised upwards in comments made on the "Today" programme on 24 April, when he described the Falklands as:

> "an outpost of empire which we seized by force from the Argentine in the last century and which Britain neglected. Britain has even failed to give the islanders an airstrip while the Falklanders themselves have developed links with Argentina, going there for medical treatment and education. Britain did not care a bit about the Falkland Islands. Then when things go wrong we mount this huge task force which will probably cost . . . £1000m. and may lead to massive loss of life."

The best solution in his view? United Nations' arbitration.

Consequences

Anger was directed not only at the Argentines in the post-invasion Emergency Debate. The Government came in for a blistering attack from all quarters for having failed to anticipate, and take adequate counter-measures against, the invasion. Conservative MPs were in the

HOW OTHERS SEE US: RUSSIAN EYES

Source: *Socialist Industry*. Printed in *Daily Telegraph*, 16.4.82.

HOW OTHERS SEE US: SPANISH EYES

Source: *El Alcazar* (Madrid). Printed in *Daily Telegraph*, 8.4.82.

QUESTION	YES	NO	DON'T KNOW	TOTAL %
Do you support the Government Falklands' policy?	78	10	12	100
Should British lives be put at risk to recover the Falkland Islands?	36	57	7	100
Should the Falkland Islanders' lives be put at risk to recover the Falkland Islands?	31	58	11	100

Results of a poll of 1000 respondents carried out by MORI for the I.T.V. programme "Weekend World" after the announcement of the Maritime Exclusion Zone.

EXHIBIT 5 : WHAT THE PEOPLE THINK

van. Edward Du Cann complained that we were "woefully unprepared" and that the assumption that the problem could be solved by diplomatic means was "fatuous". For Julian Amery the invasion was an inevitable consequence of "unpreparedness and feeble counsel".

The Labour benches, despite their support in general for the Task Force policy, lambasted the Government:

> "It seems that the British Government has been fooled . . . the Government must answer for that." (Michael Foot)

> "Is it not a fact that whenever the tinpot Fascist junta that rules Argentina is in trouble at home, it threatens the Falklands? Were the signs not to be seen some time ago? Did not the Secretary of State for Defence contribute to the invasion to some extent by his talk of scrapping *Endurance* and a large proportion of our surface fleet and thus perhaps giving the false impression that Britain might be willing − as she will not − to abdicate her responsibilities in the area? It was a collective decision of the three most guilty people in this Government. It is these three who are on trial today." (John Silkin, Shadow Defence Minister)

Such attacks were relatively mild compared with the onslaught of the Shadow Foreign Secretary, Denis Healey, delivered on 7 April. Referring to the matter as "one of the most disgraceful episodes in British history", he said:

> "If any British Government had behaved in this way on a vital British interest 200 years ago, the Prime Minister would have been impeached." (26)

Even so, it was still a formidable Commons castigation for the Prime Minister and Defence Secretary. They justified their position staunchly on the grounds that:

> (1) "The only way of being certain of preventing an invasion would have been to keep a large force close to the Falklands. No Government has ever been able to do that and the cost would be enormous." (Mrs. Thatcher)

> (2) "We were throughout seeking a peaceful solution through the United Nations and other means. To have sent a naval task force to the islands at a time when Britain might have been going to the U.N. would have seemed highly provocative." (John Nott)

> (3) "It would have been absurd to despatch the fleet every time there was bellicose talk in Buenos Aires. There was no good reason to think on 3 March that an invasion was being planned, especially against the background of constructive talks (held in February and March)." (Mrs. Thatcher)

But in the event it was not enough. Members listened attentively to a plain-speaking Dr. David Owen:

> "The question is how to restore confidence. We have heard rumours that the Secretary of State for Defence has tendered his resignation, only for it to be refused. I would say that I expect no other of him. He is a man of honour."

On the very day that the flagship *Hermes* set sail for Falklands waters, the Foreign Secretary, Lord Carrington, thought to help in the restoration of confidence by resigning. He was replaced by Francis Pym. On that day too the £ Sterling fell to a four-and-a-half-year low and almost £2.6 billion was wiped off the value of shares on the London Stock Market.

It was, however, with the utmost reluctance that Mrs. Thatcher had accepted Lord Carrington's resignation as she pointed out in a television interview:

> "If a person says to me 'It is a matter of honour and I feel I should go' that is one ground which I am not at liberty to refuse. I did so with great regret, because he's been a marvellous Foreign Secretary. He is a

sturdy and bonny fighter for Britain, a very gallant officer. We shall miss him."

Would she herself resign if she failed to regain the Falklands, she was asked. She retorted:

"Failure? Do you remember what Queen Victoria once said? 'Failure?' she said 'The possibilities simply do not exist'.

That's the way we must look at it, when you stop a dictator there are always risks. But there are greater risks in not stopping a dictator. My generation learned that a long time ago." (27)

On the Receiving End

The result of the Argentine invasion, so far as the islands' inhabitants were concerned, was an immediate loss of freedom. A set of strict regulations including a curfew and punishment for insolent behaviour — "rude gestures" would get you 30 days' jail, "disrespect to the Argentine flag" 60   — were immediately imposed by the military and by the islands' Governor, General Benjamin Menendez. Under such restrictions, with some islanders' homes damaged and others' requisitioned, bad weather, water (of all things in the Falklands!) running scarce and the knowledge that the British armada was on the way, it was little wonder that the "Kelpers" in their somewhat old-fashioned and far-off world were uncertain and apprehensive. Their "spokesmen" put forward sharply-contrasting views about what should be done. Air Commodore Brian Flow, Director-General of the Falkland Islands Office in London, fully endorsed Francis Pym's "Britain does not appease dictators" (28) line:

"In the process of escalation, I would opt for a show of strength off Buenos Aires or an assault on Comodoro Rivadavia (a big airbase and logistics centre). I may be considered a hard-liner but this is war." (29)

Another such was Bill Luxton, a deported, allegedly-subversive Falklands sheep farmer. He said his fellow-islanders would "never" accept living under an Argentine flag and would "definitely not" prefer Argentine rule to armed conflict, even with loss of life. To a European Parliament which had voted 202-28 for a withdrawal of Argentine troops, he offered heartfelt thanks.

Others were not so keen on the use of force. Edward Carlisle, for instance, brother of a former Education Minister in Mrs. Thatcher's Government. Interviewed on 9 April after returning home from the

Falklands where he had sheep farming interests, he said:

> "For God's sake, cool it. The majority of the people do not want Britain to take military action. People's attitudes have changed remarkably in the last week. We are prepared to consider Argentine sovereignty over the Islands in return for withdrawing the troops. The Argentines have promised colour TV and other benefits . . . People feel that Argentina might put more money into the Islands in five years than Britain has in one hundred and fifty. . . . The British Government has got to realise how passionately the Argentine people feel about the Falklands. There will be no backing down. Many of the islanders feel it is worth giving Argentina a chance. After all, hardly anyone in Britain knew where the Falklands were until two weeks ago." (30)

A week later Her Majesty's Government received an unusual communication with a similar message. The telegram sent by the Association of British and British-Descended Farmers in Argentina — just some of the 17,000 British passport holders in the country — read:

> "WE BRITONS AND SONS OF BRITONS FARMING IN ARGENTINA WISH TO INFORM HMG THAT FOR YEARS AND, IN SOME CASES, GENERATIONS WE HAVE LIVED AND WORKED HAPPILY UNDER ARGENTINE GOVERNMENTS OF DIFFERING POLITICAL PERSUASIONS.

> WE HAVE LED OUR TRADITIONAL BRITISH WAY OF LIFE WITHOUT ANY HINDRANCE AND OUR EXPERIENCE HAS LED US TO BELIEVE THAT THE INHABITANTS OF THE FALKLANDS HAVE NOTHING TO LOSE AND MUCH TO GAIN BY COMING UNDER ARGENTINE SOVEREIGNTY. WE BELIEVE THAT AN ATTEMPT TO REGAIN THE ISLANDS BY FORCE WOULD CAUSE AN IRREVOCABLE END TO THE ISLANDERS' WAY OF LIFE AND OFFER NO PROSPECTS FOR A SOUND AND PEACEFUL FUTURE. IT WOULD CREATE DAMAGE OUT OF ALL PROPORTION TO THE VALUE OF THE ISLANDS, NOT ONLY IN ARGENTINA BUT IN THE WHOLE OF LATIN AMERICA."

This was not a viewpoint immediately shared by the Islands' leading administrators who had been "repatriated" by the Argentines.

Passage of Arms

By late April the 70 vessels of the British Task Force were standing off the Falklands, their 8000-mile journey having taken three weeks. During this time, as can be imagined, there had been feverish diplomatic attempts to avert conflict. Neither side, however, had budged.

The Argentine forces on the Falklands surrendered on 14 June after a bloody campaign in which 254 British and 750 Argentine lives were lost and in which there was large-scale destruction of materiel. The financial cost of the British action has been put at £750m. It was an object lesson to many in the awesome capabilities of modern weaponry and in the courage of those pitted in a hard fight against a resolute foe and an inhospitable terrain.

The campaign began furiously with three separate air and sea actions, each of which had a symbolic, as well as a practical, significance. These were:

- the immense-range May-day attack on the Port Stanley airfield by ageing Vulcan bombers operating from Ascension Island. The flight would have been absolutely impossible without in-flight refuelling from tanker aircraft, itself a highly-skilled and hazardous undertaking.

- the torpedoeing of the cruiser *General Belgrano* by the nuclear submarine *Conqueror* on 2 May with the loss of 368 Argentine lives.

- the Exocet-missile attack carried out by Argentine Super-Etendard fighter-bombers on 4 May in which the British destroyer *Sheffield* sank with the loss of 24 lives and heavy injuries. This was the world's first real-life opportunity to evaluate properly in action the punch and manoeuvrability of the Exocet guided missile.

  It can be launched at any altitude between 300 and 30,000 feet at up to 40 miles' distance from the target. After launch, the missile drops quickly to a surface-skimming height of 9 feet. The target is located by a mixture of data fed into its on-board computer before launch and an updating of that information by its airborne radar. The targetting system is euphemistically called 'Fire and Forget'.

The contemplation of these events sharpened some of the divisions that existed in the House of Commons over the best way to move forward. A Commons motion, tabled on 5 May by Dame Judith Hart, attracted the signatures of one-third of the Labour membership. It read:

"That this House, deeply concerned at the escalation of conflict and loss of life . . . fearing that there are grave dangers of further escalation involving other countries, recognising that a negotiated solution will be required, believing that the UN must be involved in this, urge that there should now be an immediate truce . . . and that HM Government should fully commit itself to genuine peaceful negotiations."

This was much more elaborately phrased than the Conservative motion tabled the following day by Ian Lloyd. This called for the implementation of "whatever measures should prove necessary to eliminate the capacity of Argentine forces to inflict unacceptable losses on the British fleet".

An assistant secretary in the Ministry of Defence, Clive Ponting, was charged on 18 August 1984 under sec. ii (1)(a) of the 1911 Official Secrets Act with having communicated information to an unauthorised person on or about 16 July. MP Tam Dalyell stated the day after that it was he who had received the material and that he had passed it to the Common Foreign Affairs Committee. The material allegedly contained indications that the Government might have withheld some information about the sinking of the *Belgrano* and that this information was concerned with possible arbitrary changes in the rules of engagement. The accused was acquitted of the charge on 11 February 1985.

A Commons debate was held one week later on the motion "That this House recognises that the sinking of the *General Belgrano* was a necessary and legitimate action". It was carried by 350 votes to 0. A Labour amendment "That this House believes that, by seeking to conceal information from, and to purvey distorted and misleading information to, the House of Commons and its Foreign Affairs Committee on the subject of the *General Belgrano*, Ministers have betrayed their responsibility to Parliament" was defeated by 350 votes to 202.

EXHIBIT 6: THE BELGRANO AFFAIR

The Government did not alter course: no negotiations on anything until all Argentine troops had quit the Islands.

The plans for landing went ahead as did the Argentine attempts to strengthen their hold. The first British move was at and around Port San Carlos on 21 May. It was successful but provoked counterattacks in which the destroyer *Coventry* and the container ship *Atlantic Conveyor* were crippled.

Again a search at the UN for a diplomatic way out of the crisis. Another resolution — 505 this time — urging all sides to cooperate with the Secretary-General in finding a peaceful solution. Again failure.

A sharper tone was introduced into the multi-national deliberations by the adoption by the Organisation of American States by 17 votes to 0 (4 abstentions, including the USA) of a motion condemning the UK for its "disproportionate" armed attack and calling on the USA to stop aiding Britain. This too made no difference to the course of events in the Falklands.

The capture of Darwin and Goose Green on 28 May took the "yomping" British troops much closer to the final objective, but not without the tragic loss of the Regimental Commander of 2 Para, Lt-Col. Herbert Jones. For his bravery he was awarded the second posthumous Victoria Cross of the Falklands War, the first having gone to Sgt. Ian McKay of 3 Para.

> "Government spending on the Falklands since the invasion has amounted to more than £1m. for each of the Islands' inhabitants."
>
> Prime Minister, Commons Written Reply, 12 November 1984.

EXHIBIT 7: THE FALKLANDS PRICE

Another bridgehead was established on 6 June. But the cost of the landfall this time was heavy loss of life and injury among men of the Ghurkas, Welsh and Scots Guards as their landing ships — *Sir Tristram* and *Sir Galahad* — came under fire. It also came after Britain and the USA had vetoed another attempt in the Security Council to halt the battle.

The seizure of the high ground west of Port Stanley — Mount Tumbledown, Wireless Ridge and Sapper Hill — brought the fight to an end. On 15 June Major-General Jeremy Moore was able to report to the Ministry of Defence:

> "THE FALKLAND ISLANDS ARE ONCE MORE UNDER THE GOVERNMENT DESIRED BY THEIR INHABITANTS. GOD SAVE THE QUEEN."

A Sticky End

On a political whim an island community, remote in time and space from its guardian, had been plunged into the horrors of late twentieth century, advanced-technology warfare. Bad enough in the eyes of some of the inhabitants to have to adjust to the so-called pleasures of the age! It is little wonder that the traumatic memory of the conflict has endured, especially as it is daily reinforced by the vision of the military airstrip complex, the permanent garrison of troops, the acreage of still-uncleared Argentine anti-personnel mines and the windswept military graveyards.

> "The historical and legal evidence demonstrates such areas of uncertainty that we are unable to reach a categorical conclusion on the legal validity of the historical claims of either country. A solution acceptable to the Falklands' immediate neighbours is essential to the islanders themselves. Their prosperity must depend on having decent relations with Argentina."

EXHIBIT 8: FOREIGN AFFAIRS SELECT COMMITTEE REPORT
Chairman: Sir Anthony Kershaw (Published 12/12/84)

Some aspects of life around them began slowly to return to some semblance of normality, although no formal peace document was signed. The Eastern European factory ships returned to gather their fishy harvests in the krill-rich waters of the South Atlantic. The EEC's trade sanctions against Argentina were lifted on 21 June 1982 and Japan's on 25 June 1982. Even many of the financial restrictions imposed by Britain were removed in September 1982.

No return to life as it was in Argentina, however. The debacle of the loss of the Malvinas resulted initially in the resignation of General Galtieri as President, Commander in Chief and junta member and ultimately provoked the replacement of the military regime by a civilian administration under President Raoul Alfonsin on 10 December 1983.

> It is an immense paradox that one of the most readily identifiable symbols of Britain's Industrial Revolution and the might and majesty of its Empire — Isambard Kingdom Brunel's steamship *The Great Britain* — should have ended her life as a stranded hulk in the Falklands. She has now been brought back to Bristol and been lovingly restored as a museum piece.

EXHIBIT 9: SIC TRANSIT GLORIA

No change in British policy followed this upheaval. This had been set out in the Queen's Speech following Mrs. Thatcher's Government's re-election in 1983:

"My Government will continue fully to discharge their obligations to the people of the Falkland Islands while seeking more normal relations between this country and Argentina."

This effectively meant that no discussions of the sovereignty issue would be tolerated by Britain despite the exactly contrary thrust of General Assembly Resolution 38/12.

The advent of President Alfonsin did not alter the Argentine stance either. Indeed, in his very first policy statement on 3 January 1984, he rejected the "illegality" of the British military presence on the Falklands and alluded to the "permanent will of the Argentine people to reverse that situation". He has since won strong support from Spain, since the outbreak of hostilities a new entrant to the EEC and NATO alike, for his country's position. The Declaration of Madrid issued after a 5-day official visit to Spain by President Alfonsin in mid-1984 stated:

"Spain and Argentina, which are the victims of an anachronistic colonial situation, support their respective claims to Gibraltar and the Malvinas to restore the integrity of their national territories by peaceful means."

Life was far from normal for the three members of the military junta who had led their forces to defeat. An official investigation into their military and political conduct of the war by General Benjamin Rattenbach led to their trial and being condemned, in May 1986, to varying terms of imprisonment. General Galtieri received a 12 year sentence.

References:

1. John Miller, 'No Sailing Orders Yet', *Daily Telegraph*, 3 April 1982.
2. Ian Ball, 'Falkland Invasion Imminent', *Daily Telegraph*, 2 April 1982.
3. As 2.
4. As 2.
5. Ian Ball, 'War of Words in UN as Commando Force Strikes', *Daily Telegraph*, 3 April 1982.
6. Robert Cox, 'The Raising of the National Dream', *Sunday Times*, 4 April 1982.
7. John Miller, 'Dispute Rumbled on for 150 Years', *Daily Telegraph*, 3 April 1982.
8. Andres Wolbek-Stok, 'Jubilation in Buenos Aires', *Daily Telegraph*, 3 April 1982.

9. Ian Mather, 'Galtieri — "We will do battle" ', *Daily Telegraph*, 11 April 1982.

10. Frank Taylor, "Our flag must fly", *Daily Telegraph*, 15 April 1982.

11. As 9.

12. John Miller, 'Security Council vote is some comfort to Foreign Office', *Daily Telegraph*, 5 April 1982.

13. Richard Beeston, "Usurpers should leave", *Daily Telegraph*, 7 April 1982.

14. James Wightman, *Daily Telegraph*, 16 April 1982.

15. As 14.

16. Sir Geoffrey Howe's speech at the Conservative Party Conference, 1986.

17. "Our objective is to free the islanders" says Thatcher and Parliament, *Observer*, 4 April 1982.

18. As 17.

19. As 17.

20. As 17.

21. Colin Brown, 'PM gets rough ride in Commons', *Guardian*, 5 April 1982.

22. As 21.

23. As 12.

24. 'Government requisitions P&O liner', *Guardian*, 6 April 1982.

25. Nicholas Comfort, "Falkland Neglect" attack by Benn', *Times*, 24 April 1982.

26. 'Yesterday in Parliament', *Daily Telegraph*, 8 April 1982.

27. Ian Aitken, 'Thatcher tries to plug leaks left by Lord Carrington's resignation', *Guardian*, 6 April 1982.

28. As 27.

29. As 26.

30. Alan Osborn, "Withdrawal by junta is priority", say Euro MPs', *Daily Telegraph*, 23 April 1982.

CASE NO. 2

PIGGY IN THE MIDDLE: THE STORY OF BL's PAY DISPUTE

At the end of August 1981 came the news that British Leyland had lost £225 millions on its operations for the first half of the year. In the previous year it had lost £530 millions and the loss for the *current full year* (1981) was forecast to be about £500 millions. Responding to criticisms of company performance by Walter Goldsmith, Director General of the Institute of Directors, Sir Michael Edwardes — dubbed by *The Economist* BL's "bantam cock chairman" (1) — stated:

> "The left hopes I will advocate import controls and the right wants me to sell off parts of the business. I'm doing neither and going straight down the middle. So people at both ends of the spectrum are having a go and, in effect, they are helping each other .... If the extreme left is advocating an extreme wage claim, then the right will win because the business will be broken up. So BL is the piggy in the middle". (2)

He underlined, in his response, the certainty of the demise of BL in such an eventuality and the extent to which he would fight against an 'extreme' claim.

> "We won't be influenced", he said, "by whatever anyone else offers in industry or indeed by the unions claim. We will be influenced only by what we can afford . . . . We have to remember that every 1 per cent on pay costs us £8 million a year and anything above what we can afford will have to come out of investment . . . If the pay thing comes to a crunch, the company closes". (3)

This 'shot across the bows' of the unions at BL cars came as the unions lodged their claim for a wage increase for BL members of £20 across the board on 28 August.

Industrial Action Recommended

Management's reply to the £20 claim was an offered 3.8 per cent increase in basic pay rates, which was just under the 4 per cent specified as the limit for pay rises for public sector workers by the government for the coming year. On 2 October, union leaders representing the 58,000 BL manual workers described the offer as "shocking and disgraceful". They counter-attacked by passing this resolution:

> "In the absence of a substantial improvement to the amount of

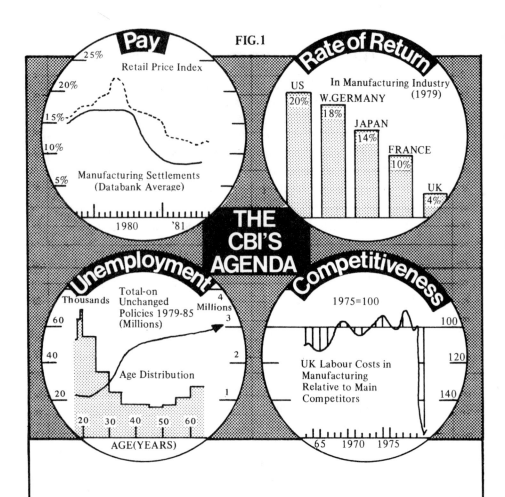

FIG.1

Pay

Retail Price Index

25%
20%
15%
10%
5%

Manufacturing Settlements
(Databank Average)

1980   '81

Rate of Return

In Manufacturing Industry
(1979)

US 20%
W.GERMANY 18%
JAPAN 14%
FRANCE 10%
UK 4%

THE
CBI'S
AGENDA

Unemployment

Total-on
Unchanged
Policies 1979-85
(Millions)

Thousands
60
40
20

Millions
4
3
2
1

Age Distribution

20 30 40 50 60
AGE(YEARS)

Competitiveness

1975=100

UK Labour Costs in
Manufacturing
Relative to Main
Competitors

100
120
140

65 1970 1975

The above figure appeared in the *Daily Telegraph* of 1 November 1981, the opening day of the CBI's annual conference and is reproduced by kind permission of the then City Editor, Ivan Fallon (now with the *Sunday Times*). It reveals a gloomy economic background to the general economy and to the BL pay dispute. The one bright spot was the level of pay settlements, which had been running three to four per cent below the inflation rate for the best part of a year. On the other hand, the competitiveness of British industry had fallen alarmingly, and typical rates of return were well below those achieved in other economies. Unemployment had struck the young particularly hard, and was expected to rise inexorably until at least 1985.

money offered on the grade rates, we are recommending industrial action to commence on November 1". (4)

The following table of price movements shows how the 3.8 per cent offer compared with percentage changes taking place during the period in question:

Price increases year to:	December 1980	July 1981
Nationalized Industries	30	20
Gas	26	25
Telephone	44	24
Electricity	30	22
Rail	41	17
Rents	23	40
Rates & Water	27	21
Tobacco	11	23
Alcohol	18	17
Food	10	8
Durables	8	5
Clothing & Footwear	6	0
Retail Price Index	15	11

Already the battle lines were being formed between the unions and BL Management with a comment from Grenville Hawley, Car Industry Negotiator for the Transport & General Workers' Union:

"We are talking about all-out strike action . . . . The offer of less than 4 per cent is totally unacceptable . . . . We are not in the ball game for percentage increases . . . . It is chicken feed". (5)

For the opposition, Geoffrey Armstrong, BL's Director of Employee Relations, flatly pronounced:

"We have told the trade unions that this is as much as we can afford and there can be no improvement . . . We cannot succeed by giving away vast sums of money in pay increases before we have earned them. We can only succeed by further improvements in the level of productivity with employees' rewards being linked to those improvements". (6)

Interestingly, however, a mass meeting of BL workers in its Bus and

Truck Division indicated, on the very same day, that they were prepared to accept a 4 per cent increase.

A Dire Warning

The call for all-out strike action made by the union negotiators was endorsed by 300 senior shop stewards from 34 BL plants meeting on 9 October. They rejected any idea of a ballot vote on the shop floor and said that mass meetings at each plant on 16 October would decide the issue.

The gravity of the situation facing the workforce was brought home to them in a letter sent by Sir Michael Edwardes to each employee on 14 October. In it he warned that, in the event of a strike over pay, the parts of the company affected would be closed and no redundancy money would be paid. He also argued his tough approach on the union's pay claim in a speech at the annual luncheon of the Fellowship of the Motor Industry on 16 October:

> "Some people say I must be courageous to take the stance I have. No one needs courage less than I do. If you haven't got the money, how can you pay it?" (7)

This attitude was backed up by the Industry Secretary, Patrick Jenkin who, speaking on television the same day, said:

> "There must come a time when the tax payer cannot go on supporting a company which is constantly subject to interruptions of this sort .... If, of course, the company were liquidated while large parts of it were on strike then no redundancy payments would be due and that would save very large sums of money." (8)

By contrast, the President of the Amalgamated Union of Engineering Workers, Terry Duffy, rejected outright the company's viewpoint on pay:

> "I fear", he stated, "we could see civil disorder in the streets. The men feel let down by Sir Michael. We have co-operated in a 40,000 job rundown at BL and productivity has gone up by 30 per cent". (9)

Calling for Sir Michael's resignation he continued:

> "We cannot lose the British Car Industry like we lost the motor cycle industry because of the obstinacy of one man and his board .... Edwardes cannot give himself a £35,000 a year rise and then say there's no money for us." (10)

Against the background of these comments, BL manual workers voted at plant meetings on 16 October by a large majority to back an all-out strike.

Terry Duffy was not surprised at this expression of the mood of the workforce:

> "We expected this vote" he claimed, "and it's the first time that Sir Michael's policy of 'Take it or Leave it' has been disregarded. This time he is wrong. The moderates and the militants have joined forces and they are going to take him on". (11)

There was, however, a willingness on the part of Grenville Hawley to get negotiations under way with company representatives at any time before 18 November. Clearly they had to be 'meaningful' and that, to him and his negotiating colleagues, meant 'money on the table'.

The Story So Far

This was not, in fact, the first time that Sir Michael Edwardes had gone direct to the workforce 'over the heads' of the union leaders, nor the first time that the threat of job losses had been used to promote low wage rises. Since his appointment as Chairman by the Callaghan government on 1 November, 1977:

- 13 BL plants had been closed with 65,000 redundancies

- Single-figure wage rises had been achieved in 1978 (5 per cent), 1979 (5 per cent) and 1980 (6.8 per cent)

- Productivity had been improved by 30 per cent with stoppages reduced from 10 per cent to 1.5 per cent of working time

- The firm had pursued a product development strategy (Metro, Honda-Triumph Acclaim and the future LM10 and 11) involving substantial investment in plant automation.

Whilst these achievements could be regarded, from a business viewpoint, as significant steps along BL's road to potential recovery, they had not been achieved without hostility. In *The Observer* (25 October, 1981), Robert Taylor pointed out:

> "To many of the shop stewards in BL, the key issue is not the pay offer but the way in which Sir Michael Edwardes runs the company . . . . Words like 'prison camp' and 'Bantustan' are freely used by stewards to describe workplace life in BL since the revival of managerial control on the shop floor".

Taylor cited the plant incentive scheme as a substantial factor in shop floor dissatisfaction with pay rates. Union officials calculated that BL's semi-skilled workers would have required a 73.2 per cent wage rise, and skilled men one of 34.4 per cent to restore their real earnings to what they had been 10 years before.

The plant incentive scheme had been imposed by management when the unions failed to co-operate in negotiations over it. It was said to be highly complex and unrelated to individual effort. There were some big bonus earners, for example, the plants at Canley, Solihull, Longbridge and the Parts Division, but even there bonus payments had fluctuated wildly. At Longbridge the bonus/man varied over the period 2–27 May, 1981 between £13.05 and £1.10 per week. The company admitted to current disparities between plants, with some bonuses as low as £3.77 and others as high as £20 or more. The average was £11.50 and the bonus ceiling stood at £22.50 per week.

Sir Michael Edwardes, these variations notwithstanding, considered the combination of wage and bonus to be attractive. Said Sir Michael:

> "In the year in which we offered a 5 per cent increase in basic, parity and incentive payments brought this to over 10 per cent. Last year we offered 6.8 per cent and we have run out at 13.5 per cent". (12)

The Next Step

A new session of negotiations between BL Cars and the unions on 22 October again ended in stalemate with Geoffrey Armstrong commenting:

> "We have exhausted all possibilities of an honourable settlement".

TABLE 1 :   **UK CAR INDUSTRY PAY/WORKER**

Company	Basic for 40 hours £	Bonus	Wage review
BL CARS Craft Production	104.60 94.00	Incentive scheme Yielding average £11.50 a week*	Due 1 November. Offer of 3.8 per cent rise plus £3.75 bonus guarantee
FORD Craft Production	114.00† 97.52†	Attendance allowance £7.09 £6.00	Due 24 November £20 a week claim submitted
TALBOT Craft Production	107.98 96.84	Incentive scheme yielding £11 - £122 a week	Due 1 January, 1982, "Substantial" claim expected
VAUXHALL Craft Production	107.20 94.20	Productivity scheme suspended because of short-time working	Due 15 September Negotiations con- tinue on 5 per cent offer

NOTE: For comparison shift premiums and fringe benefits, such as holidays and
sickness allowances, are not included.

* This is an average across 30 plants: some get nothing, others more than £20.
† Most Ford workers do alternate day and night shifts to give average weekly pay
of £133 for craftsmen and £113.77 for production workers.

Average pay for 40-hours week in West Midlands engineering industry:
skilled £107.40: semi-skilled £93.10: unskilled £80.70

Source: West Midlands Engineering Employers Association

Grenville Hawley put it more simply:

"We have run out of steam".

At this meeting BL had offered to 'guarantee' minimum bonus payments per man of £3.75 per week, an offer which the unions claimed as 'bogus' since the average bonus payments was already £11.50 per week. In putting forward the guarantee, the company said it was intending to deal with the severe problem of bonus differences, but the guarantee did have strings attached. It was not payable for overtime or layoffs or in period of dispute or sickness. Furthermore, the bonus received could not exceed £30/man/week.

Relations with the Government

On the 26 January, 1981, Sir Michael Edwardes had written to the then Industry Secretary (Sir Keith Joseph) to present BL's corporate plan for 1981. Part of his document foretold subsequent events:

"In such circumstances (a major strike) the board . . . . would very quickly initiate a review (in consultation with the Government) of the plan of the relevant business groups with consequent implications for continued Government funding". (13)

Such a public utterance - even though couched in guarded terms - tied in clearly with Sir Michael's letter to the workforce of 14 October.

In fact, if BL were shut down, either wholly or in part, as a result of a strike, 14 days grace would, by law, be given to shareholders and creditors before an application to place the company in voluntary liquidation could be made.

The Government's interest and investment in BL was substantial. Since 1975, when the Government saved BMC from collapse, aid to the value of £2,300 millions had been given to the company. The latest injection of £990 millions of non-interest bearing equity, agreed in January, 1981 when Sir Michael Edwardes had asked for £1.15 billion, was earmarked for the development of a new range of cars — the LM series. Problems had come thick and fast since 1968, when

Prime Minister Harold Wilson, and Industry Secretary Tony Benn, promoted the merger of Leyland Motors - intent on expansion under Sir Donald (later Lord) Stokes - and British Motor Holdings (makers of Austin, Morris and Jaguar). This, as BMC, had become the 5th largest non-nationalized company in Britain and, after Volkswagen the second largest motor manufacturer outside the USA.

To save BMC from commercial extinction in 1975, Sir Don Ryder, the Labour Government's Chief Industrial Adviser, proposed a new model - heavy investment - rationalisation plan based on his diagnosis of Leyland problems. According to him, the issues were:

- Substantial past lack of investment in product, plant and technology

- Lack of integration of production facilities and management systems ever since the original merger of Austin and Morris in 1951 - 1952

- Industrial Relations — difficulties relating to overmanning and restrictive practices in particular.

The apparent failure of Sir Donald Stokes to implement this plan, despite its governmental aid, led to a lack of confidence in the plan itself and to the choice of Sir Michael Edwardes by the Labour Government on 1 November, 1977 to deal with the alarmingly high level of industrial disputes and the escalating wage claims. Sir Michael was appointed with the warm approval of Labour Ministers and union

Key Factor	BMC + Leyland Motors 1966 - 1967	BL 1980 - 1981
Workforce	188,000	143,000
Manufactured Units ('000s approx p.a.) : cars : trucks and buses	750 130	390 78
Profit (£m)	38	- 535

EXHIBIT 1 : COMPARATIVE PERFORMANCE

leaders, such as Harry Urwin of the Transport and General Workers and David Basnett of the General and Municipal Workers.

Sir Michael's approach to the problems of BL involved the following plans:

- Government aid specifically for investment in new products and updating technology

- Productivity improvement, cost-cutting, de-manning and plant closures. In 1979, he requested £250 millions of aid from the Government against the closure of 13 plants and 25,000 redundancies. When these proposals were presented, they were totally rejected by the BL shop stewards, yet received 87 per cent support from the ballotted BL workforce.

In the current dispute, moreover it was already known that the BL Board, meeting on 28 October, might not submit its 1982 Corporate Plan to Government if its wage proposals were rejected.

Hopes rose over the weekend of 24/25 October, 1981, that further, more positive talks were in the offing. Terry Duffy,.before flying to Nairobi for a week-long meeting of the International Metal Workers' Federation, said he expected them. Grenville Hawley repeated his willingness to meet anywhere and with anybody to stop the strike. Pat Lowry, Chairman of the Advisory, Conciliation and Arbitration Service (ACAS), remained in informal contact with both sides.

MPs in Action

On Monday and Tuesday, 26 and 27 October, groups of MPs representing Midlands constituencies sprang into action.

Monday saw a meeting between a group of Labour MPs, including Roy Hattersley, Geoffrey Robinson, Leslie Huckfield , and Sir Michael Edwardes. Their leader, Roy Hattersley, said that they had tried to convince Sir Michael of the workforce's view that they had been "badly treated". Geoffrey Robinson, former Managing Director of Jaguar Cars, stressed that the pay dispute would end in total disaster unless the Government "bashed some heads together". Leslie Huckfield stated that Sir Michael now appreciated that his letter could be seen as provocative but that he had not changed his stance.

Seven MPs seem to have derived more reassurance from their meeting with Patrick Jenkin, who said the Government "appreciated the situation" and had "all the angles covered". Nonetheless, the depth of their concern was shown by comments from two of the team as they left Patrick Jenkin:

- "With 15 per cent unemployed in Coventry, it would be political suicide for any Tory MP here to support the liquidation of BL"

- "If war is too important to be left to the generals, then BL's situation is far too dangerous to be left to Edwardes".

However, Patrick Jenkin's view was buttressed by a Commons written reply from Norman Lamont, Minister of State for Industry, that the dispute had not yet reached the stage where the BL Board would need to consult the Government about liquidation plans.

Secret Talks

On the same day secret top-level talks were taking place at the Portman Square Headquarters of BL between a TUC team comprising Len Murray (TUC General Secretary), Sir John Boyd (General Secretary of the AUEW) and Alex Kitson (Deputy General Secretary of the TGWU) and the BL Board. The meeting produced, however, only a curt joint statement that "No progress towards a solution was made". The TUC team was due to report back to BL Cars Union Negotiating Commitee at TUC Headquarters on 28 October, the same day as the BL Board meeting.

Special Pleading

In a *Times* article on 28 October entitled "How Sir Michael can go for glory", Sir Richard Dobson, Chairman of BL during 1976 and 1977, wrote in nautical vein:

> "It is a noble sight: Sir Michael, his colours nailed to the mast, bearing down under full sail with his Admiral urging him on; the enemy on an interception course, hellbent on death or glory. Once the first gun is fired, it is highly likely that both fleets will blow each other out of the water with the loss of all hands". (14)

His solution?

> "I would say to the board of BL and to the politicians behind them, please think once more. If you are convinced that BL has no future as a major vehicle manufacturer, close it now and stop quibbling about percentage points. If, as I hope, you believe that, in the fullness of time, the company can be nursed back to health, then do what must be done to keep the patient alive in the meantime. Do not mistake rigidity for courage. Posterity will not thank you if the ship sinks for the lack of a ha'porth of tar". (15)

A pleading tone was also adopted by Michael Foot, Leader of the Opposition, with Mrs Margaret Thatcher, Prime Minister, in Commons exchanges on 27 October:

> "This is not a case of a firm", he stated, "which is on the verge of collapse, but one which could speedily be moving into a situation of profits and success . . . . Can I plead with her again not to say 'No' but come back on Thursday and see what the situation is and whether the Government would use its mediating power to assist". (16)

The Prime Minister's reply was terse:

> "Industrial relations are a matter for the company and the Government is not seeking to influence the company in these matters . . . . If there are to be increases in public spending, they have to be financed either by taxation or from borrowing and that would mean even higher interest rates . . . . The Government wants BL to succeed but does not think it right to intervene". (17)

Labour MP Tony Benn was not pleading, however, when he spoke to the BL workers. He said that:

- BL management was pursuing a confrontation course with the workforce to break up the company and that
- Sir Michael should be removed from the chairmanship of the company.

A Secret Ballot?

On 28 October, a few hours after the BL Board's decision to postpone presenting the 1982 Corporate Plan to the Government, Sir Michael appealed, on the BBC *Nationwide* programme, for union general secretaries to hold a secret ballot of their members on the BL pay offer. He said:

> "The general secretaries should hold a secret ballot so that we can be quite sure people want a strike. I am not convinced they do . . . . Are we going to allow a great company to collapse because everyone has two hands up at a meeting?" (18)

Alex Kitson's reply was short and sharp:

> "Sir Michael does not tell us how to run our business and we don't tell him how to run his. Sir Michael has nothing to do with the way we run our business. If the members call for a secret ballot, they can have one, but there has been no call". (19)

Support for this position was expressed by Ken Cure, Senior BL negotiator for the AUEW. He argued that:

> "The effect of the company's bullying tactics, which has included personal threats by foremen to the workforce, has, if anything, hardened our members' attitude". (20)

Responding to this criticism, Sir Michael offered to 'defuse' the situation by apologising for his letter.

> "I am very sorry indeed", he said, "that my letter has been seen as provocative".

The challenge and the apology came from Sir Michael after an exhausting day in which:

- Three hours of exploratory discussions between Pat Lowry and union representatives had drawn a comment from Sir John Boyd that "things look very black indeed. Only a miracle will prevent the strike".

- The BL Board had issued another statement that, in the event of a strike, liquidation and no redundancy pay were certainties.

Four Minutes to Midnight

Having rejected an Opposition request for an Emergency Debate on BL, Speaker Thomas found himself on Thursday, 29 October listening to an Adjournment Debate on the same theme (achieved via a substitution of topics by Labour MPs), featuring Patrick Jenkin and his opposite number, Stan Orme.

Calling for fresh measures and initiatives, Stan Orme said that:

> "So far as BL is concerned, we are now four minutes to midnight, within a matter of hours to one of the largest disputes in recent history". (21)

Placing the responsibility of BL - as a publicly-owned company - firmly on the shoulders of the Government, and arguing that in the event of liquidation it would be taxpayers' money which would be lost, he continued:

> "We cannot afford to sit back and wait until disaster occurs and then hope that everything will be put back again". (22)

Patrick Jenkin replied by quoting Mr James Callaghan, the previous Labour Prime Minister, who had said of Sir Michael Edwardes, that:

> "When he chooses to follow any path, we cannot tell him he should do something else. If we put him there, we must back him". (23)

Patrick Jenkin also reminded the Commons of the fact that in March 1977 Mr Eric Varley (Industry Secretary in the Labour Government under James Callaghan) had clearly outlined his view of the then situation:

"I want all workers at Leyland, including those on strike today, to be quite clear that their own future employment and the future of their company is in their hands. They can kill it or they can save it. They will have no-one else to blame or thank". (24)

His conclusion was identical to Mrs Thatcher's, namely, that the BL dispute:

"Is not, and cannot be, a matter for Government".(25)

Collapse of Peace Talks

The Adjournment Debate took place against deepening fears of a strike. Joint talks at ACAS, held after Pat Lowry had separately seen the BL management negotiators, failed after no basis for reconciliation had been found. Alex Kitson was bitter. Accusing Sir Michael Edwardes of sending 'second stringers' to the talks, he said:

"Michael Edwardes did not turn up here. We thought that his beloved BL would have forced him to come here under the circumstances. I am sure I am speaking for the whole trade union movement when I say, we are disgusted at the fact he didn't turn up . . . . There will be a strike. It's just as plain as that. Sir Michael has ensured that the strike will go ahead because of his continued stubbornness". (26)

His view was echoed by BL stewards whose comments included the following:

- "The mood of the men is stronger than ever. The strike will happen". (Jack Adams, Works Convenor, Longbridge)(27)

- "There is 100 per cent support for the stoppage and it will go ahead unless there is an improved offer". (John Newcombe, TGWU Convenor, Coventry)(28)

There was also a forceful and articulate letter in the *Daily Telegraph* (30 October, 1981), from a shop-floor worker, which made the following points:

"To the layman, the issue is a fairly straightforward trial of strength between Sir Michael Edwardes, the chairman, and the trade unions, with little, or no, consideration for the man on the shop floor except for a casual reference to pay scales and potential bonus earnings.

If you look closely at the pay scales, the majority of the workforce are in grades three and four and their *take-home* pay ranges from £60-£72 a week plus an average £5 (gross) bonus at Cowley assembly.

The difference between gross earnings, which are always quoted, and what we receive in our pay packets, is so wide that many BL employees, with children, mortgages and so on, are regarded by the Department of Health and Social Security as "low-income families". Many already qualify for rent/rate rebates.

This makes something of a mockery of our so-called "high bonus earnings" does it not? There is little annual increment for us - just 3.8 per cent; there is no "non-contributory pension scheme", we pay in £3 - £4 a week. There is no allowance for the odd day off; no work, no pay is the principle; if you are ill you are penalised - the company will not pay you for the first three days of your absence.

Our much-publicised bonus system based on plant performance is useless. Our (Cowley) average gross payment is about £5 and is calculated in such a way that few people can understand it and regard it with suspicion because the payments often bear no relation to the amount of work done; the poor rewards received clearly reflect its shortcomings. Rash statements of "high bonus earnings" will not allay our fears that we are again about to be short-changed.

One thing that riled many of the workforce was the introduction of "pay parity", whereby a man doing a job (storeman, fork-lift driver, and so on) in Cowley, would be paid the same rate as a person in similar employment at Longbridge, which is fair in principle and stops leap-frogging over wages. But what do we find? Less than a mile up the road from the Cowley assembly and body plants, at Unipart (733 plant), there are storemen, fork-lift drivers and so on in higher grades being paid more under such titles as "service parts operators" than those doing the same jobs at the assembly and body plants. This is asking for trouble . . . . Sir Michael's priority is to make BL a paying proposition. In doing so, he must make it economically viable for his workforce, otherwise he will simply stare defeat in the face. Believe me, there will be no winners then; it will be merely the beginning of the end."

THE FACTS THAT DICTATE OUR FUTURE.

An advertisement with this heading appeared in most daily newspapers on Monday 26 October 1981, as part of a persuasion exercise mounted by BL Limited ostensibly directed at its own employees but indirectly aimed at the public in general (otherwise the company could simply have written directly to its workers, which would have been cheaper and arguably more effective).

The text of the advertisement (which occupied a full page— included the following

"Twelve months ago BL Cars' employees accepted a 6.8 per cent basic rate increase together with an incentive scheme based on productivity. Consideration of the 6.8 per cent basic rise in isolation could suggest that BL Cars' employees' wages have fallen seriously behind those of other manufactuing workers.

"This is not true.

"The incentive scheme has effectively doubled the basic wage increase making a total average increase of 13½ per cent over the year, which matches the national manufacturing average. Over the same period the cost of living has risen by 11.4 per cent. So the spending power of the BL Cars' workforce has actually grown.

"It is also important to know that, even at existing wage levels, the BL car production worker's earnings are among the highest in the UK motor industry.

"So much for 1981 . . . . the year to come . . . . will be a vital year for the Company. It would have been unfair -- even insulting -- to offer any less than the utmost that the Company could afford. Especially in view of past co-operation and the fine industrial relations record that has contributed so much over the last three years.

"The most that BL Cars can offer on grade rates is £3 - £4. But the incentive scheme has been significantly improved. The scheme now *guarantees* all employees a minimum normal weekly bonus of £3.75 -- which means a wage of between £101.35 and £112.35 minimum for most employees. At the same time the bonus ceiling has been raised to a maximum of £30 a week . . . .

"This improvement was rejected by union and employee representatives on Thursday, 22 October . . . .

'What are the options?

"To pay more and become uncompetitive -- this way we wither away in the face of competition.

"To have a strike -- this would destroy customer confidence and damage market share just as new models have halted many years of decline. And we do not have the cash to stand a damaging dispute, even for a few days.

"To settle the dispute on the terms offered by the Company -- in which case the Board, with the support of the workforce, are prepared to seek the funds which are essential for the new model programme and push ahead with the plans for the Company's recovery.

"The last option is the only way to secure the future."

Reproduced with permission from *Management Monitor*.

EXHIBIT 2 : A MATTER OF FACTS

Such defiance was not, however, exhibited by the first 6,000 out of 18,000 BL white-collar staff to vote on the company's offer. The majority had clearly heeded the warning expressed by Raymond Horrocks (BL Cars Chairman and Chief Executive) as he left the ACAS talks:

> "We are not prepared to make promises we cannot meet or indeed spend money we do not have. We want to run our business on Monday and hope that people will come to work". (29)

Cause for Concern

All those involved in the dispute were by now heavily engaged in calculating the costs of a strike, to BL, to industry generally, and to the country as a whole. Among the factors to be considered were:

- BL's £2 billions per year expenditure on bought-in supplies from British motor components manufacturers

- BL's contribution, as one of Britain's largest exporters, of £1.2 billions to our balance of payments

- BL's closure (and the knock-on effects) would produce an estimated 250,000 extra jobless and reduce GNP by approximately one per cent

- The difficult position of at least eight Conservative MPs, whose seats were highly marginal. These included Jocelyn Cadbury, Anthony Beaumont-Dark and Iain Mills

Of these, perhaps the most salient feature was the sheer extent of the integration of BL's production with that of other British manufacturers. For example, 15 per cent of the British Steel Corporation's production of steel sheet was bought by BL; Lucas Girling had sold £100 millions of original equipment to BL in 1980 - 81; and an estimated 50 per cent of the production of Smiths Industries (Automotive Divisons) was attributable to BL as a customer.

Based on its analysis of the situation, *The Times* (30 October, 1981), however, argued that:

- BL's relative importance to the economy had declined in the past 10 years

- The largest British firms had already made some provisions for a BL disaster by pushing into overseas markets and/or investing abroad

- The direct job fall-out from BL (100,000 +) would be no more than two months' extra unemployment at "its present rate of increase" or, to put it another way, one tenth of the number who had lost their jobs in manufacturing over the past two years.

In the view of *The Times*:

> "The end of BL would bring catastrophic effects but in contrast to the previous occasions when BL has been to the brink and pulled the end for the battered motor giant is not now utterly unthinkable . . . . . . The consequences of Sir Michael's carrying out his threat are much disputed. The surprise to many people is that, far from being the worst possible time to wind up the troubled company, it may be the best yet".

To such a sobering pronouncement was added the warning from Labour MP Jeff Rooker - Front Bench spokesman on Social Security matters - who pointed out that, if BL were to close because of a strike, the workers involved would lose far more than redundancy money. Citing Section 19 of Labour's own Social Security Act 1975 — under which no unemployment benefit is paid to workers who lose their jobs because of industrial action — he declared:

> "I just want to warn people of an aspect of Social Security legislation so that they are not set up by the provocative action of a company. I would not want them to walk into a dispute without being aware of the other consequences of their action". (30)

The left-wing Labour newspaper *Tribune* put Geoff Rooker's point succinctly in a front-page headline - "Is this the trap that Michael Edwardes has laid for BL workers?"

Nor was there any guarantee that, in the event of the liquidation of BL as a result of a strike, parts of the company could be sold. Most commentators were of the opinion that:

- There were few bidders waiting in the wings anyway.

- Most of the big manufacturing and assembly plants would probably be unsaleable.

- Only a few, isolated, small and specialist activities might be attractive to potential buyers.

- BL's competitors would, at a time of depressed sales throughout Europe, be only too grateful for the opportunity to increase their market shares.

As Anthony Beaumont-Dark put it:

> "You could give BL away to anybody who would guarantee it as a going concern." (31)

The Nub of the Matter?

Comments from workers interviewed outside the 'K' Gate at the Longbridge plant illustrate the feeling of some of the workforce about the company's managerial approach (32):

- "BL always has this 'take it or leave it' attitude. If you don't accept what we want, you will be sacked. They simply can't go on treating us like this year after year."

- "They might as well bring the whip back."

- "Blokes have worked their backsides off for this company. This strike is not just about cash, it's about the bloody-mindedness of management"

- "We have lived with fear too long. Threats no longer have any effect on me"

- "These men do not want a strike but the time has come to say 'enough is enough' "

- "It seems to us that the company is trying to pursue 'carrot and stick' tactics without the carrot. It won't work and neither will we"

- "Call it the need to keep our dignity if you like. I can't really express it in words. But we think our very rights as free men are at stake in BL now."

The *Morning Star* editorial of 30 October was less concerned with what Pat Lowry had called 'macho management' and more with the politics of the dispute:

"This is one class waging war against another", it stated. "They plan to smash our communities, lay waste our skills, destroy our organizations".

The message of a leaflet from the Trotskyist Socialist Workers' Party, distributed at Longbridge was literally inflammatory:

"If Adolf Edwardes tries to sack us to close BL we should occupy the plant and call on the rest of the Labour movement to stop work in support of us . . . . If Edwardes and Mrs Thatcher want to play with fire, let's show them how big a bonfire they're setting on and show them we know how to light it".

A Taste of the Same

On Friday, 30 October, Ford replied to the claim of its unions for a £20 across the board wage rise, a shorter working week and improved pensions. The company offered an incease averaging 4.5 per cent. A comparison between the average production workers' wage at Ford and BL showed:-

Company	Day Shift Basic for 40 hrs (£)	Increase offered %	Bonus Guaranteed £	Attendance Allowance	Minimum Total £
BL	94	3.8	3.75	-	101.32
Ford	97.52	4.5	-	6.00	107.90

There was, however, a sting in the tail of the Ford offer. It depended totally on efficiency improvements and took no account of the unions' claimed need "for a restoration of the standard of living" within the Ford workforce. The offer was immediately rejected by Ron Todd, Chief TGWU Negotiator at Ford, as "contemptuous"(sic).

According to Paul Roots, Ford's Labour Relations Director, the rationale for the apparently low wage offer in the U.K. was that

"Britain is a very inefficient base. It costs Ford 20 per cent more to produce an Escort 'L' at Halewood than at Saarlouis in Germany." (33)

In his view, the company was seeking:

- optimum labour mobility and flexibility

- cooperation with the introduction of new technology and work systems

- avoidance of inefficient restrictions and demarcations

- full overtime flexibility

- elimination of lost working time.

A Top Level Meeting

On Saturday, Sir Michael Edwardes met Labour Leader, Mr. Michael

Foot, at the former's request. A speech on Friday at Matlock in Derbyshire had spelled out again Mr. Foot's apprehension at the possibilities of "a terrible catastrophe". He had said:

"We have used every effort we could in public and private to get the Government to intervene because it is they who will be responsible if BL closes . . . . I repeat that the scale of this catastrophe would be something beyond description and the Government must act now".
(34)

Making plain, prior to meeting Mr Foot, his willingness to meet union leaders "any time, day or night, over the weekend", Sir Michael used his time with the Labour Leader to explain why BL could not give more than a 3.8 per cent increase.

"Mr Foot", said Sir Michael Edwardes, "listened very patiently when I explained to him that we do not have the cash and he understands our problem there. Our offer is extremely reasonable. The wage level is similar to those enjoyed by Ford workers and Ford's are profitable and we are not. I have no doubt that Mr Foot is as keen to avoid a strike as are the management and Board of BL. I do not think that anyone feels that anyone is bluffing". (35)

Weekend Accommodation

The high level of activity devoted to the achievement of a solution to the BL impasse continued throught the weekend and culminated, after 13 exhausting hours of BL - union talks on Sunday, in a 'peace formula'.

All involved had the opportunity, over the weekend, of mulling over their stances. The Government had received a final plea from a four-man union team on Saturday morning but had not yielded ground. Alex Kitson complained after his meeting with Patrick Jenkin that:

"We have done everything possible to try to solve the problem but the rigidity is getting worse. Mr. Jenkin made it clear that he is not going to intervene and there is no use coming back . . . . The Government and BL between them are going to play brinkmanship to the last hour". (36)

TABLE 2 :

THE ANATOMY OF BL (1981)

Location of plant	Number of hourly paid and staff employees	Activities	Prospects for sale following liquidation
Birmingham Longbridge	18,000	Mini Metro, Allegro, engines and transmissions for these models and for Princess, Sherpa van and Ital	Doubtful
Castle Bromwich	1,500	Body shell for Jaguar and Daimler	Bad
Common Lane	1,200	Assembly of Sherpa van	Bad
Drews Lane	2,100	Transmission components for Mini and Metro	Bad
SU Fuel Systems	550	Carburettors	Doubtful
Solihull	7,000	Two plants assembling Rover, Land-Rover and Range-Rover. Due to be closed	Rover - Bad Land-Rover - Fair
Llanelli Llanelli Radiators (Unipart)	2,590	Two plants making radiators and pressings	Fair
Cardiff	620	Two plants making Land-Rover gearboxes and engine components and parts depot (Unipart)	Bad
Workington	550	Buses (50 per cent owned by BL)	Fair
Liverpool Speke	900	Body pressings for most BL models. Due to be closed	Bad
Albion	1,900	Truck transmissions	Bad
Bathgate	3,600	Trucks	Bad

Location	Number	Description	Rating
Leyland	2,800	Four plants making trucks	Bad
Chorley	1,000	Truck parts	Bad
Wolverhampton Guy Motors	700	Trucks	Bad
Leeds	350	Buses (50 per cent owned by BL)	Fair
Coventry Brown's Lane and Radford	4,800	Two plants assembling Jaguar/Daimler saloons, Daimler limousines and XJS, and producing XK6 engines and transmissions	Bad
Canley	2,000	Engineering Centre	Bad
Coventry Engines	1,500	Diesel engines and engine components. Due to be closed	Bad
Coventry Climax	1,600	Fork lift trucks	Bad
Self Changing Gears	270	Transmission systems	Good
Lowestoft	900	Buses (50 per cent owned by BL)	Fair
Oxford Cowley	10,000	Two plants producing bodies for Rover, Princess, Acclaim and Ital, and assembling Princess, Acclaim and Ital	Doubtful
Oxford Exhaust Systems (Unipart)	500	Exhausts	Good
Watford	800	Scammell trucks	Bad
Swindon	3,000	Body pressings for Rover, Jaguar/Daimler and Metro	Bad
Bristol	700	Buses (50 per cent owned by BL)	Fair

Source: Based on a diagram by John Grimwade. published in the *Sunday Times*

TABLE 3 :   **MINI METRO COMPONENTS**

Component	Source
Body pressings	Swindon (BL)
Assembly	Longbridge (BL)
Paint	International Paints (Birmingham)
Windscreen	Triplex (Birmingham)
Clutch	Automotive Products (Leamington Spa)
Carburettors	SU Fuel Systems (BL)
Engine	Longbridge (BL)
Driveshafts	Hardy Spicer, GKN (West Midlands)
Bearings	RHP Bearings (Chelmsford)
Castings	Ley's Malleable Castings (Derby)
Transmission casings	Bromsgrove Castings West Yorkshire Foundry (BL)
Radiators	Llanelli (BL)
Transmission	Longbridge (BL)
Automatic Transmission	Automotive Products (Leamington Spa)
Battery	Lucas (Birmingham)
Brakes	Automotive Products (Leamington Spa)
Brake pads	Ferodo (Chapel en le Frith) Mintex (Yorkshire)
Seats	Callow and Maddox (Coventry)
Tyres	Dunlop (Birmingham)
Wheels	Dunlop (Birmingham)
Dampers	Girling (West Bromwich
Sheet Steel	British Steel Corporation (South Wales)
Soft trim	Firth Furnishings (Coventry)

Source: Based on a diagram published in *The Guardian*

Patrick Jenkin's statement that the Government was not going to be "any final court of appeal" concluded:

"The years of agony seem to be near their end . . . . The company is now starting to pull through to viability, but we are not going to second guess the BL's Board's decisions on these matters". (37)

Michael Foot had also sought to maintain his pressure on the Government. In a speech on Saturday at a party rally in Grantham, Lincolnshire, close to the site of the grocer's shop where Mrs Margaret Thatcher was born, he again asserted:

"If the tragedy occurs and there is a stoppage and more closures at BL, I say to you that the responsibility is squarely at the door of No.10 . . . . What the nation wants is an honourable settlement. The only place you can get an honourable settlement now is No.10 Downing Street. That is where they ought to be this afternoon. Forget about the underlings . . . . The responsibility rests on Mrs Thatcher". (38)

The company also kept up its pressure by sending a further letter warning of plant closures and redundancies if a strike took place.

The Sunday talks were held at the highest level and involved:

Union Side	*Management Side*
11 union leaders including:	Sir Michael Edwardes
David Basnett (GMWU)	Ray Horrocks
Frank Chapple (ETU)	Geoffrey Armstrong
Sir John Boyd (AUEW)	and the BL Negotiating Team
Alex Kitson (TGWU)	headed by:
and the BL Union	David Andrews
Negotiating Team	plus 5 group Managing Directors
headed by:	
Grenville Hawley(TWGU)	
and Ken Cure (AUEW)	

Agreement was finally reached, in the early hours of Sunday morning, on the formula to be put to BL workers at mass meetings on Tuesday, 3 November. It comprised:

- a planned joint management - union review of the BL incentive scheme aimed at gauging the possibility of increased union/worker involvement and "localized" incentive payments.

- withdrawal of the 'Edwardes letter' if the industrial action were called off.

- confirmation of the 3.8 per cent rise in basic rate.

- consolidation of the minimum bonus offer of £3.75 into the calculations for sick pay, holiday pay and lay-off pay.

A Split in the Ranks?

There was a divergence of view on the attractiveness of the 'formula' between the Transport & General Workers and the Engineers. The AUEW view was straightforward:

- "I will be telling my members that, in my opinion, it is the limit of the concession that we can get from the company" (Ken Cure) (39)

- "It is the end of the road. There is no more money . . . I think it unwise to take any more risks and the agreement that has been reached should be accepted". (40)

For the TGWU, Alex Kitson's attitude seems to have been ambivalent. His comments were:

- "I said to my colleagues that I wasn't prepared to recommend other than the fact that the membership should consider the offer that has been made. It is an improved offer, maybe not a great improvement, but it is an improved offer. They will make up their minds whether it is enough to settle the dispute". (41)

- "I would not accept it, but it will be up to the lads. I mean they have come through three years of low improvements in their wages and conditions and if they want to fight against BL's offer then the TGWU will be beside them and prepared to fight. I think they are entitled to a lot more for the sacrifices they have made over the course of the last three years". (42)

A Stewards' Enquiry

Against a background of large-scale picketing at BL plants, BL shop stewards - faced with the task of appraising the BL offer and advising members on its acceptability - voted by 238 to 12 to reject the deal. Their meeting had started 35 minutes late since officials had first to eject unwanted demonstrators, some from the Militant Tendency and the Socialist Workers' Party. Indicative of the strength of opinion at this time were some of the protest badges and placards worn and carried at Longbridge by the protesters, including slogans like "38 per cent FOR HIM, 3.8 per cent FOR US"; BL = BREAD LINE"; "ROAST KING EDWARDES"; and "HAVE A DAY OFF ON THE DWARF".

Last Minute Pressures

BL manual workers, as they streamed to mass meetings on the Tuesday morning (3 November) to decide on the BL offer, had much to ponder. Terry Duffy had issued an impassioned last-minute plea:

> "I am backing England because, after last weekend's talks at ACAS, Sir Michael Edwardes said there was nothing more and the offer could not be improved. I am convinced by all the people who were at the ACAS negotiations that there was nothing of any substantial value to be had by continuing the strike. I believe we have reached a time of diminishing returns .... Colleagues, you have taken your stance and I hope the company has learned its lesson. I think it is in our interest to prove once more that we are responsible and take again a calculated risk". (43)

BL had taken space in the press for an advertisement which included the following text:

> "The stewards are clearly out of line with their trade union leaders who recognised on Saturday night the proposals as a basis for settle-

ment and as the company's final offer. We expect employees to take a more realistic view as their own national officials have done and to vote for the improved offer and a return to work".

Alex Kitson, in a signed leader in the November issue of TGWU's monthly journal *Record* wrote that the Tory 'wets' were 'soaking' the Government. The article continued:

"If they can achieve this purely with the power of words and the threat of losing a few votes, then surely we should be able to drown them with our protests.

It's high time we had a go. Especially on the industrial front where the Management hard-liners still regard Michael Edwardes as the new God. Up to now there have been too few efforts to use our industrial muscle to halt the Tories".

A Victory on Points

On that Tuesday, 3 November, mass meetings of BL manual workers voted by a clear majority for acceptance of the BL offer - calculated to be worth 5.1 per cent on basic - and a return to work.

Votes	Union Officials' Report		Company Report	
	No.	%	No.	%
For	25,058	55.6	38,000	73.0
Against	19,963	44.4	14,000	27.0
Total	45,021	100.0	52,000	100.0

The Next Round

On Monday, 9 November, BL's Longbridge management announced that the workforce's relaxation of 'slip' time per shift would be reduced from its present level of 52 minutes (day shift) and 55 minutes (night shift) to a consolidated time of 40 minutes to achieve a reduction in the working week from 40 to 39 hours without any cost increase. Nearly two thousand Metro and Mini assembly workers walked out immediately, to be followed later by 400 Allegro assemblers. A further three thousand workers were laid off as a result.

This action was taken by BL after a breakdown in the negotiations at a BL Cars' National Negotiating Committee meeting on 5 November, the very day the wage deal was signed by the 11 manual unions at BL, over the introduction of the shorter working week. This had been specified in the 1979 Agreement between the Confederation of Shipbuilding and Engineering Unions and the Engineering Employers' Federation.

In a letter to strikers, Brian Fox, Birmingham Operations Director for BL, stressed that:

- BL did not have the resources to offset the production loss of 2.5 per cent which the shorter working week would entail

- the unions signing the pay deal had all recognised the need to finance the lost hour by a more efficient use of working time.

Indeed, paragraph 3 of the 1979 Agreement had underlined management-union co-operation at all levels to avoid any increase in manufacturing cost when the shorter working week was introduced.

BL's announcement was made in the light of a warning from Grenville Hawley that trouble could be expected. He had said that:

"From the outset the company has not deviated on how the move should be funded. They are going ahead with their proposals. There is no sign of flexibility, of the proposed new style of management". (44)

"Tea-break Talks"

Talks held between management and union representatives after BL's announcement got nowhere; neither did further talks held on 13 November. A management offer, made by letter on 19 November, to phase-in the cut in relaxation time over four weeks, was debated by 350 shop stewards at a meeting on the 20th. Their concern was with a possible escalation of the dispute.

Strikers' meetings were held on the 19th and 22nd. Despite the fact that the latter was poorly attended, both resulted in a vote for continuation. Said Jack Adams (Communist Works Convenor at Longbridge):

"This is purely a matter concerning the conditions of our members. Our people can ill afford to go on strike as we are coming up to Christmas. They have had to consider seriously whether this dispute was worth supporting and they obviously feel it is". (45)

The situation was made even more threatening by the announcement, on 20 November, that BL's Bus and Truck Division was to lose 22 per cent of its workforce.

Informal talks between union leaders Terry Duffy and Moss Evans and Sir Michael Edwardes availed little. On 25 November, two more days of management-union discussion collapsed. The comment of the TGWU full-time official responsible for Longbridge, John Barker, was that:

"We bent over backwards at the talks to find a solution which would enable the company to fund the 39 hour week without interfering with the mens' precious break-time. We are well aware of the misery and hardship this strike is causing. We even offered to revert to the 40-hour week to get a return to work". (46)

Plant	Type of Work	Job Losses
Albion (Glasgow)	Truck, bus and axle production	140
Bathgate (Glasgow)	Medium truck assembly Diesel engines	1,365
Leyland (Lancs)	Heavy truck assembly Bus chassis	1,855
Guy Motors (Wolverhampton)	Heavy export truck assembly	740

EXHIBIT 3 : ANNOUNCED JOB LOSSES

A False Dawn

On 26 November, the TGWU followed the example set by the AUEW on 10 November by making the strike official. Union chief Moss Evans of the TGWU, which accounted for 97 per cent of the BL strikers, stated that:

> "We want to bring a speedy end to this dispute. But it will not be called off unless Leyland are prepared to enter genuine negotiations". (47)

On 30 November, in fact, there was a change in BL's approach. Having placed advertisements in the press that "The Austin will be open on Monday", BL then:

- opened the factory gates and invited all workers to return

- offered to phase in cuts over four months instead of four weeks and

- stated that those who did return would be guaranteed continued employment and those that did not would be dismissed.

Harold Musgrave explained that:

> "We have spent many hours in discussion with shop stewards and full-time union officials in an attempt to break the deadlock. Unfortunately, despite a number of suggestions on our part, it has not been possible to reach any agreement. In view of this serious situation, we have decided to call everyone at Longbridge in to work on Monday at normal working times . . . . We really cannot go on like this. We have to give a lead to employees". (48)

The union side countered by dismissing the 'open gate' move as 'a confidence trick' (John Barker), stating that strikers who did go in would

---

A recommendation that BL Cars Division should be sold within three years or closed down was made in a report by Keith Boyfield and Elizabeth Cottrell called *A Viable Future*. The report was published by the Centre for Policy Studies, established in 1974 by Margaret Thatcher and Sir Keith Joseph.

TABLE 4 :

COMPARISON OF PUBLIC SECTOR FINANCING

	State Department	Public Corporation	Private Companies with state shareholdings
France	**Post and telecoms** Capital grants, and interest free loans from Government, domestic and international bond issues and bank credits with explicit Government guarantee	**Eight sectors including gas, electricity coal and airways** Equity/debt capital, grants and subsidies, FDES loans from Government; domestic and international bank credits and bond issues with explicit Government guarantee	Many sectors including steel, banks, motor vehicles, oil and **shipping** Equity/debt capital, subsidies and FDES loans from Government; domestic and international bond issues and bank credits with discretionary Government guarantee; otherwise as a private company
Italy	**Rail and roads** Subsidies, grants and loans from Government; loans from Government credit agencies with explicit Government guarantee; domestic and international bank credits and bond issues with explicit Government guarantee	**Electricity** Grants and subsidies from Government loans from Government credit agencies with explicit Government guarantee, domestic and international bank credits and bond issues with explicit Government guarantee	**State participation system investing in may sectors and individual companies through individual management agencies (ENI, IRI, etc.)** Equity/debt capital and subsidies from management agency; domestic and international bank credits and bond issues with discretionary guarantee of management agency; normal sources of finance open to private companies to the extent that the underlying investment of the management agency is not altered

114

West Germany	**Rail** Grants and subsidies from Government; domestic bank credits and bond issues with implicit Government guarantee **Posts** Domestic bank credits and bond issues with implicit Government guarantee; self-finance from savings and deposits from the public		Over 1,000 companies in many sectors Equity from Government; otherwise as a private company
U.K.		Gas, coal, electricity, oil, airports, rail, steel, waterways, buses, telecom, posts, airline, shipbuilders, docks Grants, subsidies and loans from Government; international bank credit with explicit Government guarantee	Limited number Finance as private companies National Enterprise Board (now British Technology Group) holdings: **Rolls Royce, BL** Government rescues - equity involvement, grants and loans **BP** Equity stakes

Source: The Hundred Group. The financing of state-owned industries, December 1981

not get their £12 a week strike pay and encouraging laid-off workers to return, but only to their normal work.

Just under a third (700) of the day shift total of 2,200 (of whom 300 walked out again) and 1,000 of the night shift of 2,500 availed themselves of the opportunity, but 1,000 of the (by now) 6,000 laid-off workers voted to join the strike. As Jack Adams said:

> "The lads laid off had not had a chance to hold meetings and express their views. They were sent home early in the dispute. But they got that chance yesterday when management recalled them. BL", he went on, "had used workers to vote with their feet. Well, they have voted with their feet. There was no coercion. The lads at the gates simply handed out a leaflet from the Works Committee". (49)

The leaflet, entitled *We're Right - Sit Tight* stated:

> "This strike is not about having time off for an extra cuppa - it is about having time to perform basic human functions, minimum decent conditions free from the relentless grind that takes up every other minute of the day. We are not robots. We are not animals".

Comments on this "relentless grind" in this four-track, 4,700 Metros per week capacity output plant included: (50)

- "The foreman keeps at you all the time and the cars keep coming down the track. People don't understand the pressure we're under". (A 40-year-old Metro assembler)

- "Middle-aged men on the Metro-line tell me 'It's wicked, we can't give any more' ". (John Barker)

A Formula for Return

With no production possible during the Longbridge strike, with stocks of Allegros, Minis and Metros by now so sadly depleted, BL had good reason to seek an end to the dispute. It had lost output of 24,000 cars with a showroom value of £98 millions. The workforce was also anxious to return, having foregone pay of over £400 per employee. Twelve hours of talks ended at 5.30 a.m. on 3 December and produced a possible formula to satisfy both sides.

It contained the following points:

- Men on the day shift would get 46 minutes relaxation time, and work a 39 hour week

- Men on the night shift would get 56 minutes relaxation time but work shifts of 9¾ hours and a 39 hour week (both longer than in the past. Indeed a 38 hour night-shift week had been worked at Longbridge since 1956.)

- A 1.5 per cent tightening of work standards, i.e. rearrangement of manning and work schedules and an increase in the speed of the tracks.

Management was satisfied that costs would not increase: at an uproarious and bitter meeting, the workforce voted by a majority of only 46 for the 'formula'. The subsequent restart of production on 7 December was delayed by three hours by the refusal of some ex-strikers to work with colleagues they claimed had 'blacklegged'.

BL's Plan Approved

The Government announced approval of BL's Corporate Plan, which was made available to Parliament on 22 December. The plan - based on BL's 'break-even by 1983' aim - indicated that:

- BL's 1981 losses were greater than had been forecast but that cash flow had been contained within expected levels

- the company would require Government cash funding of £370 millions for 1982

- profits for the period 1982 to 1985 would be £300 millions lower than originally forecast, due to anticipation of lower home and export demand, plus less favourable exchange rates

- greater cost reductions and higher productivity than originally forecast had been achieved.

APPENDIX 1

Consolidated Balance Sheets (1978 - 1980) £m

	1978	1979	1980
Assets			
Inventory	1,024.0	1,040.7	946.0
Debtors and Bills Receivable	397.9	447.6	433.6
Cash Bank Balances and			
Other short-term deposits	-	24.8	18.9
Trade Investments	16.6	12.6	13.0
Net Fixed Assets	559.9	717.3	861.6
Total	1,998.4	2.243.0	2,273.1
Liabilities			
Creditors and Other Accruals	643.5	672.5	691.4
VAT and Car Tax	47.9	49.9	66.6
Bills Payable	97.7	86.9	224.5
Taxation Due	9.7	8.1	6.7
Other short-term borrowings	57.6	270.3	323.0
Long-term Loans from NEB	160.0	160.0	10.0
Other Long-term Loans	247.7	257.6	303.3
Share Capital	578.7	728.1	1,178.1 (1)
Reserves	155.6	9.6	(530.5)
Total	1,998.4	2,243.0	2,273.1

Note

(1) During the year, the company increased the authorized share capital to £1,250 millions and made share issues of 900 million shares at 50p each at par. At 31 December 1980 the NEB held approximately 99 per cent of the ordinary share capital of the company.

APPENDIX 2: Consolidated Profit and Loss Accounts (1978 - 1981) £m

	Year to 31.12.78	Year to 31.12.79	Year to 31.12.80	Half Year to 30.6.81
Sales Revenue(1)				
Car operation	2,173	2,060	1,928	n/a
Commercial vehicle operations	570	688	702	n/a
Other operations	330	242	247	n/a
Total	3,073	2,990	2,877	1,405
Trading Profit or Loss (2)				
Car operations	63	(45)	(266)	(90)
Commercial vehicle operations	12	10	(32)	(47)
Other operations	4	(11)	4	(6)
Trading Profit or Loss				
Minus Net Interest payable	56.0	66.0	93.6	47.1
Minus *Taxation payable*	12.6	6.3	3.2	2.5
Plus Minority share of profits of subsidiaries	2.1	3.0	5.8	2.9
Minus Extraordinary items (3) =Unadjusted Profit/Loss for Year	38.3 (33.8	23.0 (135.0)	139.0 (529.8)	30.3 (225.8)

Notes

(1) Sales Revenue includes VAT, Car Tax and Other Sales Taxes
(2) Costs include:

Total Wage Bill	739.9	797.8	828.2	n/a
Total Depreciation and Amortization	75,7	83.6	107.5	68.0

(3) Includes cost of redundancies

APPENDIX 3:   Operating Details (1976 - 1981)

	1976[1]	1977	1978	1979	1980	1981[2]
Vehicle unit Sales (000s)	981	785	797	693	587	272
Weekly average number of Employees (000s)	183	195	192	177	157	129
Earnings/Loss per share after Extraordinary items (p)	16.4	(20.0)	(7.8)	(12.0)	(26.2)	

Notes

(1) 15 months

(2) Vehicle production for the 6 months ending 30 June and employees as at
     30 June 1981

References:

1. *The Economist*, 24 October 1981
2. "Edwardes tell critics : we stand firm", John Fryer, *Sunday Times*, 30 August 1981
3. as 2.
4. "BL Unions plan total stoppage", John Richards, *Daily Telegraph*, 3 October 1981
5. as 4.
6. as 4.
7. Leading article, *Daily Telegraph*, 17 October 1981
8. as 7.
9. "What the end of BL would cost Britain", Robert Taylor, *Observer*, 18 October 1981
10. as 7.
11. as 7.
12. "Union Leaders reject BL Chairman's plea for ballot", Donald McIntyre, *The Times*, 23 October 1981
13. "Would anyone buy BL?", Lindsay Vincent and Steve Vines, *Observer*, 18 October 1981
14. "Now Sir Michael can go for glory", Sir Richard Dobson, *The Times*, 28 October 1981
15. as 14.
16. Report on Parliament, *The Times*, 28 October 1981
17. as 16.
18. as 12.
19. as 12.
20. as 12.
21. Report on Parliament, *Daily Telegraph*, 30 October 1981
22. as 21.
23. as 21.
24. as 21.
25. as 21.
26. Leading article, *Daily Telegraph*, 30 October 1981

27. as 26.
28. as 26.
29. as 26.
30. "MP warns BL workers to beware of financial trap", A. Bevins, *The Times*, 30 October 1981
31. as 13.
32. "4 Minutes to Midnight", Robert Taylor, *Observer*, 1 November 1981
33. "Ford pay offer is blow to BL hopes", *Guardian*, 31 October 1981
34. Paul Routledge, *The Times*, 31 October 1981
35. as 34.
36. "Late Night Peace Plan for Leyland", *Sunday Times*, 1 November 1981
37. *Observer*, 1 November 1981
38. A. J. Travers, *Sunday Telegraph*, 1 November 1981
39. *Daily Telegraph*, 2 November 1981
40. as 39.
41. as 39.
42. *The Times*, 2 November 1981
43. "Return to work for England", Duffy tells BL Striker", Clifford Webb and Douglas McIntyre, *The Times*, 3 November 1981
44. "BL cars in move to cut tea breaks", Arthur Smith, *Financial Times*, 7 November 1981
45. "Tea Breaks put BL on the brink", *Daily Telegraph*, 23 November 1981
46. "BL men's tea break strike may be official", Clifford Webb, *The Times*, 26 November 1981
47. "Tea break strike made official by Transport Union", Robert Bedlow, *Daily Telegraph*, 27 November 1981
48. "Longbridge re-opens despite strike", James O'Brien, *Daily Telegraph*, 28 November 1981
49. "BL gamble to end tea break strike fails", Clifford Webb, *The Times*, 1 December 1981
50. "BL strike - it's up to the Workers", Robert Eglin and Tony Willard, *Sunday Times*, 29 November 1981

'One . . . two . . . three'

Daily Mail, 18 June 1981 (reproduced by permission).

CONFLICT OVER COAL

A Hostile Reaction

On 10 February 1981, angry union leaders stormed out of a meeting with National Coal Board Chairman, Sir Derek Ezra, to warn of a national campaign of action over NCB plans to axe up to "50 pits and 30,000 jobs". NUM President, Joe Gormley, declared:

> "I am not going to stand it in my last year as President. I am not going to allow the industry to be raped in this way . . . . We think it is in the interests of Britain that we fight for the biggest coal industry possible in the future. And, if other people don't want to fight for Britain, the British miners will". (1)

He was supported by a united front of NUM delegates, all declaring their forthright commitment to industrial action to prevent the closures and speaking of an early activation of the recently-formed Triple Alliance of the coal-mining, steel and rail unions.

At the meeting, described as 'rumbustious' by some of the union participants, Sir Derek had outlined the basis of an NCB plan to hold down prices, increase coal sales, maintain a high level of investment and reduce coal production by between 8 and 10 million tonnes per year. Speaking of the current situation facing the NCB, he cited the fact that, by March 1981, the Board would be holding undistributed stocks of 20 million tonnes and its customers 17 million tonnes, commenting that:

> "We cannot contemplate adding to stocks at this rate. The financial burden would be insupportable". (2)

The reduced production would come about, it was stated at the meeting, through the closures of pits - which Sir Derek refused to name - where the reserves were nearly exhausted or which were geologically difficult to work. The men affected by the closures would not all lose their jobs, as some redeployment to other workable pits would take place.

The statement by Sir Derek cannot have been unexpected by the

TABLE 1 : Examples of Awards to Miners

| Redundancy Pay | | | | Ex gratia payment for incapacity of Miner from Pneumoconiosis | | Ex gratia widow's payment for death of Miner | |
| Miner aged 55 with 35 years' service | | Miner aged 50 with 30 years' service | | | | | |
Previous	From 11.3.81	Previous	From 11.3.81	Previous	From 9.2.81	Previous	From 9.2.81
n/a	£34,650	£8,790	£14,670	£150	£600	£300	£600

leaders of the three coal unions, whose members had gained dramatically from past productivity deals. Indeed, on 23 October 1980, the NUM leaders had met the NCB Industrial Relations Director, James Cowan, at NCB Headquarters in Grosvenor Place, and heard a warning that the NCB was plunging towards a substantial loss for 1980 - 81 and that there was a strong possibility that 'things could get worse'. The reason, said Cowan, was that 'the bottom had dropped out of the energy market'.(3) Union leaders were also aware of the view put forward by Philip Weekes, NCB Area Director for Wales, to a Parliamentary Select Committee on Welsh Affairs in May 1980 that, on strict business grounds, he would recommend the closure of six pits in South Wales.

What really sparked off the dramatic walk-out from the meeting, however, was Sir Derek's admission that the amount by which coal stockpiles were rising annually - nearly 8 million tonnes - was almost equal to the amount of coal imported yearly from Australia and the USA.

Trevor Bell, General Secretary of COSA and candidate for the NUM presidency, commented:

"There it was staring us in the face. There and then the resolve came over us, moderates and militants alike, not to see members' jobs sacrificed to assist the flood of cheap coal into this country". (4)

The reaction from Arthur Scargill, Yorkshire Miners' leader and another contender for Joe Gormley's job, was vociferous. He labelled

TABLE 2 :   Employment in the Mines

Miners employed	Late 1950s	Early 1960s	Early 1980s
Total	n/a	700,000	200,000
S. Wales only	150,000	n/a	26,000

the NCB plan as a recipe for 'confrontation and economic disaster', adding:

> "We have experienced the butchery of Robens. We are not going to experience the execution of Ezra". (5)

In a statement issued immediately after the meeting, the NUM said they would consider an appropriate response at a National Executive Meeting on Thursday, 19 February, at which they would review three main options:

- Ask the Government for further financial aid for the industry
- Accept the closure plan
- Hold a ballot on official strike action.

The last option was one which would attract, in Joe Gormley's view, overwhelming support, particularly since as many as 100,000 jobs in other industries could be put at risk. It was, by contrast, an option which Sir Derek Ezra, due to retire in March 1982, said he had tried to head off by being as frank as possible with the unions at the meeting and by expressing the hope that:

> "We do not go to industrial action because it will not solve our problems. It will make them worse". (6)

The Government on the Touchline

When Mr. Foot, leader of the Labour Opposition, demanded of Mrs Thatcher in the Commons on 10 February that she turn her attention to the problems of the coal mines and the results of the NCB - NUM meeting, she replied by stating flatly:

> "It would be quite wrong for the Government to attempt to manage

TABLE 3 :   **NCB COAL SALES**

Period	NCB Coal Sales (million tonnes)
1978 - 79	117
1979 - 80	125
1980 - 81 (forecast)	119

Source: *The Economist*, 21 February 1981

every nationalized industry . . . . I am not directing that industry . . . .
It is for the NCB to make the arrangements and we shall stand by
those arrangements". (7)

The Government's approach was, she added, to set the external
financing limit for the NCB - £886 millions for 1981 - and leave the
operational details to the NCB.

This pronouncement by Mrs Thatcher was a restatement of her view
(given at the 1976 Conservative Party Conference) that:

"Governments have got into doing too much. They get involved in
things they ought to leave to other people . . . . I think that with the
nationalized industries it would be far better to leave the negotiations
to those concerned with running them".

Friday the 13th

On Friday, 13 February the NCB announced the closures of pits in
South Wales, Kent and Durham. Further closures were to be made
known in accordance with the following timetable, it was said:

Monday, 16 February   - North Derbyshire
                                       South Midlands
                                       Lancashire, Cumbria and North Wales

Tuesday, 17 February   - South Nottinghamshire

Wednesday, 18 February   - Yorkshire

Thursday, 19 February   - Scotland

TABLE 4 :   Forecast Profit and Loss of Nationalized Industries

Nationalized Industry	1980 - 81 £m	1981 - 82 £m
Electricity	235	412
Gas	436	627
GPO	807	1,159
BNOC	298	438
Steel	(713)	(400)
Railways	(812)	(885)
Coal	(270)	(270)
Total	(19)	1,081

Source: Treasury Red Book (Quoted in *The Economist*, 21 March 1981)

South Wales bore the brunt of the first round of closures with five collieries all to close 'fairly soon'. These were:-

Brynlliw-Morlais (near Llanelli)   Aberpergwym (near Neath)

Coegnant (mid-Glamorgan)   Britannia (near Pengam, Gwent)

Ty Mawr-Lewis Merthyr (near Pontypridd)

Accounting for 2,800 jobs out of the total 26,000 employed in NCB's South Wales Division, these pits, said the NCB, were contributing very substantially to the Division's current yearly loss of £80 millions on the 750,000 tonnes produced. Their elimination would leave the Division with 29 pits.

Durham was to be the second largest loser of jobs, with 1,952 jobs going, out of a total workforce of 23,795. The NCB did, however, commit itself to offering alternative employment to all but 436 of those laid off. Scheduled for closure in July 1981, Bearpark and Sacriston had lost £3 millions to date in the financial year 1980 - 81, i.e. £17 per tonne produced. Houghton, to go in September 1981, was Durham's oldest pit. The fourth pit, Boldon, due to close in the spring of 1982, was running out of workable reserves.

TABLE 5 :   Government Aid to Coal Industries in EEC Countries

	1979		1980 - 81
Country	Total Aid		Aid per Tonne
	£m	per cent	£
Belgium	208	9.8	33.9
France	334	15.7	18.0
West Germany	1,386	65.4	19.5
Britain	189	9.1	1.5
Total	2,117	100.0	9.5

The earliest pit closure of all was, by contrast, in Kent. Snowdown, near Dover, was to close by the end of June 1981. Over the period 1976 - 81, this pit had lost no less than £21 millions, with £7 millions of that in the 1980 - 81 financial year alone, equivalent to a loss of £60 per tonne produced. It was planned to redeploy two-thirds of the 960 miners dismissed to Kent's other two collieries.

Pressure on the Government

Immediately after the announcement of the first cuts on 13 February, Energy Secretary David Howell received letters from Joe Gormley and Sir Derek Ezra. The latter urged a tripartite meeting to "study the very difficult circumstances facing the industry" and seek "possible solutions". The former, under some pressure from local pit leaders, who were known to be already preparing unofficial plans for flying pickets — 'in defiance of the law' — warned David Howell that it was "imperative" that talks be held on:

- The Government's cash limits for the mining industry

- Curbs on the cheap imports which were undermining British coal sales

TABLE 6 :   Falls in Coal Demand in the UK (m.tonnes)

Demand Sector	Fall in demand 1980 - 81 compared with 1979 - 80
Power stations	2.5
Steel	3.0
Industry	1.0
Domestic users	0.5
Total	7.0

Source: *The Economist*, 21 February 1981

- The huge gap between British Government subsidies to mining and those granted in other Common Market countries

It should be noted that, at the time, the then-new Employment Act measures on picketing and secondary action had not been tested in the courts.

Ezra's letter reflected the background of rapidly rising tension within the NUM since, after the meeting on 10 February, the Executive had warned of strike action and local calls for militant action - aimed at obtaining an Executive Order for a pit-head ballot for strike (an 85 per cent 'Yes' vote probability in Joe Gormley's view) - were to be discussed at an emergency meeting of the NUM Executive on Thursday, 19 February.

The Government was left in no doubt of the NUM leaders' mood about the pit closures. Trevor Bell, warning that miners were ready for a strike which would make the disputes of the 1970s pale into insignificance, illustrated this mood by saying:

"We were talking about pay in 1972 and 1974. But now it's jobs that matter and that aspect is uniting all the unions in the country".

He also made it known that, this time, a strike would involve white-collar staff from day one. This would lead to:-

- immediate and costly deterioration in conditions underground (all safety, ventilation and roof support checks would cease)

- disruption of all marketing and financial functions, including stopping the NCB computers.

The Government wasted no time in responding to the threats associated with the closure of ten pits and the associated job losses. On receipt of the letters from Gormley and Ezra, the go-ahead was given for tri-partite talks on 23 February. It was thought that Sir Keith Joseph (Industry Secretary) and James Prior (Employment Secretary) would attend.

Time and Tide

Over the weekend the atmosphere changed for the worse. On Sunday, Moss Evans of the Transport Workers, and Sid Weighell and Ray Buckton of the two rail unions, promised to back the miners if a national coal strike were called, by stopping all movement of coal. This was seen as no idle threat since dockers in South Wales had refused, after an NUM request, to unload imported coal from the Greek cargo ship, *Maria Lemos*.

Whilst the anger of the South Wales workforce resulted in the date of an Area Conference to discuss action plans being brought forward from Wednesday, 18 February to Monday, 16 February, even this was regarded by some NUM branches as grossly inadequate. On Saturday 400 men at the doomed Coegnant colliery had downed tools and walked out. They had then decided to send flying pickets to other collieries to persuade other workers not to cross picket lines.

There was also considerable rank and file pressure for a strike declaration from the Monday, applying to all 26,000 miners in the South Wales pits. As Des Dutfield, South Wales Area Vice-President, pointed out:

> "There's no difference between any of them - it's just that some of the lads are showing their anger immediately and others want to do it together".

Kent miners had also taken immediate action, with more than 2,800 men starting an overtime ban.

On the other hand, the NCB was trying to defuse the situation over the weekend by reiterating that redeployment possibilities would reduce the 30,000 announced redundancies to 10,000. The Government, for its part, was clearly hoping that the prospects of large redundancy payments would placate miners, as they had the steelmen at British Steel.

TABLE 7 :   Price Increases Compared (1980 - 81)

Index	Change in Index Figure: January 1981 compare with January 1980 (per cent)
Retail Price Index	+ 13.0
Private sector price index (based on selected price groups clothing, footwear, durable household goods - in the RPI)	+ 27.0
Public sector price index (based on prices charged by the Nationalized Industries for fuel and light)	+ 8.9

Source: Brokers Carr Sebag

A Head of Steam

The South Wales Area Conference held on Monday, 16 February at Bridgend, Glamorgan, resulted in a unanimous 'all-out' decision from the 100-plus delegates. There would be a complete withdrawal of labour, said Emlyn Williams, the South Wales miners' leader, 'until the threat of closure in all parts of Britain had been withdrawn'. Joe Gormley had, without success, opposed early and unofficial strike action at the conference. With a plea that unconstitutional action should be avoided, he had warned:

"I want to remind them (the South Wales Miners) that there are many people in the country today, even members of our unions, who have the ability to go to the law to make sure the union is brought to heel if it acts like this". (8)

His plea went unheeded. By the Monday evening five South Wales collieries had stopped working and others were expected to follow suit shortly.

The action in South Wales was also based on the supportive attitudes of other miners' leaders. In a reference to Margaret Thatcher's blunt rejection of any possibility of change in her monetarist approach - when she said at the 1980 Conservative Party Conference, 'The lady is not for turning' – the Dover NUM Executive Member said:

"Margaret will turn: the miners will turn her. We are the only industrial force that can do it because we get solidarity from other unions. Remember 1974? The team's the same, just a different captain. We're not selling the jobs of our sons. The Management are with us really because the captain's going as well as the ship's cat!" (9)

The job preservation attitudes of the South Wales and Dover miners were in stark contrast, however, with the attitude of Philip Weekes, who said that the five pits earmarked for closure were like 'sucked oranges'. He strongly supported closure on the grounds that:

- the five pits would lose £20 millions in total in 1980 - 81 and £22 - 25 millions in 1981 - 82 if they were not scrapped.

- the South Wales field presented the most tortuous geological mining problems in Britain. (10)

Certainly, more than 50 per cent of the collieries in South Wales were 70 years old and a third more than 100 years old.

Jobs were the key to the miners' reaction. Said Emlyn Williams:

"Our men will come out to the last man. We did intend to come out on February 23rd but because of the angry mood of the men we had come out immediately. We are on our way to a struggle we will win. I warn that if people in the NUM are going to discuss with the Government this week the question of fool's gold or redundancy payment, it is a non-runner. We have seen what happened to our brothers in the steel industry. It's not going to happen here'. (11)

A similar view was expressed by Hubert Morgan, Secretary of the Labour Party in Wales, who claimed:

"The miners' fight is not only for coal but in defence of our communities in Wales". (12)

Joe Gormley, though anxious to remain within the bounds of legality and to face the Energy Secretary at the scheduled tripartite meeting on 23 February with a constitutionally-taken pit-head ballot decision arising from the National Executive Meeting on 19 February, also appeared defiant. In a statement on 16 February he said that:

- there would be no sell-out by London-based members of the union (a reference to himself and the Union's General Secretary, Laurence Daly)

- if the Government could not see the amount of pressure building up, it would have to face 'a lot of grief that none of us wants.'

Emlyn Williams did not share some of the reservations expressed by Joe Gormley. His call was for immediate solidarity with an all-out national strike from the date of the National Executive meeting. He said:

"We are the area that has had the axe. Other areas will be picked off if we are defeated".

The all-out strike would not, however, make hospitals, schools or the aged suffer; they would receive supplies. "Our men will volunteer to do this work without any payment", he said. (14)

The stock market's reaction was, perhaps, predictable: a sharp fall of 8.7 points, reversing a recent advance, brought the F.T. Index down to 484.5 points.

A Change of Tune

The Conservative Government awoke on the morning of Tuesday, 17 February, to find that:

- 29,000 miners were on unofficial strike in South Wales and Kent

- a further 12,500 from the Western Area were pledged to strike from 23 February.

Further reminders of recent history came later the same day with a speech at Erith by Mick Costello, Industrial Organiser of the Communist Party, giving his praise 'for the splendid lead given by communists and others on the left in the coal fields'. He added:

> "From the initial Tory reaction to the swift action by miners, it is clear that similar action by workers at British Steel and British Leyland with other workers could stop the Tories". (15)

A statement from the Railwaymens' Union, ASLEF, came out during the morning. This announced full solidarity with the miners, reminded ASLEF members not to cross picket lines, and threatened to stop British Rail colliery freight traffic (over two million tonnes per week).

In the afternoon, Joe Gormley, Trevor Bell and Sir Derek Ezra addressed the all-party Commons Energy Committee on the current situation in the UK coal industry. Joe Gormley said that miners were not opposed to pit closures where there was no alternative:

> "We have been making strides all along. But what's raised people's hackles is that somebody, somewhere, has decided it's got to be speeded up out of all proportion".

Sir Derek, denying to the Committee that the NCB had blundered in its handling of the planned pit closures, stated:

- that he had informed the Government there would be pit closures but not how many and which ones, it being NCB policy to make the announcements first to the miners affected and

- that he hadn't met Mrs. Thatcher but that he presumed her Ministers had kept her 'fully informed'.

Almost at that moment, fresh from hearing of the latest announced closure — Hucknall Colliery in Nottinghamshire, with the loss of 600 jobs — and a pre-lunch Emergency Meeting of Ministers in Downing Street, Mr. Howell was making a statement in the Commons. He announced that the tripartite talks would be held the following day (instead of 23 February) and underlined the Government view that:

"The best hope for the industry and secure long-term jobs is investment in modern capacity. It is an extractive industry which inevitably means closures. They are inevitable and predictable".

At the same time, he also paid tribute to the miners for 'turning in a magnificent performance'.

TABLE 8 :   **Salient Operating Results**

	Examples of South Wales Pits					
	To be closed			To be kept open		
Factor	Ty Mawr	Britannia	Aberpergwym	Blaenant	Betws	Taff Merthyr
Miners employed	665	500	300	470	695	700
Coal produced ('000 tonnes p. a)	144	181	63.6	334	385	477
Productivity (tonnes/man/shift)	1.1	1.1	1.0	3.4	4.6	3.3
Yield of saleable coal (per cent)	54	n.a	n.a	92	n.a	n.a

A Piece of Peace

The tripartite talks, held on 18 February, resulted in the following agreement:

- Government undertaking to discuss, 'with an open mind and a view to movement', the tight financial constraints placed upon the NCB by the Coal Industry Act 1980. This specified that the NCB should break even by 1983 and should not exceed the financial support - the cash limit of £886 millions - already allocated by the Government for 1980 - 81.

- A withdrawal of the closure proposals by the NCB and a commitment to a re-examination of the position in consultation with the unions.

- An appeal by Joe Gormley to the men on unofficial strike in South Wales and Kent to return to work immediately.

Said Joe Gormley, after two hours of talks at the Department of Energy in Millbank:

"I am afraid we are talking about a lot of money. If my National Executive has the same optimistic attitude I have, there is no need for a conflagration. There is a new spirit of conciliation abroad".

This 'new spirit of conciliation' was to be discussed at a further tripartite meeting on 25 February.

Reactions

Reactions to the outcome of the meeting differed. Some saw the Governmental move as conciliatory:

"The miners only fired one shot and the Iron Lady became a paper doll". (Jack Collins, NUM Kent Area Secretary) (16)

"The lady said she wasn't for turning, but now she's become an expert in double somersaults". (Joe Wheeler, NUM Nottinghamshire Area Secretary)

Others were wary:

"It is all promises. There is absolutely nothing positive about it. It is far too early to call off the strike action. We must have concrete assurances in writing. There is going to be one hell of a fight in the Executive". (Mick McGahey, Scottish Miners' President) (17)

"Joe Gormley is backtracking again. How long have these pit closures been put off for?" (Eric Clarke, NUM Scottish Secretary) (18)

"If I go back to my lads with a recommendation like this, I should expect them to put a bomb on the train". (Emlyn Williams) (19)

Muted pleasure and, perhaps, thankful relief was expressed by others. Sid Vincent, Lancashire Miners' leader, commented that:

"The left is unhappy because it knows it has lost this one. Given the assurances that Joe has received . . . . it could only be construed as a political strike if we decided to continue our action". (20)

On the Floor of the House

The exchanges at Prime Ministers' Question Time on 18 February were revealing. (21)

Mr. John Watson (Skipton, Conservative):

"In view of developments in the coal industry (*loud Labour cheers*) in the past 24 hours, will the Prime Minister take time today (*Labour shouts of 'to resign'*) . . . . to confirm that the least efficient 10 per cent of all British pits are currently losing money at over £190 millions a year and that whatever may be the outcome of talks over the next few days, the most effective way of reducing costs and thereby of restoring the competitiveness of the British coal industry lies in a planned and agreed schedule of pit closures?"

Mrs Margaret Thatcher (Barnet and Finchley, Conservative):

"I understand those figures are broadly correct. (*Labour laughter*) May I stress that it is the wish on this side, and I believe on the other, to have a competitive coal industry because that puts less burden on other parts of the economy and would enable many other industries, big users of electricity which is based on coal, to have that electricity more cheaply and thereby to keep more jobs in their own industries".

Mr. Michael Foot, Leader of the Opposition (Ebbw Vale, Labour):

"I, more generously than Mr. Watson, congratulate her (*Labour cheers*) on what, on present evidence, appears to be a great victory for the miners and the nation . . . . I assure Mrs Thatcher that every time she turns she will get a nice bouquet from me. I may even ask her to dinner (*Loud laughter*). Who can tell? (*Renewed laughter*)

Is the Government thinking of including a specific undertaking to the miners of financial support in a new coal industry Bill? When will the Bill be introduced? What figure will the Government agree on to enable undertakings made to be carried through?"

Mrs Thatcher:

"On the question of dinners, Mr Foot will not need reminding that it is on occasion a lady's prerogative to say 'No'. (*Labour MPs: 'Not to the miners'*) On the amount of money, I must stick to what Mr Howell said at the meeting . . . . I am not in a position to go further. Consultations and negotiations will continue with a meeting next week".

Dr David Owen (Plymouth, Devonport, Labour) rising to Conservative cheers:

"Why did the Prime Minister ignore the repeated explanations during all stages of the coal industry Bill that this was a pit closure Bill. Who are the trimmers now? Is this slow motion Conservatism, or the first note of the Limehouse Blues?"

Mrs Thatcher:

"The action was swift and decisive". (*Loud Labour laughter*)

A Labour MP:

"Was she pushed or did she fall?"

Mr David Steel (Roxburgh, Selkirk and Peebles, Liberal):

"In her present constructive mood, will the Prime Minister turn her attention to lower interest rates?"

Mrs Thatcher :

"The House must realise that if more money is to be found, the only place it can come from is the people of this country. It either has to come out of the tax-payer's pocket or it has to be borrowed and that would lead to higher interest rates.

When people constantly ask for more money, I hope this is something they will bear in mind" . . . .

The Return to Work

The NUM National Executive Meeting on 19 February voted 15 - 8 to end the unofficial dispute and recommend an immediate return to work. The NUM communiqué made it clear, however, that if the Government did not commit itself to pump more money into the mines and curb imports, the strike would recommence.

The extra money - breaking the cash limits set down in the 1980 Act - would be used for:

- Stockpiling (the need for which stemmed from the fact that, whilst the annual pay settlements had been relatively modest - a 13 per cent settlement in October 1980 against a claim of 35 per cent - productivity bonus deals had dramatically increased productivity and output of coal)

- Improved redundancy payments

- Increased subsidies on coal to reduce prices and, thereby, cut imports

- Offsetting operational losses

- Investment.

There was a total return to work on 20 February.

TABLE 9 :   **Pit Closures Announced (by 19 February)**

Area	Pits
South Wales	Brynlliw-Morlais, Aberpergwym, Coegnant, Mawr-Lewis, Britannia
Durham	Bearpark, Sacriston, Houghton, Boldon
Western	Hapton Valley, Victoria, Newdigate
York	Lofthouse Manor, Parkhill, Orgreave
Scotland	Cardowan, Sorn, Highouse
Kent	Snowdown
Nottinghamshire	Hucknall

The Day of Reckoning

In her speech at the Annual Dinner of the Confederation of British Industry, held in London on 16 June, Mrs Thatcher said to the leaders of British industry:

> "You are poised for success. Nothing must be done to imperil your chances. This is why the Government must keep public spending down . . . . By the time we took office, the old attempts at buying jobs by more public spending and printing money had been thoroughly discredited. Our aim is nothing less than to bring inflation down permanently to low single figures . . . . Now that we have a lower exchange rate, it may be harder. So we have to redouble our efforts. For if we do not, the jobs will go elsewhere and I want them here. For us that mean keeping a discipline on the budget deficit . . . .
> I think you all now recognize the Government's determination not to provide more than can be afforded for pay rises in the public services. If necessary, we are prepared to live with the short-term consequences of that as employees adjust to the new reality". (22)

With reference to her commitment to continuing her monetarist policies, she quoted the words of an American soldier - Captain Lloyd Williams - who after landing in France in 1918 received an order to retreat. His response?

"Retreat? Hell, no. We've only just got here."

That same day Energy Secretary Howell had made a statement in the House announcing an increase of £231m in the 1980-81 NCB cash limit and giving Government policy aims as being:

- The keeping open of collieries scheduled for closure in 1981

- Encouraging men to transfer from older pits

- The subsidisation of sales to the CEGB and the BSC

- Extra subsidisation to increase exports

- The cutting of coal imports to a planned figure of 2.75 million tonnes, from their current level of 5.5 million tonnes.

All parties to the agreement were happy:

"We have an industry which has major profit potential for the future"
The changes "would put the industry in a position where it has a real
chance of offsetting its losses". (David Howell) (23)

"A positive move in the right direction . . . . I think we will find what
we undertook . . . . will be shown to be good for Britain". (Joe
Gormley) (24)

"We have done a good deal, an excellent deal". (Sir Derek Ezra) (25)

Happiness was not echoed, however, by the tone of the question put
down by Dennis Skinner (Labour MP for Bolsover) after David
Howell's statement:

> "Against the background of recession, massive unemployment and a
> run-down of factories which may have burned coal, this cosmetic of
> £231 million - it is little more - can do little to help the prospects of
> an industry set against the background of 40 million tonnes of coal in
> stock . . . . What attempts is the Minister making to run down the
> open cast mining of coal?" (26)

In this context, it is worth noting that the Yorkshire-based Mining
Intelligence Group's January 1981 Report - *A Reassessment of Open
Cast Mining* - had quoted a comment by the NCB that open-cast coal
(with a current production cost of £8.43/tonne) was 'the most profitable in Britain'.

FINANCIAL APPENDICES

APPENDIX 1

SUMMARY OF STATISTICS 1976 - 77 TO 1980 - 81

Element	1976-77	1977-78	1978-79	1979-80	1980-81
Total output (million tonnes)	120.8	120.9	119.9	123.3	126.6
Total Inland Consumption (million tonnes)	124.6	121.6	122.5	128.4	120.3
Imports - Exports (million tonnes)	1.0	.9	-	2.6	.7
Stocks at year end (million tonnes)					
- NCB	9.6	10.3	14.1	12.1	20.9
- Consumer Stock	18.5	19.5	14.7	15.8	17.5
No. of collieries at year end	238	231	223	219	211
Average Manpower ('000s)	242	240.5	234.9	232.5	229.8
Number of accidents per 100,000 man shift					
- Fatal	.07	.09	.13	.06	.07
- Serious Reportable	.98	1.0	.93	.87	1.16
Disputes - tonnage lost (million tonnes)	1.1	.8	1.5	.9	1.5
Average Cash Earnings per week (£)	76.1	84.10	101.76	119.15	140.20
Value of Allowances in kind per week (£)	5.13	6.02	6.54	7.87	9.88
Out put per man/year (tonnes)	447	441	448	467	476

Source: National Coal Board *Reports & Accounts 1980 - 81.*

APPENDIX 2

CONSOLIDATED PROFIT & LOSS ACCOUNTS FOR YEAR END

	£ millions	
	28 March 1980	28 March 1981
Turnover	3,740.4	4,186.5
Total Operating Profit Mining Activities	3.2 (23.0)	50.5 33.1
Non-mining Activities	24.5	19.8
Associated Companies and Partnerships	1.7	(2.4)
Profit on Realisation of Fixed Assets	24.4	19.0
Profit on Trading	27.6	69.5
Interest	184.7	256.2
Profit Before Taxation	(157.1)	(186.7)
Other (minority interests exchange profits, extraordinary items)	(2.2)	(.4)
Deficit for Year	(159.3)	(187.1)
Government Deficit Grant	159.3	149.0
Deficit Carried to Reserves	-	(57.8)

Source: National Coal Board *Reports & Accounts 1980 - 81*

APPENDIX 3

CONSOLIDATED BALANCE SHEET AS AT 28 MARCH 1981

	£ millions	
	1980	1981
Assets Employed		
Fixed Assets	1,795.6	2,333.2
Investment in Associated Companies & Partnerships	21.2	30.6
Deferred Interest	45.2	85.7
Net Current Assets	500.4	485.9
Total	2,362.4	2,935.4
Deferred Liabilities	234.3	279.8
	2,128.1	2,655.6
Financed by		
Loans	1,983.5	2,569.0
Reserves	102.9	99.8
Revenue (deficit) /Surplus	33.3	(21.2)
Minority Interests	8.4	8.0
	2,128.1	2,655.6

Source: National Coal Board *Report & Accounts 1980 - 81*

References:

1. Michael Edwardes, 'Gormley's last stand', *Daily Mail*, 11 February 1981
2. as 1.
3. Gordon Greig and Robert Porter, 'The truth behind the great pit disaster', *Daily Mail*, 20 February 1981
4. as 3.
5. as 1.
6. as 1.
7. as 3.
8. Keith Harper, *Guardian*, 17 February 1981
9. Stephen Cook, 'The making of a coalfield militant', *Guardian*, 7 February 1981
10. Paul Howland, 'Five doomed pits - little more to offer', *Guardian*, 17 February 1981
11. as 8.
12. as 8.
13. as 8.
14. as 8.
15. Gordon Greig and Robert Porter, 'Suddenly, it's all action', *Daily Mail*, 18 February 1981
16. Gordon Greig and Robert Porter, 'Now the big climb down', *Daily Mail*, 19 February 1981
17. as 16.
18. as 16.
19. as 16.
20. as 16.
21. Parliamentary Report, *The Times*, 19 February 1981
22. Julian Haviland, *The Times*, 17 June 1981
23. Douglas Macintyre, *The Times*, 17 June 1981
24. Christian Tyler, *Financial Times*, 17 June 1981
25. as 24.
26. as 24.

PRODUCTION, MANPOWER AND PROFIT IN BRITISH STEEL

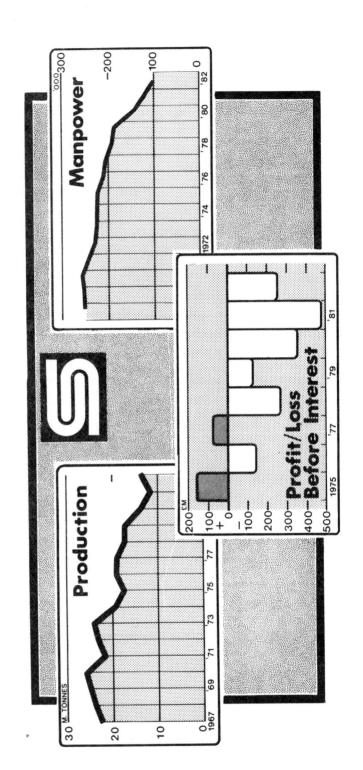

Source: Financial Times, 26 June 1982.

CASE NO. 4
BRITISH STEEL: DIVIDENDS OF SAND

Closing the Doors

It was little wonder that a comment from U.S. Steel — the leading American steelmaker — to the effect that "the devastating impact of unfairly dumped and subsidized ore has severely eroded our markets and severely depressed prices" (1) was followed by swift action. Its 1981 turnover of £7.9 billion ($13.9 billion) was suffering heavily, it asserted, not only from such predatory inroads but also from internal market competition. This had forced U.S. Steel to offer large discounts on over a third of its product line. An even worse impact on corporate profitability had resulted from General Motors decision to buy steel on a bidding system rather than source supplies (at listed prices) in the traditional way. There was no alternative but to freeze prices and to sharpen its strategy for market protection. Filing suits aimed at blocking a wide range of steel imports from the EEC and, for the first time, Korea, it alleged 'dumping'. It was certainly a grave allegation, since not less than 19 per cent of the 1981 demand for steel in the USA was met through imports (19.1 million tonnes).

TABLE 1 : METEORIC SALES GROWTH : STEEL COIL IMPORTS

Period	Imports from Argentina Canada, Brazil and Venzuela (tonnes)	Percentage Market Share by Volume
1981	71,600	0.9
1982 (first 6 months)	160,976	4.0

By June 1982 the US Government had moved to impose countervailing duties on what it perceived to be subsidized steel imports, with the British Steel Corporation singled out as the biggest culprit. These duties amounted to 40 per cent of the importers' purchase price. By December 1982, the US Government was under further pressure, through the presentation of a formal complaint accusing Japan and the EEC of collusion over the diversion of their excess steel production to the US market. David Roderick, US Steel's President, alleged at a news conference that the two parties had negotiated a 'secret treaty' for this purpose in 1978 and demanded that the Administration investigate the problem with a view to reducing Japanese imports by a third.

A meeting of EEC Ministers in Brussels on 24 - 25 July 1982 sought to find a method of settling the dispute with the USA, but was unsuccessful. The latter was unwilling either to rescind its 40 per cent tariff or conclude a bilateral agreement with any individual EEC country. The American action was bitterly criticized in the House of Commons by John Fraser (an Opposition trade spokesman) who asked of Peter Rees, (Minister for Trade):

> "Would you make it clear to the US that we cannot tolerate a situation where they want to make up the rules for other people to follow, as they appear to have in relation to steel, the Siberian gas pipeline and energy pricing? I hope you will make it quite clear that they must behave like trading partners and not trading bullies".

To this, Peter Rees responded:

> "There is a range of international agreements,which we have observed with reasonable fidelity, which are designed for the orderly resolution of these problems. We have a strong interest in the preservation of the open trading system and it is for that we must work rather than contemplate any kind of trade war between ourselves and our friends and allies . . . . We regret very much that the protectionist attitudes of a power which we regard basically as a friendly power, an ally of ours, should have clouded our relations and put at risk a range of industries and jobs in this country . . . . The various protectionist measures of the US Administration in this and other fields have been and will continue to be the subject of complaint to GATT". (2)

US Steel, however, was not the only one complaining about 'dumping'. In November 1982 Eurofer, the 'umbrella' organization representing EEC steel producers, was demanding that the EEC Commission open an anti-dumping procedure against supplies of steel coil from Argentina, Canada, Brazil and Venezuela!

Rather more direct action was being taken, meanwhile, through a picket by members of the UK steelworkers' union, the Iron and Steel Trades Confederation, at Immingham Docks. With promised support from the leaders of other unions such as the TGWU, ASLEF and NUR, the picket was seeking 'black' the import of steel on board two ships - the Panama-registered *Good Warrior* (3,700 tonnes of South African steel) and the Greek-registered *Artemis* (5,700 tonnes of

TABLE 2 :   **INDUSTRIAL OUTPUT (UK)**

Adjusted: 1975 = 100

	All industries	Manufacturing
1979	113.0	104.3
1980	105.8	95.4
1981	100.4	89.4
1982 Q1	100.7	89.3
1982 Q2	101.1	88.9
1982 Q3	101.5	88.2
1982 July	101;4	88.1
1982 August	101.4	88.1
1982 September	101.8	88.3
1982 October	101.4	87.5
1982 November	100.2	86.8
3 monthly change %	+0.1	-0.7

Source: Central Statistical Office

Japanese steel), the latter being brought in by merchant stockists, Leopold Lazarus. Union officials, however, were not hopeful of success, since the union had not been able to stop steel imports during the 13-week steel strike in 1980.

Cutting Down

The key problem underlying these moves was quite simple: a world-wide excess of capacity over demand. The main fear was equally simple: a world-wide steel war. Britain's position, facing this prospect in March 1982, was weak.

The inheritance of history was partly to blame in so far as:

- the last nationalisation of the industry in 1967 had not altered the distribution (or the scale) of steel making in the UK.

- the Government-endorsed expansion of the steel industry in 1972 foresaw increased capacity from 27 million to 33 million tonnes at a cost of £3 billions

- the expansion was based on the Japanese model of large coastal mills where optimum efficiency could be achieved through super-carriers landing huge tonnages of raw materials and adjacent mills producing long (and highly economic) runs of finished product. Five sites were chosen for this expansion: Llanwern and Port Talbot (Wales), Scunthorpe and Teeside (England) and Ravenscraig (Scotland).

More especially, the world oil crisis of 1973 and the decline of Britain's manufacturing base had wreaked havoc with demand predictions. There had been:

- a 50 per cent reduction in the number of cars produced in Britain between 1972 and 1983

- a 40 per cent reduction in the value of new construction contracts over the same period.

- a 25 per cent fall in the volume of mechanical engineering output in the eight years to 1983.

TABLE 3 : **WORLD TRADE PATTERNS ($ BILLION)**

	1973	1974	1975	1976	1977	1978	1979	1980	1981
Export value (1)	574	836	873	991	1125	1303	1635	1985	1170
Balance of Payments on Current Account (2) : Traditional oil-exporting developing countries	10	63	30	40	31	6	65	115	65
: Other developing countries	-12	-32	-37	-24	-20	-30	-48	-70	-85

(1) Source: International Trade 1981/82 (GATT)

(2) Source: OECD and IMF

Losses by BSC in the five years to 1979 - 80 had totalled £1.6 billion, despite the slashing of the workforce by 44,000 and the closure of several big plants, cutting BSC capacity to 15 million tonnes.

Ian MacGregor was hired as Chairman of the British Steel Corporation, on a contract basis from Lazard Freres, the New York-based investment bank in which he was a partner, at a price which involved an annual salary, a payment to Lazard of £675,000 a year for the three years of his term of office, and the payment of a sum ranging from nought to £1.15 million based on his job performance. Mr Mac-Gregor's appointment was seen as the first stage in a 'survival' plan involving further cut-backs. His approach, gentle in terms of plant elimination but tough in terms of manpower reductions, was aimed at achieving break-even point by 1983. By March 1982 it was clear that, due to a massive fall in demand, the original target was unattainable; orders had fallen by a third to an annual rate of 7.3 million tonnes, as against a capacity of 14.4 million tonnes, thus offsetting the earlier price increase-induced movement in finances brought about through the EEC's crisis measures on steel.

Under the 1982 'manifest crisis regime' arrangements allowed for by the thirty year old Treaty of Paris, which established the European Coal and Steel community, the EEC Commission had powers to:

- Block state financial aids (£2.3 billion in 1981) to those EEC steel industries which failed to comply with the production quota targets set for them by the Commission.

- Compensate producers who cut back on their capacity in line with the Commission's rationalization plan - involving the elimination of a further 35 million tonnes of EEC steel capacity by 1985.

- Fine recalcitrant private sector producers who failed to comply with quotas set , e.g. Alphasteel (Britain) and Kloeckner-Werke (Germany), which paid penalties of £18.4 millions for over-production in the first nine months of 1982.

Britain had done more, in fact, than its European partners in complying with the Commission's capacity-cutting directive. Italy, by contrast, had achieved relatively little. Indeed, at an informal Council of

TABLE 4 :   **VIEWS FROM THE BOARDROOM**

Note: On 29 November 1982, *The Times* published the results of a poll conducted by Audience Selection among its Business Forum, a group of 457 executive directors of companies within the private sector whose annual turnover exceeds £50 millions each, plus 79 executives of similar authority in major financial institutions. In fact, this survey consisted of a telephone interview of 253 from the total Business Forum group. What follows are relevant extracts from the results.

1: THE VIEW ON PROTECTIONISM

Do you think British industry is over or underprotected against foreign competition?

	Business Forum	Industrial members	Financial members
	%	%	%
Under-protected	42	42	42
Over-protected	7	9	–
About right	22	22	23
Impossible to generalize	29	27	35

2: VOLUNTARY RESTRAINT AGREEMENTS

Britain now has voluntary restraint agreements with countries such as Japan and similar agreements like the Multi-Fibre Arrangement to limit textile imports.
Does this kind of protectionism work to Britain's economic advantage or detriment?

	Business Forum	Industrial members	Financial members
	%	%	%
Works to Britain's advantage	43	46	31
Works to Britain's detriment	32	30	42
Cannot generalize	25	24	27

Should more such agreements be negotiated or should they be cancelled as soon as possible.

More such agreements/leave as it is	42	48	28
Should be cancelled	31	28	42
Cannot generalize	27	26	31

3: THE MOVE TO PROTECTIONISM

What controls would you like to see? Which industries should we protect? What countries should we protect against?

	Business Forum	Industrial members	Financial members
	%	%	%
Stronger protection for:			
Motor Industry	24	21	40
Textile industry	9	7	20
Other industries	39	43	25

More protection against:

The Far East	50	48	60
France	19	17	25
Spain	15	15	15
Other countries	15	14	20

*All members saying British industry in under-protected.

4: THE COMMON AGRICULTURAL POLICY

The Common Agricultural Policy is now allowable under Gatt. Gatt allows agricultural export subsidies and the limitation of access to domestic food markets. Do you agree or disagree with American demands that the level of subsidies given to EEC food exports should be severely cut?

	Business Forum	Industrial members	Financial members
	%	%	%
Should be severely cut	40	41	27
Should be cut somewhat	24	22	31
No changes should be made	23	26	13
Don't Know	13	11	19

5: NEWLY INDUSTRIALIZED COUNTRIES

Gatt has one set of rules for industrialized countries and another for developing countries. Should a third category be instituted for newly industrialized countries like Brazil and Korea?

	Business Forum	Industrial members	Financial members
	%	%	%
Yes	50	49	52
No	34	36	29
Unsure	16	15	19

And should these newly industrialized countries take on full Gatt responsibilities and freely open up their home markets to products from industrialized countries?

	Business Forum	Industrial members	Financial members
	%	%	%
Yes	73	77	58
No	12	9	23
Unsure	13	14	19

Ministers session at Elsinore in Denmark on 18 November 1982, the Italian Minister for Nationalized Industries, Gianni de Michelis, described the Commission's 1985 target as 'unrealistic' and 'politically and socially dangerous' (4). Conversely, it was agreed at this meeting that those countries which since 1980 had done least to reduce capacity - Belgium, Italy and West Germany - should now bear the brunt. The Commissioner charged with evaluating and agreeing individual national industry rationalization plans - Fran Andriessen - had set 1 July 1983 as the deadline for the next round of capacity reductions. The cuts were worth an estimated £10 billion in compensation.

TABLE 5
BRITISH STEEL INTERIM RESULTS (DECEMBER 1982)

Turnover, UK operations	27 weeks to 2/10/82	27 weeks to 3/10/81		Million tonnes	Million tonnes
			Liquid steel production	5.9	7.0
	£m	£m	Deliveries finished and semi-finished steel products		
Home	1,114	1,054	Home	3.4	3.8
Export	386	417	Export	1.2	1.5
Total	1,500	1,471	Total	4.6	5.3
(Loss) before Interest payable	(97)	(166)	*Employees:*		
Interest payable	(57)	(42)	1976 - 77	207,900	
			1977 - 78	196,900	
			1978 - 79	186,000	
			1979 - 80	166,400	
			1980 - 81	120,900	
(Loss) before			1981 - 82	103,700	
Taxation	(154)	(208)	Nov 82 (approx)	90,000	

All those Against

The Labour Party vigorously opposed the position taken by the Conservatives in acquiescing with the Commission's plans for capacity reduction and in supporting the continuation of the free trade policy in its existing form. Their rationale in so doing was rooted in their attitude towards the Government's economic policy, amply expressed in the following Commons exchanges on 23 November 1982: (4)

David Winnick (Walsall, North : Labour):

"The fresh wave of redundancies and closures sweeping the West Midlands gives the lie to any claim of economic recovery.
An answer here last week showed that the highest recorded unemployment in the West Midlands before the Tories came to office was 6.5 per cent and it is now 16.5 per cent and rising. Why should the West Midlands be turned into a wasteland because of his disastrous policies?"

Norman Tebbitt (Secretary of State for Employment):

"If the West Midlands had learnt earlier the lesson they have learned now, that it is essential to rid industry of people like Red Robbo or Mr Thornett and to get on with producing motor cars instead of calling politically-motivated strikes, there would have been a lot more West Midland jobs today."

Eric Varley (Chief Opposition Spokesman on Employment):

"Will he tell us the truth when he refers to the Government's success in bringing down the year on year inflation rate? He should admit that it has been brought about through the whip of mass unemployment, and the deliberate and systematic destruction of one fifth of our manufacturing industry."

Norman Tebbitt:

"No. I am surprised that he persists in that question because it has been explained to him more than once that the high unemployment level is not the cost of reducing inflation but the cost of having these high inflation levels which were sparked off principally by his policies and his Government when he was a Minister. During that time unemployment more than doubled . . . .
The worst possible thing for all those concerned in industry would be if anyone was barmy enough to believe that the way out of Britain's problems lay through a 30 per cent devaluation in sterling parity (as advocated in Labour's Programme for Recovery)."

On 28 November 1982, further questions pursued the matter of Britain's economic performance: (5)

Ioan Evans (Aberdare, Labour):

"To what extent has industry's competitiveness changed since May 1979

TABLE 6 :   **CITY FORECASTS OF INFLATION**

	In Aug 1982 End 82	End 82	Latest Spring 83	End 83
James Capel	7.7	6.5	5.5	6.0
Simon & Coates	8.2	6.7	5.7	6.7
Messels	7.5	5.4	4.0	n.a.
Laing & Cruikshank	7.6	6.5	6.0	7.5
Phillips & Drew	8.2	7.0	6.3	6.1
Grieveson Grant	7.5	7.0	6.5	6.7
Treasury	7.5	6.5	5	n.a.

Source: *The Times*, 27 October 1982

when the Government took office?"

Patrick Jenkin (Secretary of State for Industry):

"According to IMF figures, United Kingdom's manufacturing industry's unit labour costs were 23 per cent higher relative to our competitors in the second quarter of this year compared with the second quarter of 1979 . . . .

Ioan Evans:

"We are now more than 30 per cent less competitive than when the Government was elected. As this has been the main thrust of their policy, it represents an abject failure."

Patrick Jenkin

The pay explosion of 1978 - 79 wrought havoc in industry's competitiveness. It took time to get it under control." (*Labour laughter*)
Since 1980 higher productivity and lower inflation have begun to restore competitiveness. We must not throw it all away by profligate public spending and soaring inflation, which would be the result of Labour policies."

The issues were explored yet again on 2 February 1983. (6)

Michael Foot (Leader of the Opposition):

"In view of the appalling (unemployment) figures published today, since she has suggested that the only cure for mass unemployment she believes in is a fall in the inflation rate, when does she think her cure will start to work?"

155

Mrs Margaret Thatcher (Prime Minister):

"The figures are a great disappointment to me. Unemployment is rising the world over and in some countries - for example Germany and the United States - it is rising faster than in the UK.

Neither rhetoric nor rows nor strikes will improve the position. Only by having sound financial policies, trying to bring interest rates down, having industrial incentives and by trying to drum up orders the world over and delivering them on time at the prices and design people want shall we improve the employment situation. . . . .

Unlike him (Michael Foot), I am only prepared to advise people to buy British when British goods are best, most competitive and most suitable. The alternative course of protecting and cosseting British industry would lead to an untold increase in the cost of living, untold inefficiency in British industry and a reduction in the standard of living.

A blunt Labour view on the EEC-trade issue was given by Roy Hughes (Newport, Labour) in a debate on steel in the House of Commons on 1 December, he said:

"The major factor in the present depressed state of industry is Britain's membership of the Common Market. Steel imports are flooding into this country and 67 per cent of them are coming from Common Market countries. During the 10 years of Britain's membership, it has shown a growing deficit in manufactured goods compared with other EEC countries. Since 1979, British Steel employment has been halved from 162,000 to 84,000 but the combined steel employment in France, West Germany and Italy has only fallen from 427,000 to 375,000.

The major component of cars is steel, but 46 per cent of new cars going on to Britain's roads are from Common Market countries and these imports should be substantially curtailed. Import controls would result in Britain's car industry blossoming overnight.

A recent poll shows that 60 per cent of people in Britain are now in favour of withdrawal from the Common Market. (7)

Playing the Game

For the Conservatives, it was a hard and confusing game to play. Ian MacGregor was averse to widespread import controls and said as much in a speech launching a special issue of the *British Planning Databook* on 26 October 1982. Conversely, he did not mince words in attributing blame for the general collapse of the steel market when he stated:

"We have become totally uncompetitive and steel, as the handmaiden of manufacturing, is earning the sand dividends". (8)

On the same day, however, Peter Rees was reported as pressing his fellow EEC Ministers to adopt strict measures to reduce steel imports from the 14 nations who had special trading arrrangements with the EEC. He also adopted a tough stance at the November GATT meeting.

A study by the Committee on Invisible Exports published on 2 November argued, by contrast, that Britain should press at GATT for the removal of barriers to free trade in services like tourism, shipping, insurance and banking. These accounted for no less than one third of the UK's foreign exchange earnings and gave the UK a high place in the invisible earnings table.

Yet, at the Franco-British summit on 4 November, the British side - Mrs Thatcher, Sir Geoffrey Howe (Chancellor of the Exchequer) and Francis Pym (Foreign Minister) - was expressing disquiet about the increasingly overt French protectionist stance. Britain's past skirmishes with France over lamb and turkeys were paling into insignificance compared with France's latest action - to try to start reducing its foreign trade deficit for the first nine months of 1982 of £6.5 billion, double the amount for the same period in 1981 - to route all imports of video-cassette recorders (90per cent from Japan) through a small customs post in the provincial town of Poitiers, 200 miles south-west of Paris.

Peter Rees struck a slightly different note in a speech to international traders at Wilton Park in early November, when he said:
"There would be an advantage in establishing an independent review body to consider our trade policy towards imports in the way that the US Administration receives an independent assessment of protectionist demands from its International Trade Commission. There is a danger at present that the loudest voices heard are those of the sectoral lobby. The voice of the consumer, of importers and retailers is often insufficiently audible in our public debate. That is not to say that they should necessarily outweigh the voices for manufacturing industry, but it would be of benefit to both Ministers and Parliament if

TABLE 7 :
                                    INVISIBLE EARNINGS

	US Dollars (millions)	
Country	1979	1980
USA	27,020	28,613
UK	6,588	6,165
France	4,046	4,395
Switzerland	3,542	3,833
Italy	3,563	3,274
Spain	3,026	2,549

all voices could be clearly heard and evaluated." (9)

The 88-nation GATT Conference opened on 25 November 1982 with a warning by Jacques de Larosiere (the Director-General of the IMF) and the World Bank President, Tom Clausen, that world trade expansion was urgently needed to help third-world countries overcome their debt problems. The conference closed on 29 November with a final document declaring the evils of protectionism and a comment by Douglas Anthony (Deputy Prime Minister of Australia) that the Meeting had been 'a fiasco' since it refused to address itself to the protectionist agricultural policies of the EEC. In fact, the final document stated that the EEC would use its 'best efforts' to avoid taking and maintaining protectionist measures.

The statement to the House made by Peter Rees, on his return from the GATT Conference, and the subsequent questioning from Kenneth Woolmer, Opposition Spokesman on Trade, were revealing: (10)

Peter Rees:

> The Ministerial meeting was the first for nine years and was attended by over 80 signatories which account for over 90 per cent of world trade. The purpose of the meeting was not to revise or amend the General Agreement itself but to reaffirm support for existing obligations and to seek agreement on the examination of certain important issues which might form the basis of future negotiations.

After five and a half days and nights of negotiation the meeting adopted by consensus a document which constitutes a realistic commitment by the signatories to maintain the existing obligations of the GATT which have underpinned the open trading system since the war and strengthen their observance in the future. The document does not prevent contracting parties adopting safeguard measures under the GATT or measures with a similar effect . . . .

Throughout the meeting, the countries of the EEC consistently emphasized the need for conclusions and decisions to be expressed in realistic terms. For this reason the European Community entered a reserve on a proposal to link the study of agricultural trade with a wide commitment to re-negotiate the fundamental structure of this trade. The European Community, as did a number of other signatories, made certain other interpretative declarations.

Even with these reservations, the outcome of the negotiations - undertaken against the background of a world recession - must be regarded as an encouraging recommitment to the maintenance of the open trading system on which the prosperity of the UK as a great exporting nation depends and has helped to focus the attention of the world on the consequences of a breakdown of this system.

It was, I think, recognised that the UK through the European Community made a full and constructive contribution to this outcome without,however, compromising its right to safeguard its essential national interests."

Kenneth Woolmer:

"Has he supported the interests of British consumers, taxpayers and industrial workers in his attitude to agriculture, trade and the common agricultural policy in these negotiations?

What steps are to be taken to control unfair competition from newly industrialized countries such as Brazil and Korea and reduce the trade barriers they erect against our exports?

What progress has been made on improving and opening up GATT dispute procedures and ensuring that other countries as well as Britain are abiding by the rules of the game? What pressure in particular is being put on Japan to open up its markets as we open up our markets so frequently to them?

While we welcome any move to open up international trade in services, it is manufacturing industry in Britain which is bearing the full brunt of the Government's deflationary policy and unfair competition in dumping from abroad. Growth in banking and insurance services is no substitute for the decimated manufacturing industries such as steel, vehicle production and textiles.

The world must not adopt beggar-your-neighbour policies on trade restrictions and cumulative employment but this protectionism stems from the general problem of unemployment and excess capacity whose basic causes lie in the kind of economic policy of cutback and despair promoted by the Government.

What steps are being taken by the world's political leaders to co-operate in order to balance demand, production and employment so reducing the very fear that is leading to the threat of protectionism? What is being done about increasing the borrowing capacity of developing nations which still provide vital markets for our industry?"

Peter Rees:

"Trade issues cannot be completely divorced from economic and monetary issues, but it is not within the remit of GATT to conduct such a wide-ranging review although there were perceptive contributions from representatives of the Fund and the World Bank . . . . "

SAFEGUARDS: Switzerland and the Nordic countries want to develop a code which will limit and identify restrictive trade agreements.;
DEVELOPING COUNTRIES: They are looking for ways of getting their goods into industrialized countries while still protecting their own infant industries. They won't tolerate discussion of their export subsidies but will tolerate an extension of multi-lateral trading agreements.;
TRADE IN SERVICES: The Americans want to bring service industry restrictions such as airline cartels within the scope of GATT.;
AGRICULTURE: The big up-coming issue. The Australians and Americans want to open up at Europe's Common Agricultural Policy (CAP).;
DISPUTE SETTLEMENT: Canada is pressing for a speed-up of the settlement of disputes at GATT.;
RECIPROCITY: A general term to describe equality of treatment in trading relations. Some countries, including Britain, feel this is breaking down and want to restore it.;
MORE DEVELOPED COUNTRIES: The Taiwans and South Koreas of the world, which are now pushing agressively into export markets. Western countries want them progressively to lose the exemption from GATT rules enjoyed by the other developing countries.;
IMPORT SURGES: GATT allows countries to prevent low price import surges: the problem is how to define these surges and limit action once the problem has been solved or ameliorated.;

EXHIBIT 1 : GUIDE TO THE MAIN ISSUES AT GATT
Source: Observer, 21 November 1982.

EXHIBIT 2 : A LETTER TO THE TIMES

Sir, Mr Michael Grylls may be Chairman of the House of Commons Industry Committee, but if he wants to pronounce on steel (letter, 15 December) he had better get his facts right. It was not Sir Charles Villiers but Sir Monty Finniston who was overruled, first by Mr Benn and then by Mr. Varley, over 'realistic' plans to cut back British Steel Corporation capacity to the size of the market. The home market was then strong (one third larger than it is today). When the Scholey-Villiers plan came in 1979-80 it cut BSC to *less* than the size of the home market.

Moreover we are not faced with 'the reduction of the British steel industry to that of our Continental neighbours'. United Kingdom steel output was surpassed by France and Italy as long ago as 1974 and since 1979 we have made less steel than Belgium/Luxembourg. Under this Government the United Kingdom has sportingly cut back one third of BSC's manned steelmaking capacity, yet European Coal and Steel Community forecasts are for Community over-capacity to remain at today's levels in 1985. The United Kingdom industry has been closing plants regularly since 1977 and the only noticeable result has been to produce a situation where Mr Grylls wants more cuts.

Mr Grylls says our markets have declined more than other countries' markets. In 1979 the United Kingdom, consuming 368 kg/head, was at least in the same league as Belgium/Luxembourg (376), France (395) and Italy (400). Two years later the United Kingdom figure was 264 kg/head compared to Belgium/Luxembourg (319), France (325) and Italy (345).

This is merely another way of expressing the impact of the icy blast of monetarism on British industry, which cut its demand for steel by 18 per cent in the two and a half years from 1979. He wants BSC in line with the market: has he ever considered putting the market back in line with the nation's invested capacity at BSC?

Finally, Mr Grylls repeats third hand the old saw about Ravenscraig being far from its markets. True it is some distance from his seat at Surrey, North-West, where doubtless they are well-placed to comment on unemployment in the North. But Ravenscraig diversified its markets long ago, before the Linwood closure and this ought to be the cause for praise, not blame.

Besides, is there a single firm or country in the world where Mr Grylls would call for closure because they were far from their markets? Would he say it to the Japanese, who exported 28 per cent of their output, or to West Germany which exports 46 per cent, or to Belgium/Luxembourg which exports nearly 80 per cent? Perhaps you, Sir, will keep open a space in your columns for his reply.

Yours sincerely,
MARTIN UPHAM, Research Officer,
The Iron and Steel Trades Confederation,
Swinton House, 324 Gray's Inn Road, WC1.

Source: Times, 7 January 1983.

Radical Surgery?

The collapse in UK steel demand was, by June 1982, so large that questions were being publicly raised about the viability of British Steel's five 'integrated' mills. Additionally, it was feared that some private UK steel makers would be forced out of business. As Ian MacGregor pointed out:

> "The great tragedy of British Steel is not the decline of the BSC but the decline in the British manufacturing industries." (11)

Ravenscraig, in Scotland, was rumoured to be a closure 'favourite' but Scotland itself had suffered much in recent years with the spectacular closures of the Linwood car plant, the Wiggins Teape pulp mill at Fort William and the British Aluminium smelter at Invergordon.

Cuts in steel-making capacity in other European countries were meanwhile beginning to be announced:

- *Cockerill-Sambre* (Belgium), reduced from 8.5 million tonnes to 6.1 million tonnes with 3,900 redundancies (May)

- *Usinor & Salicor*, the two French giants, cut back capacity by 4.7 million tonnes with a job loss of 20,000 (June)

- *Krupp Stahl* (subsidiary of the Fried, Krupp Group) lost 3,600 jobs over two years (December) through the partial closure of its Rheinhausen Works at Duisburg in the Ruhr

- *Finsider* (the Italian giant whose subsidiaries included Italsider, Almine & Terni with mills at Toronto, Genoa-Cornegleano, Naples Bagnioli and Prombino) cut capacity by 2.38 million tonnes and jobs by 11,000 over three years (February 1983).

One steel company in Germany - Arbed Saarstahl, the German subsidiary of the Luxembourg steelmaker Arbed - provided an object lesson. Faced with a dramatic slump in orders, and the loss of 30,000 jobs if it closed, the company - as the second largest employer in the Saarland where unemployment averaged 10 per cent - had applied to the West German Government for a loan to cover wage and other costs to the end of 1982. The Government decided in November 1982 that

The following advertisement was placed in the *Christian Science Monitor* on Thursday, 11 August 1983 by the United Steelworkers of America:

DEADLY TARGET PRACTICE

The ability of foreign governments to flood United States consumers with below-cost products results from policies known as 'targeting'. Briefly, targeting works like this:

A government makes a conscious decision to promote a chosen industry by giving it preferred treatment. This may mean government ownership. It usually includes tax breaks, low-interest loans on favorable terms, outright grants, research and development assistance, import protection, and subsidies not available to other industries.

The targeted industry develops rapidly with this kind of government nourishment. Soon it has the capability to produce far more goods than its domestic market demands. At this point the subsidized industry looks for foreign markets to dump its excess production. Because of our high standard of living, the strength of the dollar, and generous 'free trade' import laws, the United States is the obvious dumping ground.

When this happens, American manufacturing industries and their workers are the victims. They become targeted for extinction. On top of that, we lose those manufacturing jobs and the industries that werve them are also forced to lay off workers.

Don't think that low wage industries are immune. The consumer elctronics industry in the United States is a case in point. Though its wages were not high, that industry lost 63,000 jobs to targeting by the Japanese and other governments.

Because of international targeting, free trade in free markets has become an illusion - a myth in which only the United States government continues to believe. Our European and Asian trading partners have learned to regulate trade to protect themselves from one another's targeting practices, while promoting their own preferred industries.

The latest example of targeting is unusually dramatic. It threatens the whole American steel-making industry - and the iron and coal mines which supply it. US Steel is negotiating to import 3½ million tons a year of steel slabs from the government-owned British Steel Corporation for finishing at the Fairless Works near Philadelphia.

STEEL-MAKING FURNACES which employ 3,000 workers at Fairless would be closed. Worse, competitive pressure would soon force other domestic companies to close their furnaces and import subsidized semi-finished steel from Brazil, Korea, Taiwan, Europe or Japan. There's plenty available from the target steel industries which foreign governments have sponsored.

US Steel spokesmen have announced that the Company is asking British Steel for a 600 million dollar investment, as its price for this piece of the American steel market. The British government is thus able to take dead aim at this target. No long range planning will be needed - just pay the money and ship the steel.

If the US Steel - British Steel deal is ever finalized, it will violate US trade laws. We will oppose it on this and other legal grounds. But win or lose on this case, the basic problem will still exist.

America's international trade problem is international targeting.

Let's understand it . . . . let's discuss it . . . . let's solve it.

its loan of DM 75 million (£14.48 million) would have to be matched by acceptance of the following conditions:

- An equal subsidy from the Saarland Government

- The banks holding Arbed debt would forego the receipt of interest

- The 26,000 strong workforce would go without half their yearly bonus

The capacity cutback required by Bonn as the price of this aid - 20,000 tonnes and 3,500 job losses - was in December rejected as too low by the European Commission, who demanded 500,000 tonnes and gave the company until 30 April 1983 to come up with restructuring proposals. Eventually, despite opposition from IG Metall (West Germany's largest union) and the company itself, which had since 1977 cut its capacity for crude steel by 37 per cent and that for rolled steel by 26 per cent, the Commission's formula had to be accepted.

Meanwhile, announcements of cuts in BSC capacity proceeded apace:

- Mid August 1982 : Closure of London Works re-rolling mills, West Midlands - 480 jobs
- November 1982 : Closure of Round Oak Steel Works, West Midlands - 1,286 jobs
  : Job cuts at the Special Steel products jobbing shop at Craigneuk, Scotland - 427 jobs
  : Axing of 1,700 jobs in the Special Steels section in Rotherham and Sheffield
- December 1982 : Teeside Works - 1,800 jobs
  : Llanwern - 350 jobs
  : Orb Works, Newport - 200 jobs
  : Shotton, North Wales - 172 jobs
  : Scunthorpe and Orgreave - 573 jobs
- January 1983 : Teeside - 630 jobs

The total reductions over this period reached almost 7,000. At Shotton, it is worth noting that 10,500 workers had been employed until steel making was stopped in 1980, at which time over 8,000 were made redundant.

Simultaneously, the private steel-making sector in the UK was suffering a 'shake-out'. A similar pattern was evident in three sectors:

- *Steelmaking.* Instead of accepting a consortium's offer of £16 millions for the closure of its subsidiary Manchester Steel, Oslo-based Elkem decided on a survival plan based on the loss of 170 jobs out of a workforce of 810. Other loss-making steel companies - like Sheerness Steel in Kent - came under the 'possible closure' spotlight as a result.
  The survival plan for Manchester Steel involved a one year pay freeze, a reduction in capacity to 300,000 tonnes and a lump sum payment of £4,000 to workers over 50 on top of statutory EEC funded payments.

- *Wire Drawing.* The rationalisation scheme put forward by accountants Touche Ross to members of the industry involved nine major companies which between them accounted for 80 per cent of the UK capacity of just over one million tonnes a year. With demand running at 550,000 tonnes a year the decision to cut over 1,500 jobs would reduce capacity by 212,000 tonnes. Said Leonard Kerr, the General Secretary of the Amalgamated Society of Wire Drawers and Kindred Workers, whose membership had fallen from 12,500 to 7,000 in the period 1981 - 83:

  "We would rather see some of the industry remain than have nothing."
  (12)

- *Castings.* Under the scheme arranged by Lazard Brothers, the merchant bank, 15 foundries were to close with the loss of 30 per cent of Britain's 200,000 tonne casting capacity. Those left would pay to the companies closing a three per cent levy based on their turnover for the next five years. Government compensation was available out of the £22 million fund set aside by the Government to aid all private sector steel rationalization moves.

The Big Battalions

On 20 December, Patrick Jenkin made his long-awaited announcement about the future of BSC's integrated plants. They were to be kept open for another five years. And BSC - losing £8 million per week and having already exceeded its 1982-83 External Financing Limit of £365 million - was given until March 1985 to break even. In a later reply in the Commons to a question raised by Sir Peter Emery (Conservative, Honiton), Jenkin confirmed that:

- if BSC had had to adhere to the profit targets that had been set previously (i.e. break-even point by 1983) some 'very 'brutal and drastic steps' indeed would have been necessary.

- keeping the five plants open would involve an estimated £160 million in Government aid over the next three years.

It was wiser, he said, for the Government - as owner of the nationalized steel industry - to 'stretch it out a little longer' (Labour shouts of 'until after the General Election'). (13)

With this position Sir Anthony Meyer (Conservative, Flint West) disagreed:

"Why should this Government", he asked, "of all Governments, need reminding that the way to save jobs is to make industry as a whole competitive and that to massively subsidize the steel industry will drag down with it into the pit many other industries and many other jobs?" (14)

In January 1983 it was revealed that the UK's total steel output - at 13.7 million tonnes - had fallen to near the 1947 level. This disclosure provoked the following vitriolic Commons exchange between the two party leaders on 7 February. (15)

Michael Foot:

"When she took over her office in May 1979, we were the seventh biggest producer of steel in the world. Now we have sunk to fifteenth. We are producing less steel than they produce in Poland. Is that what she calls doing a superb job?"

TABLE 8 : EMPLOYMENT, CAPACITY AND PRODUCTION IN THE STEEL INDUSTRY

Employment in the steel industry and crude steel capacity and production in million tonnes

	74	75	76	77	78	79	80	81	Oct 82*	Estimate 85**
Belgium										
Jobs	63,700	59,300	57,200	49,752	48,541	48,665	45,220	44,106	42,800	
Capacity	17.8	19.0	18.5	19.2	20.0	19.7	19.7	17.9		
Production	16.2	11.6	12.1	11.3	12.6	13.4	12.3	12.3	8.5	19.1
Denmark										
Jobs	(2.500)	2,600	2,800	2,500	2,500	2,800	2,181	1,743	1,700	
Capacity	0.6	0.7	0.7	1.2	1.2	1.2	1.1	0.9		
Production	0.5	0.6	0.7	0.7	0.9	0.8	0.7	0.6	0.5	0.9
Germany										
Jobs	232,037	222,824	219,142	209,465	202,801	204,813	197,406	186,685	180,700	
Capacity	60.4	62.9	65.8	67.7	68.8	68.8	66.9	67.8		
Production	53.4	40.4	42.4	39.0	41.2	46.0	43.9	41.6	31.3	66.6
France										
Jobs	157,833	155,775	153,948	142,992	131,595	120,555	104,940	97,305	96,300	
Capacity	30.6	33.7	33.3	33.3	32.4	32.0	32.5	29.7		
Production	27.0	21.5	23.2	22.1	22.8	23.4	23.2	21.3	15.9	30.1
Ireland										
Jobs	800	800	700	700	700	700	700	700	600	
Capacity	0.1	0.1	0.1	0.1	0.1	0.1	0.1	0.3		
Production	0.1	0.1	0.1	0.1	0.1	0.1	0.0	0.0	0.0	0.3
Italy										
Jobs	95,656	96,140	98,015	96,593	95,591	98,720	99,528	95,651	95,200	
Capacity	28.9	32.7	33.7	34.2	35.7	37.0	39.4	40.8		
Production	23.8	21.8	23.4	23.3	24.3	24.3	26.5	24.6	20.5	39.9
Luxembourg										
Jobs	23,603	21,447	21,755	17,437	16,774	16,351	14,904	13,419	13,100	
Capacity	6.7	7.5	8.2	8.2	8.2	7.6	7.3	6.4	6.4	
Production	6.4	4.6	4.6	4.3	4.8	5.0	4.6	3.8	3.1	5.9
Netherlands										
Jobs	25,100	25,400	25,100	20,529	21,295	21,248	21,047	20,911	20,500	
Capacity	6.1	6.3	7.7	8.2	8.3	8.4	8.5	8.6		
Production	5.8	4.9	5.2	4.9	5.6	5.8	5.3	5.5	3.8	8.6
United Kingdom										
Jobs	194,347	183,140	180,384	176,953	165,361	156,579	112,120	88,247	79,300	
Capacity	27.8	27.0	29.2	28.9	27.9	28.9	28.0	25.4		
Production	22.32	20.2	22.3	20.4	20.3	21.6	11.3	15.6	11.9	25.3
EEC										
Jobs	(795,476)	767,426	759,044	716,921	685,158	620,431	598,046	548,767	530,200	
Capacity	178.9	189.9	197.7	200.9	202.1	203.5	202.5	197.7		
Production	155.5	125.7	134.1	136.1	132.6	140.3	127.8	125.3	95.3	196.8

Figure in brackets close estimate as Danish figures not available for this year.
*Figures at end of October.
**Estimate of capacity based on national projections.

Source: Eurostat (published in The Times, 20 November 1982).

167

Margaret Thatcher:

"He has neglected to say that our steel industry is over-manned and over-priced. He has neglected to mention that his own Government had to close down the Ebbw Vale Steel Works. They ducked many of the difficult decisions that we eventually had to take . . . . I believe that on the whole Mr MacGregor has done a superlative job."

References:

1. Paul Betts, 'US Steel freezes price of sheet products', *Financial Times*, 10 April 1982.
2. William Weekes, 'US accused of acting like trading bullies over steel imports duty', *Daily Telegraph*, 27 July 1982.
3. Giles Merritt, 'EEC Ministers agree on stringent steel closures', *Financial Times*, 19 November 1982.
4. Parliamentary Report, *The Times*, 24 November 1982.
5. Parliamentary Report, *The Times*, 29 November 1982.
6. Parliamentary Report, *The Times*, 3 February 1983.
7. Parliamentary Report, *The Times*, 2 December 1982.
8. Edward Townsend, 'MacGregor says "No" to import controls', *The Times*, 27 October 1982.
9. George Clark, 'Minister wants a body to consider import controls', *The Times*, 15 November 1982.
10. as 5.
11. Ian Rodger, 'A crippling lack of demand', *Financial Times*, 28 June 1982.
12. Robin Reeves and Ian Rodger, 'Steel Industry's job losses reach 6,000 in a week', *Financial Times*, 4 November 1982.
13. Ivor Owen, 'Jenkin's steel verdict seen as stay of execution', *Financial Times*, 21 December 1982.
14. as 13.
15. Parliamentary Report, *Financial Times*, 8 February 1983.

CASE NO. 5

FARES FAIR

It's all in the Manifesto

> "It was perfectly reasonable to publish it. We are very concerned that there should not be a gap after the election while the new council's officers find out what the new council is doing." (1)

Thus spoke Andrew McIntosh, 'moderate' leader of the Labour Opposition on the Greater London Council, of his party's abnormal success in having the 70,000 word Labour Manifesto printed - at a cost to the GLC of £2,200 - in the GLC's agenda for the council meeting on 3 March 1981. His defence of the move was made necessary by the attacks of the ruling Conservative party in the GLC on what they saw as its highly provocative content.

The key plank in the Manifesto, apart, that is, from pledges to create an extra 10,000 jobs per year and to restore the housing cuts that had been carried through by the Conservatives, was an unequivocal statement that the fares for bus and underground services operated by the London Transport Executive would be cut by an average of 25 per cent in October 1981 in the event of a forthcoming Labour victory in the GLC elections to be held on 7 May 1981. The Labour party's ability to take this step was inferred from the 1969 Transport (London) Act which set up the London Transport Executive under the control of the GLC as the grant-making body. Previously, public transport in London had been governed by the Transport Act 1962, as amended by the Transport Finances Act 1966. Whilst the former specified that the LTE's predecessor - the London Passenger Transport Board - had to balance its revenue account, taking one year with another, the latter allowed grants to meet deficits on revenue account to be made by the Minister out of national revenue.

EXHIBIT 1 : CITY OF WESTMINSTER CHAMBER OF COMMERCE RATE RISE ATTITUDE SURVEY

Responses to survey (Member firms)	Percentage stating they would 'probably have to reduce staff as a result of rate rise'
227	20

Source: Christopher Warman, *The Times*, 9 October 1981.

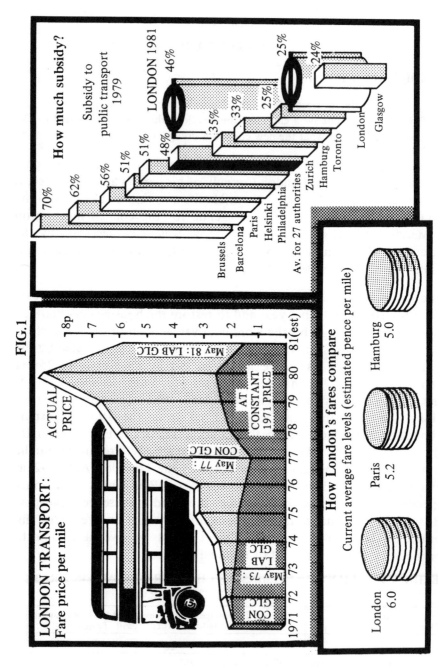

FIG.1

How much subsidy?

Subsidy to public transport 1979

LONDON 1981

- Brussels 70%
- Barcelona 62%
- Paris 56%
- Helsinki 51%
- Philadelphia 51%
- Av. for 27 authorities 48%
- 46%
- 35%
- 33%
- 25%
- Zurich 25%
- Hamburg
- Toronto
- London 25%
- Glasgow 24%

LONDON TRANSPORT:
Fare price per mile

8p
7
6
5
4
3
2
1
81(est)

ACTUAL PRICE

May 81: LAB GLC

AT CONSTANT 1971 PRICE

May 77 : CON GLC

May 73 : LAB GLC

CON GLC

1971 72 73 74 75 76 77 78 79 80 81(est)

How London's fares compare
Current average fare levels (estimated pence per mile)

London	Paris	Hamburg
6.0	5.2	5.0

Source: *The Times*, 18 December 1981.

The fare-cutting policy itself had been approved after lengthy deliberation by Labour members and was considered to cost the equivalent of an extra 16p/£ rates for each household in London by 1983 - 84 (approximately £1 extra per week). It was justified in the Manifesto by the Party's statement that:

"We believe Londoners will get good value for their money in the form of support for the London Boroughs most in need, better public transport, less congestion and more and better jobs." (2)

Whilst there was very strong resistance to the cost to the rates of such a policy - the GLC's revenue grant to the LTE resulted from rate precepts demanded by the GLC of the London Boroughs - there was little doubt about the level of traffic congestion in London.

TABLE 1 :
ATTITUDES OF OVERSEAS VISITORS TO LONDON TRANSPORT FARES BEFORE GLC FARES FAIR POLICY

Mode	Percentage of sample stating fares were:			
	Very Expensive	Expensive	Average	Cheap
Tube	40	33	26	1
Bus	-	44	31	25

(Figures based on a British Tourist Authority survey)

Source: Dennis Barker, *Guardian*, 5 January 1982

Is London Choking to Death?

This was the gloom-inspiring title of an article by Peter Gillman in the *Sunday Times* (15 November 1981) in which he produced frightening statistics on London's traffic problems:

- Traffic speeds in Central London had slowed down from an average 14.2 m.p.h. in 1974 to 12.1 m.p.h. in 1981, during which period the number of vehicles had risen by 12 per cent.

- A report (issued in September 1981) by a group of environmental consultants indicated that, in a recent survey, 80 per cent of vehicles in the London W1, WC1 and WC2 districts were parked illegally. It also stated that Westminster

Borough's 9,500 car parking meters were jammed in 1980 on no less than 63,458 occasions (of which ring-pulls from cans accounted for 22,973 and match-sticks 10,447).

- In November 1981, the Camden Parking Zone had only 61 traffic wardens - out of an 'optimal' complement of 115 - available to service 38 'beats'.

TABLE 2 :   **TRAFFIC INFLOW STATISTICS**

	Years	
Arrivals in Central London between 07.00 and 10.00 daily	1976	1981
Vehicles:		
London buses	3,200	2,600
Cars	119,200	131,000
Motor/Pedal cycles	21,600	25,000
Passengers ('000s)		
LT Underground	424	468
LT buses	151	105
British Rail	401	393
Private transport	187	199

Source: LTE *Annual Report*, 1981.

This concern was also sharply reflected by LTE itself in its Annual Report for 1981. It spoke of:

- the increase in 1968 in the scheduled running time on bus route 29 from Victoria to Wood Green from 54 to 72 minutes because of increased road congestion

- the degree of congestion, militating strongly against economies in operations, since 'operating costs are incurred primarily against the journey time, whereas revenue is earned according to the distance travelled. Slower speeds mean higher costs and reduced productivity'.

These notwithstanding, LTE recorded, for its bus operations, an improvement of a quarter of a minute in the average passenger bus-stop waiting time in 1981 over 1980. This was achieved predominantly by the increase in mileage operated and by better control of services.

TABLE 3 :
AVERAGE PASSENGER WAITING TIME (MINUTES)

Wait type	Bus		Underground	
	1980	1981	1980	1981
Scheduled wait	4.3	4.4	2.5	2.5
Excess waiting time	3.4	3.1	0.8	0.7
Total	7.7	7.5	3.3	3.2

Source: LTE *Annual Report*, 1981.

Note: 'Excess waiting time' is the additional waiting time which passengers experience because of deficiencies and irregularities in the service.

Such an improvement was doubly welcome in view of what LTE saw as the 'near anarchy' which existed with illegal parking in London and the fact that, in 1981, traffic congestion resulted in nearly three per cent of the total scheduled mileage being 'lost' because buses were so late they could not complete their journeys.

Into Action

The high-level electioneering campaign of the Labour Party brought victory at the polls in the GLC May election. Their eight-seat win in the contest for control of the largest local authority in Europe was hailed by the Parliamentary Labour Party Leader, Michael Foot, as:

"An absolute condemnation of monetarist policies and policies that have led to mass unemployment." (3)

Within days Ken Livingstone had become the GLC leader - defeating Andrew McIntosh in a secret ballot for the role - and Labour's commitment to reducing London Transport fares was starting to be implemented with a public statement of intent. On 12 May, Ken Livingstone met the LTE Chairman, Sir Peter Masefield, to discuss the issue. Whilst there were apparently no minutes of this dicussion, a report (dated 2 June) to the GLC's Transport Committee recorded that the LTE had been instructed to submit proposals, by 1 July, for an

TABLE 4 :
LANDSLIDE VICTORY PREDICTED FOR LABOUR IN GLC ELECTION

Polling organization	Forecast percentage of vote for parties:		
	Labour	Conservative	Liberal/SDP Alliance
Opinion Research Centre	71	20	1
National Opinion Poll	70	20	2

Source: C. Warman, *The Times*, 2 May 1981.

Note: The NOP poll disclosed that 19 per cent of respondents in its survey did not know that an election was forthcoming.

approximate reduction in fares of 25 per cent, to be brought in at the earliest possible date. LTE developed several options to meet this requirement and these were discussed at a number of public meetings where bus and tube users were invited to express their views. By early July the GLC had completed its consideration of LTE's final proposals.

Financial calculations by the GLC officers were taking place in parallel, and on 10 July the GLC's Comptroller of Finance, Maurice Stonefrost, set out a total supplementary rate precept of £117.3m (to be collected by the London Boroughs and handed over to the GLC) of which:

- £69 millions were made up by the fares reduction and equalled a rate of 6.1p/£

- £48.2 millions were the result of the intended write-off of the the accumulated LTE deficit which had been inherited from the previous Conservative administration. This amounted to 5.8p/£.

Thus the total rate burden which the Boroughs had to levy on the GLC's behalf was 11.9p/£ on top of the Boroughs' own rate levels.

This rate resolution was passed by Council on 21 July and a letter requiring payment by instalments sent to the Boroughs the next day.

Following the agreement between British Rail and LTE over fares on routes where they operate side by side, and the GLC's assurance to the

LTE that 'adequate funds to pay for the increased services at the reduced fares' would be generated by the GLC, the 'Fares Fair' policy was scheduled for launch on 4 October.

The key fare decreases - averaging some 32 per cent - were heralded by a major 'Fares Fair' advertising campaign using TV, radio, press advertisements, posters and 500,000 leaflets.

Storm Clouds

'You have been warned', was the laconic comment with which the previous Conservative GLC leader, Sir Horace Cutler, had greeted the publication of the Labour Manifesto.

Frequent attacks were mounted by the Conservatives - based on the view that Labour's policies would result in an increased rate burden of 25p/£. Typical was the onslaught of the Conservatives' Deputy leader, Richard Brew:

> "The manifesto is the length of a short and poor novel and is as thick as two short planks. It draws its inspiration from Karl Marx." (4)

There was also the vociferous pre-election opposition challenge to the Manifesto by the Acting Council of London Ratepayers (formed on 10 March with the intention of cohesively fighting rate rises).

On the other hand, these were minor irritations for the GLC socialists compared with the court action brought by Bromley Borough Council against the GLC on 28 October.

Against a background of claims that the cost of the 'Fares Fair' policy to London rate-payers could rise in a full year to over £200 millions - partly because of the supposed loss in Central Government Grant support that the GLC would suffer by having overstepped appropriate spending limits and some withholding by rate-payers of the supplementary rate payment - the hearing of 'Regina v. The Greater London Council. Ex parte Bromley Borough Council' commenced. Bromley applied in the Queen's Bench Division Court before Lord Justice Dunn and Mr Justice Philipps for:

- An order of *certiorari* to quash a supplementary precept for the levying of a rate of 6.1p/£ applicable from 1 October 1981 to 31 March 1982

EXHIBIT 2 :   **TRAVELLERS' TALES**

"Reduced Fares? They must be off their heads. They should be paying us to travel in conditions like these. And now there will be more people than ever trying to get on the buses and probably fewer buses for them to get on". *Passenger on a heavily-laden No.6 Bus.*
"My single fare from Belsize Park is 40p. It was 60p. But I would not say I was happy about it. I shall be paying the difference in my rates. The money has got to come from somewhere. It doesn't take a lot of intelligence to work that out". *Passenger at Oxford Circus.*
"Never again! I have come from Wimbledon for 40p, but it has taken hours. I would willingly spend a couple of quid on petrol and risk another £18 or so in car fines than go through that purgatory again". *Wimbledon shopper.*

Source: Robin Young, *The Times*, 6 October 1981.

- a declaration that the supplementary rate was *ultra vires*

- An injunction to restrain the GLC and the LTE from implementing or continuing to implement the decision to operate the reduced fares.

The hearing started with a ferocious assault by David Widdicombe, Q.C., and Harry Sales, both appearing for Bromley. The former accused the GLC of treating ratepayers as 'a milch cow, a bottomless well of funds'. (5) They contended that:

- under the 1967 General Rate Act, supplementary rates are unlawful if they are made for a purpose for which Borough Councils have no power to make a rate

- Bromley believed that Parliament, in passing the Transport (London) Act in 1969, intended London Transport to be run as a business, rather than on social welfare principles

- "Having won the election, the new administration had proceeded with its fares policy in blindly following an election pledge, without, so far as we know, any legal advice and ignoring the true effect on financial consequences." (6)

- The financial loss to the GLC as a result of the policy would be £61.4 millions in the first 6 months and £123 millions in the first full year. This would involve the following forecast results:

	Rate precept for public transport (p/£)	Cost to ratepayers with premises valued at a rateable value of £300 (p.a.)
Former Conservative GLC policy (1981-82)	2.4	£7.20
Labour GLC policy (1981-82)	13.5	£40.40
Labour GLC policy (1982-83)	20.0	£60.00

- "You may think these figures are quite staggering and it will be our case that this is a policy of deliberate loss-making on transport at the expense of the ratepayer." (7)

- Hence, the decision to levy the supplementary rate because of lower bus and tube fares was contrary to the statutory duties of the GLC, and unlawful exercise of their discretion, and a breach of their duties to the ratepayers of Greater London.

The GLC's case was put by Peter Weizman, Q.C., and James Goudie. It rested simply on the GLC's perception of its primary duty to make provision for a public transport system which would meet the needs of London and people travelling within it. Given that it was not possible to run the public transport system at a profit, the GLC saw their role as providing a social service.

Round One: GLC 1 Bromley Borough 0

The court found, on 3 November, that the GLC's supplementary rate was lawful and rejected Bromley's three applications. In reaching the decision, the judges had not concerned themselves with value judgements about how public transport systems should be run. Lord Justice Dunn commented:

> "One view was that it should be run as a social or welfare service, financed predominantly by taxation at minimum cost to the user. The other view was that the system should be run so far as was practicable as an ordinary business concern and that the bulk of the revenue should be provided by those who used the service, although it was accepted that some financing from taxation was inevitable in present conditions. Both these views were strongly and sincerely held by their respective protagonists. They raised wide political, social and economic issues with which the Court was not concerned." (8)

Referring to Sections 1, 3, 5 and 11 of the Act, the judges stated their view that the issue before the court was one of the degree to which the GLC was empowered to subsidize the LTE. Cutting the fares by 25 per cent and then freezing them for the life of the Labour administration (as specified in the Manifesto) produced a case which, in the words of Mr Justice Philipps, was 'at the margin of what is permissible." (9)

Lord Justice Dunn found, however, that the applicants had failed to show that the GLC had acted outside, or abused, their powers in view of:

- The linkage between the power to fix fares or to approve a particular fares structure *and* the discretionary power to make grants

- The role of the GLC in deciding how far transport was to be paid for by user or taxpayer

- The fact that the LTE was not expected to make a profit.

The First Replay

Two days after the Queen's Bench Division Court ruling against Bromley Borough, David Widdicombe, Q.C., was in action again pleading the Borough's case in the Court of Appeal before Lord Denning (Master of the Rolls), Lord Justice Watkins and Lord Justice Oliver. The case for Bromley, he said, turned on the exact meaning of Section 1 of the Transport (London) Act, in which the GLC's duty of promoting 'the provision of integrated, efficient and economic transport facilities' is stated. He referred their lordships to the Oxford English Dictionary definition of 'economic' - 'run on business principles' - as opposed to 'economical', which signified the avoidance of waste. This latter meaning, he said, had been stressed in the Divisional Court. He cited the famous Poplar case of 1925, in which George Lansbury and other Labour leaders in Poplar were legally restrained from pursuing altruistic policies at the ratepayer's expense, in accusing the current GLC leaders of pursuing 'eccentric principles of socialist philanthropy." (10)

For the GLC, David Weizman, Q.C., countered by stating that:

- "All the relevant considerations" had been weighed before the GLC's decision. "It was not a simple commitment to the Manifesto but a considered decision based on reports they had received." (11)

- No authority could run a public transport system at a profit. "If LT were not run as a service, it would be easy to make it pay. They would simply close all the unprofitable stations where there were few passengers." (12)

The unanimous decision by the Appeal Court judges that the GLC's supplementary rate precept decision was *ultra vires* and that the LTE was under a duty to carry out its functions in a business-like way resulted in the order of *certiorari* sought by Bromley council. Commenting that he thought Ken Livingstone had acted 'very foolishly' (13), Lord Denning justified the verdict on the following grounds: (14)

1. 'A Manifesto issued by a political party in order to get votes is not to be regarded as gospel. It is not a covenant. Many electors do not vote for the Manifesto, they vote for the party. When a party is returned to power, it should consider what it is best to do and what is practical and fair. To cut fares by a half or a quarter is a gift to the travelling public at the expense of the ratepayers. The GLC has to hold the balance fairly.'

2. 'LTE is entrusted with the task of running London Transport. They have to do it on business lines so as to break-even. If they cannot do so, the Council can make grants.'

3. 'LTE is the charging authority, not the GLC. Council has to approve LTE recommendations on fare policy, not the other way round.'

4. The GLC had failed to observe two procedural requirements of the 1969 Act: failure to give LTE appropriate written directives and failure to consult six neighbouring councils.

"I realise,' said Lord Denning, 'that this will cause much consternation to the GLC. They will be at their wits' end to know what to do about it, but it is their own fault. They must unscramble the affair as best they can.' (15)

The GLC immediately said they would appeal against the decision in the House of Lords.

TABLE 5 :

LONDON LABOUR COUNCILLORS' PUBLIC SECTOR TIES				
Authority	Trade Union officials	Economically inactive	Local Government and similar	Total
Camden Borough	6	4	14	33
Lambeth Borough	3	4	8	27
Islington Borough	2	9	17	43
Lewisham Borough	1	3	17	33
Southwark Borough	0	9	14	48
GLC	8	13	20	47
Total	20	42	90	231

Source: David Walker, *The Times*, 23 August 1982.

Mrs Thatcher, the Prime Minister, left no doubt as to where her sympathies lay during Question Time on 10 November. (16)

Bromley's Conservative MP, Mr. J. Hunt had asked: "Has she (the Prime Minister) had time to study the judgement in respect of the GLC supplementary rate? Will she commend the initiative of Bromley Council which alone among the London Boroughs had stood up against the rapacious demands of the GLC? Will she lend her support to its continuing efforts of behalf of London's hard-pressed rate-payers?"

In reply, Mrs Thatcher stated categorically: "I join in congratulating Bromley Council upon its initiative. I did see the judgement which will have been greeted with relief by many people."

She continued in the same vein with a sharp rejoinder to the point made by Mr Alexander Lyon (Labour, York) that: "Although it may be one thing to say that the Council has exceeded its statutory powers it is quite another to say that, even if it has the statutory powers, it acted unreasonably in balancing the interests of ratepayers and tax-payers. In such circumstances, the judges were making political and not judicial decisions."

To Conservative cheers and Labour shouts of 'Rubbish', Mrs Thatcher replied: "I wholly reject that. Judges give decisions on the law and the evidence before them. They do so totally impartially."

This firm tone notwithstanding, no less than 100 MPs signed a Commons Motion on 10 November stating that 'Lord Denning is wrong and dangerously wrong to say that election policies and election mandates are to be disregarded." (17)

Such also was the view advanced by Ken Livingstone, who told an audience of 120 members of the Camden Town Amenity & Transport Group, that 'I would not mind if people who did not implement their election pledges got this sort of clobbering'. (18)

Having criticized the press coverage of the hearings as 'ill-informed and bigoted', he continued by saying that, if the Appeal Court's decision were upheld by the Lords, there would be 'chaos and confusion' and 'irreparable damage to the quality of life in London'. London would end up, he thought, with the sort of skeleton service provided for the poor and deprived in cities like Los Angeles since 'people are just going to give up and say this is the end of London Transport'. (19)

'Game, Set and Match'

Robert Alexander, Q.C., opened the batting for the GLC in its appeal before the Lords' Appellate Committee consisting of Lords Wilber-

TABLE 6 :
ACCIDENTS IN THE LONDON METROPOLITAN POLICE DISTRICT

Year	Fatal	Serious	Slight	Total	Casualties per 100 accidents
1976	722	8,252	43,984	52,958	125
1977	692	8,046	46,465	55,203	124
1978	726	7,933	45,039	53,698	124
1979	627	7,528	42,153	50,308	124
1980	599	6,998	41,041	48,638	122

Source: Metropolitan Police Statistics Analysis for 1980.

force (presiding), Diplock, Keith of Kinkel, Scarman and Brandon. He argued that:

1. The judgments of two of the three Appeal Judges had 'contained some of the rhetoric of forensic advocacy to a degree greater than that normally heard in the reasoned tones of judgement.' (20)

2. As the GLC's decision had been reached by an elected body after proper opportunity for debate, it was not 'lightly to be interfered with.' (21)

3. The decision was 'looked into pretty thoroughly and pretty carefully.' (22)

4. If the Lords were to rule the scheme invalid, there would be a very substantial fares rise.

After repeating his previous arguments on the demerits of the GLC approach, David Widdicombe, Q.C., countered his opponents' last point by saying that 'what they have not pointed out is the quirk of arithmetic that, if you reduce fares by 33 per cent, when you put them back to where they were before, that percentage works out at 50.' (23)

The unanimous verdict of the Law Lords was that the Fares Fair scheme was 'a breach of the GLC's duty to the ratepayers'. Lord Diplock said:

"It cannot be too emphatically stated that the house is not concerned with the wisdom or fairness of the GLC's decision . . . . All that their Lordships are concerned with is the legality of that decision . . . .

It is well-established by the authorities that a local authority owes a general fiduciary duty to the ratepayers from whom they obtain monies needed to carry out their statutory functions and that includes a duty not to expend those monies thriftlessly but to deploy the full financial resources available to the best advantage . . . . As the GLC well knew when they took the decision to reduce the fares, that would entail a loss of rate grant from the central government funds amounting to about £50 millions which would have to be made good by the ratepayers . . . . That would clearly be a thriftless use of monies obtained by the GLC from ratepayers." (24)

Lord Scarman added that the 1969 Act 'required LTE to follow, so far as practicable, a financial policy of break-even. Grants in support of revenue from fares were envisaged; but as a necessity and not as an object of social or transport policy . . . . It is plain that the 25 per cent reduction was adopted not because any higher fare level was impracticable but as an object of social and transport policy . . . . It was not a reluctant yielding to necessity but a policy preference. In so doing the GLC abandoned business principles.' (25)

Dennis Barkway, leader of Bromley Council - 60 per cent of whose territory was a patchwork quilt of green-belt villages and whose nearest tube station was seven miles away at Brixton - was cock-a-hoop at the final verdict. He said:

"What we have seen today is the fully panoply of the law at work in our society, which is a democracy under the law. It is game, set and match to us." (26)

So was the Tory leader on the GLC, Sir Horace Cutler, who , in demanding Ken Livingstone's immediate resignation, thundered:

"Livingstone and Co. are totally discredited. The Manifesto on which they fought and won the election in May is in shreds - shot to pieces. They must resign. There is no place in London's affairs for Livingstone and his ilk. One by one his madcap policies have been exposed for the follies they are. Now the maddest of all has been pronounced illegal by five of the country's most eminent judges." (27)

The comment of David Howell, Transport Minister, was quieter in tone but not out of tune with Sir Horace's:

> "This crisis is entirely the fault of the GLC who have managed in seven months of folly to create financial chaos. It is now up to the GLC to decide how it proposes to clear up the mess it has created. The Government is delighted this unnecessary extravagance has now got to end." (28)

There were strong calls in the Commons on 17 December for an Emergency Debate on the situation. That of James Wellbeloved (SDP, Bexley, Erith & Crayford) is of particular interest, given the defection of Labour members to the SDP since the May election:

> "What is at issue is not the right of the GLC to provide a subsidy but the responsibility which they exercise in providing that subsidy. It is advisable to have a debate so that Ken Livingstone and his Marxist friends on the GLC, and some of them are here, can be made aware that his irresponsible attitude is unacceptable to Londoners and that he needs to exercise responsible management of London's affairs." (29)

Mrs Thatcher firmly rejected all such calls - including one from Mr Foot. She declared:

> "What I understand the main burden of the judgement to be . . . . is that LTE has a duty to budget, to make a reasonable effort to break-even, recognising that, in present circumstances, it may well not do so. The previous year's budget, set on the basis that there would be an £80 millions subsidy from the GLC, constituted such a reasonable effort and that subsidy is not in itself unlawful." (30)

The Labour reaction was hostile, Sidney Bidwell (Labour MP for Ealing, Southwell) said that:

> "Mrs Thatcher's references to breaking even are out of line with the running of public transport in any other major city in Western Europe. This judgment will be treated with widespread dismay by thousands of ordinary folk in London." (31)

Albert Booth, Labour's Transport spokesman, had enunciated his party's approach to Transport policy in a speech on 27 November to the National Council for Inland Transport as: (32)

- "A deliberate policy of pricing private motoring at a level to make people switch to public transport "

- "Decisive action" against the company car. "It is estimated that 60 per cent of all new car purchases are made by companies, which is robbing the Treasury and the public transport system of revenue on a very large scale."
- At least a doubling of investment and subsidies for public transport.

Booth now criticised the Law Lords' interpretation. According to him, it 'is such that it denies the voters of London the democratic right to choose a fresh policy to be operated by their own selected body.' (40)

This view was shared by Norman Atkinson (Labour MP for Harringey, Tottenham), who claimed:

"There is widespread opinion that the legal judgement made by all of their Lordships will be considered to be an extra-parliamentary political instrument." (34)

The correct answer was widely seen in the Labour party to be a change in the law on London transport. Ken Livingstone supported such a strategy:

"The Lord's decision turned back 60 years of social provision by local authorities and puts us back into a climate of opinion that says a councillor's prime aim is to keep the rates down. London will face a devastating position if we cannot in a short space of time achieve an amending Act of Parliament. There is no public transport system on this planet that breaks even let alone makes a profit . . . . There will be no surrender, no resignations. We are determined to fight for our manifesto. We are not giving up, going away or keeping the seat warm for Sir Horace Cutler." (35)

Albert Booth reiterated his statement of 27 November that:

"New legislation will be enacted by the next Labour Government to preclude a similar outrageous intervention by the judiciary." (36)

He was speaking in the Emergency Debate (22 December) on the situation facing the GLC, when:

- He praised the results of the cheap fares policy since its launch - increases of 11 per cent and 7 per cent in bus and tube passengers

- He warned of the dire consequences of fare increases

- He criticised the Transport Minister's approach, stating "If he is not prepared to do anything, he will be a Nero fiddling while Rome burns, sitting in his ivory tower while the transport system in London goes from bad to worse and creates enormous problems for those who live and work in the city." (37)

To this David Howell, Transport Minister, responded:

"If a sharp rise (in fares) is now needed it is a reflection not just of the reversal of the low fares policy but the inefficiencies and cavalier GLC attitude to cost which has prevailed since May. They were warned repeatedly that their policy was misguided and could lead to difficulties. It has done so. It is now for LT to propose and for the GLC to approve what provision of subsidy is reasonable and legal. If the GLC find themselves incapable of sorting out their difficulties, let them come and see me." (38)

TABLE 7 :
PROVISIONAL FIGURES PUBLISHED BY THE GOVERNMENT FOR REVENUE GRANTS AND ESTIMATES OF SUPPORT PLANNED BY THE TRANSPORT AUTHORITIES

Authority	1982-83 (£m)	1983-84 (£m)
Greater London	220	188
Greater Manchester	46	45.9
Merseyside	40	50.6
South Yorkshire	40	57.4
Tyne & Wear	18	20.6
West Midlands	28	28.3
West Yorkshire	44	46
Total	436	436.8

Source: Hazel Duffy, *Financial Times*, 6 November 1982.

Options

Difficulties were certainly facing the parties in their appraisal of action possibilities. On the one hand, Sir Peter Masefield announced in a message sent to LTE staff on 23 December that, at the end of the Fares Fair policy:

- Fares would be doubled
- There would be cuts in bus miles (15 per cent) and tube miles (3 per cent) but no route cutting
- There would be a 4 per cent cut in London Transport's staff by natural wastage.

These moves would be based on the availability of the same level of GLC subsidy as before and on a five-year loan to cover the added deficit arising from the Fares Fair Policy. On the other hand, GLC officials, early in the New Year, reported in confidence to the council's Committee Chairman and Vice Chairman that:

- A doubling of fares on the 21 March would produce a drop of about 25 per cent in patronage and a rise in revenue in 1982 of £166 millions
- This would, however, still leave a legally unacceptable level of deficit and, hence, a further rise in fares (together with cost reductions) would be needed as soon as possible to bring in an extra £80 millions
- Since an LTE loss for 1982 was unavoidable, the estimated level of GLC grant needed would be £160 millions
- A proposal to cut services by 15 per cent was to be resisted. It 'may well undermine the confidence of the travelling public and this, together with the consequences of major fare increases and cost reductions which prove to be necessary, could seriously undermine the capital's public transport system'. (39)

By contrast, for Larry Smith (TGWU Executive Officer and Chairman of the TUC's Transport Industry committee) the key option was resistance to the Law Lord's decision by a campaign 'uniting all those who work in, and use, public transport'. He contended that:

"If we had a strike in London which lasted more than one day it would stop London because you cannot move in the metropolis merely by using personal transport. The whole thing would become a glue pot." (40)

The fare increases/service cuts/defiance/direct action option range was discussed at rumbustious meetings of the GLC on 11 and 12 January 1982.

At the first, a meeting of the ruling Labour Group, Councillors were told that they could be surcharged or even banned if they refused to increase fares. Ken Livingstone sought to be conciliatory on the issue:

"The position is that we have a party policy of non-compliance. But we accept that many members of the Labour Group - because of impossible burdens imposed by a surcharge and bankruptcy - are not in a position to join us in a vote of non-compliance." (41)

The group vote was 23 - 22 in favour of defying the Lord's ruling and a refusal to increase fares.

This vote was reversed at a seven-hour Council meeting the following day by 27 votes to 24. Twenty-one Labour members, led by the Deputy Leader of the GLC, Illtyd Harrington, were joined by the three SDP members and three Conservatives in opposing the motion. One of the Labour member was Andrew McIntosh, the author of the Fares Fair Policy, who said:

"We must vote in favour of obeying the law because that is the right thing and the Socialist thing". (42)

Among the 24 resolved on defiance were Ken Livingstone and Dave Wetzel, former bus driver and the GLC Transport Committee Chairman. The Tory Leader, Sir Horace Cutler, had asked Conservative members to abstain rather than assist in getting 'Livingstone's chestnuts out of the fire'. (43)

The end result was agreement on two fares increases, in March (100 per cent) and in June (about 50 per cent) and a motion 'to inform the London Boroughs and the Government that, in the light of the Law Lord's decision, it will be illegal for the council to continue the present concessionary travel scheme for the elderly beyond March 31, 1982.'

TABLE 8 :
PERCENTAGE OF COSTS COVERED BY SUBSIDY

Total Revenue and Capital Grants as a percentage of Total Expenditure			
Overseas		London	
Milan	83	Pre October 1981	29
New York	70		
Brussels	66		
Stockholm			
Copenhagen	53	October 1981	54
Chicago			
Paris	52		
Hamburg	40		
Toronto	36		
Munich	35		
		Post March 1982	27

Source : LTE Annual Report 1981

Notwithstanding Ken Livingstone's 'oil on troubled waters' stance within the GLC meetings, in the February issue of the left-wing *London Labour Briefing* he (and his council colleague, Valerie Wise) wrote, adamantly supporting overt defiance, that:

> "There must now be a massive campaign to ensure that fares do not go up. The GLC must campaign alongside the London Labour Party and the Transport Unions and all other sections of the Labour movement. There must be full support for the Labour Group for any industrial action taken by LT workers to ensure that the Lords' decision cannot be implemented." (44)

The Governmental View

The Governmental reaction to the GLC's position was given by David Howell in a letter sent to Ken Livingstone and in exchanges in the Commons on 18 January. In his letter he stated:

> "There is no question of London's old people losing their travel concessions . . . .(45). It is ridiculous to indulge in wild talk of dismantling public transport. What we have said is that resources for transport

like those for anything else, are not infinite. Nor can ratepayers continue to be treated as they were in recent months. Resources must be used to keep the essential services going and cater for real needs and not be dissipated in indiscriminate low fares subsidies adopted for political reasons." (46)

In addition he offered:

- Legislation to enable the GLC to continue providing concessionary travel for Senior Citizens and the disabled

- A loan of £125 millions, repayable over five years to enable London Transport to avoid a second large fare increase.

In exchanges with Albert Booth and William Pitt (Liberal MP for N.W. Croydon), David Howell maintained his stance. Whilst the Government were quite willing to legislate to give the GLC the same powers as other local authorities for the operation of a concessionary fare scheme, it was a question of the level of support given:

> "The Government has long accepted the case for a degree of revenue support for public transport. The problem with the GLC is they didn't know when to stop. I reiterate it remains the clear view of the Government not to propose legislation to allow the GLC to go on crushing the ratepayer.
> He (William Pitt) is quite unjustified and unwise to speak about chaos
> . . . . I can only assume that he would like to see low fares, low rates and low taxes as well. But there happens to be a matter of deciding who pays and who pays when a major bungle has been made by the GLC." (47)

He followed his comments by announcing that, since the GLC had decided to reduce the level of subsidy to former levels, the block grant payable to London Boroughs in 1981-82 would be increased by £60 millions.

Confusion Worse Confounded

> "We very much regret these cuts which will mean more traffic on the roads. We are not happy about the proposals which are the result of being forced to act in a business, rather than a social way." (48)

Thus a spokesman for the LTE on the changes, announced on 22 January, which were said to underlie the LTE's budget for 1982. They consisted of:

- The closure of seven Tube Stations

- The consideration of the closure of three more branch lines, involving a threat to sixteen other Stations

- Later starting (6.00 rather than 5.30 a.m.) and earlier finishing (12.00 rather than 00.30 a.m.) of bus and tube services

- Cuts in services of 10 per cent in buses and 5 per cent in the underground.

The effect of these service cuts, for which, said Sir Peter Masefield

"We have no appetite, especially as current low fares have increased our business" (49)

was estimated to be a saving of £22 millions on running costs in a full year and a capital investment saving of £32 millions over four years.

A GLC meeting - described as 'incoherent and chaotic' - on 26 January threw out this proposal of cuts - and also voted against increasing fares. Sir Peter Masefield declared disconsolately:

"If we don't put the fares up on the 21 March, which is the earliest practicable date required by the Law Lords' decision, we shall be acting unlawfully. And if we do put them up without the GLC's authorisation, we may be acting unlawfully. We can't be in the position of breaking the law if we put the fares up and breaking the law if we don't. What I'm trying to do is to play this absolutely non-politically" (50)

This result was once again overturned on 16 February, when the GLC approved its budget for 1982-83, involving expenditure of £1,077 millions, of which the GLC contribution to LTE for 1982 was to be £240 millions. A fares increase was to take effect from 21 March and there were to be some service cuts but no closures of stations. The advice from the Attorney-General, Sir Michael Havers, to the Government indicated that this level of subsidy did not breach the GLC's fiduciary duty.

TABLE 9 :
RESULTS OF LOCAL AUTHORITY ELECTIONS (MAY 1982)

a) London Boroughs

Party Gaining Seats	Party Losing Seats			Total
	Con	Lab	Liberal and SDP	
Conservatives	-	45	12	57
Labour	16	-	57	73
Liberal and SDP	28	33	-	61
Total	44	78	69	191

b) Outside London

Party	Seats Gained	Seats Lost	Net Results Seats changed
Conservative	227	202	25
Labour	183	232	(49)
Liberal and SDP	230	141	89
Independents	8	56	(48)
Others	-	17	(17)

This very substantial increase in the rate burden in the London Boroughs drew the comment from Dr Tony Hart (Chairman of the GLC Finance Committee) that:

> "Much of the increase is the price we are forced to pay as a result of the House of Lords' decision to outlaw our cheap fares policy . . . . The decision today puts London Transport and the council in a position to carry on in 1982. It leaves London Transport on the same slippery slope towards being the worst big city transport service in the world that it was when we came in last May." (51)

On Campaign

The agreement of the GLC budget and the final LTE budget in mid February did not bring any relaxation in the campaign that had been waged by the opponents of the Law Lords' ruling. Rather the reverse.

On 25 February, Sir James Swaffield (Director General of the GLC

TABLE 10 :   **BUDGET COMPARISONS**

Element	1981-82 Budget	1982-83 Budget
Administration Setting	Conservative	Labour
Average London ratepayer pays GLC as part of his rate bill (£/week)	.99	1.89
= p/£	18.2	34.8
Average ratepayers' payment from rate bill for public transport (£/year)	7.20	27.04

Source: James O'Driscoll (*Daily Telegraph*, 29 October 1981) and David Walker (*The Times*, 17 February 1982).

and Clerk to the Council) and Sir Peter Masefield took the unusual step of holding a press conference at County Hall in ostensible support of the 'Keep Fares Fair' campaign that had been launched on 30 January by Dave Wetzel. Sir James was accompanied at the conference by his senior staff:

- Maurice Stonefrost (Comptroller of Finance)
- Miss Audrey Lees (Controller of Transportation)
- John Fitzpatrick (Director of Administration and Solicitor to the Council).

Sir Peter Masefield gave the results of the Fares Fair policy:

- A 7 per cent increase in Tube passengers
- A 12 per cent increase in Bus passengers
- The restoration of fares to the 1969 level
- A loss of £65 millions in the six months to 31 March 1982.

Backing up Sir Peter, Dave Wetzel said:

"We want to alleviate the effects of the Lords' ruling and we want the Press to hear the facts from the horse's mouth.' (52)

Another Press Conference was held on 27 February at London's Dominion Theatre. Called 'the London Assembly' it was attended by 1,500 delegates from trade unions, pensioners groups, the unemployed women's organisations, ethnic minorities and the homeless. Bitter condemnation of the ending of the Fares Fair policy was expressed by many speakers. David Moore from the Methodist Mission in Tower Hamlets contrasted the access to transport facilities of inhabitants of Bromley and Tower Hamlets:

Percentage of Households

	Owning No Cars	Owning 1 Or More Cars
Bromley	31	69
Tower Hamlets	71	29

Another - Vincent Burke of the Society of West End Theatres - said that the entertainment industry in Central London was organising its own campaign in support of cheap fares. This would include a benefit performance of the Italian farce *Can't Pay, Won't Pay*.

And then there was the London Transport strike held on 10 March. Of the plan to call this the first total shutdown of public transport in London since the General Strike in 1926, David Howell said:

"I do not think the balance of consideration we need (to pilot the Travel Concessions (London) Bill through Parliament) is helped at all by conducting a senseless publicity campaign at the ratepayers' expense (£200,000) and encouraging absolutely pointless action by the staff which can only make matters worse. Campaigns and slogans are no substitute for getting down to the job of dealing with the real problems of public transport in London.' (53)

The campaign and the strike plan raised the tempo in the Commons during the second reading of the Bill to give the GLC the same powers as other authorities to make travel concessions to the elderly and disabled not awarded by the 1969 Act. There was uproar from the Labour benches when John Hunt called Ken Livingstone 'A Marxist madhatter' (54) and from the Conservatives when Robert Hughes (a Labour spokesman on Transport) said:

"The Government is not entitled to hide behind the skirts of the Law Lords and impose its policy as a by-product of a decision by unelected judges." (55)

Your correspondent William Otley (February 25) asks for an explanation as to how a 25 per cent decrease for six months leaps to 100 per cent fares increase on March 21 with drastic cuts in services.

Indeed he asks someone to own up. I am disappointed that Lord Denning and the five "Vandal in Ermine" did not respond.

The result of the House of Lords ruling is that London Transport now has to be financed by the GLC on the basis that everything practicable is done to break even. This naturally includes steep fare increases and cuts in expenditure.

Ratepayers will have to meet the extra bills as fewer people travel on London Transport services. There will be an extra 180,000 car and motorbike journeys into London every day. This will create more road congestion, more accidents, more pollution (noise and fumes), more parking problems and will result in additional expenditure on fuel, traffic management, hospitals, police time, new roads, insurance, road repairs, car parks and the extra cost of longer journey times for lorries, buses and cars. - Dave Wetzel, Transport Chairman, Greater London Council, County Hall, SE1.

This tempo was kept up when the House of Commons came to the Third Reading of the Bill on 1 March. Kenneth Clarke (Parliamentary Under Secretary for Transport) said:

> "I fear that the people who have come to power at County Hall are better at campaigning than they are at administration . . . . The streets of London are full of empty buses between the peak hours and services are being provided which pay no regard to the level of demand . .
> . . . At the moment there is too much campaigning, political rhetoric, people putting up stickers, presenting petitions." (56)

The response from the Labour front-bench was a stated intent to legislate to make a cheap fares policy legal when Labour returned to power.

> "I believe", said Roger Stott, "we ought to rise to the challenge and attempt to draft legislation which is at least Denning-proof. It is the House of Commons that makes the law and not the judges." (57)

Where to get off

The 'Keep Fares Fair' campaign with its 'Can't Pay, Won't Pay' slogan was by now well under way with over 100,000 signatures. Run by Valerie Wise, it was aimed at the approximately 75 per cent of users of

TABLE 11 :   **EFFECTS OF FARE CHANGES**

Date	Fares	Passengers	Revenue	Ratepayers' Contribution in a full year	Total Grants as Total Revenue
4 Oct. 1981	Down by by 32%	Up by 10% from 5½ to 6m a day	Down by 25%	Up by £125m	Up from 29% to 54%
21 Mar 1982	Up by 96%	Down by 18% from 6 to 5m a day	Up by 65%	Down by £206m	Down from 54% to 27%
Total Effects	Up by 33%	Down by 6½% from 5½ to 5m a day	Up by 23%	Down by £81m	Down from 29% to 27%

Source: LTE *Annual Report* for 1981

London Transport who came from the GLC area. Dave Wetzel kept stoking the fuel with comments such as:

> "It's a bad law that stops us having cheap fares, and bad laws are there for the breaking." (58)

In a speech to students at the North East London Polytechnic at Barking, he said:

> "I am a supporter of the "Can't Pay, Won't Pay" campaign. It's illegal. You can be fined or even sent to prison, but I urge people to get involved in the campaign. I am inviting you to break the law." (59)

To 300 campaign supporters outside County Hall, Wetzel claimed:

> "Government Ministers are sitting on their hands with gleeful smiles on their faces. We have got to take the grin off their faces." (60)

The date for the raising of LT fares duly arrived, with Dave Wetzel publicly pledged to ride on a bus from Portland Place to Oxford Circus, tendering the old fare. When the conductor told him at Trafalgar Square to pay up or get off, he asked his fellow passengers whether or not he should leave the bus.

> "I voted that I should stay but the majority were against me. I accept a democratic decision, so I got off the bus." (61)

APPENDIX A

Salient Features of the Transport (London) Act 1969

Section 1

The GLC is under a duty 'to develop policies and to encourage, organise and, where appropriate, carry out measures which will promote the provision of integrated, efficient and economic transport facilities and services for Greater London'.

Section 3

The GLC has power to make grants to the London Transport Executive 'for any purpose.'

Section 4

The London Transport Executive is set up 'for the purpose of implementing the policies which it is the duty of the Council under section 1 to develop.'

Section 5

'Subject always to the requirements of section 7(3) of this Act, it shall be the general duty of the Executive to exercise and perform their functions, in accordance with principles from time to time laid down or approved by the Council, in such a manner as, in conjunction with the Railways Board and the Bus Company, and with due regard to efficiency, economy and safety of operation, to provide or secure the provision of such public passenger transport services as best meet the needs for the time being of Greater London.'

Section 7

'(3) The Executive shall so perform their functions as to ensure so far as practicable -

(a)   that, at the end of each such period as may from time to time be agreed for the purpose of this paragraph between the Executive and the Council, the aggregate of the net balance of the consolidated revenue account of the Executive and any subsidiary of theirs and the net balance of the general reserve of the Executive is such (not being a deficit) as may be approved by the Council with respect to that period and

(b)   that, if at the end of any accounting period of the Executive the said aggregate shows a deficit, the amount properly available to meet charges to revenue account of the Executive and their subsidiaries in the next following accounting period of the Executive exceeds those charges by at least the deficit.

'(6) The Council, in exercising or performing their functions under this Act, shall have regard -

(a) to the duty imposed on the Executive by subsection (3) of this section . . . .
and where the requirements of paragraph (b) of the said subsection (3) fail
to be complied with by the Executive, the Council shall take such action in
the performance of their functions under this Act as appears to be necessary
and appropriate in order to enable the Executive to comply with those
requirements.'

Section 11

(2) The LTE is required to submit to the GLC and obtain their approval of 'the
general level and structure of the fares to be charged for the time being for the
carriage of passengers by the Executive or any subsidiary of theirs on railway services or London bus services.'

APPENDIX B

Financial Data on LTE's Operations

1. LTE Revenue Accounts for 1980 and 1981
(To year ending 31 December)

Element	1980 (£000s)	1981 (£000s)
Income	466,308	468,057
Expenditure	551,799	621,057
Depreciation & Renewal Charge	70,124	80,200
Deficit on Traffic Operations	(155,615)	(233,968)
Net Revenue from ancillary businesses	6,571	7,089
Deficit for year before grants	(149,044)	(226,879)
Grants from GLC		
- Revenue Support	80,000	82,000
- Depreciation & Renewal	70,124	80,200
Deficit/Surplus	1,080	(64,679)
Balance brought forward from previous year	(3,676)	1,080
Transfer from General Reserve	3,676	24
Deficit/Surplus carried forward	1,080	(63,575)

2. LTE Balance Sheets for 1980 and 1981
(As at 31 December)

Assets	1980 (£000s)	1981 (£000s)
Current		
Cash & Bank Balances	8,303	6,746
Debtors (Central Government, GLC, Other)	47,515	42,937
Stores	40,792	39,837
Other Short-term deposits & interest in subsidiary company	2,506	756
Term deposits	9,140	7,980
Fixed Assets (Net)	1,163,167	1,326,635
Total	1,271,428	1,424,891
Liabilities	£000	£000
Current Creditors	96,542	130,208
GLC Loan		22,500
Bank Overdraft	4,130	7,364
Term Loans	10,254	9,023
Equity Corporate Capital	1,150,495	1,311,350
Provision for renewal of non-depreciated Assets	8,898	8,021
General Reserve	24	
Deficit/Surplus Carried Forward	1,080	(63,575)
Total	1,271,423	1,424,891

Source : LTE *Annual Report*, 1981

3. LTE Statement of Source and Application of Funds

Sources	1980 (£000s)	1981 (£000s)
Operations Total Income	472,879	475,146
Other Sources Sale of Assets	5,048	8,286
Central Government Direct Grants	11,049	10,405
GLC Grants	207,323	228,813
Total	696,299	722,650
Applications		
Operations Staff Costs, materials & services	551,459	621,542
Additional Fixed Assets, renewal expenditure, loan repayments	123,875	148,008
Increase (Decrease) in Working Capital	20,965	(46,900)
Total	696,299	722,650

APPENDIX C

The Objectives of the Main Board of London Transport as Foundations for the 1981 Budget

1. To meet, so far as possible, the needs of London for a satisfactory level of public passenger transport service at acceptable fares.
2. To operate those services as efficiently and as economically as possible, consistent with a high standard of safety and performance.
3. To manage London Transport's affairs so as to achieve, financially, a break-even position, taking into account the combined income from commercial revenue and from the grants of the GLC . . . . £160 millions in all.
4. To provide, within these resources, a satisfactory combination of bus and underground services, looking not only to 1981 but also beyond.

Note: The 1981 Budget was approved by the GLC in December 1980.

Source: LTE *Annual Report*, 1981.

References:

1. *The Times*, 3 March 1981.

2. as 1.

3. Craig Seton and Christopher Warman, *The Times*, 9 May 1981.

4. *The Times*, 4 March 1981.

5. 'GLC cheap fares policy challenged in the High Court', *The Times*, 29 October 1981.

6. 'Ratepayers used as milch cows for cheap GLC fares', James O'Driscoll, *Daily Telegraph*, 29 October 1981.

7. as 5.

8. Law Report, *The Times*, 4 November 1981.

9. 'Judges warn GLC over fare cuts out of rates', David Walker, *The Times*, 4 November 1981.

10. 'GLC Chiefs accused of acting like eccentric 1920's Socialists', David Walker, *The Times*, 6 November 1981

11. 'GLC Fare Cuts were "a considered decision". *Daily Telegraph*, 7 November 1981.

12. as 11.

13. 'Dennings Law', *Economist*, 14 November 1981.

14. Law Report, *The Times*, 11 November 1981.

15. 'GLC Fares Chaos as Denning rules rate levey is illegal', *The Times*, 11 November 1981.

16. Parliament, *The Times*, 11 November 1981.

17. as 15. .

18. 'Livingstone says LT facing break-up if rates appeal is lost', Sarah Segrue, *The Times*, 12 November 1981.

19. as 18.

20. 'Drastic rise in Fares if GLC loses, Lords told', John Grigsby, *Daily Telegraph*, 23 November 1981.

21. as 20.

22. 'Fares decision not hasty, says QC', Frances Gibb, *The Times*, 26 November 1981.

23. G.L.C Case is sign of rates revolt, QC says', Frances Gibb, *The Times*, 1 December 1981.

24. Law Report, *The Times*, 18 December 1981.

25. as 24.

26. 'Fares will jump, GLC warns', Frances Gibb and David Walker, *The Times*, 18 December 1981.

27. 'GLC asks for help over its fares muddle', Richard Holliday, *Daily Mail*, 18 December 1981.

28. as 27.

29. 'MPs demand fares debate', *The Times*, 18 December 1981.

30. as 29.

31. as 29.

32. 'Labour plans to "price motorists off the road" ', John Petty, 28 November 1981.

33. 'Thatcher welcomes fares judgement', *Guardian*, 18 December 1981.

34. as 29.

35. as 27.

36. as 32.

37. 'Howell blames fares rise on GLC's cavalier attitude', Peter Pryke, *Daily Telegraph*, 23 December 1981.

38. as 37.

39. ' "Double London Fares in March" GLC officials advise', John Carvel, *Guardian*, 5 January 1982.

40. 'LT strike is threatened in Fares Fair battle', David Felton, *The Times*, 24 December 1981.

41. 'Labour Defiance on Fares', John Grigsby, *Daily Telegraph*, 12 January 1982.

42. 'GLC votes for 150% fares rise', John Grigsby, *Daily Telegraph*, 13 January 1982.

43. 'Labour splits as GLC votes to double London's fares', *Daily Express*, 13 January 1982.

44. 'More on London fares for elderly', *Financial Times*, 15 January 1982.

45. as 44.

46. '£125m loan offer to stop London's second fares rise', John Grigsby, *Daily Telegraph*, 15 January 1982.

47. Parliament, *The Times*, 19 January 1982.

48. 'London Transport to close Tube Stations and cut buses', Michael Bailey, *The Times*, 23 January 1982.

49. as 48.

50. 'L.T. threatens GLC over fares', *Observer*, 31 January 1982.

51. 'GLC rate almost doubles', David Walker, *The Times*, 17 February 1982.

52. 'GLC Chiefs Defend Cheap Fares', Michael Bailey, *The Times*, 26 February 1982.

53. 'Strike planned over fares ruling is condemned', William Weeks, *Daily Telegraph*, 25 February 1982.

54. as 53.

55. as 53.

56. 'GLC advised to stop "daft" fares campaign', Peter Pryke, *Daily Telegraph*, 2 March 1982.

57. as 56.

58. 'London soars to top of fares league as subsidy row grows', *Sunday Times*, 14 March 1982.

59. ' "Risk Jail" call in LT fares protest', Robert Bedlow, *Daily Telegraph*, 19 March 1982.

60. 'Travellers risk fares protest chaos today', James Allen and John Grigsby, *Daily Telegraph*, 22 March 1982.

61. 'Bus folk tell Dave where to get off', David Hewson, *The Times*, 23 March 1982.

CASE NO. 6
FLEXIBLE ROSTERING

'Rail Policy'

The publication of *Rail Policy* - a statement by the British Railways Board of its policies and potential for the 1980s - was a bold step. It was also, in the Board's view, a necessary and overdue step. It spelled out that:

> 'A crucial decision has to be taken soon about the future of British Rail. BR must prepare to take either the path of progress by re-equipment and modernisation, or that of decline through a gradual but deliberate run-down of the system. We cannot continue as we have done in the past. We are reaching the dividing of the ways.' (1)

Whilst the Board recognised the need to make better use of existing resources, it diagnosed that the heart of the problem was the need for 'a new financial regime'. (2) Under the prevailing system it had been impossible, stated the document, to undertake the long-term investment programme which the railways required. Financial ceilings, shortage of cash, the need to direct 'investment' money to meet shortfalls on current account had all militated against such a course. Of these constraints the principal issue threatening the very role of the railways was seen as the Government's cash limits policy.

> 'In our Corporate Plan 1981 - 85 recently published we asked what needed to be done if, in those years, we had to live within the External Financial Limits current in 1980. On the assumptions then made in relation to the railways we could have survived, though only by stern measures towards our customers and our employees. The prospect was not attractive. Now, with the recession deeper than expected and no likelihood of significant growth in the economy until 1982, we can no longer regard even that limit as either attractive or realistic.' (3)

The need for more funding was urgent.

> 'The watershed year is 1983. If major expenditure or replacement is not started by then, the inevitable consequence will be a rapid run-down of the whole railway system. We could postpone until that date, continuing with some replacement and with much "make do and

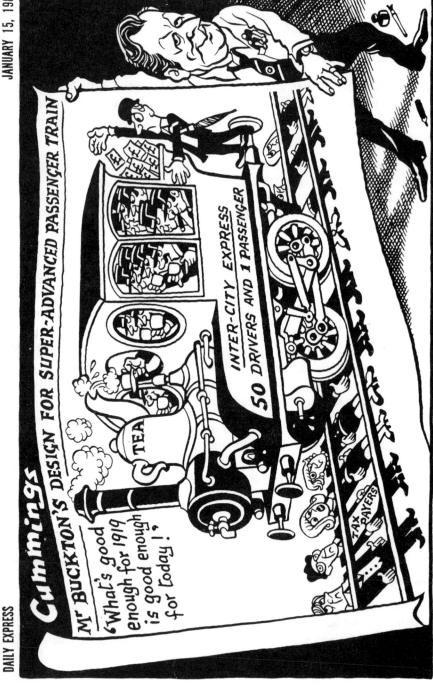

Daily Express, 15 January 1982 (reproduced by permission)

mend" at present investment levels, but not beyond. In 1981 we must have started the design and planning work and have placed orders for materials if major re-equipment is to commence in 1983 - so the year for decisions is 1981 . . . . and the single most significant decision is Electrification'. (4)

The capital cost of this programme (which takes into consideration a net reduction in railway personnel of 38,300, calculated on then current conditions of service) was given in *Rail Policy* as £287 millions in 1981, rising to £461 millions in 1987 (all figures at 1980 prices).

This 'expanding investment programme . . . . would substantially exceed our current investment ceiling and in present circumstances our External Financing Limits'. (5)

What are External Financing Limits?

Each year the Government stipulates the amount of funds each nationalised industry will be permitted to borrow to make up any difference which exists between what the industry invests and the finance it can generate internally and through Governmental grants. These stipulations on borrowings - called External Financing Limits - are a mechanism of primary importance in the Government's control of public expenditure.

Given the sources of British Rail income, shown in Table 1, it will be noted that British Rail's investment capacity is highly susceptible to changes in the level of Government grant (in 1979 - 24.7 per cent) and the amount the Government allows it to borrow, especially as:

- A substantial portion of BR's investment in 1979 was subject to a Government-imposed ceiling
- A Government cash limit was placed on the PSO (Public Service Obligation)
- An EFL was placed on borrowing.

So, any state corporation which cannot raise sufficient funds internally through the sale of their product/service at profitable prices must inevitably rely on grants and borrowings to make up the deficit. If these two latter are too strictly controlled, then policy changes on operations and/or investment will naturally have to take place.

TABLE 1 :   **MAIN SOURCES OF RAILWAY INCOME**

Income Source	£m
(a) from customers	799.7
freight	432.1
parcels	130.8
other	38.0
(b) from Central Government Public Service Obligation [1]	419.0
Special Replacement Allowance	56.9
(c) from Local Government [2]	46.6

Source : *Rail Policy*, 1981.

NOTES

(1) The Public Service Obligation (PSO) is the form of compensation by the Government towards the net cost of providing a public railway service which does not pay for itself through fares and of which one part - the 'Social Railway' as opposed to 'Inter-City' - is 'very unprofitable'.

(2) The cost to the GLC and the Passenger Transport Executives outside London of buying railway services on a contractual basis on behalf of local communities.

Crying Wolf?

Was the gloomy note sounded in *Rail Policy* warranted? Read what Jack Simpson (Executive Director of British Rail Catering) said of the demise of restaurant car facilities on the Hastings, Ramsgate, Margate, and Clacton to London services:

"These units have all but expired. They need extensive refurbishment and that means a considerable sum of money. On the SE lines we are talking about it would cost £1.2m just to do a cosmetic facelift putting new interiors up to modern hygenic standards into old shells with no hope of a return on the money and still ending up with an old vehicle . . . . Do not think we like withdrawing services. Do not think it makes us happy. None of our services pay their way, except one or two isolated exceptions . . . . Morale is low. But a principal factor is the constant battery of complaint and criticism that we get from the public. Isn't it time that the public started to try to help us rather than trying to destroy us? The days when catering people were paid peanuts for all sorts of hours no longer apply. Industry gets people to work unsocial hours by paying them considerable sums in their pay packets. The public walks into a shop and pays £400 for a TV set, but no one questions whether that set is worth the money. Yet they question if a boiled egg is worth 35p because they think they know what is involved." (6)

Whilst this particular cri-de-coeur is unmatched in *Rail Policy*, the view presented in it is uncompromisingly harsh. The system is ageing:

- The average age of the diesel locomotive fleet mainly used for freight services is 17 years; that of the DMU (Diesel Multiple Unit) fleet employed on local passenger services is 22; that of the EMU (Electrical Multiple Unit) fleet, used in the London, Glasgow, Manchester, Liverpool and Birmingham area, is 20.

- The current rate of renewal of signalling falls £30m per annum short of that assessed as necessary to eliminate semaphore signalling from the system by the year 2000 and to renew earlier electrical and electro-mechanical systems.

If investment is not carried out, says BR, there are three inevitable inter-connected consequences:

(1) *Service standards would fall.* 'It would be possible to amend published timetables for progressive deterioration in the track and its effect on train speed. But the effects on reliability would not stop there; . . . . breakdowns and failures would increase. Rail travel will become less reliable, less saleable'.

(2) *A reduction in the scale of the railway business:* 'to bring it within the capacity of available assets at acceptable standards of service'. This is not current BR policy, however.

(3) *The closure of lines on a significant scale.* This was stated to be an option not open to BR at that time.

Sir Peter Parker, Chairman of the British Rail Board, did not, even in the face of such predictions, lack confidence.

"I personally have never been more confident of a rail future since I came to this job. In an energy-conscious world, railways must prove the winning way to go . . . .Electrification is the one thing we need to weld together all our opportunities, the glittering prize paramount." (7)

TABLE 2 : EFFECTS OF LACK OF HEAVY REPAIR OR LIFE–EXTENSION INVESTMENT PROGRAMME

Service Element	1981	1991
Track mileage withdrawn from traffic	-	3,000 rising rapidly
Mileage carrying temporary speed restrictions	180	800
Annual failure rate of mechanical signalling systems (per cent)	4	10 rising
Resultant annual duration of train delays (hours)	5,000	8,500 rising
Availability of locomotives (per cent)	75	50

Source : *Rail Policy*, 1981

Sir Peter came to British Rail in 1979 after a highly successful career with Philips Electrical, Booker McConnell, Associated British Maltsters and the Rockware Group. On his arrival, he found that:

"This great industry was being shamed. The chaps were not buttoning up their uniforms. Deficit financing is demoralising. It makes a proud outfit look crummy . . . . Mind-boggling overcentralisation in the taking and clearing of decisions, terrific slowness and loss of time . . . . A stewpot of industrial relations." (8)

Sir Peter Parker's plans for dealing with the situation of decay and decline did not only focus on the need for more funding to support strategic change. He made considerable organisational change; sought the Government's permission to raise money on the open market to fund major projects; put much muscle behind the final stages of the Advanced Passenger Train's development and plans for the Channel Tunnel. And he began the fight for productivity on BR.

"It doesn't grow on Trees"

Productivity was, in the Government's view, not only the salient issue for British Rail but also one of the key factors in the management of the entire economy. Norman Tebbitt, referred to by his political opponents as 'a political skin-head' (9) on his appointment as Employment Secretary in place of James Prior on 15 September 1981, declared:

> "All the talk about less hours and more money is moonshine. The only way to bring unemployment down is to counteract foreign competition with more productivity, better quality and lower prices".
> (10)

Nor can Sir Peter Parker have had any doubts about the implications of this thinking for his own organisation, given the responses of David Howell, Transport Secretary, to questions about the financial situation at BR in the Commons on 20 October 1981:

> "I am aware", he said, "of the Board's desire to maintain high investment levels. The investment ceiling still stands at £325m as set by the last Government. But investment must be influenced by business performance and the Government is keen that the Board should achieve economies so far as possible from operating costs and not from cutting into investment. Under present pressures nothing can be protected . . . . The reality is that investment funds do not grow on trees."
> (11)

And, if this message were not enough, there was the 28 October Commons debate on the Labour motion that:

> 'This House has no confidence in the economic policies of the Government which have pushed the registered total of unemployed people to shameful levels, have dealt a series of damaging blows to British industry and offer no hope of recovery.' (12)

During this debate, Michael Foot, Leader of the Opposition, argued:

> "The UK economy has been subjected to an unprecedented fiscal, monetary and foreign exchange squeeze and all this must be directly laid at the door of Government. It was all done, we have been told, in order to deal with inflation . . . . The medium-term financial strategy - that wondrous phenomenon - was supposed to decelerate the growth in the money supply and be the key method by which the country should proceed. By now, under the strategy announced and laid down, the Prime Minister had planned to print £7,000 millions of money - yes she prints money sometimes when she wishes to - but she has printed something like £17,000 millions. That is the extent to

which the money supply has grown in the last 18 months. In her own tests, it does not look like very good house-keeping . . . . The economy has reached such a stage of crisis that conventional reflation will hardly scratch the surface. It would hardly do more than relieve the increasing scale of unemployment. To have any hope of recovering anything like full employment, rapid economic growth must be created . . . . We must look, for example, at our nationalised industries and other public authorities, some of which are being throttled by the Government's policies . . . . The nationalised industries chairmen should be brought together here and now to discuss their role in recovering and how they could get people more jobs . . . . The short-term strategy for starting on the road to full employment must be the conventional Keynesian reflation and an ambitious one. Of course, this would suck in imports and measures would have to be taken to deal with this. There would be problems with inflation which would have to be contended with. Above all, we shall strive to secure, and will secure, a new understanding with the trade unions . . . . 'Diseases desperate grown by desperate remedies are relieved' or not at all. This Government has proved that it has not the competence, the will, the imagination or the humanity to deal with these problems. We, therefore, invite this House and the country to throw them out." (*Labour cheers*) (13)

To this eloquent onslaught, Mrs Thatcher, Prime Minister, replied:

"Unemployment is a scourge, a social evil and soul-destroying for the young, who are bound to feel that they have been trained for a world which does not know how to use their talents. It is a sentence often passed on those who have done nothing to deserve it sometimes by those whose industrial behaviour damages the whole economy and destroys other peoples' jobs.
At the depths of every recession, Britain has been more stricken with the curse of increased unemployment than the majority of our international competitors. The steadily growing weakness has suffered further because of three years of excessive pay increases culminating in the 1979/80 round in which earnings rose by more than 20 per cent in a year.
To a large extent this reckless jump in wages - at a time when output did not grow over the period - represented the cashing of post-dated cheques which Mr Callaghan scattered around him in his attempt to escape from the winter of discontent. Mr Foot's recipe is to spend more, borrow more, tax less and turn a blind eye to the consequences. Higher and higher budget deficits are no solution to the problem of

unemployment. Savers at home and abroad cannot be force-fed with unlimited government debt . . . . This Government has redeemed a great part of the overdraft left behind by Labour. It has reduced the official overseas debts from £22 billions when it took office to about £14 billions now, the lowest figure in real terms since the war. The route of Whitehall-led inflation is denied to us as a remedy for the dole queue not out of dogma, not out of pre-occupation with monetary aggregates but because it wouldn't work.

There are three aspects to the Government's financial strategy -

(1) To maintain the financial discipline necessary to reduce inflation

(2) To restrain the level of public borrowing

(3) To control public spending.

The nationalised industries, protected from the disciplines of the market place, can impose their costs on consumers of their products or on the taxpayer. That is why the Government places such emphasis on measures to introduce into the public sector the same commercial disciplines which the market enforces in the private sector." (14)

A False Dawn

BR negotiators' high hopes of successful progress on the productivity front when they reached 'understandings' with the three rail unions — the NUR (National Union of Railwaymen), ASLEF (The Associated Society of Locomotive Engineers and Firemen) and TSSA (Transport Salaried Staff Association) — on 20 August 1981, were dashed by ASLEF's subsequent flat rejection of the major productivity element — Flexible Rostering — and the start of a campaign of national strikes on 12 January 1982. Certainly, the 'understandings' (given in Appendix A) had been a welcome relief to the pain caused to BR by the 1981 pay dispute. This had involved the unions' refusal to accept BR's offer of seven per cent and a later recommended award by the Railway Staffs National Tribunal of 11 per cent (eight per cent payable from 20 April 1981 and a further three per cent from 1 August 1981). BR had agreed to this proposal on the proviso that the three per cent would be conditional on productivity agreement and had been very optimistic that all three unions would accept the principle of negotiating on productivity.

This optimism had been fulfilled at first. The key issues were:

(1) The open station concept;
(2) The manning of passenger trains;
(3) Variable rostering hours;
(4) Single manning on traction units;
(5) The manning of freight trains;
(6) The trainman concept.

Talks on those problems had started on 3 September, with progress monitored by ACAS, and continued, in the case of NUR and TSSA, until successful completion on 22 December. Not without hiccoughs, however. The NUR General Secretary, Sid Weighell, had threatened withdrawal from the productivity talks on 6 November on the grounds that the pledge of additional support for the railways made by David Howell's predecessor, Gerald Fowler, had not been met.

> "How far can the Government expect the rail unions to cooperate with British Rail management in productivity proposals while Ministers fail to honour their obligations to the industry and renege on ministerial promises made?" (15)

This complaint was backed up with a further protest on 10 December:

> "Unless we get paid for the productivity changes being made, we will pull out of the talks. If the Board is so starved of resources that it cannot pay for changes it is not going to get them. We are not giving something for nothing . . . . Increased productivity depends on improved investment." (16)

His union had disassociated itself, on the other hand, from the unofficial action taken (and official strike action planned for 21 October but avoided at the last minute) by ASLEF, in reply to service cutbacks introduced by British Rail. Their financial state by November was extremely parlous — 'because of the serious effect of the exceptional deterioration in rail passenger revenues for 1981', as David Howell said when making a further £110.4 millions in the Public Service Obligation grant available.

Not so, ASLEF. Their publicly expressed attitude was that the three per cent extra pay was *not* conditional on a productivity agreement and that BR was breaking its 'agreement' by insisting that it was. Ray Buckton, ASLEF's General Secretary, made his case in an open letter to *The Times* addressed 'Dear Commuter'', which said:

'Prolonged discussion in mid-August between all the parties concerned resulted in two separate agreements, on pay and on productivity. The agreement on pay was in line with the award of the industrial tribunal. It was specific and unconditional . . . . The understanding on productivity provided for discussions to be resumed within the railway negotiation machinery . . . . ASLEF have attempted to use this procedure to discuss the issue. The BR Board has consistently refused and instead it has unscrupulously tried to bind the two separate issues together despite the ACAS agreement.

On 23 December the Board told the union that because it considered that there had not been sufficient progress on certain productivity matters, it would not pay footplate staff the agreed three per cent increase. The BR Board has unilaterally reneged on an agreement, using as a pretence for its action ASLEF's alleged refusal to make progress on productivity, particularly on the issue of Flexible Rostering, which would bring about the elimination of the eight hour day, a principle enjoyed by most British workers." (17)

The productivity talks between ASLEF and BR were, in fact, grinding to a halt at the start of December and it was early recognised that an ASLEF strike on the issue was probable. By the end of December, Ray Buckton was stating:

"There is a serious danger of industrial action. I have never known BR renege on an agreement like this before. They are inviting trouble."
(18)

By 11 January, when the strike was 'on', the ASLEF President - Derek Fullock - was stating categorically the other facet of ASLEF policy:

"There is no intention whatsoever of compromising on the eight hour day."

The BR Board's pleasure at their success with NUR and TSSA was matched by their bitterness over the way ASLEF had acted. BR's Industrial Relations chief, Clifford Rose, grew more and more exasperated the nearer loomed the ASLEF action:

■ 'ASLEF has displayed a continued negative attitude to changes in working practices. The action which ASLEF proposes will bring even more uncertainty to our passengers and cause serious damage to our business prospects. It is important to understand that ASLEF has shown absolutely no willingness to accept any variation to the eight hour day.' (19)

- 'There was a commitment in August from ASLEF to accept Flexible Rostering otherwise we would not have signed the pay deal. The Board is standing firm because we are convinced we must deliver improved productivity. There will be no concessions and we are not moving until we are satisfied that ASLEF will agree to Flexible Rostering.' (20)

- 'We are determined to deliver these improvements in productivity and prove to the Government and the public that we can run a viable service. ASLEF is failing to come to terms with what is required to run a modern railway system in the 20th century. If the union decides to shut down the railway network, that would be tragic but we are not prepared to throw money away in return for nothing.'

Obstacle Races

Whilst BR was stalwartly fighting the productivity battle, it was beset by three other, well-publicised problems, all of which had serious financial ramifications.

The first was the particular difficulty of keeping open highly unprofitable lines for which there was a moral or other non-financial case. An example of this is the Cambrian Coast line, the only link between the main line railway system at Shrewsbury and some of Wales' finest coastal and mountain scenery, itself served by three narrow gauge railways: the Talyllyn, the Festiniog and the Vale of Rheidol. Not only did the line lose £1.25 millions a year, but the cost of keeping it open in future included £1.5 millions to be spent soon on repairing the Barmouth viaduct - built in 1867, rebuilt in 1903 and found in 1980 to have been severely attached by the Teredo Norvegica (a marine boring worm previously responsible for extensive damage to old wooden sailing ships). Commented Geoffrey Myers (BR Board Member for Marketing) :

> "The simple truth of the matter is that the financial input does not now meet the physical output. There is no money for the Barmouth viaduct without work being cancelled on some other routes." (22)

The second problem was that of British Rail's Advanced Passenger

Train, the very symbol of railway modernisation. Its launch, on 7 December, came over two months after the inauguration of France's Train de Grande Vitesse, linking Paris and Lyon on a brand-new track (costing £850 millions) in 2 hours 40 minutes and reaching a top speed of 162 mph. In his speech at the TGV-launching ceremony, President Mitterand - himself the son of a station-master at Angouleme - stressed:

- The pursuit of the modernisation policy.
- The leading role of the railways in French transport policy.
- The comfort and reliability of the TGV.

He concluded by saying:

"I hope that preliminary studies for a high speed link with Northern France and Belgium, and later on - and it is no dream on our part - with Britain, will prove successful". (23)

TABLE 3 :   ASLEF'S ASSETS

Asset	£
Cash	184,923
Owed by other unions	160,842
Stocks & Shares (as at 31.12.81) of which Treasury Stock £462,570. Associated Dairies £14,286. Beecham £30,976. Arthur Bell & Sons £23,285. Boots £22,261. Bowater £6,849. BP £25,198. Broken Hill Pty £14,908. GEC £49,620. Hall, Mathew & Co., £47,586. Land Securities £31,722. Marks & Spencer £23,436. Shell Transport £22,200. Total	1, 190,872
Union Headquarters	1,250,000
Total Funds	2,786,637

Admittedly, BR's APT - conceived over 17 years ago at Derby - was still classified as 'experimental' but its first experiences in service were highly problematic in comparison with those of its French rival. For instance:

(1) Because of the enormous power needs of the power car, it wasn't safe for some passengers to walk through it on their way to the restaurant car. This was especially true for passengers with electric pacemakers for heart conditions. Hence the decision was taken that no passengers would travel in the front two cars (before the power car and the restaurant) and only the cars behind would be used, giving a capacity of 258 seats as opposed to 450 on current Inter-city Trains. (24)

(2) On the first day return trip from Glasgow to London, the famous tilting mechanism failed three times, spilling drinks and jamming electronically-controlled doors. As the £37 million train got into its majestic stride at 137 mph, passengers felt the full exhilaration One passenger remarked, "We must get used to having our breakfast seeing the ground out of one window and the sky out of the other." Asked how she coped with the tilting mechanism, a 'drinks stewardess' said, "I just stand with my legs open". (25)

(3) Power failures and icing compounded the initial problems. (One year's trouble-free service was required before the APT - or a modified version - could be released into full service).

The third issue - and the most significant from BR's viewpoint - was the steps being taken by the Government on electrification, or rather the lack of them. In June 1981, opening the only electrification scheme to come into operation in that year, a £1.1 million project linking Stockport and Hazel Grove, Sir Peter Parker had remarked on 'how pathetically under-electrified we are' and the facts that:

- The only electrification work under way at the time was the line from Bedford to St. Pancras (popularly known as the 'Bedpan Line'), which was scheduled for single-manning operation to start in Spring 1982.

- The only future electrification plan of substance was for that linking Luton and Bedford.

It was a major shock to BR, therefore, to learn on 20 November that the Government had apparently ruled out, for the near future, a £13 million BR proposal for the electrification of a 27 mile main-line stretch from Hitchin to Huntingdon.

In fact in June 1981, Norman Fowler had invited BR to submit a 10 year programme of schemes on:

> "Only those potentially profitable main-line routes where it is clear that the benefits could justify the investment in question and on the achievement of necessary improvements in productivity." (26)

As BR could not show that the main-line business would become profitable by 1985 - the apparent target date - it had not placed before the Department of Transport its full scale ten year programme, and had put forward its Huntingdon Scheme as a stop gap. The rejection was a major blow. Indeed, a BR spokesman said, as the Board's meeting on 4 December, that there would be discussion of a 'massive attack' on the Government for 'its entirely negative response' (27) to BR's claims for £5.67 billion investment funds over the next decade. What was perhaps worse was that BR were obliged to inform Balfour Beatty - the electrification contractors working on the Bedford - St. Pancras scheme - that, as from Spring 1982, there would be no more work for the 80 highly-skilled workers and they would be laid off. (28) Apparently, only on the East Coast Line from Kings Cross to Newcastle was it at all possible to meet the Government's insistence on a prospective seven per cent real rate of return. (29) The result was, according to one senior BR executive, "a Berlin Wall" between BR and the Department. (30)

ASLEF Strikes

On 12 January, a beleaguered Sir Peter Parker said that the BR Board was considering the suspension of striking ASLEF drivers, a move which ultimately would have meant closure of the 11,000 mile network. Suspension would, however, have been an act of suspect legality in view of the public obligation to provide train services under the Act of Nationalisation. Also, it would have caused difficulties in respect of the other rail unions, since BR did not have a 'lay-off' agreement with them which allowed it to send home workers indirectly affected by industrial disputes. In fact the 'guaranteed week' arrangement ensured that all who were not directly involved in the dispute could continue to report for duty and receive their pay for a basic 39-hour week.

Sir Peter was adamant about the correctness of the BR Board stance over the productivity deal made in 1982:

- ■ "We mixed sweat in the summer and no-one is going to take the country down the path of saying these agreements were separate." (31)

- ■ "The dispute is one of principle and good faith. We cannot fall at the first hurdle. This is the Grand National of change and this really is the first fence. There is no going back on that." (32)

Ray Buckton was equally adamant about the need for BR to pay the disputed three per cent without reference to productivity commitments:

> "If they pay ASLEF the same money on the same basis as they have said they will pay the NUR, the strike will not be on." (33)

Buckton was emphatic in placing the blame for BR's threat at the door of the Government. The suspension threat, he said, was 'obviously political' and the British Rail Board was 'being pushed by the Government' (34). His union would regard suspensions as 'a direct attack on the whole trade union movement' (35). This view was shared by other members of the ASLEF executive, notably Bill Ronskley, who commented:

> "I think myself it is now quite clear that this is not just a question of productivity but of Parker and the Board going out to destroy ASLEF. There is a feeling that Parker is acting on Government orders." (36)

Both Sir Peter Parker and Ray Buckton were hard at work justifying their stances to the public. On 13 January, the former was on the BBC *Nationwide* programme stating that the strikes were 'totally unnecessary and totally unexpected in view of the understanding we had in August,' (37) and that BR could not afford to pay the disputed three per cent to ASLEF drivers 'unless we spun some more money out of our own guts'. Meanwhile, Ray Buckton appealed to BR:

> "Why make the situation worse? I say to Sir Peter and his colleagues, let us get ourselves together and pull ourselves out of a conflict which the Railways Board has deliberately created." (38)

He also apologised to rail travellers:

"On behalf of all Society members, I would like to apologise to members of the public for the inconvenience they are suffering as a result of the dispute.

I want them to be very clear about its causes. They are suffering because the BRB has torn up the agreement with the Society on pay.

It has refused to carry the subject of a completely separate agreement - the issue of productivity - to higher stages of the machinery of negotiation and has deliberately provoked our action by rejecting all attempts to get discussions going again. All Sir Peter has to do is keep his side of the bargain and pay the three per cent increase and ASLEF members will be back at work tomorrow." (39)

Such differences in viewpoints were made more pointed by BR's offer of the three per cent extra to the NUR - on the basis of progress made in bargaining on the introduction of Flexible Rostering - and the NUR's attitude that the three per cent was advanced with no productivity preconditions attached. As Russell Tuck, the NUR Assistant General Secretary, pointed out:

"The fact that the offer has been made does not imply acceptance . . .
We did not discuss the dirty word of productivity at all. They said they were prepared to offer us the money with no strings attached."
(40)

The NUR, in fact, had apparently insisted that the increase be offered to its members but had decided not to accept it whilst the ASLEF dispute was in progress. Certainly, whilst the NUR had made abundant progress with BR on the Flexible Rostering issue, ASLEF had still not changed its position - despite protracted discussions and the 31 October deadline for them - by December 1981.

Each side also had its allies to publicise its case. In a speech in Edinburgh on 15 January, Sir Geoffrey Howe, the Chancellor of the Exchequer, stated:

"It must be right for the BR Board to take the stand they have and for us to give them our full backing. The Government has all along been ready to play a full part in helping modernisation on the railways provided it goes hand in hand with productivity . . . . There is much to be done - not by Government but by management and unions - to impose efficiency and give better value for money to the taxpayer and the customer in great public corporations if future large-scale investment is to be provided." (41)

TABLE 4 : AGE OF THE TRAIN DRIVER

Age Band	Number of Drivers within Age Band
50 - 54	4,500
55 - 59	5,500
60 +	1,500

Source : 'BR on the track of the Trainman' by David Felton
The Times, 16 August 1982

Supporting the ASLEF case, Len Murray, General Secretary of the TUC, by contrast, argued that:

"The Railways Board is at fault both by failing to pay the balance of the pay award and by failing to use the established machinery to find acceptable methods of inproving productivity." (42)

But Murray also proposed a 'peace' formula based on:

- BR's payment of the disputed three per cent; and
- A recommencement of the BR-ASLEF negotiations on Flexible Rostering.

This, at a time of growing tension and initiative, particularly in view of the warning by the BR Board - losing £6 millions for every ASLEF strike day - that NUR members would not be allowed to work on Sundays from 24 January onwards, was widely welcomed. (Sunday working was outside the guaranteed working week and was paid for at overtime rates). Talks at the Arbitration and Conciliation Service were scheduled to start at 10 a.m. on 19 January.

Stop-Go Talks

The ACAS talks did indeed commence on 19 January but collapsed the next day. They restarted on 22 January and broke up again almost immediately. A further attempt on 26 January was unsuccessful in getting ASLEF to participate in a proposed arbitration attempt by a Committee of Inquiry, comprising the members of the Railway Staff

National Tribunal (RSNT) which, in 1981, had recommended the original 11 per cent pay deal. Of ASLEF's unwillingness to accept Len Murray's suggestion of an independent ACAS Inquiry or one carried out by the RSNT, Ray Buckton said:

> "It's not a matter of being afraid to go to the Tribunal. We could agree now. But what's the good of an agreement? It would not be implemented because the men wouldn't work iι." (43)

Not only was ASLEF intransigent on this score, but, on 20 January, it reportedly only took 20 minutes of the Executive's time to decide to continue with the 'alternate day' strike action. Commented Ray Buckton:

> "We are not going to give way on the fact that the Board has broken an agreement. The money should be paid. We cannot give way to the form of blackmail that to get the money we have to accept the disappearance of the eight hour day." (44)

The BRB's exasperation at ASLEF's position was voiced by Sir Peter Parker:

> "The ASLEF position is now clear. They will accept an umpire's decision as long as he rules in their favour . . . . Why, when it comes to accepting a binding commitment, does ASLEF melt away like snow?" (45)

This was more than matched by the views of the NUR's Sid Weighell, who declaimed:

> "If his (Ray Buckton's) case is as good as he says it is, how the hell can he lose? (46) I am fed up to the back teeth with the dispute. I have been in on all the discussions. We made two agreements under the chairmanship of ACAS and signed them simultaneously. They are separate, I accept, but the point is, you cannot pick and choose about agreements which you have signed." (47)

It was, however, unfortunate for Sid Weighell that not all his members shared his view on the acceptability of the Flexible Rostering principle. They showed their disapproval by taking unofficial strike action on 20 January (Kings Cross guards), 26 January (London - Kent guards) and 29 January (NUR guards at Shoeburyness, Slade Green and Plumstead).

Meanwhile, the political furore in Parliament continued unabated, with:

- The Speaker's rejecting for the third time in a fortnight a demand from Leslie Huckfield (ASLEF-sponsored Labour MP for Nuneaton) for an Emergency Debate.

- Sir Geoffrey Howe's supporting the BR stance with the comment that 'Given the blatant disregard of ASLEF to realise there must be a link between pay and productivity, it must be right for the Board to make a stand'. (48)

- The National Executive Committee of the Labour Party's blaming BR for 'failing to honour its signed agreement which is specific and unconditional'. (49)

- Criticism by William Rodgers (former Labour Transport Secretary and now a leading SDP member) of ASLEF's 'Bloody minded' and 'suicidal' attitude. 'The great majority of railwaymen', he said. 'are fed up with the strike and know where their own interests lie. They will be the victim if ASLEF pulls down the house around them'. (50) To which Ray Buckton responded, 'If Mr Rodgers has expressed these comments, I'm even more confident our case is right.' (51)

Such contention was, however, overshadowed in the public debate - as indeed was the BR Board offer made, on 23 January, that the three per cent would be paid to ASLEF members if they accepted binding arbitration on the dispute - by the reaction of ASLEF members at King's Cross and St. Pancras to an article which appeared in the *Sun* on 22 January in which allegations were made about some drivers 'drinking, fiddling (rosters) and cheating' at work.

A potential substantiation of some such allegations was given in a *Guardian* article on 26 January entitled 'Frauds netted BR employee £2,851', in which Mr Stephen Parrish, solicitor for Robin Dandy (a BR timekeeper accused of fraud and corruption, tried and found guilty at Portsmouth Crown Court), stated:

> "Dandy believed that making claims for unworked overtime was a tradition on the railways and he fell in with it. Sometimes workers would not turn up for scheduled overtime and Dandy would enter his

name in their place. It was regarded as timekeepers' perks. It was a widespread practice in the industry." (52)

The allegations contained in the *Sun*, made by two railmen - Max Wallace and Geoff Leighton - provoked a furious reaction and the 'blacking' of the News International (Rupert Murdoch) papers - the Sun itself, *The Times*, *The Sunday Times* and the *News of the World*. Criticism of the action was immediately voiced by Arthur Brittenden (Director of Corporate Relations, News International) who said:

"We deeply regret this form of censorship. We are extremely sorry that they are taking this sort of action but we are totally satisfied with the accuracy of the story." (53)

Mrs Thatcher used a sharper tone:

"No-one in this country, whether member of the union or not, must be allowed to jeopardise the freedom of the press. All industrial action loses jobs. It does not create them." (54)

Not until 27 January, the day after BR suspended all non-essential Sunday working, was the 'blacking' limited and only after:

- A High Court action by News International, resulting in an agreement by two ASLEF officials, Dennis Cadywould and Steven Forey, to read out this statement to their assembled members:
  "In accordance with the undertaking given in court before Mr Justice Glidewell, I am bound to make the following request. I request all employees here to ignore any resolution, instruction, direction, advice or request already issued to black the *Sunday Times*, *Sun*, *Times* or *News of the World*."
  The request was not complied with although it represented a considerable shift in Steven Forey's pre-court view that:
  "The men are incensed by this legal action. They see it and the *Sun* article as an attempt to divert us from the main issue, which is that we want our three per cent and we will not accept Flexible Rostering. This struggle goes on . . . . we still want an apology and we want a full page retraction." (55)

- A 300-7 vote by King's Cross train crews to resume handling, after the *Sun* and *The Times* had printed the railmen's side of the story.

The Judgement of Solomon

Despite immense pressure to do so, ASLEF refused to attend or even give evidence to the ACAS-inspired Inquiry which commenced (after being postponed repeatedly from 3 February onwards) on 9 February and ended two days later. In addition to objecting in principle, it also denounced the Inquiry's terms of reference, which were:

'To consider the terms of the 1981 pay and productivity understandings ratified by agreements by the Railway Staffs National Council, and taking into account the agreement to introduce a 39 hour week, to make recommendations to resolve the differences over the payment of the further three per cent pay increase to footplate grades and over clause (c) of the productivity understanding on Flexible Rostering and related matters.'

When a formula was found which was acceptable to ASLEF, it was rejected by the other three parties to the Inquiry - BR, NUR and TSSA. Indeed by 4 February, Ray Buckton was telling the Inquiry's Chairman, Lord McCarthy, that ASLEF would attend only if the BRB agreed to pay the three per cent beforehand.

It was clearly a chaotic situation for the Committee, whose other two members were George Doughty (former General Secretary of the Technical, Administrative and Supervisory Section of the AUEW) and Ted Choppen (former Managing Director of Esso), to resolve. It was not made any easier by BR's strike-breaking attempt to run a London-Aylesbury service on 3 and 4 February, an attempt described by Ray Buckton as 'another example of BR's inept publicity stunts backfiring on them' (56). Nor was the situation helped by ASLEF's uncompromising attitude, as exemplified by Ray Buckton's statement that:

"The strike will carry on until the BR Board say they are wrong, because they are wrong. I've never been so sure of anything in my life. Our supporters realise this is an attack on the Trade Union movement and that, if the management gets away with it here, look out the next trade union that comes along. We are much stronger now than we were when we had far more members, if power is judged by the ability to stop the railways. This union is not involved in any battle for survival. As long as trains are driven in Britain, there will always be ASLEF." (57)

The position of the BR Board was presented by Clifford Rose:

> "There is no chance at all of our giving in. BR is determined to move
> this forward positively." (58)

Conversely, one aspect of the situation had been simplified, as BR's
message to passengers made clear:

> "We are running a railway today because we believe that a railway
> which operates on four days out of seven is more help to you than a
> railway that doesn't run at all. Some of you may agree with the call
> that we should suspend ASLEF drivers and, in effect, shut down the
> railway until the issue is resolved. But there is no evidence that a shut-
> down would magically solve everything and bring the drivers back to
> work. Indeed it could even have the opposite effect." (59)

The message of the Government was also clear. Robin Cook (Edinburgh Central, Labour) had put the following question:

> "Any investment in modernisation will have to come out of the
> External Financial Limits, which he (David Howell) has increased by
> substantially less than the rate of inflation anticipated by the Tories.
> The increase in that limit for next year will be wiped out by the
> borrowings over recent weeks.
> As it is the Government which encouraged BR to go ahead with that
> borrowing, will he at least make sure that it is not penalised by an un-
> realistic level of external financial limit for next year which will mean
> there is no modernisation, no investment and little maintenance?"(60)

David Howell replied:

> "The limit for next year has been maintained in real terms. The need
> is for all concerned, including those in other railway unions to urge
> ASLEF to end their totally destructive strike and recognise, along
> with other unions, that increased pay and productivity and investment
> go hand in hand. That is where the future of the railways lies. That
> was the way we were going before this wretched strike." (61)

What was far from clear, however, was the attitude that the Inquiry
would take in respect of BR's position. In his final submission to the
Inquiry, Clifford Rose, in fact, conceded that the pay understanding :

> 'Was not conditional in the narrow sense of productivity being
> achieved, although it did include a very important clause referring to

the continuance of negotiations . . . . We are having to face the issue of survival in the railways in the form that we know them. We have no chance of surviving if we do not face squarely the issue of self-generated productivity and co-operation in minimising costs." (62)

Sir Peter Parker was also anxious. In a statement on 12 February, he said:

"I do not want to be told to pay the three per cent for nothing. It is absolutely vital that we are not told to pay the three per cent and go into more talks and more talks and more talks. We are anxious to hear what the three per cent is for. It is quite specifically, in our minds, for the productivity commitment that ASLEF made and the other unions have lived up to." (63)

His fear was not unfounded. The RSNT Inquiry Report, published on 16 February, found that:

- There was nothing in the two agreements which made the payment of the three per cent conditional on BR's view of the extent of progress in the productivity discussion. 'In effect,' stated the Report, 'the Board was not provided with a veto which they alone need interpret.'

- Although the agreements were related, 'nothing has been placed before us to suggest that the Society has formally has formally reneged on the understandings reached with the assistance of ACAS'.

The Inquiry recommended, on the basis of these findings, that:

(1) BR should pay the disputed three per cent.

(2) ASLEF should call off its strike action.

(3) There should be a tight timetable for negotiations over productivity and, if no agreement was reached by 19 March, at National Council, there should be an arbitration hearing at the RSNT before Lord McCarthy.

Reactions

The BR Board was suspicious of the Inquiry's view that their proposals offered 'the best prospects of tracing a way out of the present differences between the parties in dispute. Sir Peter Parker said:

"We do not want the same problems in six months time. We want the commitment before we pay the three per cent . . . . ASLEF are not getting anything for nothing." (64)

A statement issued subsequently by the Board showed a slightly different tone:

'The settlement of the dispute represents a major move from the position on November 30 when negotiations on productivity came to a halt after ASLEF said it was not prepared to alter the present eight-hour agreement in any way. The position now is that after six weeks of damaging strikes and a committee of Inquiry which ASLEF refused to attend, the blockage in negotiations has been removed. The Board's firm stand has won back the commitment to productivity which was the crux of the recommendations of the Committee of Inquiry.' (65)

Ray Buckton rounded on the BR Board:

"We are back to square one. While saying they are accepting the recommendations, in reality they are not. They have got to come clean. They have got to accept or reject the findings. They can't have it both ways. They are still insisting on the very thing that caused the dispute in the first place.' (66)
"We want to know whether the three per cent is to be implemented. Once this is done we will call off our industrial action . . . . But you just cannot trust them . . . . So far as our position on the eight hour day is concerned, it is very very clear and we have not changed.' (67
"It is not just a victory for ASLEF. It is a victory for common sense and for the whole trade union movement of this country." (68)

The NUR's initial reaction, as expressed by Sid Weighell, was a plaudit for the Inquiry team. He said:

"I think Lord McCarthy has done an excellent job. He has done precisely what an arbitrator should do - condemned both sides and come up with a solution." (69)

By the end of February, however, Sid Weighell's feelings were less positive. He then described the BR-ASLEF conflict as 'an unnecessary and crazily expensive confrontation. We have all lost. For anyone to regard the outcome as some kind of victory takes some believing. It would be like cheering your own execution." (70)

David Owen,, the Parliamentary leader of the SDP, spoke for many bewildered train travellers when he stated in a speech at Northampton on 17 February:

> "Fudge and mudge . . . . Agreements are solemnly made in the full knowledge that the parties have different interpretations. It is a form of national Micawberism. One just hopes something will turn up." (71)

For Cyril Bleasdale, newly-appointed as BR's Inter-City Director, such pessimism was misplaced. With BR's agreement to pay the three per cent (backdated to 3 August 1981) and the ASLEF action called off, he declared:

> "Our aim is to win back customers . . . . We shall be embarking on a major exercise with staff to give a better service. We have discovered that rail travel is more relaxing than we thought. Once we have continuity of peace on the horizon, we shall go headlong into a Marketing attack." (72)

'Have a Good Trip!'

In mid-March 1982, all parties were giving evidence to the (by now) familiar members of the RSNT - Lord McCarthy, George Doughty and Ted Choppen - whose task was to give a non-binding recommendation as to whether ASLEF should accept BR's Flexible Rostering proposals. For the first time in the dispute, ASLEF's detailed position was being put forward in a 126-page submission by Ray Buckton:

> "Members of ASLEF will not be bludgeoned into acceptance of arrangements which will reduce their standard of living further, impinge on the little social and domestic life they already have and could well put their own and passengers' safety at risk.
> During the course of the recent rail dispute, it was stated on a number of occasions by no less a personage than the Chairman of the BR Board that my Society was clinging to outmoded agreements (the 1919 Agreement on the eight hour day) and hanging on to the last vestiges of the steam age . . . . I repeat, elimination of the eight-hour guaranteed day arrangement has little to do with the more efficient use of manpower. Its abolition would be principally a device to reduce the pay of footplate staff and the Chairman's rhetoric is a mask to cover the Board's true interest.
> If the Railways Board is able to produce convincing arguments that a

reduction in wages brings efficiency and does not merely reduce operating costs then I would be happy to examine its proposals in a different light (73) . . . . That one in ten footplate staff is unfit for normal duties suggests that the peculiar combination of stressful and irregular work is even more damaging than the research, which has so far been done, would indicate . . . .

In your findings you should categorically state that the present rostering agreements for this group of grades (train drivers) must continue as they are now. If you should award otherwise, it is not me or my Executive Committee you will have to convince that the Board's arguments are valid but the 24,000 or more footplate staff on BR who make up the membership of the Society." (74)

The BR Board, by contrast, considered its proposed scheme of 7-9 hour shifts over and eight week cycle (involving 312 hours per cycle and a potential 7½ per cent average increase in working time) as perfectly feasible, a point with which the TSSA and NUR spokesmen agreed. Stressing the fact of the other two rail unions' agreement to Flexible Rostering, Clifford Rose — whose speeches in evidence were interrupted by jeers, catcalls and abuse from spectators — declared:

"Much of the footplate staff opposition to variable day rosters has been based on a combination of misinformation, rumour and unquestioning adherence to the policies promulgated by the ASLEF headquarters and officials. You will not be surprised when I say that this Board regards the outcome of this Tribunal hearing as critical to the whole future of the industry, indeed to the very survival of the railway system as we know it in this country." (75)

Adjourned after 2 days of taking evidence, the Tribunal restarted its work on 29 March, only to confess that it found itself in a quandary on its recommendations. This it hoped to resolve by undertaking a trip around the country (against the advice of the BR Board) to hear the drivers' own views at depots in York, Glasgow and Bristol. Meanwhile:

- The *Daily Mail* published on 27 March details of what it claimed to be a top-secret BR document listing 34 lines (more than 13 per cent of BR's current 21,811 mile network) which were under closure threat.

- David Howell announced on 31 March that Mr. P. J. Butler (Senior Partner in accountants Peat, Marwick, Mitchell)

BR off the rails

The following letter was published in *The Observer* on 7 March 1982:

With reference to your editorial (21 February) 'No Permanent Way for BR', I wish to point out that as well as registering a famous victory in trade union history, more important was the fact that the Society completely vindicated its stance, despite all and sundries attempts to either prejudge or influence the dispute's essential outcome.

Thankfully, the Society's position throughout the dispute remained firm with the insistence that the BRB had to firstly pay the 3 per cent pay settlement awarded last August by the industry's independent tribunal (RSNT) and secondly negotiate other matters relating to productivity through the railways industry's own machinery of negotiation. Factors which, even without ASLEF's attendance at the ACAS Commission of Enquiry, Lord McCarthy and his team of arbitrators recognised and agreed were violations by British Rail of both RSNT and later the ACAS Understandings signed in August 1981.

All of this makes one reflect on why commuters were subjected to the misery and inconvenience of the previous six weeks. Perhaps the view given by some members of the Board which described the ASLEF Executive as acting like Kamikaze Pilots would be more appropriately used on themselves as their reference to this group seems to indicate that they know more about certain aspects of the Wartime Japanese Air Force, than they do about the British Railways Industry.

Contrary to what some may have people believe, the ASLEF Executive Committee are not Luddites refusing to accept change. We accept that with new technology will come new methods of work. To justify this, take a look at our record on negotiations over the years. Our aim all along has not been to retain a 1919 agreement, it's been a refusal to accept a return to pre-1919 conditions. Honesty, loyalty and common sense demand that we guard the conditions of employment of the workers we represent.

Lew Adams, ASLEF, Executive Committee Member.

would be joining the team headed by Sir David Serpell, which was set up in December 1981 with the remit of investigating railway finances. James Butler would act as a consultant to the team alongside Alfred Goldstein - a senior consultant with R. Travers Morgan & Partners. The Report was published on 20 January 1983 and considered the scope for action between running a 'commercial railway' and continuing to run a 'social' one.

- On the same day, the Government announced an effective cut in its subsidy to BR for the coming year. It was to be £804 millions, an increase of £50 millions on the previous year, but representing in fact a cut of £15 millions after inflation had been allowed for. David Howell also pointed out that any over-run of the 1981-82 cash limit would be deducted from that for 1982-83. BR had asked for £885 millions. Whilst the BR Board described the figure as 'tough but manageable', (76) Ray Buckton said 'With a stroke of a pen the Government have now effectively destroyed the future of the railway industry. By cutting cash aid they are forcing up fares and driving away business. If they think this will lead to a nil pay-settlement, they are living in dreamland." (77)

■ The BR Board proposed on 22 April the closure of its Engineering workshops at Shildon (Durham) and Horwich (Lancs), and a partial run-down of its workshops at Swindon (Wilts) as part of a plan to cut a further 3,500 - 4,000 jobs. Shildon, lying in a pit closure area, was a village with a population of just over 15,000. The works employed 2,600. Interestingly, it was the village whence, in 1825, George Stephenson's 'Locomotion' set off for its historic journey to Darlington.

Commented Sid Weighell, "The situation is pretty grim. We don't go to the barricades every Monday morning but there comes a time when you have to say 'enough is enough' . . . . We will call out at least 250,000 in the whole of BR to oppose any threat to the jobs and livelihood of members (as at Shildon) . . . . If someone does not shift, there is bound to be a conflict. If nothing is done, then there will be nothing left." (78)

■ BR published its Annual Report for the year ending 31 December 1981 at the end of April.

Decision No. 77

The RSNT published its long-awaited 72-page report entitled *Decision No. 77* on 7 May.

'It has not been possible to arrive at simple and easily stated conclusions . . . . There must be willingness to consider new avenues to advance or we cannot hope to arrive at an acceptable settlement . . . . Nothing we have said is intended to justify unilateral action or confrontation.'

TABLE 5 :
PERFORMANCE INDICATORS FOR THE RAILWAYS

	1977	1978	1979	1980	1981	% change 1981 with 1980
Passenger miles per loaded passenger train mile	94	97	102	97	95	- 2.1
Average fare per passenger mile - pence	3.24	3.66	4.00	4.82	5.33	+10.6
Government grant per passenger mile (at 1977 price levels) - pence	1.99	1.78	1.88	1.91	2.30	+20.4
Average wagon load (all traffics including Freightliner and National Carriers) - tonnes	22.99	24.52	25.20	25.83	27.17	+5.2
Freight revenue per wagon (at 1977 price levels) - £	1,890	2,043	2,188	2,099	2,743	+30.7
Net tonne miles per loaded freight train mile	324	331	343	338	358	+5.9
Loaded train miles per train crew member	6,602	6,647	6,536	6,700	6,914	+3.2
Train running and terminal cost per loaded train mile (at 1977 price levels) - £	3.30	3.33	3.43	3.36	3.23	- 3.9
Track maintenance costs per track miles (at 1977 price levels) - £	4,511	4,611	5,173	4,928	4,890	- 0.7
Total administration costs per loaded train mile (at 1977 price levels) - pence	83.0	83.5	87.8	89.9	94.6	+5.2
Passenger miles/net tonne miles per member of staff employed (Rail and Rail workshops) - 000's	140.9	144.7	147.8	142.9	146.2	+2.3
Revenue per £1,000 of paybill costs (Rail and Rail workshops) - £	1,297	1,351	1,305	1,244	1,200	- 3.37

Source: British Railways Board *Annual Report* (1981)

The forecast loss for 1982 was estimated as £165 millions.

From its analysis of the evidence, it understood why ASLEF regarded the 1919 agreement as 'something of a sheet anchor' and just how much 'real and widespread resistance to the Board's proposals for Flexible Rostering' existed on the part of ASLEF members. Nonetheless, it found firmly in favour of the BR Board position.

> 'We realise that, in the case of both the BR and ASLEF, they (the proposals) involve a change of position, plus a readiness to try something new. Unless progress is made on this question, the future outlook for the railway system and railwaymen is bleak and uncompromising. We have made it clear that we believe there is not much time left. The BR Board was justified in believing that if they are to obtain the necessary capital for investment and modernisation which they require from Government, they must be able to demonstrate that they are making progress in implementing the 1981 understanding.'

Ray Buckton lost no time in condemning the findings that the eight-hour day should be abandoned and that Flexible Rostering, coupled with negotiations over safeguards and (as in the case of the NUR and TSSA) bonus, should be introduced. He stated:

> "I have never in my life seen such a jumble of words that mean nothing coming from intelligent people." (79)
> " .... We are not Luddites. We want the railways to work." (80)
> " .... It's an unworkable compromise, which if introduced would quickly bring the railways to a halt." (81)

It was certainly a far cry from his reaction to the last McCarthy finding which had been exuberantly welcomed with the words:

> "I'm laughing. It's total victory. This completely vindicates almost word for word, what we have been saying over this issue. Right is right." (82)

By 12 May, the ASLEF executive had backed their General Secretary's view that the recommendations were 'totally unacceptable'. Indeed, at an ASLEF delegate conference, called to discuss the situation on 18 May, the union President, Derek Fullick, threw down the gauntlet in no uncertain terms:

> "If I am confident of anything at this conference, it is that there will be no movement on the rigid eight-hour day . . . . If they (BR Board) want a bloody nose, they are going about it in the right way . . . . BR

should not delude itself because the strength of feeling that exists within our ranks will again be transformed into action should the need arise . . . . Without the Government, the BR Board would not have had the stomach for the fight that took place." (83)

Clifford Rose by contrast, along with the leaders of TSSA and NUR, welcomed the report as giving 'a very clear steer towards Flexible Rostering'. The BR Board's determination to proceed was now reinforced by their refusal to negotiate the 1982 pay deal with the unions until ASLEF had fully accepted Flexible Rostering.

Not without reason did the chairman of the Central Transport Consultative Committee (the public 'watchdog' for the railways) write in his Annual Report for 1981, which was released on 19 May:

'The railway is suffering from the Dwindles.'

Of Pelion and Ossa

Anger within the NUR over the BR Board's moves on closure threats and pay led to the calling of a special Union Executive meeting on 21 May. According to Sid Weighell, the consequences of these moves were dire. The day before the meeting he was in action at the National Union of Mineworkers' Blackpool conference with a ringing challenge:

"We will be giving notice to the Rail Board that they must come to terms with the Union's policy or face the consequences. Failure to respond in a constructive way within the time limit laid down by the NUR will result in the union using its industrial strength to force an acceptable solution . . . . We will take action in such a way as to create havoc . . . We have come to a stage which we can tolerate no more. I hope we don't have to fire a shot but tomorrow we will be laying down the law about what we are going to do." (84)

And so it was. The meeting decided that unless BR withdrew its closure plans and made a reasonable pay offer, action involving all the NUR's 170,000 members to 'create maximum disruption' would result. The Board responded to this threat by producing statistics to back up their closure rationale:

Scheduled Demand	1980	1986
Number of locomotives in use	3,695	2,798
Number of carriages in use	21,168	15,150
Number of waggons in use	132,000	34,000
Waggons in repair	19,500	8,000

On 28 May, BR offered NUR and TSSA members a five per cent pay rise rigidly conditional on further productivity improvements. Quite apart from the disparity between the 15 per cent claim lodged in February and this offer, it was also stipulated by BR that the increase would be brought in on 6 September (not, as due, 18 April), thus reducing its value over the year from five per cent to 3.08 per cent. It was also made plain, at the RSN Council, that:

- If there were any more strikes which halted a continuous customer service, the offer would be withdrawn.

- The deadline for successful completion of negotiations on the other productivity points was 31 July.

The offer was rejected as 'derisory'. (85)

ASLEF were in a mood to tangle with BR also. A Delegate Conference on 21 May had passed the following motion:

'The Society remains committed to the retention of the eight-hour day and instructs the union Executive Committee to continue its policy that there should be no worsening of staff conditions.'

In the knowledge that the BR Board was seeking to impose its new rosters on ASLEF members, the Executive issued a statement on 3 June that any attempts to act along these lines would be 'in complete abrogation' of the 1956 agreement which set up the industry's negotiating machinery. 'It would call into question the future of industrial relations in the industry . . . . The Board alone will be responsible for the industrial action that the Society might take to support our members' interests.' (86)

The Heat of the Summer

There was a sharp rise in the industrial relations temperature in mid-June. Despite the successful bonus deal negotiated with NUR for Flexible Roster working by its members and BR's postponement of cutbacks in its engineering workshops (announced on 3 June), the NUR issued a threat of a strike call from 28 June. BR responded by:

- Warning its major customers that, unless there were a breakthrough on pay and productivity talks with the unions, there would be a rail shutdown, lasting possibly four weeks.

- Sending a letter from Sir Peter Parker to all employees. This said: "We are in deep trouble. You could say we're broke. This time the threat to jobs could affect you all. Think seriously . . . . If we fight the competition instead of each other, we can still save many of the jobs which are at risk." (87)

- Rejecting a union call to divorce pay from productivity negotiations. Said BR Board member James Urquhart: "We need the rail unions to accept that things have got to be different." (88)

After fruitless day-long talks on this issue with the Board, an exasperated Sid Weighell said:

"From this day on, I'll be preparing my army to fight." (89)

The following day, detailed guidelines on the planned action were sent out to branch officials from union headquarters.;

Guidelines of a somewhat different nature, according to a report in the *Observer* of 20 June, were sent out in a confidential memorandum to the General Managers of BR's five regions on 28 May. The memorandum (composed by two BR directors, Gerry Orbell and Sidney Hoggart), was quoted as saying:

"The Board's position is firm, as you know, in the general context of its policy for change, that there will be no giving up this principle (Flexible Rostering) even at the price of lasting stoppages . . . . On the date of implementation, if (ASLEF) staff refuse to work the rosters, they will be seen by management and they will be given a final opportunity to change their minds. If they still refuse, they will be sent home . . . . We shall persist with this action indefinitely while continuing to bring pressure to bear on the trade unions for the negotiation of a national agreement on FR."

The BR Board's attention was more taken up, nevertheless, with the immediate problems posed by the NUR. Sid Weighell was in a bitter mood. Of BR's claim that investment depended on progress with productivity, he said:

"They have been telling me that story for months. If you deliver on parcels, deliver on marshalling yards, deliver on this . . . . we can get some understanding. We deliver and deliver and deliver and nobody benefits. Up to now they have reneged on every understanding." (90)

To ASLEF, who had said they might join NUR in a strike, Weighell replied:

"I don't need anybody to help me stop the railway. When we stop, everything stops. What I need is help from the broader movement." (91)

Sir Peter Parker also took a hard line. In a letter to the BR workforce headed *You, your family and your job*, he wrote:

'It is now one minute to midnight. Unless common sense from ordinary railwaymen takes over, the railways are now due to start the most disastrous strike in their history. For your sake, for the sake of your family and the future of the railway system, help me to stop this strike before it starts.' (92)

'Nobody regrets this head-on clash with responsible trade union leaders more than I do. But, on this occasion, they are wrong and I am writing to you to urge you to ask your union leadership to think again . . . . Think about it - is it worth the risk? . . . . (93)

'If you decide not to strike, the Board will not accept loss of trade union membership as a cause for dismissal.' (94)

Sid Weighell, similarly, wrote to his members:

"I am confident that members will be loyal to the NUR because if they desert the union, there will be nothing left to defend them . . . . We are going to win. I will use all the resources of this union. This will be a rough, tough battle which I prefer not to be in. It is not of my choosing." (95)

Despite the intervention of ACAS and talks at the Railways Staff National Council, the strike was still on. Sir Peter Parker warned, as the minutes ticked by:

"This could be a very long strike indeed - one month, two months, three months." (96)

TABLE 6 :   NATIONAL BUS RESULTS - 1980 AND 1981

	1980	1981
Operating Profit (£m)	5.8	25.3
Interest Payments (£m)	17.1	9.8
Profit before Tax (£m)	(11.35)	5.45
Turnover (£m)	581.9	618.4

Source: *Financial Times* 17 June 1982.

Note: National Bus controls 35 regional and local coach and bus services.
In 1980 Government's relaxation in coach licensing ushered in a large
expansion in long-distance coach services.

Wars and Rumours of Wars

On 28 June the NUR strike commenced. By the 29th it had ended.
The NUR conference, expected to back the Executive's strike decision
(17 votes to 6), actually overturned this result by 47 votes to 30 and
by passing the resolution that:

> 'This AGM, having regard to all the circumstances and the strength of
> the union's claim, instructs the General Secretary to refer the NUR
> case to the RSNT. We believe the NUR's record in negotiation with
> the BR Board will stand the test of examination by an impartial
> body.'

There had been straws in the wind suggesting opposition to the strike -
from Derby, York, Central Wales, Shrewsbury and Holyhead branches
- but the scale of rejection of the union approach had not been foreseen. Sid Weighell remarked after the vote:

> "It is not a climb down. It is a suspension. It is not a defeat for the
> Executive. The strike could go on again, my members do not run for
> cover. If the RSNT goes against the NUR we will pull the whole lot
> out again." (97)

BR welcomed this somewhat surprising turn of events in a statement
on 29 June, which stated:

'The NUR conference has shown good sense in lifting the strike, but we are still to make progress on the outstanding issue of productivity. Both from ASLEF and NUR there are unfulfilled commitments from last year's settlements. There can be no pay increase until these are delivered and the trade unions have until July 30. In no way can the timetable decision be prolonged. Nor the issues kicked once again into touch. Every day that passes is a day lost. The sooner we clear the productivity commitments, the stronger our case for investment in the industry.' (98)

A football metaphor was also used by the spokesman who announced the unanimous ASLEF Executive decision to call an all-out indefinite strike from midnight within 24 hours of the end to the NUR action on

What British Rail *has* achieved
From Sir PETER PARKER

SIR - Two factors invalidate the picture projected by Mr Graham Paterson in his report about job reduction in nationalised industries (June 28).

The first is that he understates the reduction in railway staff by nearly 50 per cent. Between the end of 1977 and the end of 1981 the reduction in the railway work-force was 11,892 and the latest figures raise that total to 15,500, against the 7,842 quoted.

The second factor is the failure to relate job reductions to levels of output, a crucial factor in any comparison of this sort.

Take British Steel: employment fell by some 42 per cent, over the five-year period, matching a fall in output of some 40 per cent. British Leyland cars' record is one of a fall in output of some 20 per cent, and job reductions of some 40 per cent, but this reflects a substantial programme of investment and modernisation.

Against this, British Rail's record was one of an increase in passenger miles of 5 per cent and a reduction in freight tonne miles of some 13 per cent - in terms of units of output, a reduction of 1 per cent overall. Yet over the same period our workforce fell by more than 6 per cent.

The market for rail has *not* collapsed in the same dramatic way as the markets of the other great industries with which we are so frequently compared. Bearing in mind that we run an integrated network - far different from a series of industrial plants - which in the case of passenger services requires statutory procedures before we can reduce its size, this is a record of no mean achievement.

PETER PARKER
Chairman, British Railways Board,
London, N.W.1.

3 July. Said he:

> "It's not the Cameroons they're playing this time. It's Brazil!" (99)

Sir Peter Parker called the decision 'deplorable' and 'shameful' (100) and wrote immediately to all ASLEF members:

> 'Earlier this week, the good sense of ordinary railway workers pulled us back from the brink of a real disaster. Now your union has put us back there. I need your help to save the railway .... Let me be blunt. The Board is absolutely determined to introduce Flexible Rostering .. .... For the sake of your own future and that of the railway, consider that if this strike goes ahead thousands of jobs will go, perhaps yours .... What we are asking is not unreasonable. And it is vital. Give it a chance. Convince your union leaders to see sense.' (101)

The Board also withdrew its conditional five per cent offer to ASLEF members.

The planned strike was called in response to BR's announcement that, as no progress on negotiating the introduction of Flexible Rostering had been made, the new rosters would be imposed sequentially in depots throughout the country. Ray Buckton blamed the management for it:

> "If this strike takes place it's because there's some bloody-mindedness on the part of the BR Board. They will not lift their unilateral action and so we cannot lift the threat of a strike." (102)

Clearly, trouble was in the offing. Equally clearly the BR Board was not going to compromise. Sir Peter Parker said:

> "The country has every right to be fed up with this nonsense. This issue must be put to bed. We are not going to end up with any fudged situation. This is one fudge too far." (103)

Ray Buckton was also taking a hard line in a letter to ASLEF members:

> "This is not just an ordinary industrial dispute. We're fighting for more than the eight-hour day. We're fighting for the survival of strong trade unions on the railway." (104.

And in a statement on 3 July, Buckton added:

EYE WITNESS:

Tony Donaghy, Guard at St. Pancras, Branch Secretary of St. Pancras NUR and a Communist Party member:

"I liked it immediately. I liked the people and the people in those days were part of the system. You could climb promotional ladders - engine cleaner to fireman, fireman to engine driver, ticket-clerk to station master. Now that kind of family inheritance is non-existant. The system has changed and the railway worker has changed. Most of the management staff are out of universities and management training centres. It's all had an effect on the long standing railway worker - there's a greater tendency to be selfish because we don't belong to the industry in the way we used to. People see it as just another job . . . .'

Source: 'Life on the Bedpan Line', by Ian Jack, *Sunday Times*, 27 June 1982.

> "The whole trade union movement should recognise that the Board has declared war on ASLEF . . . . If the Government believes that is the way to run a nationalised industry. I ask - who is giving the orders?" (105)

He also cast doubt on the validity of the rosters which BR were issuing He wrote:

> 'New rosters posted at some depots may seem harmless. Some of them contain few turns over eight hours or none at all. This is because BR have been careful not to exploit the potential for depot closures, redundancies among drivers and drivers' assistants and the transfer of work from depot to depot. What you are seeing is not Flexible Rostering as the Board wants it, not what we were on strike for 17 days to prevent. It is a fake.' (106)

As can be imagined, there was much party political controversy surrounding ASLEF's and BR's actions. Particularly strong messages came from:

- *The Prime Minister*, in a speech celebrating 'Victory in the Falklands' at Cheltenham, who said, "We are no longer prepared to jeopardise our future just to defend manning practices agreed in 1919 when steam engines plied the tracks of the Grand Central Railway and the motor car had not yet taken over from the horse . . . . Increasingly, this nation

241

TABLE 7 : **RAIL SERVICES - PROFIT AND LOSS**

In the financial year 1980-81 BR's income - including a Government subsidy of £810m - was around £2,900m. After outgoings, the board had a trading loss of £37m. Some 58% of BR's overheads went in staff costs. The table below lists key services and which did or did not make money.

	Income £m.	What it made or lost £m
Passengers:	1,022	+140
(including inter-city	(472)	(+128)
London/South East)	(423)	(+107)
Freight, including parcels and mail	615	- 25
Freightliners (container traffic)	71	+ 0.1
Workshop Sales	25	+0.2
Station catering	48	+1
Train catering	21	- 7
Property	55	+37
Sealink	202	- 4
Hotels	37	- 2
Consultancy services	5	+0.2

Source: *Sunday Times*, 27 June 1982.

won't have it. Our people are now confident enough to face the facts of life. There is a new mood of realism in Britain. That too is part of the Falklands factor. The battle of the South Atlantic was not won by ignoring the danger or denying the risks. It was achieved by men and women who had no illusions about the difficulties, faced them squarely and were determined to overcome. That is increasingly the mood of Britain. And that is why the rail strike won't do." (107)

■ *Peter Shore (Shadow Chancellor)*, addressing the National Union of Mineworkers' Conference, who warned: "Trade unions must always be ready to defend their legitimate interests. Their leaders, like good commanders, must always be ready to fight. But they must first choose the right ground make sure their troops are prepared and trained and soberly appraise the reserves of public goodwill that are available. And they must remember that this Government, which has slaughtered 20,000 firms in the last three years and presided over the loss of two million jobs is not one that has much tenderness for industrial casualties, particularly in the public sector." (108)

■ *George Gardiner (Conservative, Reigate):* "The travelling public's determination not to be beaten by the strike is fuelled not only by a gut rejection of ASLEF's bloody-mindedness . . . . but by an awareness that the time has come to break the backs of those forces that stand in the way of improvements and defend to the bitter end their restrictive practices . . . . If it is a fight to the death, as the ASLEF leader has described it, it would be the death of ASLEF and what a welcome that would be. It epitomizes all that holds back BR and British industry. It is a union which even its own members could do without. Let BR put this union dinosaur out of its misery." (109)

The Ultimate Sanction

With BR trying desperately to run a skeleton service (using NUR and strike-breaking ASLEF drivers) and continuing to post rosters in depots, it was losing £8.5 millions per day by 9 July. It was not prepared to continue in this vein and, on 13 July, announced its decision to sack all ASLEF drivers then on strike. Following intervention by ACAS and the TUC, drivers were to be given up to 20 July to make up their minds on whether to work the new 7 - 9 hour rosters. Then , on 14 July, Sir Peter Parker announced that the entire network would close as from midnight on 20 July, if there were not a substantial return to work. It would be the first entire closure in the history of the state-owned railway. Said Sir Peter:

"The decision is a sad, black day for British Rail but I think an inevitable one. I cannot go on spending public money on an inadequate service." (110)

There was considerable pressure on both sides to arrive at a settlement. Sid Weighell appealed to Ray Buckton to take the issue to the RSNT:

"We are now at the cross-roads. The future of BR will be decided this week . . . . Thousands of jobs and 27,000 track miles will go down the plughole. The train drivers will go down the plughole like everyone else." (111)

David Howell, in a statement to the Commons, referred to Michael Foot as 'the striker's friend', for a speech issued at the Durham Miners Gala which denounced the Government for 'planning to break the spirit of working people in this country . . . . to smash the unions and create a servile workforce." (112)

Howell's statement continued:

> "it is the duty of all those who believe the public should be protected and the railways and all who work in them saved from disaster - to urge the ASLEF executive from their futile course." (113)

Support was shown for the ASLEF position by Len Murray of the TUC and, particularly, by the miners' union President, Arthur Scargill. Labour MPs like Stan Orme, Neil Kinnock and Eric Heffer added their voices. Michael Foot pressed the need for intervention on Mrs Thatcher during Commons exchanges on 15 July:

> "It is an outrage that in such a major national crisis none of her ministers have seen the parties concerned." (*Labour cheers*)

Foot got short shrift:

> "No. I think it is an outrage that Mr Foot will not appeal to the drivers to return to work." (*Conservative cheers*) (114)

After it became clear on 16 July that the BR Board position was unmovable, the entire ASLEF executive was called to meet the TUC's Finance and General Purposes Committee. This meeting led to marathon 'peace' talks on 17 July involving all parties (with TUC and ACAS representation) which led to a settlement. The major provisions of this agreement were:

- An end to the strike.
- Negotiations on the introduction of Flexible Rostering within a strict timetable.
- The calling of special ASLEF delegate conference within 10 days to approve changes in the eight-hour day.

On leaving the talks, Jim Urquhart acknowledged 'the great help we had from the TUC in reaching the peace proposal' (115); Sir Peter Parker said simply:

> "A very good night's work. I'm going off to get breakfast - eggs sunny side up." (116)

Said Ray Buckton, as his Executive ordered drivers back to work from midnight on 18 July:

"We have to face reality. The battle could not be won without the support of the whole trade union movement, which was not forthcoming." (117)

On 30 July, agreement was finally reached at the RSNC on the introduction of Flexible Rostering, clearing the way for the 1982 pay round. These began on 3 August at the RSNT under Lord McCarthy. They promised to be difficult since agreement was needed on all the five remaining productivity points outstanding from the 1982 'understandings'. And, as Sir Peter Parker had pointed out:

"The Kitty is barren." (118)

References:

1. *Rail Policy*, British Rail Board.
2. as 1.
3. as 1.
4. as 1.
5. as 1.
6. 'Why BR's "Meals on Wheels" will vanish', by Franklyn Wood, *Now Magazine*, 18 February 1980.
7. 'The electrifying flair of Sir Peter Parker', by Paul Johnson, *Now Magazine*, 6 March 1981.
8. as 7.
9. 'Better work in Tebbit's recipe', *Daily Telegraph*, 16 September 1981.
10. as 9.
11. Parliamentary Report, *The Times*, 21 October 1981.
12. Parliamentary Report, *The Times*, 29 October 1981.
13. as 12.
14. as 12.
15. 'Curbs on overtime threatened by railwaymen', by Robert Bedlow, *Daily Telegraph*, 7 November 1981.
16. 'BR's cash crisis could lead to a new row with unions', by Robert Bedlow, *Daily Telegraph*, 11 December 1981.
17. 'Dear Commuter: an Open Letter from Ray Buckton', *The Times*, 11 January 1982.
18. 'Guerilla threats to trains', *Sunday Telegraph*, 27 December 1981.
19. 'Go slow and strike by rail drivers', by Robert Bedlow, *Daily Telegraph*, 30 December 1981.
20. 'Train chaos will start on Monday', by Robert Bedlow, *Daily Telegraph*,
21. as 20.
22. 'A three-cornered fight over rail lines' future', by Michael Baily, *Times*, 12 October 1981.

23. 'France-Japan race into the age of the train', by Charles Hargrove and Peter Hazelhurst, *The Times*, 23 September 1981.

24. 'Full tilt for Dec.7 launch', by Nigel Hawken, *Observer*, 15 November 1981.

25. 'BR unveils train with a leaning to high speed', by Michael Smith, *Guardian*, 8 December 1981.

26. 'Rail electrification team to be laid off', by Lynton McLain, *Financial Times*, 21 November 1981.

27. as 26.

28. 'Buses times and fares cut to beat BR', *Daily Telegraph*, 21 November 1981.

29. Editorial in *The Times*, 15 December 1981.

30. 'BR clashes with Howell on electrification rail plan', by Roger Eglin, *The Times*, 22 November 1981.

31. 'BR may suspend striking drivers', by Ian Black, *Guardian*, 13 January, 1982.

32. 'Strikers face suspension', by John Richards, *Daily Telegraph*, 13 January 1982.

33. 'BR offers NUR drivers 3%', by Philip Bassett, *Financial Times*, 15 January 1982.

34. as 33.

35. as 31.

36. 'Hopes of a solution to rail dispute hinge on ACAS', by Christine Tyler, *Financial Times*, 18 January 1982.

37. 'No hint of rail peace as freeze hampers attempts to beat strike', by John Ardill et al, *Guardian*, 14 January, 1982.

38. 'Strike until we win" say drivers', by David Felton, *The Times*, 14 January 1982.

39. 'Rail battle lines are drawn up', by Peter McHugh, *Daily Mail*, 14 January 1982.

40. 'Buckton hits back over NUR offer', *Daily Express*, January 1982.

41. 'Howe backs BR in row with ASLEF' by Nicholas Comfort, *Daily Telegraph*, 16 January 1982.

42. 'Rail "Pay Now" call by Murray', by Robert Bedlow, *Daily Telegraph*, 16 January 1982.

43. 'NUR blames train drivers', *Observer*, 24 January 1982.

44. 'ASLEF's wildcats threaten more chaos', by Robert Bedlow, *Daily Telegraph*, 21 February 1982.

45. as 43.

46. as 43.

47. 'Rail drivers plan more disruptions', *Daily Telegraph*, 25 January 1982.

48. 'BR right to take a stand', *Daily Telegraph*, 29 January 1982.

49. 'Miners back railmen', by Robert Bedlow, *Daily Telegraph*, 28 January 1982.

50 'S. Region Chaos Today?', *Daily Telegraph*, 1 February 1982.

51. as 50.

52. 'Frauds netted BR employee £2,857', *Guardian*, 26 January 1982.

53. 'Rail summit on plan for arbitration', by Robert Bedlow, *Daily Telegraph*, 23 January 1982.

54. 'Railmen lift *Sun* blacking', by Ian Glover, *Daily Telegraph*, 27 January 1982.

55. 'Murdoch papers go by road and air as blacking continues', by John Ardill and Angela Singer, *Guardian*, 26 January 1982.

56. 'BR's hopes of special service dashed', *The Times*, 4 February 1982.

57. 'Spokesman for the age of steam', *Observer*, 7 February 1982.

58. 'Train strikes keeping 25% off work', by David McKie, *Guardian*, 9 February 1982.

59. *Daily Telegraph*, 11 February 1982.

60. Parliamentary report, *The Times*, 11 February 1982.

61. as 60.

62. 'Peace with honour for BR', by Robert Taylor, *Observer*, 14 February 1982.

63. 'Parker firm on pay guarantee', by John Richards, *Daily Telegraph*, 13 February 1982.

64. 'BR back to square one', by Robert Bedlow, *Daily Telegraph*, 17 February 1982.

65. 'Talks on train drivers' rostering to begin on Thursday', by John Richards, *Daily Telegraph*, 22 February 1982.

66. *Daily Mirror*, 17 February 1982.

67. as 64.

68. 'Train drivers reject ACAS peace moves', by John Ardill, *Guardian*, 17 February 1982.

69. as 64.

70. 'Weighell condemns "crazy" stand by train drivers', by Robert Bedlow, *Daily Telegraph*, 1 March 1982.

71. *Daily Telegraph*, 18 February 1982.

72. 'Cheap fare idea for BR campaign to woo travellers', by Michael Bailey, *The Times*, 22 February 1982.

73. ' "ASLEF will not budge", Buckton insists', *The Times*, 16 March 1982.

74. 'Buckton pledges "no surrender on rail rostering" ', by David Felton, *The Times*, 16 March 1982.

75. 'Train drivers consider new rosters unworkable', *Financial Times*, 16 March 1982.

76. 'BR accepts "tough" cost constraints', by Lynton McLain, *Financial Times*, 2 April 1982.

77. 'BR faces £15m aid cuts and inquiry', by Michael Smith, *Guardian*, 1 April 1982.

78. 'Strike threat by NUR in fight to secure jobs', by Robert Bedlow, *Daily Telegraph*, 30 April 1982.

79. 'Luddite denial as rail threat grows', by Robert Taylor, *Observer*, 9 May 1982.

80. 'Buckton damns "unworkable" roster Report', by Robert Bedlow, *Daily Telegraph*, 8 May 1982.

81. 'McCarthy report backs BR on rostering', by David Felton, *The Times*, 8 May 1982.

82. Trevor Kavanagh, *Sun*, 17 February 1982.

83. 'ASLEF chief works up full head of steam', by Robert Bedlow, *Daily Telegraph*, 19 May 1982.

84. 'NUR threatens "havoc" over 5000 lost jobs', by Robert Bedlow, *Daily Telegraph*, 21 May 1982.

85. 'BR offers 5% rise and plans to enforce Flexible Rostering', by Philip Bassett, *Financial Times*, 29 May 1982.

86. 'Rail rostering dispute continues', by David Felton, *The Times*, 4 June 1982.

87. 'Hopes for new rail pay talks', by Graham Patterson, *Daily Telegraph*, 17 June 1982.

88. 'Railway strike nearer after talks deadlock', by Graham Patterson, *Daily Telegraph*, 18 June 1982.

89. as 88.

90. 'NUR pressing ahead for all-out strike', by John Ardill, *Guardian*, 21 June 1982.

91. as 90.

92. 'Parker offers job support to strike breakers', *Guardian*, 24 June 1982.

93. ' "BR ready to abandon closed shop if strike goes ahead" says Sir Peter Parker', by Donald Macintyre, *The Times*, 24 June 1982.

94. as 92.

95. 'National rail strike more likely as NUR refuses compromise', by John Lloyd, *Financial Times*, 26 May 1982.

96. 'Rail strike on as peace talks fail', *Daily Telegraph*, 26 June 1982.

97. 'Revolt in NUR stops strike', *Daily Telegraph*, 29 June 1982.

98. 'ASLEF turns the screw', by John Richards, *Daily Telegraph*, 30 June 1982.

99. 'Now ASLEF calls all-out strike from Sunday', by Paul Routledge and David Felton, *The Times*, 30 June 1982.

100. as 99.

101. 'TUC talks fail to break deadlock over rail strike', by Paul Routledge and David Felton, *The Times*, 1 July 1982.

102. 'Rail strike on as BR reject peace plan', by John Richards, *Daily Telegraph*, 2 July 1982.

103. 'BRB takes tougher position', by Philip Bassett, *Financial Times*, 3 July 1982.

104. as 103.

105. 'BR ready to sack drivers', by Robert Taylor, *Observer,* 4 July 1982.

106. 'ASLEF and BR face long fight', by Robert Bedlow, *Daily Telegraph*, 3 July 1982.

107. 'The Faint Hearts were wrong', by Michael Jones, *Sunday Times*, 4 July 1982.

108. 'Buckton hails drivers' solidarity as BR keeps 1250 trains running', *Guardian*, 6 July 1982.

109. Parliamentary report, *Guardian*, 6 July 1982.

110. ' "Black Day" says Parker', by Robert Bedlow, *Daily Telegraph*, 15 July 1982.

111. 'ASLEF go to peace talks', by Robert Bedlow, *Daily Telegraph*, 14 July 1982.

112 'Foot slams Parker; "I back ASLEF" ', *Sunday Times*, 11 July 1982.

113. as 110.

114. Parliamentary report, *The Times*, 16 July 1982.

115. 'BR peace offer goes to drivers', by Robert Taylor, *Observer*, 18 July 1982.

116. as 115.

117. 'ASLEF's bully boys cave in', by Tom Condon, *Sun*, 19 July 1982.

118. 'ASLEF strike collapses', by Robert Bedlow, *Daily Telegraph*, 19 July 1982.

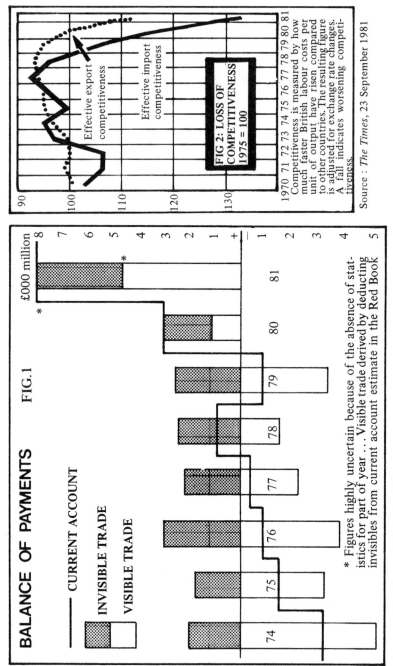

BALANCE OF PAYMENTS FIG.1

£000 million

— CURRENT ACCOUNT

INVISIBLE TRADE

VISIBLE TRADE

* Figures highly uncertain because of the absence of statistics for part of year … Visible trade derived by deducting invisibles from current account estimate in the Red Book

Source : *The Times*, 11 March 1982.

Effective export competitiveness

Effective import competitiveness

FIG 2: LOSS OF COMPETITIVENESS
1975 = 100

1970 71 72 73 74 75 76 77 78 79 80 81
Competitiveness is measured by how much faster British labour costs per unit of output have risen compared to other countries. The resulting figure is adjusted for exchange rate changes. A fall indicates worsening competitiveness.

Source : *The Times*, 23 September 1981

CASE NO. 7

THE DE LOREAN DREAM

The Best-Laid Plans

On 24 November 1982 eleven brand-new, dull-grey, stainless-steel, gull-winged, 125 m.p.h. sports cars came under the hammer. Products of the once-proud De Lorean Motor Cars Company, of Dunmurray, Belfast, they were auctioned on the orders of the Receivers, Sir Kenneth Cork and Paul Shewell of Cork Gully, the UK's largest insolvency practice. It was an ignominious end to the dreams of the company's American founder, 58 year-old John Zachary de Lorean.

One of the largest crowds ever to attend a British Car Auctions sale watched as, under the glare of TV cameras, £141,850 was added to the assets of the Receivers. In fact:

- The De Lorean Motor Cars Company had been set up, with substantial Government finance backing, as recently as July 1978 and in the year to November 1981 it had lost £23 millions. Its total accumulated deficit was £26.6 millions.

- The car had originally retailed in the USA at a list price of £13,700. Its ex-Belfast works value was put at £10,000.

- The company owed the UK Government an estimated £85 millions, including an equity stake of £17.7 millions.

- Obligations to the company's trade creditors exceeded £41 millions net.

- DLMC's parent had net negative assets and total debts of £94.8 millions.

Given this background, the sum realised at the auction constituted no more than 'eleven small drops falling into an almost empty bucket'. (1) A further indignity was that the cars were purchased by motor traders for 'their investment potential as extinct rarities' (2) rather than their value-in-use.

TABLE 1 : Parliamentary Representation 1974 - 1983

Election Date	Seats in Parliament Won By						
	Con	Lab	Lib	Plaid Cymru	Scottish Nationalist Party	Ulster Parties	Total
1974	277	319	13	3	11	12	635
1979	339	269	11	2	2	12	635
1983	397	209	23*	2	2	17	650

* Includes six social Democrats (SDP)

The final act in the Greek tragedy of DLMC had not been long delayed once a decisive meeting between Northern Ireland Secretary, James Prior and John de Lorean, former Vice President of General Motors and DLMC's president and owner, had resulted in the company's being put into receivership on 19 February 1982.

Whilst DLMC was, in fact, insolvent, receivership was preferred to compulsory liquidation because of the need to keep the company in existence as a going concern so as to explore all possible rescue avenues.

Despite strenuous efforts by John de Lorean and some inital optimism on the part of the Receivers, there had been few interested parties and no takers.

- Budget Rent-a-Car's interest in acquiring 2000 cars waned quickly after the Bank of America filed suit on DLMC's parent - the De Lorean Motor Company Inc., of New York - alleging that DLMC had defaulted on repayment of part of an £18.2 million loan to finance the sale of DLMC cars in its only market - the USA.

- A leasing deal between DLMC, Consolidated International and the Group Investors Corporation of Columbus, Ohio, fell through.

- A rescue bid by one of New York's largest landlords, Peter Kalikow, proved fruitless. Terminal negotiations coincided with disclosures that the American Internal Revenue Service had been carrying out a probe into DLMC's affairs.

- A last-minute mission by a UK consortium failed, once it became known on 18 August 1982 that the UK Government could make no adequate promises of extra aid.

Initial setbacks had not deterred John de Lorean from continuing desperately to seek funds to refinance operations. Indeed, as late as 6 p.m. on 18 October he was telling the BBC that funding was available and that the cash needed to stave off liquidation would be lodged by the Receivers' final deadline of 10 p.m. that day. It wasn't and, on the same day (19 October) as John de Lorean was arrested by the FBI on a drug trafficking charge involving 220 lbs of cocaine valued at $14 millions, the closure of the Dunmurray plant was announced by James Prior.

According to the prosecution's evidence, John de Lorean had been recorded on video tape holding a package containing South American cocaine and saying:

"This is better than gold. It came just in the nick of time . . . . It's better than gold. Gold weighs more than that, for God's sake." (3)

Another Day, Another Dollar?

Not for John de Lorean, M.Eng., MBA, son of a millwright at the Ford Motor Company in Detroit. His dream of producing 'an ethical car in an ethical company' (4), which had started when he set up DLMC in October 1975, was over. Nor for the workforce in the DLMC factory which had been, in its heyday, Northern Ireland's No.1 exporter.

No blame could be attached to either the factory itself nor the workforce for the company's demise. In fact, Sir Kenneth Clark had waxed eloquent about the former - a 72 acre plant on the Twinbrook Industrial Estate in West Belfast - during his rescue attempts.

"The factory itself is marvellous. De Lorean completely succeeded in that, at least. We have a charge on it and it's a wonderful facility. If necessary, it could be used for other things, perhaps making other vehicles or boats. Looked at one way, if you up-ended the chassis of the existing car, you could have the start of quite a reasonable boat." (5)

And John de Lorean was unstinting in his praise for his workforce:

"They are the most fabulous people I have worked with. I have not seen a workforce like this in 25 years. There is nothing like it in the United States today. They really care." (6)

No matter. Out of a workforce of 2600 (well above the original 1500 jobs specified in John de Lorean's agreement with the UK Government at the production start-up in February 1981), 1100 were made redundant on 12 February 1982 and a further 1300 dismissed at the end of May. Production had dropped from 400 to 200 cars/week only on 10 January 1982.

The union reaction to the situation was one of resignation, well summed up by the comment of one member, who said:

"People are happy to take their week's wages (£86 - 114 per week in 1981) as long as they are on offer. Nobody expects it to last. Dreams don't come true.' (7)

The TGWU District Officer, George Clark, had early on warned John de Lorean:

"We told him he'd have to be realistic. We told him to keep his feet on the ground. But he's overshot the mark with too much production." (8)

When the first redundancies were mooted in January 1981, Clark could do no other than accept the company's liquidity shortage.

"We know it's not a ploy when they say they haven't got it (cash for redundancy payments) but both the Company and the Government have a legal obligation and we're not going to let them get off that." (9)

His meeting, on 31 January 1982, with Michael Foot, Dame Judith Hart (Labour Party Chairman) and Alex Kitson (Chairman of Labour Party's Northern Ireland Study Group) bore no fruit as did the symbolic fight to save the factory by union officers, Sean O'Neill and Jim Nicholson. The last 16 staff were sent home on 16 October 1982.

And they were not the only ones. The knock-on effect of the DLMC crash on the fortunes - and labour forces - of small suppliers, like the part-DLMC owned CP Trip of Northern Ireland and Scott Engineering of Nuneaton, was severe. Sadly, it was made worse by their forbearance in refraining (as unsecured creditors) from petitioning for the winding-up of DLMC in March 1982 (on the grounds that they might get nothing) only to find that, when Renault pressed for this in October, they did get nothing. They were last in a queue comprising, apart from Renault (DLMC's engine supplier and owed £10.5 millions) GKN, Courtaulds, Lucas, BTR, Girling and may other important suppliers.

For Bruce McWilliams, DLMC's Marketing Chief, it was also the end of the line. He resigned in August 1982, painting a revealing picture of an American company's last days.

> "I resigned for several reasons. In particular, I believed the company will collapse. Things are coming to a crunch. In the California office we ran out of coffee money, stamp money; we owed $330 (£190) for water that we couldn't pay. We just ran right out of money."

His remarks on John de Lorean himself are worthy of note:

> "I don't believe that the company can be salvaged with de Lorean running it. Many changes are necessary, including the exiting of the man who brought the whole enterprise into being. John is a discredited person, he is not going to revive the company. The gold bath taps at the guest house outside Belfast did not bring the company's collapse but they symbolised a point of view and a method of operation that led to it. John de Lorean was a terrible manager with no sense of prudence, financial restraint or organisation. He behaved less than graciously. Except for rather occasional flying visits and overnight stops at the Connaught Hotel, John did not much trouble with the constituency that made his dream come true. He called in at London and Belfast only when absolutely necessary to seek additional funds." (11)

'Disaster City' was John de Lorean's own term for the company's demise. (12) That it certainly was.

'Miracles can Happen

'I fought long and hard,' wrote Roy Mason, Northern Ireland Secretary of State in the Labour Government in 1978, in a *Times* article on 12 October 1981, 'for the establishment of new industry in North-

TABLE 2 :   **Voting Patterns 1974 - 1983**

Votes Cast for Parties (Thousands)									
Election Date	Con	Lab	Lib	SDP	Plaid Cymru	Scottish Nationalist	Others	Communist	Total (m)
1974	10,501	11,457	5,347		166	840	897	17	29.2
1979	13,698	11,532	4,314		133	504	1,024	17	31.2
1983	12,991	8,437	4,205	3,570	125	331	952	10	30.6

ern Ireland, including the de Lorean project . . . . At the time the de Lorean project was launched, social conditions in the province were awful, housing was disgraceful and, in West Belfast, the Bogside and Londonderry unemployment was appalling . . . . de Lorean happened at a time when no private enterprise would have entered West Belfast without Government intervention, Government cash . . . . and had not bold decisions not been taken by Ministers . . . . de Lorean are now producing cars. Royalties are coming into the Government.'

'More than 2000 people are employed; breadwinners in their homes, pride in their breasts and purchasing power in their areas. It is the re-vitalisation of West Belfast.'

'The de Lorean Board got what they were entitled to . . . . and there were two members of NIDA on the de Lorean Board. I do not know, of course, since the deal was made, whether individuals are making money out of the project. To me, that matters not, provided all is legal. What matters is the survival of the project.'

'One had to recognise that when talking about money, *orthodox* Treasury economics never recognises the part it might play in under-mining the terrorists' recruiting drive by providing jobs. Damn it all, what an achievement! From virgin ground, green labour, a break-

TABLE 3 :   **Unemployment in Northern Ireland (13)**

Year	Month	Men ('000)		Women ('000)	
		In Work	Jobless	In Work	Jobless
1979	June	228.5	43	225.2	19.8
1980	June	280	49.5	223.4	23.5
1981	June	255.4	73.3	213.9	30.5

TABLE 4 :   **Who's Who in Ulster Job Creation**

NIDOC	The Northern Ireland Department of Commerce whose Industrial Development Organisation section was responsible for attracting inward investment.
NIDA	The Northern Ireland Development Authority promoted and assisted the development of firms.
IDB	The Industrial Development Board was set up by the UK Government in March 1982 to replace the industry establishment functions of NIDOC and NIDA. It has a similar 'one stop shopping' approach to attracting investment as Eire's Industrial Development Authority.
LEDU	Local Enterprise Development Unit set up by the UK Government in 1971 to deal with companies with less than 50 employees.*

*   In the year to 31 March 1981, it created 1055 jobs at a cost of £3,433/job. For the same period in 1982, the figures were 1613 jobs and £3,217. (13)

through in motor car design and the demand such that they are fighting and squabbling in the UK for the product for which customers are offering $5,000 above list price.' (14)

The Cabinet decision which Roy Mason so enthusiastically supported against the criticisms levelled in October 1981, was fully in accord with the advice given by Dr George Quigley (Permanent Secretary to NIDOC) in a Report on Northern Ireland to the Labour Government in 1976. In this he recommended that the public sector had to take unprecedented risks to attract foreign investment to Ulster. Interestingly, it was Dr Quigley who played a large role in starting the process for the establishment of DLMC in Ulster after NIDOC had approached John de Lorean (15) and after Eire had rejected the latter's plans for an Eire base as 'too risky'. (16)

The enthusiasm of Roy Mason, however, was not shared - either at the time or since - by his ex-Cabinet colleague, Joel Barnett, Chief Secretary to the Treasury (17). Interestingly, he was in the position, in 1982, of being chairman of the Commons Public Accounts Committee charged with carrying out a full investigation into the circumstances surrounding Government backing, one of which was the cost of policing the province (£384 millions in 1982 - 83).

It was scarcely the case that the risks involved in the de Lorean project

TABLE 5 : Terrorism in N. Ireland (18) - New Ireland Forum Report

Violence resulting in	Number with place of Birth			Number in Category		Estimated cost to UK Exchequer in direct cost and loss of output (1970 - 1981) from all forms of violence in Northern Ireland (£ billion)
	In Northern Ireland		Outside Northern Ireland	Prison Service and British Army	Others	
	Catholic	Protestant				
Deaths	1043	864	393	722	1578	9

258

were not appreciated. Indeed, it was known that:

- John de Lorean, when making DLMC a public company in 1978, had warned the American Securities and Exchange Commission that 'only investors who can afford a total loss of their minimum investment of $25,000 should apply for shares'. In fact the SEC had noted 17 'high risk factors' for the firm. (19)

- The small British car firm of Jensen had collapsed and Aston Martin had enjoyed a very turbulent history.

- John de Lorean's volume targets at 20,000 cars/year were higher than the highest sales ever achieved by such direct competition as BMW, Porsche, MG, Cadillac and Corvette Stingray.

- A report by McKinsey, commissioned by the Government and presented on 18 July 1978, said the scheme was 'extraordinarily risky' and its chances of success 'remote'. (20)

However, de Lorean was demanding a rapid decision in principle from the Government by 28 June 1978, in view of offers under discussion from:

- Puerto Rico : A package of £64.75 millions in aid if de Lorean raised $25 millions privately.

- Detroit : A total of $68.5 millions in assistance from city and federal grants and loans.

There clearly were serious uncertainties involved in the engineering development of the concept (undertaken by Lotus) and the initial plan for the assembly of:

- A French transmission and engine
- A stainless steel body from Argentina
- Brakes from the USA
- Tyres from Italy (21)

Additionally, there was the question of consumer acceptance to ponder. Mercedes had rejected the 'gull-wing' door idea for sports cars and

FIG.3
ORGANISATION STRUCTURE OF DE LOREAN COMPANIES AS AT
FEBRUARY 1981

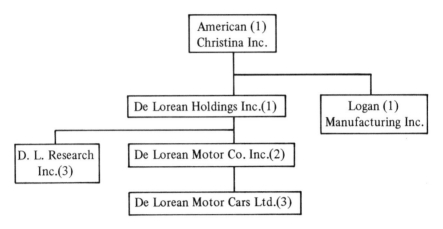

Notes: (1) 100% owned by John de Lorean.
         (2) 83% of shares owned by John de Lorean.
            (Johnny Carson had a $500,000 share)
         (3) Ownership and operating control in the hands of John de Lorean.

the Bricklin project for a gull-wing car strikingly similar to the de Lorean design and backed by the Canadian Government was on the point of collapse in 1978.

And there was the issue of the fact that, despite the UK Government's funding of the project, ownership and operating control of DLMC remained in the hands of John de Lorean. There were only two NIDA-appointed directors on the Board of DLMC: the solicitor Alex Featherstone and banker James Sim. Intriguingly, these two were referred to in a *TV Eye* programme on 8 March 1984 by Peter Taafe, a DLMC production worker, as 'Daffy Duck' and Bugs Bunny'.

Despite the collapse of DLMC, Ray Mason was unrepentant. In a Commons written statement on 20 October 1982, he stated that the venture was:

'A tremendous achievement . . . . It starkly shows the difference between a caring Government and one that doesn't care at all. I feel very sad that the De Lorean company in Northern Ireland has collapsed -

TABLE 6 : The De Lorean Deal (June 1978)

Initial Aid	£17.8m equity provided £18.7m Factory Grant £6.7m loans £9.75m Employment Grants
Employment	Minimum level of employment to be achieved : 1,500
Royalties	£185 to be paid to the UK Government on each of the first 90,000 cars produced. Thereafter £45/car for 10 years
Other Clauses	An inflation-proof arrangement A currency depreciation arrangement No money lending to Parent Transfer pricing agreement Share conversion right for UK Government

sad for Northern Ireland and especially for the people of West Belfast. West Belfast, a Catholic community, is like an enclave of the third world within the UK . . . . They needed a will to live - I gave them hope." (22)

His attitude was fully endorsed by the then Minister at the Northern Ireland Office, Don Concannon:

"We knew investment was the only answer. We had to change the economic base from the old declining trades like shipbuilding and textiles before we could offer Northern Ireland the good government of the British counties with a reasonable prospect of jobs, housing and so on." (23)

Roy Mason blamed the collapse on 'the lethargy, hopelessness of the political deadbeats in the Northern Ireland Office who have sat back and let the area once more sink back and flounder in despair.' (24)

The Government was the target of Don Concannon's criticism :

"The whole thing was that the policy in Northern Ireland was to bring jobs to the people. Nobody has disagreed with the proposition that only Government will bring jobs to Northern Ireland. We were trying to do it on the cheap. Neither they (the present Government) nor the people in the Treasury, want this sort of project to succeed. If it did it would be against their entire economic philosophy." (25)

TABLE 7 : **Jobs with Major Employers in N. Ireland**

Employer	1950	1976	1977	1982
Harland & Wolff	24,000			6,000
Man-made fibre industry		9,400		1,880
James Mackie : Jute processing machinery			4,000	1,600

Mrs Thatcher's Government's answer to such charges was a £90 million economic booster package for Ulster, produced in January 1982. Aimed at the creation of 5,500 jobs, it included spending plans for housing, agriculture and commercial premises. This was part of a double strategy, the second element being the creation of a Northern Ireland Assembly.

Said James Prior, in introducing the strategy:

> "I long for the time when I can go to the USA and say 'Look at what we have accomplished. We've got political stability. Put some money in.' " (26)

Certainly, in contemplation of the level of political turmoil, terrorist violence and economic decline in the province's main employers, such steps were no more than realistic.

John De Lorean : The Lad Himself

John de Lorean initially collaborated with Patrick Wright in writing a book entitled *On a Clear Day You Can See General Motors*, which was published in 1980. Whilst he later backed out, he left in the book a clear imprint of his idealism and the force of character which led to such pronouncements as:

- "We are going to bootstrap ourselves back into operation. All we need is intestinal fortitude." (27)

- He created his own companies "because I never have to kiss anyone's fanny. I never have and I never will." (28)

He certainly made such an impression on trade unionist, George Clark, who stated:

> "John is a very serious businessman and not the American playboy some of us could make him out to be. His flamboyant reputation works against him here but it's what we need in America and that's what counts." (29)

This was how John de Lorean himself saw his ultimate rise to high status in General Motors:

'I had been General Motors' fastest-rising executive. When I joined the Pontiac Division in 1956, I came under the tutelage of Simon E. Knudsen, who was head of the division. He taught me the business as he transformed Pontiac into the hottest car division of the 1960s. We gave it a youthful image by producing a new range of sporty cars.

From Pontiac, in early 1969, I became General Manager of the Chevrolet division. Except for insiders, no-one knew the depths of the troubles there. America's most popular name-plate was out of control and heating into the red. The 3½ years which followed were the most difficult and challenging in my business life.

I put together an energetic young management team which got its arms round this unwieldy giant and turned it round. We extracted billions of dollars profit where there had been little. In 1972, we set a divisional sales record for the industry, 3.1 million cars and trucks. The next year was even better, 3.4 million.

I baulked at becoming a group vice-president when the job was first offered in September 1972. But after two weeks of ceaseless pressure from my bosses, I relented and went upstairs. It was a horrible mistake.

About a week after I took up my job on the fourteenth floor, I was in the office of Elliott M. Estes, executive vice-president of operations. He said, "I've always told them that it's good for GM to have someone like you in the ranks. It shows how democratic we are".

Until then, I had deluded myself into thinking I was held in high esteem by my superiors, even if they didn't like me, because I was a business success. I was shocked to realise that this was not the case. Just as the corporation at the time had token blacks, token women and token chicanos, I was their token hippy.

The fact that I had been divorced, was a health fanatic and dated generally younger actresses and models didn't go down well with the executives or their wives.

I didn't pay much attention. I figured I was loyal and dedicated to General Motors. I did my job well. The company had a right to know

TABLE 8 :Belfast Crime Rate

Royal Ulster Constabulary	Belfast Area	Population Predominantly	1980 Crimes	
Division:			Reported	Solved
B	West	Catholic	5097	479
E	East	Protestant	3287	843

Source: 'Knee cappings tighten the IRA grip on the ghettos',
      Observer, 6 September 1981.

how I was spending my business life, but it had no right to know how I was spending my private life.

Nevertheless, my clothing and lifestyle were increasingly rattling my superiors, as was the publicity my personal and business lives were generating. I was being resented because my style of living violated an unwritten rule that no personality could outshine General Motors.

If your appearance, style and personality were consistent with the corporate stereotype, you were well on your way to being a "loyal" employee. But loyalty demanded more.

The practice of fawning over the boss gave birth to a secret network to find out his likes, dislikes and idiosyncracies . . . .

It was a shocking experience for me "upstairs". After eight years of running car divisions, I suddenly found myself in a non-job with no business to manage directly. Soon after I moved into top management my boss started giving me little, stupid, make-work kinds of assignments, things which I thought should have been decided further down the line.

Some of these things, which had little or no impact on the business, were an insult to a person's intelligence, especially if that person was a manager with 17 years in the company and a good track record. They were things which any secretary, could have done . . . .

In January 1973, I wrote a stinging and critical analysis of General Motors' management and system. If at all possible, I wanted to jar management into realising the deep rooted problems upstairs. I was pretty sure this would not be effective - but at least it would demonstrate to management that we could no longer exist together and that it was best to let one resign on my terms.

The process of separation had begun long before. I had the feeling that "what I am doing here may be nothing more than perpetuating a a gigantic fraud". A fraud on the American consumer by promising something new but giving only surface alterations - a couple of extra horsepower and an annual price increase. A fraud on the American economy, because the annual model changes may be good for the auto business in the short term but not for the economy of the country. Couldn't the money we spent on styling changes be better spent in reducing prices and in improving service and reliability? Or seeking solutions to the social problems which our products were creating in pollution, energy consumption, safety and congestion?

And a fraud on our own company because we were kidding ourselves that these slight annual alterations were innovative. They were not.

It seemed to me, and still does, that the system of American business often produces wrong, immoral and irresponsible decisions, even though the personal morality of the people running the businesses is often above reproach. The ultimate measure of success and failure of these businesses isn't their effect on people but rather their earnings per share.

TABLE 9 :   **Living Standards**

Country	1978	1979	1980
USA	132	132	129
Germany	104	106	107
Japan	91	93	96
UK	89	88	87
Ireland	59	58	58

(Indices of gdp/head. OECD Average = 100. Converted at purchasing power parities)

Sources : 'The rich get richer and the British get poorer', by Mervyn Westlake,
          The Times, 22 March 1982.

In such a completely impersonal context, business decisions of questionable personal morality are easily justified. When someone is forced into early retirement by management power-play or a supplier is cheated out of a sale by under-the-table dealings, the public reaction is generally, "Oh well, that's business". And management's reaction is often, "It's what's on the bottom line that counts".

"A person who shoots and kills another is sentenced to life in prison. A businessman who makes a defective product which kills people may get a nominal fine or a verbal slap on the hands, if he is ever brought to trial at all."(30)

TABLE 10 :   **Unemployment Levels In The UK (February 1982)**

Area	Total Unadjusted	% of Workforce
Northern Ireland	110,800	19.5
Wales	170,300	16.1
North	212,700	16.0
Scotland	333,100	15.2
West Midlands	344,400	15.1
North West	422,800	15.0
Yorks and Humber	272,700	13.2
South West	183,600	11.2
East Midlands	175,400	11.0
East Anglia	74,000	10.5
South East	692,600	9.2

A Time And Place

The first Lorean sports cars were supplied at Easter 1981 and went on sale in the USA in June. The project had commenced in June 1978. From the start of 1978 onwards the announcements of home market results of American car producers became increasingly gloom-laden. A loss for Chrysler of $448 millions in the first quarter of 1980; a further loss of $436 millions in the first nine months of 1981. Losses by Ford in the USA amounted, in 1981, to no less than $1.06 billions and, world-wide, to $89 millions in the first quarter of 1982.

For the whole US car producing industry the picture was the same: in 1980 and 1981 they collectively lost a massive $5 billions. Only General Motors recorded a profit in 1981 - a minute £333 millions in the light of its position as the world's second largest corporation.

TABLE 11 :   **US Car Production By Major Producers (31)**

Domestic Product	1978	1979	1980	1981
American Motors	170,739	162,057	149,438	136,682
Chrysler	1,146,258	949,598	660,017	729,873
Ford Motors	2,582,702	2,140,368	1,475,232	1,380,600
General Motors	5,385,282	4,917,911	4,116,482	3,796,696
Total	9,284,981	8,169,934	6,401,169	6,043,851

TABLE 12 : Japanese Car Imports to USA (000s) (32)

Japanese Producers Sales in USA Market	1980 Rounded	1981 Rounded
Toyota	582	576
Nissan	517	465
Honda	375	371
Mazda	162	166
Subaru	143	152
Mitsubishi	129	111
Total	1,908	1,841

Such stark statistics showed the poorest industry performance levels since 1970. Indeed, Detroit's whole production in December 1981, of 368,700 cars, was the lowest since December 1959.

The picture for imports was not quite so bleak. In fact, they slightly improved their volume market share in 1981 from the 1980 level of 21.2 per cent to 21.5 per cent.

What had gone wrong? A host of factors was influencing the car market place adversely. For one thing the population mix had significantly changed, and was continuing to change. For another, the US market was nothing if not mature with 83.5 per cent of households owning one or more cars (34). The price of petrol, at $1.25/gallon in 1981, was almost double the pre-1973 level. Average retail prices of domestically produced cars had risen steadily from $6,476 in 1976 to $7,676 in 1980, and $9,020 in 1981 (35) and compared unfavourably

TABLE 13 : USA Age Distribution Patterns (33)

Age Group	Per cent of population in Age Group in				
	1910	1950	1980	2000 (Forecast)	2000 (Forecast)
up to 18	38	32	28	27	25
18 - 54	52	51	51	53	47
55 - 64	5.5	9	10	8	13
65 +	4.5	8	11	12	15
Total	100	100	100	100	100

with those of Japanese imports. There was an estimated wage differential of \$8/hour between the US production worker's rate (\$20/hour) and his Japanese counterpart in 1981 (36).

To try to cope with the decline-in-demand problem, US car manufacturers had since 1980 mounted a formidable counter-attack.

- *New models:* e.g., the introduction by Chrysler of its new 'K' class of small cars (and the phasing out of large models) in July 1980 and the Ford launch of its Lynx and Topaz models in August 1980 and Spring 1982 respectively.

- *Labour layoffs:* by mid-1981 some 200,000 production workers had been laid off.

- *Dividend passing:* by Ford, Chrysler and General Motors.

- *Price cutting:* from January 1982 Fords were offering a 5 per cent price cut plus a two-year free-maintenance deal. GM were giving a 10 per cent discount.

- *Plant closures:* including the giant Ford Mahwah plant.

Despite this ostensibly potent combination of measures, it had been clear, since November 1981, that it was insufficient to get the industry moving again. Democrat President Carter's 1980 aid package consisting of an easing of Federal emission regulations, a temporary delay in introducing safety laws and £1 billion in Government loan guarantees and tax breaks, had also not worked. Indeed, it was only action by the US Treasury (which included putting the President of the United Autoworkers Union, Douglas Fraser, on the main board) which had saved Chrysler from bankruptcy.

TABLE 14 :   Leading Companies Working Capital (37)

Companies	Working Capital (S Billions)	
	Start of 1979	End of 1981 (Forecast)
Ford, General Motors, Chrysler, American Motors	13	(- 9)

TABLE 15 :   Swings and Roundabouts

Ford : WORKERS	General Motors : WORKERS
(1) Forego 3% annual wage increase for 2½ years	(1) Forego 3% annual wage increase for 2 years
(2) Take 8 fewer days paid holiday over a 2½ year period	(2) Give up the equivalent of 10 days paid holiday per year
(3) Accept a 9 month freeze on cost-of-living increases	
Ford : COMPANY	General Motors : COMPANY
(1) Extends the guaranteed income scheme for long-service workers who are laid off	(1) Extends the guaranteed income scheme for long-service workers who are laid off
(2) Extends the profit sharing scheme	
(3) Promises a 2 year moratorium on plant closures	(2) Increases coverage of GMs lifetime job security experiment to 4 more plants

It was the union which took the most significant step in seeking a solution. A direct answer was made to a call by Commerce Secretary, Malcolm Baldridge (at a congressional hearing on 5 November 1981) for greater productivity. He stated:

"Let's face it. We have got to become more competitive by elimination of some of our wage cost disadvantage." (38)

The Executive Council of the UAW voted on 9 December to allow members to reopen wage contract negotiations with manufacturers in advance of the normal re-negotiation date in September. Peter Pestillo , Ford's Vice President for Labour Relations, welcomed the move as:

"A preliminary but potentially positive step which may result in the negotiation of a new contract if the national Ford Council approves. Ford would like to replace the existing contract with a new long-term agreement. The need to resolve the labour cost issue is urgent and should be addressed now. We are prepared to proceed." (39)

Ford's haste was understandable:

■ They had a five month stock of Lynxes (as against a normal two months)

- Their US market share had fallen from 17.3 per cent in 1980 to 16.6 per cent in 1981
- They had lost $1,060 billions (£576 millions) in 1981.

And so was that of General Motors, whose President (Roger B Smith) said that a deal which would permit price cuts:

> "Could usher in a new era of labour-management co-operation because it addresses the heart of the problem in our industry today - non competitive labour costs and inflated car and truck prices." (40)

The results of the negotiations are given in Table 15. The Ford deal, which saved the company an estimated $1 billion (£540 millions) in costs, was ratified by no less than 73 per cent of the workforce. A union statement read:

> 'We are extremely pleased at the margin of ratification. It is clear evidence that our members at Ford understand and support the historical breakthrough contained in the agreement that will lead to greater security for themselves and their families.' (41)

The GM-AUW deal had been harder to negotiate; not surprisingly, in the view of one anonymous union leader, who said:

> "With Ford and Chrysler you know there is trouble. But with GM you suspect the company is trying to take advantage of the tough economic times to break the union." (42)

Talks had initially stalled over the balance and amount of direct wages and benefits, the level of outsourcing (buying in components and subcontracting manufacture) and threatened plant closures, but an acceptable deal (valued by General Motors at $3 billions) was concluded.

Problems at Source

Most commentators agreed that the major cause of the decline in demand facing Detroit was the US Administration's economic response to the nation's economic difficulties as it perceived them. Specifically criticised was the combination of Republican President Reagan's deflationary budget-cutting approach and the Federal Reserve's tight money policies. The period from September 1981 to February 1982 is illustrative.

Having pushed through budget cuts of $35 millions in July 1981,

President Reagan announced further cuts of $16 billions for the fiscal year 1982, and a total of $80 billions over the following three years. A tax rise of $3 billions was also included in the July package. In a television speech on 24 September, President Reagan explained:

"We have no choice but to continue down the road to a balanced budget - a budget that will keep us strong at home and secure overseas . . . . Interest payments are, at $96 billion, more than the combined profits of the 500 biggest companies in the country."

Such cuts were hardly music to the ears of the military ($13 billions out of the $80 billions cut) or to the 36 million Americans in receipt of social security benefits (food stamps, welfare payments, housing assistance, college student loans, etc) and the 51 million who drew Federally-supported health assistance benefits (Medicaire and Medicaid).

The President saw no alternative to his policy:

"I have no reverse gears (43) . . . . I will not be deterred by temporary economic changes or short-term political expediency." (44)

Indeed, in February 1982 he sent a further highly controversial $50 billion cuts package for 1983 to Congress. For opponents of the President's policies, it was not just the cuts which were difficult to swallow, but the forecast of budget overruns on which they were based.

Official Budget Deficit forecast for fiscal year 1982/3 (Forecast made in February 1982 before the announced cuts package)	157

TABLE 16 :   **Forecast Budget Deficit ($ billions) (45)**

The other side of the coin was the tight-money policy of the Federal Reserve Bank under its Chairman, Paul Volcker, who repeatedly emphasised the Fed's determination to stick to its high interest rate/ restricted credit creation approach. Unfortunately, the money supply did not seem to be under the degree of control necessary for the

TABLE 17 :   **Borrowing Rates & Share Values**

Element.	14.9.81	24.11.81	17.2.82	8.3.82
Dow Jones Industrial Share Index	866.15	870.2	824.3	795.47
Chase Manhattan Bank's Prime Borrower's Rate %	20	15¾	17	16

policy to be widely seen to be working. For example, fluctuations in M1 amounted to the difference between:

- A fall of $3.3 billions in the week ending 28 October 1981

- A rise of $9.8 billions in the week ending 15 January 1982.

Democrat Senator, Edward Kennedy, spoke for critics of the Administration's economic approach by labelling it 'schizophrenic' and saying that the President had given the nation 'the worst economic mess since the Great Depression'. (46) To the President's statement of 4 December 1981 that the announced unemployment figure was 'a tragedy for the country and the people involved' (47) - backed up by a rider from a White House spokesman that unemployment was 'the price you have to pay for bringing down inflation' - Senator Kennedy retorted that the Administration was 'playing Santa Claus for the wealthy and Scrooge for the working people'. (48)

His Democratic colleague, Congressman Leon Panetta, joined in the chorus by remarking that:

"This budget is not going to fly - anyone who believes that is nuts'. (49)

While the UK Government adopted a muted approach to such a 'monetarist' approach - not dissimilar from the Conservatives' containment of public sector spending and control of the PSBR - Shadow Chancellor, Dennis Healey left no doubt on his views on 'supply side economics'. He wrote that President Reagan 'has done for Monetarism what the Boston Strangler did for door-to-door salesmanship'.

TABLE 18 : Effects of Reagan Administration's Policies

| | | 1981 | | | 1982 | |
Element	Sept	Oct	Nov	Dec	Jan	Feb
Percentage change in composite Index of 10 leading indicators (Rate of layoffs, number of new orders, average work week length, level of liquid assets, prices of raw materials, etc)	(2.2)	(1.8)	n/a	(.3)	(1.2)	(.3)
Overall USA unemployment level	7.5	8	8.4	8.8	8.5	8.9
Year on Year inflation Rate (%)	11	10.2	n/a	8.9	8.4	n/a

Dancing on wet cement

The crisis position which provoked the renegotiation of labour contracts in the US car industry coincided almost exactly with the sales
drive for the de Lorean car. Production had started in February 1981
and by the autumn was in full swing. The first cars sold at 10 per cent
above list price and initial reaction was favourable. The TV commercial enjoined listeners to:

> 'Drive the de Lorean -
> *Live the dream today'*

One year later - in February 1982 - it was clear that the dream had
turned into a nightmare and disaster was staring DLMC in the face.
Out of a total production of 8,333 cars, only 52.5 per cent had been
retailed, and break-even point was later assessed as 7,000 cars per year
by accountants Cooper and Lybrand. The segment of 'randy, West
Coast bachelors hurtling towards the age of 30' at whom the product
was said to be targeted (50) did not seem all that attracted to the car,
even with the substantial '10% off' discount which came into force
from January 1982.

In fact, the cash drain on the company which operated at full production for the three months starting on 3 October - 80 cars/day - was of
haemorrhage proportions.

The company's financial difficulties were not new. To get production started in August 1980, a further loan of $14 millions had been negotiated with the UK Government. By February 1981, the Government had guaranteed a further £10 millions in bank loans. It was, however, just after the delivery of DLMC's second dividend cheque for £395,500 on 2 October 1981 (bringing its total dividend payments to NIDOC to £599,700) that its real problems began to be well known and fully appreciated.

One problem for DLMC was funding the wage bill - £17 millions in 1981.

For the US parent - receiving the cars at transfer prices as DLMC's only customer - there was the additional need for funds to stock the cars until their sale to the 350 dealers, who were all shareholders in DMC.

John de Lorean's fund-raising attempts were legion and highly imaginative. Among the most significant were the following:

(1) *Raising Equity*

Plans for raising equity for the company were originally made in mid-summer 1981 but had to be shelved temporarily because of negotiations on other forms of funding with the UK Government. The first attempt - a planned public offering of 2.25 million shares at $12 each in the newly formed De Lorean Motors Holding Co - had also to be called off because of the depressed state of the US market. John de Lorean spoke of this setback on 9 October 1981:

> "Our ability to raise public funds has been seriously injured and this has driven us back to the position we did not want to be put in. We either get it from the public or from the Government." (51)

Having previously made clear (on 4 October) the pressure on him:

> "If banks cut off our credit and the dealers' credit, then closure could very well happen." (52)

By December the purpose and scale of the planned flotation had changed. On 9 December, DMH filed with the Securities and Exchange Commission to exchange its common shares for outstanding common and preferred shares of DMC and to raise $12 millions from a pro-

TABLE 19 : The De Lorean Chronology

*	*October 1975:* De Lorean Motor Company is formed in Michigan by John Z De Lorean Corporation to design and develop the De Lorean sports car and set up a US dealer network.
*	*July 1978:* DMC enters agreement with the Labour UK Government to set up manufacturing subsidiary in Belfast with £53m in loans, grants and equity.
*	*October 1978:* First ground broken at Dunmurray, Belfast, site.
*	*1979:* Lotus Cars used to develop final version of car for production.
*	*July 1980:* De Lorean misses scheduled production start-up as a result of development problems.
*	*August 1980:* A further £14m loan is negotiated with Government, leading to political criticism of Government's decision to provide it.
*	*February 1981:* Production getting under way, but row breaks out over De Lorean claim that the £14m loan of the previous year should have been treated as grant. Relations between the Government and De Lorean become strained.
*	*February 1981:* Government agrees to guarantee £10m in bank loans.
*	*May 1981:* Car launched in US to some criticisms of quality but starts to sell at a premium.
*	*July 1981:* First royalty of £¼m paid to Government.
*	*August 1981:* Public share issue to raise S28m prepared but postponed.
*	*October 1981:* Police probe allegations of financial irregularities, but company is cleared of criminal misconduct.
*	*November 1981:* Sales start to falter, provoking cash flow difficulties.
*	*January 1982:* More modest share flotation abandoned. De Lorean applies unsuccessfully for £35m in export credits. At end of month, company makes 1,100 workers redundant.
*	*18 February 1982:* De Lorean board meets Northern Ireland Secretary, James Prior, for 'decisive' meeting on company's future.
*	*19 February 1982:* Voluntary Receivership announced.

Source: *Financial Times*, 20 February 1982.

* *16 August 1984:* John de Lorean is cleared of charges at the Drugs Trial.

Source: *The Times*, 11 August 1984.

posed flotation of 1m common shares and one million warrants to purchase an equal number of common shares. One intention was that DMH would buy out the De Lorean Research Partnership, which at the time was entitled to 23.4 per cent of corporate profits. This too was not proceeded with, on the advice of the brokerage house, Bache, Halsy, Stuart and Shields Inc., because of a lack of interest in the offering and the state of the market. There was also comment from leading investment analysts to consider, for example, Wall Street's David Healey, who said:

> "I have frankly come to the conclusion that potential investors would be a great deal better off if they put their money into booze and broads because the return would be the same and they'd have more fun." (53)

(2) Rolling loans forward

From September 1981 onwards, DMC was locked in an epic struggle to try to roll forward a Bank of America loan (£21 millions) to cover US operations. The company was unsuccessful despite the pledging of unsold US car stocks and UK loan guarantees as collateral. Part of the difficulty was the fact that by the end of March 1982 DMC owed DLMC more than £10 millions for cars supplied (54). Interestingly, DMC was a secured creditor of DLMC.

(3) Pressing the UK Government for more funds.

Whilst they were prepared to consider John de Lorean's request for more cash aid and loan guarantee extensions in December 1981, NIDA and NIDOC baulked at his plan that they should underwrite a new £35 million credit guarantee he sought in January 1982 from the Export Credits Guarantee Department.

(4) Reliance on supplier credit.

By 20 February 1982 this had exceeded £41 millions.

(5) Assorted claims for compensation.

This included help in 1979 with adverse exchange rate variations, a loan of £14 millions from the UK Government as compensation for DLMC's dropping a controversial inflation-proofing clause from the June 1978 agreement, and a claim for £10 million compensation for destruction of property and loss of production due to terrorist activity in 1981. Particular reference was made to the consequential riot damage suffered on 5 May 1981, the day of the death of Bobby Sands, the IRA gunman who had led the hunger strike in the Maze Prison. Settlement of this claim was agreed at £425,000. (55)

(6) *A new royalty deal*

On 29 January 1982, John de Lorean put forward a restructuring proposal whereby the UK Government would give up its investment in DLMC in return for a higher royalty payment/car. James Prior, Northern Ireland Secretary, rejected this out of hand.

It was not the first attempt at renegotiation. In the summer of 1980 John de Lorean, believing that under the agreement with Roy Mason he was entitled to a further £22 millions, had sought a similar change. In a company memorandum written at the time, he described such a result as 'an idealised scenario fraught with potential problems and pitfalls.' (56)

(7) *Sale of unused tax allowances*

In early February 1982, John de Lorean attempted to sell the right of £40 millions of unused tax allowances granted by the Government to DLMC. To take advantage of these allowances (which could be used to offset tax on profits earned elsewhere in the UK on other activities), the buyer would have had to take control of the company. These allowances had not been used since DLMC had never made profits. The asking price was 20p in the £.

Whilst all these attempts were being made, John de Lorean made statement after statement to the press to ensure that his position was recognised. The tone of his remarks changed as his difficulties grew.

> "I want it to succeed. I would have been pleased not to have had this public controversy. We took a swamp and built a factory on it. There are 2,000 people there who now have jobs who would not have and they work like hell for it . . . . " (57)

> "We are here to stay. What you see is a miracle and we are proud of it. Nothing is going to stop us. We will survive." (58)

> "From a personal standpoint, I really don't need all this aggravation. This project is really nothing to do with my life style. Even today I am making considerably less than half of what I made at General

Motors eight years ago. I know how to sell automobiles. Unfortunately, it's like trying to dance on wet cement. We are completely surrounded by a set of impossible circumstances." (59)

"Our company has been undercapitalised since its founding. This has prevented us from operating on a smooth and steady basis. A typical automobile manufacturer runs its assembly lines on a constant rate to accumulate a modest inventory during the slow winter months to be ready for the spring upsurge in sales. Unfortunately, we lack the capital or export finance to build this winter inventory." (60)

"It is impossible to continue as a Government-owned company because we have become such a political hot potato. Nobody dares touch us . . . . People keep talking about the deal and the financial arrangement we made. We did not negotiate anything. All we did was to accept what was offered . . . . In November we had firm dealer orders for about 5,000 cars for the following quarter. We felt cool, calm and confident that everything was wonderful . . . . Suddenly the industry went into the ash can. It was a mistake to allow NIDA 'to talk me into' launching the company in Belfast." (61)

Whispers

The difficulties that John de Lorean was facing in raising finance were not helped by disclosures of alleged misdemeanours.

The first was made by Miss Marianne Gibson, John de Lorean's ex-private secretary in Belfast, who made a statement at Slough Police Station on 9 October regarding the level of John de Lorean's personal investment in DLMC. She passed two files of documents to Conservative MP, Nicholas Winterton, which were thought to substantiate her comment that:

> "I was concerned that, with the small amount of money he had put into the company compared with the British investment of £80 millions, he would come out on top and the British would lose control. It concerned me as a patriotic subject."

An investigation, ordered by the Prime Minister, was carried out by Scotland Yard and John de Lorean was cleared of any impropriety in a statement made by the Director of Public Prosecutions on 12 October.

Miss Gibson's complaint was as smoke to the fire started by William Haddad, a former Vice President, with his publicity for allegations that:

- The prospectus backing up the DMH's share offer in 1981 was inaccurate. It said that the 350 dealers had 'committed themselves to purchase an aggregate of approximately 43,000 vehicles during the first two years'.

- John de Lorean was enjoying excessive personal perquisites from his companies.

- The manner in which the company had sought to modify its original agreement with the UK Government was improper.

- The effect on DLMC shareholders (company executives, private investors and car dealers) of the share offer being made through DLMH rather than by DMC was intentionally disadvantageous, adversely affecting the value of their holdings and stock options.

- Payments to GDP, a Panamanian-registered Swiss-based partnership in Geneva - for the engineering development of the car - were somehow irregular.

Writs for libel were filed by John de Lorean on 13 October.

John de Lorean countered Miss Gibson's allegations at a Press Conference in the DLMC canteen on 12 October 1981, stating that it was a lie that he had agreed to invest $4 millions in the Belfast company and had put up only £750,000. Not only had he been contractually bound to put in $1 million in cash, he had also brought to the company the design asset of his 'dream car', valued at $5.7 millions. In terms of salary, he contended that he was 'getting only what I am entitled to by contract demanded by the Government at the time of signing our agreement.' (62)

From the UK Government's viewpoint, it was William Haddad's allegation about GDP which was the most serious, since it was known that:

- Lotus Limited were supposed to be paid from this source for the engineering development of the de Lorean car.

- Under an agreement signed in November 1978, the De Lorean Research Limited Partnership - set up as a tax shelter by Wall Street Brokers, Oppenheim and Co., and numbering among its 125 shareholders such celebrities as Sammy Davis Junior and best-selling author Ira Levin - contracted to pay GDP $12.5 millions against a UK Government contribution of £5.15 millions. The total of $17.65 millions was intended as the payment to Lotus.

- The relationship between the Research partnership and GDP was under tax investigation at the start of 1981.

After the collapse of both DMC and DLMC, the seriousness of this allegation became apparent. None of the $17.65m ever reached Lotus - it was paid for its work directly by DLMC - and $8.9m had gone, in the word of the Receiver, Sir Kenneth Cork, 'walkabout'. The balance apparently had been used by de Lorean himself to repay a personal loan he had taken out to buy the Logan Division (a manufacturer of snowploughs and snowmobiles) of the Thiokol Corporation. These funds had passed through the hands of no fewer than five different banks since October 1978:

- Barclays Bank (International), London
- Rothschild Bank, Zurich
- Mellon Bank, New York
- Citibank, New York
- Pierson, Amsterdam

Storm Cones

The Government had been warned. Following the resignation of Mr Walther Stryker, DLMC's £100,000/year Treasurer in December 1979 - 'not competent' in NIDA's view - NIDA called for the setting up of a financial reporting system enabling 'effective measurement of results and cash flow' (63). Also, NIDA had ensured the appointment of Shaun Harte - a NIDA executive - as Director for Programming and Planning Co-ordination. This was necessary in view of the research development which DLMC had on hand in 1980. These included a DLMC equivalent of the Land Rover and a bus (the DMC 80, 'Transbus'). Dennis Faulkner, NIDA's Chairman, wrote to John de Lorean to warn him that:

> 'The cost and cash effect of a slippage in shipping and invoicing cars would be very substantial and could not be met from the company's current cash resources.'

This letter was sent at the start of 1980 (64) but as late as 17 January 1982 Faulkner was still complaining about the lack of 'financial controls within the group as a whole'. (65)

The crunch came for the Government on 27 January 1982. The previous day, James Prior,had voiced his anxiety:

> "I am extremely concerned about the future of the company, its employees and the great sums of money that have been put into it." (66)

On the 27th itself, Adam Butler (Minister of State for Northern Ireland) spelled out in the Commons that:

> "There is a point beyond which one cannot go. We have an acute responsibility to the taxpayers in the way money has been used, and have to take that into account as well as the situation of the workers and employment in the province.
>
> Nothing in the Government's present words should be taken as committing any further assistance or comfort to the De Lorean companies." (67)

The debate provoked by suspicions of De Lorean's parlous financial situation which resulted in Adam Butler's announcement of an independent Cooper and Lybrand survey of DLMC affairs, was pointed.

Mr Robert Cryer (Keighley, Lab.):

> "Would he *(the Minister)* agree that, with the massive public contribution to this company, there ought to be a majority shareholding on behalf of taxpayers . . . . It is a disgrace that, after contributing £83 millions, the taxpayer does not even own the car. The only way to provide certain future jobs is by public ownership under the NEB *(National Enterprise Board)*. Does he accept that this particular private enterprise venture appears to be a rip-off for the directors and a potential disaster for the workers?"(68)

Mr Adam Butler:

> "It was the Labour Government of which he was a member which came to the arrangement with Mr De Lorean and if that Government, with its philosophy of nationalisation, was not prepared to have a majority shareholding, he won't be surprised if I do not agree with his proposal." (69)

Mr Alan Clark (Plymouth Sutton, Con.):

> "He and his predecessors were warned consistently from both sides of the House about the commercial prospect of this enterprise and the financial integrity of Mr De Lorean.

Mr De Lorean boasts openly in New York that he has a headlock on the British Government and that it will always pay up in the end.

If the Minister wants to use taxpayers' money on job creation schemes in Northern Ireland, would it not be better to find a way without subsidising the life-style of a lot of American con-men?" (70)

The Cooper and Lybrand study indicated gross liabilities of £106.4m as against gross realisable assets of £91.7m, of which £45.2 m were assets specifically pledged against secured creditors' claims. One of these was DMC, itself!

References:

1. 'Eleven small drops fall into the de Lorean Receivers' empty bucket', John Griffiths, *Financial Times*, 25 November 1982.

2. as 1.

3. 'Half de Lorean firm offered to drugs agent', *The Times*, 22 October 1982.

4. 'The tribulations of trying de Lorean' Ivor Davies, *The Times*, 3 March 1984.

5. 'New deal hope for d.L.', *Daily Telegraph*, 20 February 1982

6. ' "We will survive" says cleared de Lorean', Craig Seton and Christopher Thomas, *The Times*, 13 October 1981.

7. 'How de Lorean's wings were clipped', Roger Eglin, Christopher Hurd and Chris Ryder, *Sunday Times*, 24 January 1982.

8. as 7.

9. 'De Lorean cannot pay off jobless', Patrick Bishop, *Observer*, 31 January 1982.

10. 'John de Lorean has to go', Michael Gillard, *Observer*, 1 August 1982.

11. as 10.

12. 'Ulster: an economic disease which may yet prove fatal', Brendan Keenan, *Financial Times*, 17 March 1982.

13. *Financial Times*, 11 May 1982.

14. *The Times*, 12 October 1981.

15. 'De Lorean - The End', Steve Vines and Jane McCloughlin, *Observer*, 21 February 1982.

16. 'Gull-wing dream car cost taxpayers £84m', Graham Patterson, *Daily Telegraph*, 21 October 1982.

17. 'Positive interest in D.L. plant?', Lisa Wood and Margaret von Hatten, *Financial Times*, 22 October 1982.

18. 'Ulster violence has cost UK £9 billion', Richard Ford, *The Times*, 4 November 1982.

19. as 16.

20. ' "De Lorean Talks were a Poker Game", man who endorsed project says', Anthony Bevins, *The Times*, 22 November 1983.

21. 'The Fast Tycoon', Paul Keel, *Guardian*, 21 October 1982.

22. *The Times*, 21 October 1982.

23. as 12.

24. 'The scandal of de Lorean', Gordon Greig, *Daily Mail*, 21 October 1982

25. as 12.

26. 'Can the Prior jobs plan save Ulster?', Chris Ryder, *Sunday Times*, 21 February 1982.

27. as 12.

28. 'Rise and fall of a Detroit superstar', Henry Miller, *Daily Telegraph*, 21 October 1982.

29. 'Common de Lorean - By an MP', Robert Porter and David Norris, *Daily Mail*, 29 January 1982.

30. Patrick J. Wright (1980). *On a Clear Day you can see General Motors*, London: Sidgwick and Jackson.

31. 'Why Detroit is praying for an economic upturn', Bailey Morris, *The Times*, 26 February 1982.

32. 'World car markets', *Financial Times*, 10 February 1982.

33. 'Uncle Sam is showing his age', Nicholas Ashford, *The Times*, 15 December 1981.

34. 'Road to disaster for US car giants', Paul Johnson, *Now*, 11 July 1980.

35. 'Idle hands threatened by G.M. robots', Alex Brummer, *Guardian*, 13 January 1982.

36. as 35.

37. as 35.

38. 'US manufacturers' losses mount. Reagan pressed for cars summit', *The Times*, 6 November 1981.

39. 'Autoworkers open door to pay concessions', Ian Hargreaves, *Financial Times*, 10 December 1981.

40. GM & Unions join hands to cut prices', *The Times*, 14 January 1982.

41. 'US Ford workers back pay freeze for landslide vote', Henry Miller, *Daily Telegraph*, 2 March 1982.

42. 'GM wants more cuts from car workers', Bailey Morris, *The Times*, 15 March 1982.

43. 'Reagan stands by spending cuts policy', James Srodes, *Daily Telegraph*, 7 November 1981.

44. 'Reagan's recession', Robert Farrell, *Observer*, 22 November 1981.

45. 'Sweeping Reagan cuts to keep Budget pledge', Nicholas Ashford, *The Times*, 25 September 1981. 'Reagan slashes welfare as budget deficit soars', Bailey Morris, *The Times*, 8 February 1982.

46. '8% jobless as US slump worsens', Richard Beeston, *Daily Telegraph*, 7 November 1981.

47. 'US jobless at highest point in over 6 years', Reginald Dale, *Financial Times*, 5 December 1981.

48. 'Why Reagan may lose this time', Reginald Dale, *Financial Times*, 22 February 1982.

49. Article in the *Sunday Times*, 17 January 1982.

50. John de Lorean, quoted in 'Why the jigsaw didn't fit', Neal Ascherson, Hugo Davenport, Eric Dymock, Patrick Bishop, Michael Gillard, Charles Scobie, *Observer*, 24 October 1982.

51. 'Attorney General to clear de Lorean', Philip Robinson and Craig Seton, *The Times*, 12 October 1981.

52. ' "Allegations stupid", says de Lorean', *The Times*, 5 October 1981.

53. as 12.

54. 'De Lorean in car rental talks', Barbara Conway, *Daily Telegraph*, 2 March 1982.

55. 'De Lorean claims £10m "IRA Riot Compensation" ', Colin Brady, *Daily Telegraph*, 5 February 1982.

56. 'De Lorean tries to squeeze out Government', *Observer*, 31 January 1982.

57. 'Attorney G

58. as 6.

59. £84m in public funds already gulped down', Barbara Conway, *Daily Telegraph*, 29 January 1982.

60. 'De Lorean hints at sale', Henry Miller, *Daily Telegraph*, 30 January 1982.

61. ' "I was wrong to launch a Belfast firm," says de Lorean', Christopher Thomas, *The Times*, 1 February 1982.

62. as 51.

63. 'De Lorean - two years of doubts and misgivings', Stella Shamoon, *Sunday Telegraph*, 7 February 1982

64. as 63.

65. 'De Lorean's secret memo on cash chief', Michael Gillard, *Observer*, 7 February 1982.

66. ' "Car plant plight very serious" admits Prior', Bob Redwell, *Guardian*, 26 January 1982.

67. *The Times*, 28 January 1982.

68. as 67.

69. as 67.

70. as 67.

G.C.H.Q.: THE SEAMLESS ROBE

The End of the Affair?

Never before in the life-time of Mrs. Margaret Thatcher's Conservative Government had the initial media comment on one of its policies been so universally and consistently damning. 'A certain dank ineptitude', in the *Guardian*'s caustic view (1), was shown by the moves made by the Government on 25 January 1984.

- to stop staff at the top-secret Government Communications Headquarters from continuing to belong to trade unions; and

- to remove from them the protection afforded by employment legislation.

In exchange, they were to receive an individual pre-tax hand-out of £1,000. In the *Observer*, Alan Watkins argued that:

'Over Cheltenham enlightened public opinion has few doubts. It is not just that freeborn British men and women are being denied the right to belong to the union of their choice. There is also the element of squalor, of bribery and corruption, of money changing hands. There is further the callousness, the insensitivity, the brutality even of the Government's action. Decent people being confronted with the choice of something they do not wish to do or . . . being dismissed without redundancy payment. Whatever the rights and wrongs, the whole operation was bungled from the start.' (2)

Even strong traditional supporters of the Conservative Government's policies were highly critical. 'The Government's handling of the ban has been little short of shambolic' announced the *Daily Telegraph* (3) and its sister publication, the *Sunday Telegraph*, pursued the same theme in its editorial of 5 February:

'So many have been the Government's mishaps over the Cheltenham Intelligence Centre that it is now, to use an Americanism, in a "no-win" situation. After all this confusion, even if GCHQ is eventually de-unionised — and that is quite a big if — the political price will be needlessly high. Can it really be that Ministers did not appreciate the politically-explosive nature of what they were doing? . . . And now the initial misjudgement has been followed by a series of flounderings which amount to the biggest flop in policy presentation in years.' (4)

Initial misjudgement? Series of flounderings? Absolutely not, in the

TO BE COMPLETED BY ALL GCHQ STAFF.

Complete either A or B.

A. I . . . . have read and understood General Notice 100/84 and wish to continue to be employed at GCHQ.

I agree to resign from membership of any trade union to which I belong. I also undertake not to join a trade union or to engage in its affairs or to discuss with its officers my terms of employment or conditions of service or any other matter relating to any employment at GCHQ. I understand, however, that I may join a departmental staff association approved for the time being by Director, GCHQ.

B. I . . . . have read and understood General Notice 100/84. I do not wish to continue to be employed at GCHQ. I wish to be considered for a transfer elsewhere in the Civil Service.

EXHIBIT 1: SIGN HERE PLEASE (5)

view of the Prime Minister quizzed during a visit to Budapest about the possibility of the resignation of Sir Geoffrey Howe, the Foreign Secretary, over the matter:

> "Goodness me, no. I have every confidence in the Foreign Secretary. I have worked with him. I have negotiated with him. He is splendid. He is an absolutely master of negotiations." (6)

But in spite of such a positive view, the Conservative Government was still having problems with its GCHQ ban eleven months after its announcement and after it had scored a virtual 'knock-out' legal victory in the House of Lords. Norman Willis, newly-elected General Secretary of the TUC, said on hearing the Law Lord's verdict:

> "If the Government think this is the end of the GCHQ affair, they are badly mistaken." (7)

He, six 'rebel' GCHQ staff members who had refused to be deunionised and a phalanx of human rights supporters planned, as of November 1984, to take the union-ban case to the European Court of Human Rights in Strasbourg. Willis continued:

> "Despite what their Lordships say, it remains morally wrong for the workers to be denied the right to union representation." (8)

And, if this were not enough of a worry for the Government, there was the prospect to consider of the merger of two of the civil service unions which had been prominent in rejecting the union-banning policy. If the plan were agreed at their respective annual conferences in 1985, the Society of Civil and Public Servants (executive grades) and the Civil and Public Services Association (clerical grades) would merge into one union with almost a quarter of a million members. (9)

> "I think this is a struggle for the survival of civil liberties in Britain and, if you allow the right to join a voluntary organization to be taken away, the next stage is the loss of the ballot paper."

EXHIBIT 2: TONY BENN'S VIEW (10)

The most ironic result of all occurred, however, when − with 67 GCHQ staff still unionised, according to the Government − the Treasury began negotiation of a special GCHQ pay claim in December 1984. Of the five members elected by staff as their negotiating team:

- one was a trade unionist who had refused to renounce his membership,
- one had rejoined his union after the ban came into force on 1 March 1984, and
- one had been politically very active before the ban.

So the Treasury was placed in the invidious position of having to negotiate directly with a team dominated by Civil Service trade unionists from a top secret Government establishment who were patently flouting a legal ban. (11) Hardly an enviable situation!

Nor was there pleasure for the Government in the three-day series of meetings and rallies launched by the TUC on 25 January 1985 to commemorate the anniversary of the ban . . .

Hush-Hush Stuff

According to Tom King, Secretary of State for Employment, "The Government action in respect of the Cheltenham Communications Centre was taken solely in the interest of national security." (12) Certainly, so secret was the nature of the work of the Centre that, not until the revelations involved in the trial of the spy GCHQ-linguist Geoffrey Prime, was its very existence as an intelligence agency publicly acknowledged. After the hugely-important Prime affair it was widely known that:

> "The Government Communication Headquarters is a very special organisation with a very special product . . . Intimate and continually-updated information on the diplomatic and military intentions of potential enemies, which only signals of the highest quality can provide, is of inestimable value for those charged with making foreign and defence policy." (13)

It was also known, but by no means so widely, that:

> "Under a secret 1946 treaty (known in Whitehall as You-Koo-Sah) Britain and the USA parcel out the world between them for the purpose of . . . electronic intelligence. The National Security Agency, the US equivalent of GCHQ, funds a substantial proportion of the British effort . . . It provides advanced equipment and seconded personnel for Cheltenham's world-wide network of listening posts known as the Composite Signals Organisation." (14)

Also under the treaty:

> "Every Wednesday morning an American, a Canadian, an Australian and a New Zealander join offices and civil servants from our security and intelligence establishments and the Ministry of Defence, the Treasury, and the Cabinet Office" for a meeting of ". . . the Joint Intelligence Committee." "The meeting deals with assessments of current intelligence." (15)

It is estimated that 7,000 staff are employed at the Cheltenham Centre and 2,000 elsewhere in 'electronic intelligence-gathering' posts (16) which range from Cyprus to Scarborough, Little Sai Wan (Hong Kong) to Bude, and Ascension Island to Singapore. (17) They include specialised linguists, cryptographers, radio monitor and computer staff. (18) The last named group of personnel faces an even greater degree of interdependence with their American counterparts, since:

> "A new computer system, code-named 'Platform', is due to link more than 50 separate systems and, more significantly, will integrate GCHQ more closely with the NSA at Fort Meade, Maryland." (19)

The enormous significance of uninterrupted intelligence from GCHQ was considered by the Government to be obvious. (20) Hence the extent to which past disruptions of the system (see Table 1) had caused the Government considerable alarm, although it was stressed by all parties in the union ban debate that only a tiny minority of GCHQ

Dates	Disruption
23 February 1979 and 22 June 1979	One day strikes.
September 1979	Work to rule and overtime ban took place just after the invasion of Afghanistan.
20 December 1979 to 13 February 1980	Disruptive action.
27 November 1980	Protest meeting.
9 March 1981	One day strike followed by disruptive action which occurred during the period of the unsuccessful attempt to assassinate President Reagan and the solidarity strike in Poland.
10 June 1982 to 26 August 1982	Overtime ban at outstations.

TABLE 1 : **DISRUPTIONS RECORDED** (21)

personnel was involved at any one time and that the service was never placed in jeopardy. On the other hand, Sir Geoffrey Howe declared in a series of Commons written answers on 30 January 1984 that union action might even have affected operations during the Beirut refugee camp massacre and the Falklands War. (22) Furthermore, it was asserted by the media that the Americans had communicated their dissatisfaction to the UK Government about industrial disputes, particularly in respect of 'crisis monitoring'. (23) For example, Washington was said to have been 'incensed' on 8 March 1981 − the first day of a five-month Civil Service pay dispute − when technicians disrupted the working of the Ascension Island station and the tracking station at Bude, which feeds its data to the National reconnaissance Office in Washington. The ensuing months of sporadic upsets also had a bearing on WINTEX, the biannual exercise in which NATO partners simulate the transitional stages to war with Warsaw Pact forces. (24)

Whilst the Government was at pains to reject the notion that American pressure lay behind the ban, (25) it is crystal-clear that concern with the effects of the 1981 disruption greatly influenced the thinking of Sir Brian Tovey, then Director of GCHQ and now advisor of Plessey, the telecommunications firm. His verdict was:

> "It made us look ridiculous. We (i.e. the British and the Americans) do not interfere with each other, but having said that, Americans could not be unconcerned if a major partner fell down on the job . . .

We noticed a reluctance to enter into work-sharing and we read this as a message. It was the beginning of a reluctant feeling that 'Oh Lord, we don't know whether we can rely on the Brits'." (26)

This sentiment was clearly shared by his GCHQ predecessor, Sir Arthur Bonsall. (27)

> "Inevitably, the already jaded parallel with George ('Big Brother is watching you') Orwell's image of 1984 was paraded yesterday. Britain is not on the road to tyranny: it is where it has been poised for a century, poised between the requirements of popular democracy and the ancient practices of an oligarchical, secretive system of government which has never quite come to terms with the extensions of the franchise."

EXHIBIT 3: A GUARDED GREETING FOR THE LAUNCH OF THE 1984 CAMPAIGN FOR FREEDOM OF INFORMATION ON 5 AUGUST 1984 (28)

There was absolutely no denying the purposive nature of the planned trade union disruption. The announcement made by them at the start of their action on 8 March 1981 read:

> "There will be a range of selective and disruptive action which will affect Britain's secret communications surveillance network. There will be both national and international repercussions." (29)

EXHIBIT 4:   **THE INTELLIGENCE WEB** (30)

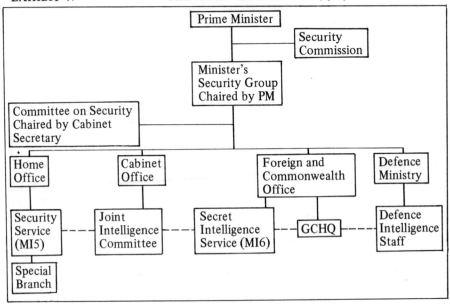

Lies, Damned Lies . . .

Behind the union ban lay, it was claimed, a 'de-unionisation' plan that had been drawn up and submitted to the Government by Sir Brian Tovey in 1982. It took account of what he called the 'subtle relationship' with the Americans and the fact that it would be, in the words of Vice Admiral Bobby Inman, ex Director of NSA, a "marvellous move". (31) The Americans, explained Sir Brian:

> ". . . had always been puzzled by the presence of the unions. They have a cast-iron organisation at NSA. If anyone goes on strike, they get the sack." (32)

| Donald Maclean |
| Guy Burgess |
| Kim Philby |
| John Vassall |
| Anthony Blunt |
| Geoffrey Prime |

TABLE 2:   KEY POST-WAR CIVIL SERVICE SPIES

A quite different viewpoint was given, on the other hand, by John Sheldon, General Secretary of the Civil Service Union. He claimed:

> "This is a cover-up. The real reason for the announcement (of the ban) is that they are having pressure put on them to introduce the polygraph (lie detector). It is the USA putting the pressure on the Government about its security system." (33)

This opinion was shared by Jeremy Windust, a member of the Coordinating Committee of GCHQ Trade Unions (34) and Ken Jones of the Society of Civil and Public Servants.

It was indeed the case that the Security Commission investigation of the case of Geoffrey Prime — jailed in November 1982 for 35 years for selling secrets to the Soviet Union — had recommended the use of the lie detector and General Notice 100/84 had specified, in Paragraph 7, that staff would be subject to 'any recommendations of the Security Commission accepted by Government'. Even so, the prospect does not seem to have been viewed with great enthusiasm by the authorities. The minutes of a meeting on 8 July 1983 between Sir Robert Armstrong, Cabinet Secretary and Head of the Home Civil Service, and a Civil Service Trade Union team called in to discuss the matter, were quoted as stating (35) that Sir Robert 'would not find the use of the

> "The polygraph has four long, thin pens which are attached to highly sensitive instruments measuring breathing, pulse rate and skin moisture. A belt is placed around the subject's chest to monitor respiration. A blood pressure cuff goes around the arm, while electrodes round the first and middle fingers measure sweating. The readings are transferred electronically and trace wavering lines on a moving belt of graph paper. Operators are trained to interpret significant variations in these lines while the subject is being questioned. The theory is to measure physical reaction to three types of questioning: relevant, irrelevant and control."

EXHIBIT 5: 'NOW, WHAT DID YOU SAY YOUR NAME WAS?'(36)

polygraph attractive. But the Security Commission said it was the one thing that might have deterred Prime'. Also, in a letter dated 9 January 1984 to the Council of Civil Service Unions about the purely experimental use of the polygraph, Sir Robert had affirmed that:

> "There is no decision to proceed from that (pilot scheme) to a scheme for the definitive introduction of the polygraph in security screening. That decision remains entirely open and will be for consideration when we are in a position to assess and analyse the results of the pilot study." (37)

The experiment was proceeded with but did not, in fact, run smoothly or quickly. The first stage was, according to an Intelligence Report by the American Bar Association, a visit by two members of MI5 for training at the US Polygraph Training School in Alabama. (38) The second was the purchase in October/November of six 'Ultrascribe' (39) polygraph sets from the Chicago manufacturer, Stoelting, two of which were later found to be faulty and had to be returned. The third stage was the polygraph testing of senior GCHQ managers — nearly all of whom had volunteered — which was under way in May 1984 at MI5. (40) At this time, no machines were based at Cheltenham and no middle/lower-ranking staff had apparently been tested. (41)

Part of the difficulty involved in getting the pilot scheme under way must have been the high degree of resistance shown, on technical grounds alone, by some interested parties. Whilst the 1500-strong American Polygraphers Association claimed up to 95 per cent accuracy with their equipment and approach (42) — and they should have had evidence for their view since all CIA staff must take lie detector tests — there were many powerful detractors, for example:

- Dr. John Beary, US Assistant Secretary for Health: "The polygraph does not work . . . It is an excitement-detector, not a lie detector'. (43)

- Professor David Lykken, a psychologist from the University of Minnesota and a leading USA critic of the polygraph: "It is dangerous and counter-productive and wrong at least a third of the time. It is a menace to be suppressed". It is "asinine". (44) "Apart from the damage to the careers and reputations of innocent persons, this decision (to use the polygraph at GCHQ) is likely to result in the loss to the Government of some of its most conscientious civil servants, replacing them with under-socialised types." (45)

- Dr. Douglas Carroll of Birmingham University: "The device is inaccurate and likely to jeopardise the lives of conscientious civil servants. Its introduction should be resisted by all trade union members". (46)

Such views had received powerful support from American researchers, Dr. Benjamin Kleinmuntz and Dr. Julian Szucko of the University of Illinois, who had found "unacceptably high" error rates in their experiments with polygraphs. (47)

Neil Kinnock, Leader of the Opposition:

"The Prime Minister is travelling to Hungary this afternoon. While she is there, will she be discussing the right of people to belong to independent trade unions?" *(Labour cheers)*

Mrs. Thatcher, Prime Minister

"If I did, I should also discuss the right not to belong to trade unions." *(Conservative cheers)*

House of Commons, 2 February 1984.

EXHIBIT 6:   **TIT FOR TAT (48)**

Trade unionists were made aware of these broadsides at a Society of Civil and Public Servants Polygraph Conference at the Festival Hall in London on 26 January (addressed by Professor Lykken) (49) and at a Cheltenham meeting in late March 1984, when Dr. Carroll stated that, unless trade unions successfully rejected the lie detector's use at Cheltenham, it would be brought in by institutions throughout Britain.(50)

Attacks were not restricted to those from the technically-qualified, however. Charles Irving, Conservative MP for Cheltenham, joined the fray by insisting that "the polygraph has a record of proven failure. The trained infiltrator will get round the test" (51) by self-hypnosis, yoga-type meditation, or thought-transference. For former Home Secretary, Merlyn Rees, who sought to introduce a bill in the Commons to monitor the polygraph's use, it was "pseudo-scientific".(52) Dissatisfaction with the credibility of the performance of the machine was also expressed by the Commons Employment Committee which, after a 10 month inquiry, produced a report which stopped just short of calling for a ban on the polygraph's use in business. John Gorst, Committee member, declared:

> "The evidence was all there to justify calling for an outright and immediate ban on the use of the polygraph in the private sector." (53)

Intriguingly, Sir Brian Tovey had claimed that, before the Security Commission's investigation of the Prime affair, he did not know what a polygraph was! (54)

An Offer You Can't Refuse

Sir Geoffrey Howe's statement to the House of Commons on 25 January 1984 was restrained in expression, sober in delivery and wholly unexpected in content. He declared:

> "As the House knows, the Employment Protection Acts contain provisions which enable the Government to exempt Crown employees from the application of the Acts. These provisions can be used only for the purpose of safeguarding national security and reflect the acknowledged need for particularly sensitive functions of government to be protected so far as possible from the risk of exposure of disruption.
>
> Government Communications Headquarters is responsible for intelligence work of crucial importance to our national security. To be effective this work must be conducted secretly. Moreover, GCHQ must provide a service which can be relied on with confidence at all times . .
>
> The House will wish to know that, for these reasons, I have today signed certificates excepting GCHQ employees from the application of the relevant provision.
>
> The certificates have immediate effect and new conditions of service are at the same time being introduced at GCHQ. Under these new conditions, staff will be permitted in future to belong only to a departmental staff association approved by their Director . . . The Government fully respects the right of civil servants to be members of a trade union and it is only the special nature of the work of the GCHQ which has led us to take these measures. I can assure the House, therefore, that it is not our intention to introduce similar measures outside the

field of security and intelligence. GCHQ staff are being informed this afternoon. Those who decide to remain at GCHQ will each receive a payment of £1,000 in recognition of the fact that certain rights which they have hitherto enjoyed are being withdrawn from them in the interests of national security." (55)

This utterance was greeted with incredulity by some MPs and fury by others. Dennis Skinner (Labour) — known to media commentators as 'The Beast of Bolsover' — led the latter group in a full-blooded onslaught. He thundered:

"All fascists throughout the ages have used the cloak of national security and national interest in order to chip away at hard-won liberties and freedoms, especially among the trade unions. What evidence is there that those who belong to trade unions are more likely to hinder national interests than those who come from Eton and Harrow and that belly of the establishment? How many shop stewards have betrayed the country?" (56)

Sir Geoffrey Howe gave a sharp response:

"It is a measure designed to uphold the very freedoms that would be threatened by fascism, not least fascism of a socialist kind. The evidence which justified this measure is the evidence that convinced the last Labour Government of the need to include these measures in the employment protection legislation." (57)

Ex-Foreign Secretary, Dennis Healey, was in the van of those who could hardly believe their ears:

"The House must be told why the Government decided after all these years to deprive employees of GCHQ of rights enjoyed by Civil Servants in the Ministry of Defence and the Foreign Office who are doing work of national importance too.

This is depriving them of rights to industrial organisation which are enjoyed by the Royal Ordnance Factories and in private factories like Vickers and Plessey which are doing work involving security control to the nation's security. What consultation did he have before taking this decision, with the elected representatives of the GCHQ? . . . with the Security Commission? . . .

This is a very grave decision he has announced . . . I would appeal to him not to implement that decision before he has consulted the representatives of the employees concerned . . . " (58)

The Foreign Secretary's reply to this was equally terse, and definitive. He declared that it was not a matter for the Security Commission and that "it would not have been appropriate in a matter of this kind" for there to have been consultations with the trade unions at the GCHQ. He continued:

> "I appreciate the importance of the matter and for that reason there has been long and careful consideration of, for example, the need to avoid a repetition of the industrial action which took place in the three years 1979 to 1981 which faces staff doing this kind of work with severely conflicting loyalties . . . I remind the House that the provisions which I have invoked are already applied to other aspects of the Security Service (i.e. MI5 and MI6) and are bound in statutes passed by the last Labour Government of which Mr. Healey was a member." (59)

The trade unions' angry reaction to this removal of their GCHQ members from the protection of Industrial Courts and Tribunals and to the loss of membership by 1 March 1984 was predictable:

- "An unprincipled onslaught on basic trade unions and human rights which is of the utmost gravity to the trade union movement as a whole. There must be a real danger that the rights of many thousands of other workers dealing with security issues in private industry as well as other Civil Servants will then be at risk." (60)

- "This decision . . . is an appalling and unacceptable denial of human rights. It is grossly offensive for the Foreign Secretary to imply that the fact of Trade Union membership poses any threat to national security . . . The most extreme measure . . . the offer of a tame, state-controlled union backed up by a £1,000 bribe is no alternative to the right of genuine trade union membership." (61) *(Len Murray, TUC General Secretary)*

- "Judas money . . . an offensive bribe." (62) *(John Sheldon, General Secretary of Civil Service Union)*

- "I would have expected this from General Jaruzelski in Poland but not from the Prime Minister of a democratic state. I do not believe that people's civil and trade union liberties can be bought for £1,000." (63) *(Alistair Graham, General Secretary of Civil and Public Services Association)*

- "An extra-ordinarily inept piece of mismanagement . . . entirely counter-productive." (64) *(John Astin, Chairman of the Cabinet Office Branch of the First Division Association)*

Fuel was added to an already roaring fire when it became known, through a Commons reply by Barney Heyhoe (Minister of State at the

Element	Year			
	1983-1984	1984-1985	1985-1986	1986-1987
Total Cash provision (£bn.)	15.716	17.031	18.060	18.66
% rise over previous year		8.4	6.0	3.3
Provision on Falkland Islands (£bn.)		0.684	0.552	0.450
% of total public spending		13.5		
% of Gross Domestic Product		5.2		
Per capita expenditure (£)		300		330
Defence Manpower (thousands)				
— Services	320		329	
— Civilian	209		179	

TABLE 3:   PUBLIC EXPENDITURE ON DEFENCE (65)

Treasury) to a question from Alan Williams (Shadow Deputy Leader of the Commons), that some GCHQ employees who refused to leave their union and would not accept alternative positions would be treated as if they had resigned. (66) "Political dynamite" was the description of this matter by Williams, and Sir Geoffrey Howe wasted little time before attempting to clarify the Government's position. His statement said:

'Every effort will be made to transfer to other departments staff who are unwilling to remain in GCHQ under the new conditions. And GCHQ will continue to employ them while this is being done. Staff for whom it proves impossible to arrange a transfer to another department will be eligible for premature retirement on redundancy terms.

Those who refuse to move to an alternative suitable post . . . as was made clear on January 25 . . . will not be treated as redundant nor be be entitled to any compensation. The existing conditions of service relating to redundancy provide that a civil servant who refuses to move to a suitable post anywhere in the country in the case of a mobile officer and anywhere within daily travelling distance of his home in the case of a non-mobile officer is treated to all intents and purposes as if he had resigned.' (67)

This did nothing to assuage Alan Williams' wrath:

"That is the most brazen, unrepentant and incompetent response I have ever heard from a Minister . . . Is it not incredible that, in his statement of last month . . . the Foreign Secretary thought there were only three options available to civil servants and seemed to be utterly unaware of the fourth, critical and penal option he has just spelled out to the House? . . . He has revealed a level of incompetence that would be unforgivable in the greenest and newest parliamentary secretary."

(68)

Neil Kinnock followed this diatribe with one of his own:

"The civil servants are being forced to surrender their civil rights and we are now learning that if they don't surrender they will lose their financial rights . . . This is not a matter of usual practice, this is a matter of calculated victimization of people against whom the Government is using the worst sort of financial coercion. In this form it is despotism, no more and no less." (69)

Sir Geoffrey replied by stating that the chance of employment termination had been made perfectly clear in the notice received by GCHQ staff on 25 January. He also remarked:

"Mr. Kinnock has an infinite capacity for destroying such case as he has by exaggeration and by hyperbole. His case simply will not wash."

(70)

"Jaw-Jaw and War-War"

It had been the first time in two years that Len Murray, TUC General Secretary, had been inside 10 Downing Street on official business — and it had not been a fruitful visit. (71) Despite what was regarded as a major concession, the TUC's attempt at negotiation on 1 February had failed. Bill McCall (Chairman of the Main Policy Committee of the Council of Civil Service Unions and a member of the 16-strong trade union deputation led by Len Murray) said:

"We told the Premier we were not offering a no-strike agreement for the whole of the civil service but a no-disruption agreement in an area which the Government says is vital for security. We say that such an agreement should remove all uncertainties and all conflict of loyalties." (72)

The Prime Minister did not agree. She countered uncompromisingly by listing four factors of especial concern which she considered could only be satisfied by the action the Government had taken. (73)

Said Sir Geoffrey Howe:

"The Prime Minister made clear that the Government position and the offer to GCHQ staff stands. We believe our position is right." (74)

Bill McCall was not optimistic about future prospects, particularly as Mrs. Thatcher had confirmed that she could not withdraw the certificates. (75)

No disclosure	Management cannot explain/justify its actions in cases brought before Industrial Tribunals on the grounds of security.
No disruption	The GCHQ's total efficiency must be maintained at all times.
No intrusion	External trade union officials pose a major difficulty. Security problems may be posed by their negotiating over internal labour problems.
No loyalty conflict	Avoidance of any loyalty conflict during external industrial disputes.

TABLE 4: THE PRIME MINISTER'S FOUR POINTS (77)

The rejection of the TUC team's offer — "I don't think she quite understands the enormity of what she has done" (76) was the view of Alistair Graham — unleashed a flood of protest moves. Within the Civil Service sphere of action, plans were being drawn up for legal action in the High Court and protest meetings of staff at Cheltenham and outstations.

By contrast the Government was clearly intent on reviewing the possibilities of a solution based on Section 18(4) of the Trade Union and Labour Relations Act 1974 which states that agreements to prohibit strikes and disruption can be legally binding provided they are in

"All the democratic validity of an Albanian General Election."

EXHIBIT 7: NEIL KINNOCK'S COMMENT ON THE GCHQ TALKS
(78)

writing. Notably, a no-strike agreement had already been concluded in respect of Britain's Polaris submarine activity at Rosyth and Faslane on the Clyde. (79)

Further discussions between the unions and the management side did produce, however, a seemingly positive result (80), despite reservations from Alistair Graham that "She wants total slavery here" (81) and Sir Robert Armstrong's view that "The GCHQ is a seamless robe". (82)

The document which resulted from the further meetings was a remarkable one. The unions pledged:

- not to instruct, or even ask, their members to take industrial action.

- not to 'put at risk the continuous maintenance, 24 hours a day, seven days a week of essential security and intelligence services at GCHQ'.

These pledges would come into operation if the union membership ban were lifted. Mrs. Thatcher — dubbed 'The Iron Lady' by the media — and the unions discussed the document at a meeting held on 23 February (preceded by a lobby of Parliament). During the meeting, the Prime Minister was informed by Len Murray that:

- there was no basis in law for her action

- there was nothing in the Conservative's last election manifesto to support her decision

- the Conservative Government's own Green Paper on Trade Union Immunities had emphasised that the freedom of employees to combine had come to be accepted as a hall-mark of a free society. (83)

According to Bill McCall, the 'cast-iron' proposals included a statement that:

"There shall be included in the conditions of service of staff in GCHQ a provision that they will take no action which would or might interfere with the uninterrupted operation of essential security and intelligence services." (84)

The omens did not look good, however, as the Commons skirmish that took place before the meeting indicated:

Neil Kinnock:

"It is possible to get a solution which guarantees civil rights and security because union members there (at GCHQ) are fully and irrevocably dedicated both to civil liberties and security."

Mrs. Margaret Thatcher:

"I hear what he said. I believe that the Government decision announced on 25 January remains the only effective guarantee of our objectives which, I believe, are widely shared."

Neil Kinnock:

"She is seeing the unions. If she is stubborn in that view, precisely what is the point of a further meeting? She would be pre-occupied with the values of democracy and the interests of national security entirely . . . clearing her mind of any desire to defend what was initially an ill-advised and thoroughly perverse decision." (85) It was, he contended, "A question of personal vanity". (86)

The subsequent failure of the meeting resulted in the immediate call by the unions to their 600,000 Civil Service members (excepting those at GCHQ) for a half day strike on 28 February as "a demonstration of repugnance and anger". (87)

Mike King, Secretary of the Cheltenham Branch of the First Division Association, put the supposed view of his members by refusing to sign on for the new "1984-style" GCHQ and writing in his union magazine that:

"I am insulted that my membership (of FDA) is represented as a threat to the security of the state for, like the rest of those at GCHQ, I consider myself a loyal, responsible and patriotic citizen." (88)

Even the organisation of Conservative Trade Unionists was hostile to the Government's approach, which they thought had led to "adverse consequences and damage to the Conservative Party". (89) What was particularly paradoxical was that it had coincided with a Conservative Trade Unionists' membership drive and that the new booklet produced for the drive (called by its critics *The Infiltrators' Bible*) contained in its preface — written by John Selwyn Gummer, the Party Chairman — the statement:

"I want to see trade unionists play an increasingly central part in all that we do." (90)

In the face of these attacks and a blast from Lord Bancroft, former Head of the Home Civil Service, that the Government's conduct had been "breathtakingly inept — a further exploration of the bloody fool branch of management science", (93) the Government stood firm. Nor

David Owen (Plymouth Devonport, SDP):

"In order to reach a settlement of the dispute at GCHQ, will she (the PM) consider a 3-fold package in which certification under the Employment Protection Act remains on the table, a no-strike agreement is negotiated with the unions and the Government withdraw its administrative decision to deprive any of the people at Cheltenham of trade union rights."

Mrs. Margaret Thatcher:

"The principle that members of organisations concerned with national security should not be members of national unions is a familiar one which already applies to the police and intelligence services. I believe the proposals we made are the only ones which will fully reach the Government's objectives." (92)

Martin Flannery (Sheffield Hillsborough, Labour):

"Coming out against the working people at GCHQ having the right to be in unions is seen as a continuation of the anti-trade union groups like the pro-Nazi group which is deeply embedded in the bowels of the Tory party. *(Conservative protests)* It is bigger than I thought."

Mrs. Margaret Thatcher:

"Mr. Flannery must be hard put to it for a question. People from all over this House fought against Nazi-Socialism . . . and we all resent any implication to the contrary . . . The majority of those at GCHQ have accepted the Government offer and a minimal number have refused it." (93)

EXHIBIT 8:   **PRINCIPLES & PRACTICES**

was its stance affected by the blistering onslaught from the Opposition's spokesman on Foreign and Commonwealth matters, Dennis Healey, during a 6½ hour Commons debate on 27 February. He called the decision 'a kick in the teeth' for union leaders, like Len Murray, who had sought a constructive relationship with Government, and he accused Sir Geoffrey Howe of being "the laughing stock of the world". He also lampooned the Prime Minister by referring to the "Mephistopheles behind Sir Geoffrey's shabby Faust" and the "Great She-elephant" and "Catherine the Great of Finchley".

More pertinently, he quoted Sir John Nott who, as Secretary of State for Defence, had stated in April 1981 that the civil service action taken in 1981 had in no way "affected our operational capabilities". (94) Former Labour Prime Minister James Callaghan referred similarly during the debate to the fact that previous Conservative Foreign Secretaries Lord Carrington and Francis Pym had also not felt the need to act in respect of union membership.

The Foreign Secretary responded with a critical quotation from the Civil Service Campaign Report of 1981, which stated that "our (i.e. the Civil Service Unions') ultimate success depends on the extent to which defence readiness is hampered . . . by this and further disruptive action". (95) He then argued that, whilst the union proposals did represent an undoubted effort at improvement, they did not deal with the key factor of the monopoly position for union representatives at GCHQ.

Another element in this viewpoint had been previously dealt with by John Selwyn Gummer who had declared that:

> "If the security of the whole nation is in some way imperilled by the use of GCHQ as a pressure point of Government, then the Government has got to make sure that the defence of the nation comes first." (96)

Mrs. Thatcher, evidently pleased with the vote victory (201 to 25), despite numerous Tory abstentions in her high-majority Government ranks, told the Commons in what the *Daily Telegraph* correspondent, Edward Pearce, deprecatingly called her "tin duchess drawl" (97):

> "A majority of 176 is good enough for me . . . I agree that I am stubborn about pursuing matters of national security. The people of this country expect no less." (98)

The TUC-supported half day of protest on 28 February 1984 caused widespread but relatively low-key disruption in public transport, London newspaper production, vehicle plants, docks and shipyards. The

---

The Fleet Street branch of the engineers union, the AUEW, took a decision tonight to withdraw their members' labour from all Fleet Street offices . . . An irrational and totally unjustified decision whatever the views may be held in regard to the current Cheltenham dispute. There appears to be an unaccountable and totally cynical disregard for the future of the industry which provides the AUEW members in Fleet Street with a very good living. It will be the intention of all NPA members to pursue all possible legal remedies to obtain maximum damages that can be recovered in the circumstances. (99)

**EXHIBIT 9:   THE VIEW OF THE NEWSPAPER PUBLISHERS
ASSOCIATION**

union message was rammed home at rallies in major cities. At Manchester, Alistair Graham proclaimed:

> "When it comes to a defence of basic trade union rights, there will be no moderates in the trade union movement. We are all extremists now." (100)

It did not impress the Government to learn that a union spokesman described the result as "probably the biggest piece of industrial action that the Civil Service has ever seen". (101) The newspaper headlines on 29 February indicated that 'Thatcher rules out more talks on GCHQ ban'. (102)

Short Shrift . . .

The report by the Commons Select Committee on Employment, on its investigation of the GCHQ union ban, made interesting reading. Its recommendations were greeted enthusiastically by the civil service trade unions as giving a much needed fillip to their campaign to achieve a

---

1. The union ban should be withdrawn on the proviso of a satisfactory accord between the Government and the unions which maintains 'both the essential continuity of operations at GCHQ and also freedom of association and the right of membership of a trade union'.
2. The procedure for implementing the ban should be immediately 'frozen'.
3. The unions should give whatever 'legally-binding' assurances the Government requires.
4. Whatever the agreement made in respect of the GCHQ, it should not be regarded as a precedent for use elsewhere.
5. The Prime Minister's invitation to talks should be taken up immediately by TUC leaders and the Council of Civil Service Unions.

EXHIBIT 10: THE COMMITTEE'S RECOMMENDATIONS (103)

negotiated settlement of the dispute. Mike Barke, Cheltenham Coordinator for the CCSU, commented:

> "The Select Committee Report has put the ball in the Government's court and appears to open the way to a negotiated settlement and that will bring great relief. However, local union representatives at GCHQ will want to look very carefully at the precise terms of any proposed agreement to make sure that unions at GCHQ are not emasculated."
>
> (104)

The official CCSU statement was less guarded. It welcomed the "positive lead" given by the committee and stated "Their report fully vindicated our approach in seeking a negotiated settlement". (105) For Len Murray it was a welcome boost to his position:

> "The Select Committee has recognised that the Government cannot remove the right to trade union membership by diktat." (106)

The Government, by contrast, saw little in the report issued on 15 February to cause it to alter course, as Mrs. Thatcher made plain in her first question time in the Commons after returning from a visit to Russia on 16 February 1984. Labour MP Geoffrey Robinson had stated:

> "The reckless bungling by Sir Geoffrey Howe . . . has caused enormouse and unnecessary damage to the international standing of our security system and to the individual integrity of employees" and "the six point programme in the recommendations of the report represents a reasoned and constructive basis for an agreement to be reached." (107)

The Prime Minister, who was suffering from a bad cold, replied hoarsely:

> "I note that the Committee endorsed the Government's objectives but take a different view of how to achieve them.
>
> The Committee is entitled to its views but we remain convinced that the Government's approach provides the only effective guarantee to meet those objectives." (108)

Virtually the same reply was given in an exchange with Neil Kinnock, who had asked:

> "Can I sympathise with the Prime Minister with her throat difficulty? I promise privately to offer the name of a very good lozenge which I have found to be efficacious . . .
>
> The Select Committee produced not only a constructive but a unanimous report. In the light of these developments, does she not realise that failure to adopt a course like the one suggested by the Select Committee would be to abandon fair play and common sense and to neglect the national interest?" (109)

The Prime Minister's concern with the avoidance of any sort of disruption at GCHQ was further highlighted by her response to a question from Conservative MP Michael Howard:

> "Is it not remarkable that, during all of the many exchanged which have taken place across the floor of the House on GCHQ since 25 Jan-

uary, not a single member in any of the Opposition benches has utter-
ed a word of condemnation of the industrial activity which disrupted
activities there, including those activities which took place between
February and April 1979 when Dr. David Owen had direct ministerial
responsibility for these matters?" (110)

Conservative

Anthony Baldry (Banbury)
John Gorst (Hendon N.)*
Gerard Neale (Cornwall N.)
Mrs. Elizabeth Peacock (Batley Spen)
Andrew Rowe (Kent Mid.)
Peter Thurnham (Bolton N.E.)

Labour

Ronald Leighton (Newham N.E.)**
Gordon Brown (Dunfermline E.)
Donald Dixon (Jarrow)
Kenneth Eastham (Manchester, Blackley)
Greville Janner (Leicester West)

* Resigned as leader of the Tory group on 9 February
** Chairman of the Committee

TABLE 5:   EMPLOYMENT COMMITTEE MEMBERSHIP

The Commons Select Committee had laboured long and hard at its
task of reviewing the GCHQ policy move. It had sought evidence from
a wide range of participants and had been successful except in the
cases of Peter Marychurch (GCHQ Director) and Jack Hart (Chairman
of the trade union side of the Civil Service Whitely Council at GCHQ)
whom the Government did not allow to participate in the enquiry. It
had learned a lot.

Bill McCall, for example, in answer to the question of whether the
unions at GCHQ had disrupted security, had told committee members:
"I would say that the straight answer to that is, yes we have". (111)
They had been informed of the secret no-strike deals on Polaris. (112)
Sir Geoffrey Howe had revealed, during a two-hour grilling at the
Committee, the nature of the disruption in March 1981 and the fact
that in 1980 informal attempts were made to try to get a no-strike
deal at GCHQ, but these had proved sterile. (113) Gerry Gilman, General Secretary of the Society of Civil and Public Servants, had been

Dick Pinhey, Engineer "I will not work for any organisation that denies me basic human rights." *Dave Blogg, Design Engineer* "As a body we have strength, but I don't know. With a wife and family, who can afford principles?"

EXHIBIT 11: A VIEW FROM INSIDE CHELTENHAM GCHQ (115)

ready to guarantee the maintenance of 'essential services' but was not a supporter of "a blanket agreement covering everybody". (114) Alistair Graham saw the Government's move as a gigantic bluff (116) since, in his view, it would take five years before some of Cheltenham specialists could be replaced with others equally trained. Despite the linguistic decorum of the Report, the Committee had not been greatly impressed on four points in particular.

- *The imposition of the ban*
  "We do not wish to add further to the criticisms that have been made by others: we would simply observe that the handling of this issue could not be described as a model of its kind."
- *The tardiness of the Government's response to the problem*
  "Does this mean that, but for the exposure of a spy, which led to the avowal, the Government would have continued indefinitely to be seriously disturbed about possible threats to national security at GCHQ and yet be prepared to take no action?"
- *The way in which the 'ban decision' had been taken*
  Apparently without full cabinet consideration.
- *The acceptability of the union plan*
  A 'key passage' in Sir Brian Tovey's evidence suggested that the union alternative plan would have "met all the requirements that were necessary" at the time when he was drawing up his plan.

Some of its authors were even more forthright when interviewed. Ronald Leighton called the Government's conduct 'ham fisted'. (118) John Gorst, champion (in the 1976-1977 Grunwick dispute) of the right not to belong to a union, described the ban as "the nasty thin wedge of Fascism" adding "I am not accusing the PM of Fascism, but it is a horrible precedent". (119)

Downing Street was unabashed. Less than two hours after the Committee's recommendations were known, it issued the following statement:

> "SINCE IT MIGHT AFFECT THE DECISIONS OF THOSE AT GCHQ, THE GOVERNMENT MUST MAKE CLEAR NOW THAT THE OFFER MADE TO GCHQ STAFF AND ACCEPTED BY A SUBSTANTIAL NUMBER OF THEM STANDS." (120)

Going to Law

On 1 March 1984, the date by which GCHQ staff should have completed their response to General Notice 100/84, CCSU sent out to all staff who had not signed 'A' or 'B' a letter which stated categorically:

> "We are determined not to concede the principle of free trade union organisation and representation at GCHQ. This fight isn't going to end now, we are determined to keep it going for as long as necessary to obtain justice." (121)

This was backed up by statements from Len Murray that the complaint against the Government would be pursued at the International Labour Organisation and by the CCSU itself that it would apply for a full judicial review of the union ban decision. This cannot have been good news to Mrs. Thatcher who, on the same day, was being congratulated in the Commons by Conservative MP Sir Anthony Meyer for the "courage and determination with which she had won a great victory at Cheltenham. In its way . . . no less significant than the victory she won in the South Atlantic." (122)

June and July 1984 fulfilled the best expectations of the unions regarding their grievances. The International Labour Organisation found that the ban contravened Convention 87 of its Code — of which the UK is a signatory — and demanded the reopening of negotiations between the two sides. This had not been anticipated by Ministers, who had reckoned on the ILO's acceptance of the Government's view that Convention 151 had great specific relevance to the matter.

Len Murray was delighted with the judgement. He declared:

> "The British Government has been found in violation of a solemn international undertaking. In one of the most clear-cut decisions ever issued by the ILO, the report completely upholds the complaint made

EXHIBIT 12:   **ILO CONVENTIONS**

by the TUC." The ruling placed the British Government "alongside
some of the most odious regimes in the world through the violation of
a basic human right. The Government can only remove this stain on
Britain's good name by acting on its recommendation." (123)

Tom King, Secretary of State for Employment, made it clear in response that there could be "no prospect of reopening this matter". (124)
Indeed, the ILO's ruling was described as "absurd and simplistic" by
Government lawyer Simon Brown in his defence of the Government's
move in the judicial review action brought by nine civil service unions
to challenge the validity of the ban. He stated further that in matters
of national security, the Crown had "an untrammelled power". (125)

The Government's case was upheld on all counts save one. And that
was the one that mattered, according to Mr. Justice Glidewell. He concluded a 64 page judgement by ruling that:

> "The instruction purportedly issued by the Minister for the Civil Ser-
> vice (The Prime Minister) on 22 December 1983, that the terms and
> conditions of civil servants' service at GCHQ should be revised so as to
> exclude membership of any trade union other than a departmental
> staff association . . . was invalid and of no effect." (126)

The key point at issue? "Fairness" he stated "and the rules of natural
justice, required that the decision should not finally be made until the
staff or their representatives . . . had been consulted and their views received and considered". (127) He noted that staff could have had a
"legitimate expectation" about consultation since Sir Robert Armstrong had discussed a range of sensitive issues (including lie detecting)
in 1983 and had promised the unions to do so again by letter on 9
January. Given that the unions had not contested the Government's
move on removing staff from the protection of the Employment Acts

– but only the membership ban – he found, moreover, that it was appropriate for the power conferred on a Minister by an order in Council to be subject to the same scrutiny and control by the courts as a statute would be.

The Prime Minister had, in fact, used an article of the 1982 Civil Service Order in Council – which allows specific instructions relating to changes in civil servants' conditions – for the imposition of the ban. Hence the employment of prerogative powers, rather than a statute, was at issue in this case.

To complicate matters, Mr. Justice Glidewell also concluded that:

> "Any decisions as to what constitutes a matter of national security, and whether particular activities do or might pose a threat to national security, are solely for her Majesty's Government." (128)

The judge's ruling that the ban was illegal provoked a noisy hue and cry in the House of Commons. (129) Neil Kinnock led the chase.

> "The Government has been found guilty of breaking the law . . . will she now admit that . . . the judgement of the High Court . . . makes it clear that responsibility for a major breach of natural justice and offence against civil rights rests with her and her alone? It was she and she alone who issued instructions for the compulsory removal of trade union membership . . . Why did she allow a month to elapse during which consultation could have taken place before leaving the Foreign Secretary as a punch bag to try and cover up her trail of guilt?

> How will she defend this country when she is so obviously prepared to make such breaches of natural justice? Will she conclude this £5m. farce by apologising to loyal civil servants for the insult to their integrity and instruct Government lawyers to withdraw the appeal? In the light of this experience, will she, just for once, let humility and reason replace her extremism and prejudice?"

He was closely followed by Ronald Leighton, who enquired:

> "Is she capable of pausing for reflection *(Labour shouts of "No!")*. Is she capable of thinking she might not have been right? Is she capable of saying she might have been in error, instead of opting for an immediate appeal which could lead to an ever bigger fiasco? Will she encourage an agreement acceptable to both sides rather than proceed by authoritative diktat?"

Neil Kinnock drew a sharp rejoinder from the Prime Minister to the effect that four ministers in the last Labour Government had had their actions declared illegal by the courts and that she did not think "any-

Support Recorded In MARPLAN Surveys for:	1983		1984		
	Nov.	Dec.	Jan.	Feb.	Mar.
Conservatives	42	41	42	39	38
Labour	35	37	38	40	38
Alliance	22	21	19	20	22
Total as % of respondents	99	99	99	99	98

TABLE 6:   WHOM WOULD YOU VOTE FOR IN A GENERAL ELECTION TOMORROW? (130)

one would deny the right to go to the Court of Appeal to get the matter satisfactorily settled". Ronald Leighton's dig was side-stepped.

There then ensued an intervention from Dennis Skinner (Bolsover, Labour) of quite a different character, namely:

Dennis Skinner:
"As the stakes are extremely high and it could, if it went the wrong way, end in her resignation as PM, how can we be assured that the PM would not go to the extent of bribing the judges who will take the decision?" *(Conservative protests)*

The Speaker (Mr. Bernard Weatherill):
"Order. Every MP must take responsibility for his question, but I think that question is out of order."

Mrs. Thatcher:
"I must ask that that allegation be totally and unreservedly withdrawn."

The Speaker:
"I gave Mr. Skinner the opportunity to do that. Would he now do that?"

Dennis Skinner:
"She is quite capable of doing that."

The Speaker:
"I put Mr. Skinner on warning that, unless he is prepared to withdraw that allegation, I shall be forced to take extreme action."

Dennis Skinner:
"I have no intention of withdrawing that allegation because the Prime

Minister would do anything to save her own neck."

The Speaker:
"I name Mr. Dennis Skinner for persistent disobedience of the chair."

The motion that Dennis Skinner be suspended for five days was moved by John Biffen (Leader of the Commons) and was carried by 218 votes to 84.

The furore did not die down. Later that day (17 July 1984) The Master of the Rolls, Sir John Donaldson refused − despite forceful arguments from the Treasury − to issue a statement which would have prevented unions from starting to recruit members at GCHQ pending the Government's appeal. The situation, so far as the Government was concerned, was "manifestly unsatisfactory". (131)

Employment Act 1980
The Government will provide funds to independent trade unions towards the costs of unions' conducting secret ballots on, for example, industrial action . . . Unionised employees, in workplaces where there are union membership agreements have the right no to be unreasonably excluded or expelled from a union. This new right will be in addition to common law rights. Complaints of infringement will be heard by industrial tribunals.
Picketing is lawful only if it is carried out by a person attending at, or near, his own place of work . . . violent, threatening or obstructive behaviour goes beyond peaceful persuasion and is, therefore, unlawful.

Employment Act 1982
Increases the protection of individuals dismissed for not being trade union members in a closed shop . . . makes trade unions liable to pay damages if they organise unlawful industrial action . . . Restricts lawful trade disputes to those between workers and their own employer.

The Trade Union Act 1984
Provides for union leaders to be elected by secret ballots. Secret and properly conducted ballots before strike action are necessary for unions to be immune. Enables trade union members to vote at regular intervals on whether their union should continue to spend money on party political matters.

EXHIBIT 13: KEY POINTS IN INDUSTRIAL RELATIONS LEGISLATION 1979−1985

Front-bench spokesman Gerald Kaufman saw it as the day on which Mrs. Thatcher crossed her Rubicon. It was, he declared in a *Times* article on 31 July:

> "the most uncomfortable day Mrs. Thatcher had endured in Parliament since she entered Downing Street five years previously."

> "All Governments", he wrote, "endure setbacks. All Prime Ministers suffer ups and downs. Governments can recover. Prime Ministers are extraordinarily resilient. However, in every Government's life, in every Prime Minister's career, there may come a moment when the public's tolerance snaps, when the willingness to forgive or to understand is withdrawn, when an invisible line is crossed . . . Whether the leader knows it or not, the prospect of defeat lies ahead. I believe that Margaret Thatcher had crossed that line by 17 July 1984."

Less than one month later, however, it was the Government's turn to rejoice. The three Appeal Court Judges ruled that the Courts had no jurisdiction over actions taken by the Government under the Royal Prerogative "taken in the interests of national security to protect this country from its enemies or potential enemies". (132) The same argument was later used, after the unions had taken their case to the House of Lords, by Lord Diplock:

> "National security is the responsibility of the executive. What action is needed to protect its interests is a matter upon which those upon whom the responsibility rests – and not the courts of justice – must have the last word. It is par excellence a non-justifiable question." (133)

The union reaction to the Appeal Court verdict was one of sadness. Peter Jones, Secretary to the CCSU, said:

> "They (the judges) came down totally on the Government's side. They have said that ministers can do what they like on grounds of national security and that is a worrying thing for everyone in this country. It is now becoming an issue of personal freedom." (134)

This feeling was shared by the unofficial GCHQ Trade Union Group. (135)

Houses Divided

After the union ban at GCHQ, morale there was said by one staff member, Christopher Dagleish (Assistant Language Specialist) who resigned, to be "devastated". (136) Even before it morale throughout the Civil Service was not regarded by commentators as more than mediocre. Consider, for example, the opinion of the former head of the Home Civil Service, Lord Bancroft. Giving the Suntory-Toyota lecture at the London School of Economics on 1 December 1983, he had no doubts as to where the fault lay:

> "It's no good blaming the media or society or the politicians generally. The tone setters are the employers, i.e. the Ministers. The ritual words of praise, forced out through clenched teeth in public, deceive no one if they are accompanied by noisy and obvious cuffs around the ear in semi-private. The popular view of Whitehall, and therefore of the civil service, is still that of a few Oxbridge mandarins whispering hexameters into Ministers' ears. This is, of course, rot." (137)

Evidence of morale-affecting issues in the Civil Service was, indeed, not hard to find.

- There was the question of senior civil servants' leaving Whitehall to take up posts in industry, the number in the top three grades (permanent, deputy and under secretaries) having almost doubled in the eighties. Doubly significant, when it is borne in mind that the Prime Minister's Efficiency Unit — headed by Sir Robin Ibbs, an Executive Director of ICI — had been asked to find out why the Civil Service had been failing to discover sufficient middle-ranking talent for rapid promotion to Whitehall posts. (139)

Name	Last Civil Service Post	Current Business role(s)
Sir Brian Tovey	GCHQ Director 1983	Security Consultant, Plessey.
Lord Bancroft	Head of Home Civil Service and Secretary to the Cabinet 1979-1981.	Non-Executive Director of Bass, Rugby-Portland Cement, Grindlays Bank, etc.
Sir Michael Palliser	Head of the Diplomatic Service 1975-1982	Vice-Chairman Samuel Montagu, Non-Executive Director of United Biscuits, Shell Transport & Trading, etc.
Sir Douglas Wass	Permanent Secretary to the Treasury 1974-1983	Head of Economic Strategy Unit, Coopers Lybrand, Non-Executive Director of De La Rue, Equity & Law, etc. Adviser to 1984 Campaign for Freedom of Information.

Note: Many of the above do voluntary work in the public service as well.

TABLE 7:   EXAMPLES OF OUTSIDE APPOINTMENTS OF SENIOR CIVIL SERVANTS LEAVING WHITEHALL SINCE 1980 (138)

- The introduction of new technology was posing severe difficulties. The DHSS computerisation strike in Newcastle which lasted from 8 July to 17 December 1984 and cost the Government an estimated £85m. was indicative. (140)

- While one aspect of the industrial relations climate was perceived by the unions as favourable – the political levy payment deal struck in respect of the 1984 Trade Union Act between Tom King and the TUC on 15 February 1984 – others were not. For example, the Government was openly speaking of the possibility of trying to abolish Wage Councils (set up originally by Winston Churchill to set minimum wages in a range of traditionally low-pay industries) and there was a hint from Lord Donaldson (former President of the 1971 Industrial Relations Court) that there was more Government legislation in industrial relations on the way. (141)

- The particular level of, and orientation towards, efficiency and effectiveness demanded in the Civil Service's administration by the Government was symbolic of a new and harsher 'work culture'. It was noteworthy also that some traditionally neutral civil servants felt antipathetic towards some Government measures and showed their disaffection by 'leaking' information, e.g. Miss Sarah Tisdall (the date of arrival of Cruise missiles from the USA) and Clive Ponting (the affair of the sinking of the cruiser *Belgrano* in the Falklands war).

Such factors may have contributed indirectly to the hostility felt by the civil service unions towards the ban decision and to the calling of the first meeting in five years of the Civil Service National Whitley Council, the top forum for the discussion of industrial relations issues in Whitehall. The purpose of the latter was, in Bill McCall's words, to express:

> "the severe adverse effect on Civil Service industrial relations generally of the arbitrary action taken by the Government in Cheltenham . . .
> The reverberations are being felt throughout the Civil Service." (142)

Indeed, they were – and considerably exacerbating prior union splits. Alistair Graham arrived at his CPSA annual conference, for instance, to find no less than 91 censure motions facing him for having participated in the joint Civil Service union offer of a no-strike agreement at GCHQ. One of the motions call for his resignation "for bringing the union into disrepute by refusing to carry out conference decisions." (143) In a variety of statements, he made his position clear:

> "I suspect that much of that response is activist-based rather than membership-based . . . I am not about to change my style of leadership . . . we would be grateful if the conference was more sensitive to the realities of the outside world and recognise the difficulties we face." (144) "I am always wary of the conspiracy theory but it is true to say that in some of the resolutions you can see the Militant Tendency at work . . . It is also true that the broad left — made up of Communists, Trotskyists and Left-wing Labour supporters — holds separate unofficial, unconstitutional conferences to decide which issues to pursue through the annual conference." (145)

Whilst he successfully held off the threat to his position as General Secretary, he did not sway the conference towards his viewpoint that "those who peddle the view that somehow this Government can be toppled by industrial confrontation are seriously wrong". (146) Nor did he dissuade it from adopting a policy of opposing any no-strike agreement in the Civil Service. He had certainly pleaded:

> "If you care about getting trade unionism back, if you really care, you will defeat this motion, even if it makes you puke."

But Conference accepted the motion proposed, and the viewpoint advanced, by Jonathan Baume (Secretary of the Union's Broad Left) whose main argument had been that:

> "Our members were victims of a pipe-dream of so-called new realism.
> It was all very well at the TUC last September but when it came to the crunch what we got from the Government was old realism." (147)

What was this 'new realism'? A cogent expression of it had been given in a 6000-word document entitled *Strategy for the Future* prepared by Len Murray for consideration by the TUC's Inner Cabinet — its Finance and General Purposes Committee — and then for wider discussion, ultimately at the September 1984 TUC Conference in Brighton.

"Ministers cannot be the sole judge of what is national security. They are not above the law."

(Larry Gostin, NCCL General Secretary)

**EXHIBIT 14 : THE VIEWPOINT OF THE NATIONAL COUNCIL
FOR CIVIL LIBERTIES** (148)

The recommendations made in *Strategy for the Future* were stark:

> "It (the Trade Union movement) must accept that workable compromises have to be found between the claims of the people it directly represents and those of other groups . . . The process of government in a democratic society cannot be carried out in the isolation of the Cabinet Office and Whitehall nor can the need to broaden government by effective, responsible and open consultation in which both sides of industry participate be contemptuously rejected as a form of Corporatism to be compared with the fascist corporate state. The trade union movement seeks involvement in order to strengthen parliamentary democracy not to weaken it. (149) . . . Unions must be ready to change to continue to advance the interests of working people and their families . . . Workers should have the right to strike but when strikes do occur they not only hurt the business and the community. They hurt the workers involved." (150)

Five days after the publication of this document came the announcement of the GCHQ ban.

National Union	1983 Political Fund Expenditure (£)	% of Membership Paying Political Levy
TGWU	1,354,478	98
GMBATU	1,436,176	82
NUPE	1,260,727	98
AUEW	781,524	65
NUM	477,465	60
USDAW	442,909	92
NUR	303,280	96
COHSE	274,036	92
UCW	251,136	94
EETPU	206,375	78
TOTAL	6,788,106	n/a
TOTAL (all 47 UK Unions): 8,639,336		81

Notes: The total number of union members is eight million. Seventy-nine per cent of the Labour Party's income comes from the unions; 82.5 per cent of the political fund was given to the Labour Party in 1983. (151)

TABLE 8:   **TOP 10 UNIONS**

On 29 February the TUC's Finance and General Purposes Committee decided to withdraw the union representatives from the National Economic Development Council until GCHQ employees were allowed to retain their union membership.

The NEDC is a Government-Management-Trade Union forum for the discussion in general and strategic terms of UK industrial policies. A boycott was regarded as a serious threat to its survival by the Prime Minister. (152)

> "The question now is whether the TUC will be content with having blown off a little steam or whether it will carry out its threat to sever all relations with the Government. It is a decision which is of little consequence to the Government but of some importance to the Trade Union movement. Unlike her post-war predecessors, Mrs. Thatcher has never felt the necessity to court the unions' favour or involve them in the minutiae of policy making."

EXHIBIT 15 :   **WHERE TO NEXT?** (153)

This policy — which did not involve a boycott of the important Economic Development Committees of the NEDC nor some of the tripartite bodies on which TUC members served (e.g. the Manpower Services Commission) — was reviewed periodically but stayed unchanged until a full-scale debate took place at the TUC's September Conference (held half-way through the coal strike over the NCB's pit closure programme) on the motion that:

> 'Given the Government's legislative and repressive attack on the trade union movement and its unbending commitment to economic policies which create mass unemployment and reduce the standard of living of our members, Congress instructs the General Council not to participate in the NEDC.'

The motion was rejected (5.6 million to 4.0 million) despite the advocacy of the proposer of the motion, Ken Gill, General Secretary of TASS, who claimed:

> "There is not a lot of evidence that our gold-plated six (i.e. the six trade union members of NEDC), which is what we call them among ourselves, have had the slightest effect on any policy since 1979. There is no moral, political or economic justification for going into Neddy — this rich man's monetarist club — again." (154)

And on 24 October 1984 the TUC General Council voted 22-19 to end the NEDC ban. (155)

References

1. Editorial, *Guardian*, 25 February 1984.
2. Alan Watkins, 'Fighting the war of Thatcher's face', *Observer*, 5 February 1984.
3. 'Cheltenham Pie', *Daily Telegraph*, 4 February 1984.
4. Editorial, *Sunday Telegraph*, 5 February 1984.
5. Craig Seton, 'GCHQ is silent on union ban', *Times*, 4 February 1984.
6. George Jones, 'Mrs Thatcher says Howe is splendid', *Sunday Telegraph*, 5 February 1984.
7. Frances Gibb and Paul Routledge, 'Law Lords uphold GCHQ ban', *Times*, 23 November 1984.
8. Richard Norton-Taylor, 'Backlash threat to GCHQ ruling', *Guardian*, 23 November 1984.
9. 'Civil Service unions launch merger campaign', *Times*, 15 January 1985.
10. Anthony Bevins, 'Democracy threatened after Cheltenham union ban, Benn claims', *Times*, 28 February 1984.
11. David Brindle, 'Banned union men in GCHQ pay talks', *Financial Times*, 12 December 1984.
12. John Kesby, 'Ban attacked', *Sunday Telegraph*, 3 June 1984.
13. 'GCHQ', Leading article in the *Times*, 4 February 1984.
14. Peter Hennessey, 'Intelligence efforts are imperilled', *Times*, 26 January 1984.
15. Peter Hennessey, 'The foreigners who share British intelligence', *Times*, 3 April 1984. Peter Hennessey, 'More evidence of GCHQ disruption', *Times*, 9 March 1984.
16. Keith Harper, 'Signals Centre unions win TUC backing', *Guardian*, 31 January 1984.
17. As 14.
18. Richard Norton-Taylor, 'Redundancy maze puzzles union', *Guardian*, 4 February 1984.
19. Richard Norton-Taylor, 'Murray calls for national action on GCHQ', *Guardian*, 25 February 1984.
20. As 12.
21. Richard Evans, 'Ban on unions essential, former GCHQ Chief says', *Times*, 6 February 1984.
22. Peter Hennessey, 'Can this web catch them all?', *Times*, 16 April 1984.
23. As 16.
24. Hugo Davenport, 'Special units at GCHQ may hold key to conflict', *Observer*, 5 February 1984.
25. As 14.
26. As 24.
27. Barrie Penrose and Simon Freeman, 'GCHQ Chief — Why unions had to go', *Sunday Times*, 5 February 1984.

28. Editorial, *Times*, 6 January 1984.
29. As 27.
30. Paul Routledge, 'US demand for introduction of lie detector blamed', *Times*, 26 January 1984.
31. Barrie Penrose, Simon Freeman and Donald Macintyre, *Sunday Times*, 5 February 1984.
32. As 31.
33. As 30.
34. Jeremy Windust, 'GCHQ: The lie test that failed', *Times*, 25 January 1985.
35. As 14.
36. David Rosenberg and David Shears, 'Does the lie detector have the ring of truth?', *Sunday Telegraph*, 5 February 1984.
37. As 14.
38. 'MI5 will study lie detector', *Sunday Telegraph*, 29 January 1984.
39. John Kesby, 'GCHQ revolt by Tory unionists', *Sunday Telegraph*, 15 April 1984.
40. Peter Hennessey, 'Senior staff take GCHQ lie tests', *Times*, 12 May 1984.
41. As 40.
42. As 36.
43. As 36.
44. As 36.
45. As 36.
46. Pearce Wright and Tim Jones, 'Polygraphic lie detectors are inaccurate and unreliable, scientists say', *Times*, 31 March 1984.
47. As 46.
48. Parliamentary report; 2 February 1984, *Times*, 3 February 1984.
49. As 14.
50. As 46.
51. As 36.
52. Richard Norton-Taylor, 'Industrial Relations review for civil service', *Guardian*, 29 March 1984.
53. Richard Evans, 'MPs stop short of urging business ban on lie detectors', *Times*, 21 February 1985.
54. As 27.
55. Parliamentary report; 25 January 1984, *Times*, 26 January 1984.
56. As 55.
57. As 55.
58. As 55.
59. As 55.
60. As 16.
61. As 30.
62. As 30.
63. As 30.

64. Richard Norton-Taylor, 'Cabinet Advisers' fury at GCHQ union ban', *Guardian*, 3 February 1984.
65. *Government's Expenditure Plans 1984/7*. London: HMSO. Published 17 February 1984.
66. Ian Aitken, 'MPs expect signals centre compromise', *Guardian*, 3 February 1984.
67. Parliamentary report; 3 March 1984, *Times*, 4 March 1984.
68. As 67.
69. As 67.
70. As 67.
71. Richard Norton-Taylor and Keith Harper, 'Thatcher bends a little during row over union ban at GCHQ', *Guardian*, 2 February 1984.
72. Maurice Weaver, 'Thatcher firm on banning GCHQ unions', *Daily Telegraph*, 2 February 1984.
73. As 71.
74. As 72.
75. As 72.
76. As 2.
77. As 72.
78. Barrie Clement, 'Murray suggests wider action over GCHQ ban', *Times*, 25 February 1984.
79. As 31.
80. David Felton, 'Unions offer unique guarantee', *Times*, 23 February 1984.
81. Robin McKie, Adam Raphael and Robert Taylor, 'Ban threat to radio officers at spy HQ', *Observer*, 19 February 1984.
82. As 80.
83. Richard Norton-Taylor and Julia Langdon, 'Thatcher rules out deal on GCHQ', *Guardian*, 24 February 1984.
84. As 83.
85. Parliamentary report; 23 February 1984, *Times*, 24 February 1984.
86. As 83.
87. David Felton and Anthony Bevins, 'Thatcher rejects options over trade union ban', *Times*, 24 February 1984.
88. Richard Norton-Taylor, 'Rank and file show depth of anger at union ban', *Guardian*, 24 February 1984.
89. Parliamentary report; 7 February 1984, *Times*, 8 February 1984.
90. Parliamentary report; 21 February 1984, *Times*, 22 February 1984.
91. Adam Raphael, 'Howe may be forced to back down', *Observer*, 5 February 1984.
92. As 39.
93. As 39.
94. Parliamentary report; 27 February 1984, *Times*, 28 February 1984.
95. As 94.

96. As 10.
97. Edward Pearce, 'Not even aspirin city', *Daily Telegraph*, 29 February 1984.
98. James Wightman, 'Thatcher not to give in', *Daily Telegraph*, 29th February 1984.
99. 'Fleet Street halted', *Daily Telegraph*, 29 February 1984.
100. As 99.
101. As 99.
102. 'Thatcher rules out more talks on GCHQ ban', *Daily Telegraph*, 29 February 1984.
103. Philip Webster, 'Thatcher ignores MPs call to lift GCHQ ban', *Times*, 16 February 1984.
104. Craig Seton, 'Unions are relieved by Report', *Times*, 16 February 1984.
105. James Wightman, 'Ban at spy centre will stay', *Daily Telegraph*, 16 February 1984.
106. As 105.
107. Parliamentary report; 16 February 1984, *Times*, 17 February 1984.
108. As 107.
109. As 107.
110. As 107.
111. As 31.
112. John Kesby and Norman Kirkham, 'Unions secret dockyard pacts', *Sunday Telegraph*, 5 February 1984.
113. Philip Webster, 'Safety of GCHQ "ensured by ban" ', *Times*, 9 February 1984.
114. 'Only 1 in 4 opt for £1,000', *Observer*, 12 February 1984.
115. As 31.
116. Maurice Weaver, 'Howe under fire as MPs say "Scrap ban" ', *Daily Telegraph*, 16 February 1984.
117. As 116.
118. As 105.
119. As 81.
120. As 103.
121. David Felton, 'Defeated GCHQ unions try to pick up pieces', *Times*, 2 March 1984.
122. Parliamentary report; 1 March 1984, *Times*, 2 March 1984.
123. Donald Macintyre, 'Government snub former ruling on GCHQ', *Observer*, 3 June 1984.
124. As 12.
125. Raymond Hughes, 'GCHQ ban "within code of freedom" ', *Financial Times*, 28 June 1984.
126. Richard Norton-Taylor, 'GCHQ ban on unions rules out', *Guardian*, 17 July 1984.

127. Richard Norton-Taylor, 'Judge defends workers rights over GCHQ ban', *Guardian*, 17 July 1984.
128. As 127.
129. Parliamentary report; 17 July 1984, *Times*, 18 July 1984.
130. *Guardian*, 29 March 1984.
131. David Felton, 'Judge declines to forbid unions' recruiting among staff at Cheltenham', *Times*, 18 July 1984.
132. 'The national security incantation', *Guardian*, 7 August 1984.
133. Michael Zander, 'Law Lords backing for GCHQ ban on unions', *Guardian*, 23 November 1984.
134. Will Bennett, 'No end to battle in courts on GCHQ', *Guardian*, 7 August 1984.
135. As 134.
136. Peter Hennessey, 'Russian specialist resigns over "failure" to tighten GCHQ security', *Times*, 10 August 1984.
137. Peter Hennessey, 'Ministers blamed for sapping Whitehall morale', *Times*, 2 December 1983.
138. 'When civil servants take business posts', *Times*, 6 March 1984.
139. 'Whitehall promotion failing', *Times*, 21 January 1984.
140. Nicholas Timmins, 'Benefits strike ends but pensioners must wait for cash', *Times*, 18 December 1984.
141. 'Unions laws "hint" worries TUC', *Daily Telegraph*, 16 February 1984.
142. Peter Hennessey, 'Whitehall unions forum to examine GCHQ ban', *Times*, 23 March 1984.
143. 'Civil service union chief attacks the militant plotters', *Daily Telegraph*, 11 April 1984.
144. 'Left threat to moderate chief of CSU', *Times*, 10 April 1984.
145. As 137.
146. Philip Bassett, 'Civil servants rout left bid to oust moderate leader', *Financial Times*, 17 May 1984.
147. As 146.
148. As 134.
149. Paul Routledge, 'TUC document calls for compromise with Government and society', *Times*, 20 January 1984.
150. Donald Macintyre, 'Unions are now out of touch', *Sunday Times*, 22 January 1984.
151. Barrie Clement, 'Trade unionists "misled" on levy', *Times*, 13 March 1985.
152. Andrew Taylor, 'Second boycott of NEDC meetings by union leaders', *Financial Times*, 5 April 1984.
153. Editorial, *Daily Telegraph*, 29 February 1984.
154. John Winder, Derek Barnett and Stephen Goodwin, 'Engineers' defeat keeps open possibility of unions' return to Neddy', *Times*, 6 September 1984.
155. 'TUC General Council votes 22-19 to end Neddy Ban', *Guardian*, 25 October 1984.

THE INNER CITY TIME BOMB?

Whatever Next

There was much speculation in Britain in early February 1986 about the imminent statement by Mrs. Thatcher's Conservative Government on its Inner City Policy. Would it involve a substantial increase in public expenditure — an explosive economic policy U-turn? Would it, by contrast, follow the lines of the Conservatives' previous approach? Would there be any change in the politico-administrative partnership between Central and Local Government which handled the very serious inter-related social, economic and ethnic minority problems posed in some of Britain's major cities? What impact would *Faith in the City*, a detailed report into the state of such cities produced by the Archbishop of Canterbury's Commission of Inquiry, have on the Government's thinking?

Such speculation was fuelled by the eruption of serious civil disorders in Brixton and on the Broadwater Estate in Tottenham in September and October 1985 respectively. These occurred at a time when the temperature of the relationship between Central Government and City Government was already high as a result of the culmination of the 'Rates Rebellion' staged by a consortium of left-wing Socialist/Militant Tendency-led authorities. Point was added to the debate by the fracas at Bradford University (a) in early February 1986 in which Conservative MP John Carlisle had his finger broken. It was thought that members of the non-University 'Asian Youth Movement' were responsible for the injury to the MP, who was due to speak on the theme of politics and sport. (1)

The Government announced its Policy Review on 23 October 1985. It was aimed, said Chancellor of the Exchequer Nigel Lawson, at making an urgent study of the workings of the Urban Programme.

This was the complicated and extensive system whereby Central Government allotted funds to local authorities — through Urban Development and Derelict Land Grants and through Enterprise Allowances — for specific projects. No less than £1.3 billion had been spent on the programme since 1982 and funding for 1985/6 amounted to £338m. Of this, one quarter was to be spent on environmental clean-up and land-reclamation schemes and the balance split almost equally between

Year	Unemployment level in the UK (Unemployment as % of the workforce)
1961	1.3
1971	3.3
1976	5.5
1979	5.3
1980	6.8
1981	10.4
1982	12.1
1983	12.9
1984	13.1

TABLE 1 :   **GROWTH IN UK UNEMPLOYMENT** (b)

Source: Social Trends 16th Ed. HMSO.

social and economic uses. Job-creation and work-training initiatives run by the Manpower Services Commission, such as the Youth Training Scheme and the Community Programme, lay outside the scope of the Urban Programme. (b)

However strange it might appear at first sight, it is a matter of record that the Urban Programme had, as a whole, been underspent since 1983/4. Analysing evidence on Inner City aid spending, the Commons Public Accounts Committee concluded (2) that a key reason for this was a shortfall in the number of projects that qualified as suitable for the Urban Development Grant on grounds of private sector involvement. This was a salient feature of the American model on which the Grant (introduced in 1983 by the then Environment Secretary Michael Heseltine after the experience of the Toxteth riots in 1981) was based. The Committee's overall view was far from complimentary. And this despite the programme's 17-year track record!

> "The information we have received does not convince us that the Urban Programme yet represents a well-designed policy document based on a clear understanding of the problems and what needs to be done."

It had been launched with a purposeful clarion call by Labour Home Secretary James Callaghan in 1968:

> "to provide for the care of our citizens who live in the poorest or most overcrowded parts of our cities and towns . . . to reverse the downward spiral which affects so many . . . to deal with the deadly quagmire of need and apathy." (3)

The subsequent history of the programme did not seem to reflect such clarity of aim, however. There had been a surprising plethora of extra appraisals, such as Inner Area and Cycle of Poverty Studies. There had been an abundance of schemes: Educational Priority Areas, Community Development Projects, General Improvement Areas, Housing Action Areas, Neighbourhood Schemes . . . And no shortage of underpinning evidence for the problems either, with contributions from Commissions of Inquiry like Plowden (Primary Education), Seebohm (Personal Social Services) and Milner-Holland (London's Housing). And the 1977 White Paper on the Inner Cities!

Two particular features of the Urban Programme are of interest in the light of the original aim. Firstly, that Urban Aid has never been an extra grant; it consists of funds taken out of the yearly Rate Support Grant that Central Government pays towards the expenditures of local authorities and put into a special category. Secondly, 'deserving' inner city areas have been chosen according to a complex 'need assessment' formula based on:

- the proportion of 'stress households' (minimum 20%) in an area
- the proportion of 'new Commonwealth-immigrant' population in it (minimum 33%)
- the % of unemployed in the area's workforce (minimum twice the national average), and
- the proportion of households living beneath the DHSS' Supplementary Benefit Poverty Line (minimum 'high').

It should be noted that there are many examples of Urban Aid Projects which have been of significant 'community value', for instance the Muhammed Ali Sports Centre in Handsworth, the Newskills Training Workshop in Lambeth and the conversion of the Bon Marché department store in Brixton into unit workshops. Another was a £1.7m. Craft Centre in Newcastle opened in December 1985 by the Environment Secretary, Kenneth Baker.

This Craft Centre had, in fact, been identified as a priority need by the Newcastle City Action Team. This was one of a group of inner-city based 'task forces' of civil servants from the Departments of Environment, Employment and Trade and Industry as well as from the Home Office, stationed in Urban Programme Partnership Areas. The task of each CAT was to concentrate attention on need situations and to coordinate necessary aid efficiently and effectively. The system is based on the CAT set up by Michael Heseltine in Liverpool, also after the Toxteth (Liverpool 8) riots in 1981.

Winning Ways?

Interest in the forthcoming statement on Inner City Policy to be made by the Policy Review sub-committee (Douglas Hurd — Home Secretary: Kenneth Baker: Lord Young — Employment Secretary) had also been raised by several other important and related developments. These were:

(1) the publication on 25 January 1986 of the Housing and Planning Bill which included provision for a brand new grant — the Urban Regeneration Grant. This differed markedly from the existing Urban Development Grant in that it could be given (in the form of grants, loans and/or guarantees) to private developers of innter city schemes. No increase in funding would be entailed if the new grant were employed, stated the Bill. Indeed, the publication of the Bill preceded by two days an announcement of a substantial cut in the Urban Development Grant (payable to local authorities) for 1986/7.

New Housing Construction by:	1979	1980	1981	1982	1983	1984
Local Authorities	79	80	58	36	37	35
New Town Corporations	9	8	10	4	2	2
Housing Associations	18	21	19	13	16	16
Government Departments	1	1	1			
Total Public	108	110	88	53	55	54
Total Private	144	131	118	127	148	158
Total New	252	241	206	170	203	212

TABLE 2 :   NEW HOUSE CONSTRUCTION IN ENGLAND
AND WALES ('000)

Source: Social Trends, 16th Ed. HMSO 1985. Quoted in *Times*, 11.11.86, 'Ownership Boom as Home Stock Grows', Christopher Warman.

(2) the rejection of any idea of "guaranteed job quotas" for ethnic minorities by Alan Clark, Junior Employment Minister, on 14 October 1985.

(3) the new Public Order Bill which extended the offence of in-

citement to racial hatred to the publication or distribution of material likely to or intended to stir up racial hatred. The Bill also made it an offence to possess such material if there was intent to publish or distribute it. This built on the Race Relations Act of 1976.

(4) the Wages Bill, published on 31 January 1986. This was aimed at repealing the Truck Acts, restricting the operations of the Wage Councils to workers over the age of 21 and abolishing the payment of redundancy rebate to employers with 10 or more employees. Paymaster-General Kenneth Clarke introduced the Bill by stating its central purposes as:

"to create job opportunities, particularly for young people . . .
The so-called protection of the wage councils is worthless to a young person who cannot get a job because it is illegal to pay him a wage he is prepared to accept"

(5) the implementation of the Police and Criminal Evidence Act 1984 on 1 January 1986. Critics of this legislation, like Joseph Handley (member of the Brixton Legal Defence Group and "liaison" with the Broadwater Farm Estate Defence Committee) and Pamela Hayers (Broadwater Farm Neighbourhood Council worker and Defence Committee coordinator), were said to regard its "Stop and Search", "Arrest", "Intimate Body Search", "Interrogation and Access to Legal Advice" provisions as "draconian" (4). By contrast, the government had no doubts as to the appropriateness of the measure. Said Nigel Lawson:

"There can be no economic or sociological justification for throwing a petrol bomb, that is crime and must be dealt with as such" (5)

Element	Year	
	1951	1984
Private ownership as % of total housing stock	29	61
Total housing stock (m. dwellings)	14	22

TABLE 3 :   **PRIVATE HOME OWNERSHIP**

Source: Social Trends, 16th Ed. HMSO.

Such differing perspectives on the issue of public order and the role and equipment of the police were thrown into stark relief by the disorders in Brixton and Tottenham in late 1985. (c) These followed two tragic incidents: the accidental shooting of Mrs. Cherry Groce in her Brixton home by armed police officers searching for her son whom they suspected of a felony and the death of Mrs. Cynthia Jarrett who suffered a heart attack during a police raid on her home, again in search of her son who was also a suspect.

The Broadwater riots resulted in the dreadful hacking-to-death of P.C. Keith Blakelock at the foot of one of the linked stairways that connect the maze of ziggurat-like blocks that make up the estate. A Metropolitan Police report, prepared for the Haringey Police-Community Consultative Group by Deputy Assistant Commissioner Michael Richards, maintained that the brick and petrol bomb attack on the police was premeditated and followed a particular pattern. Its main finding, given in a *Guardian* article of 13 January 1986, was that the riot plan had been "prepared months in advance".

A memorial march — reputedly the largest-ever by black people in Britain — took place on 11 November 1985 in support of the Groce and Jarrett families. Joseph Handley, one of the organisers of the Brixton-Hyde Park protest march, made an horrifying claim about the background to the march:

> "I walked onto the Farm the other day to meet with the Defence Committee. A Police Officer approached and said to me 'This is not an eye for an eye, coon. It runs much deeper than that . . . They will not be satisfied until they have taken at least one black head on the Farm.' (6)

Even more significant, perhaps, was the spontaneous outburst from Bernie Grant, the leader of Haringey Council, after the Tottenham riot. Laying the blame squarely on the police, he stated:

> "What they got was a bloody good hiding." (7)

Rising Damp

> "I find it particularly obscene that the same Prime Minister whose economic and social policies keep so many of my constituents homeless can afford to go out and spend £400,000 on a neo-Georgian bunker in Dulwich."

Thus Tony Bank MP (Newham NW, Lab), opening a debate on homelessness in the House of Commons on 20 December 1985. No stranger to oratorical flourish, he continued:

"The stable in Bethlehem would offer more comfort than some of the bed-and-breakfast accommodation that many mothers and their children will enjoy this Xmas." (8)

The cause of the scandal in his view? The Government's cuts in public sector housing investment.

Evidence for Tony Banks' critique was not far to seek. Firstly, as Table 2 indicates, there had been a substantial and inexorable shrinkage in new public sector house building since 1980. When this is coupled with the increase in the number of council houses and flats sold by local authorities in line with the Government's 1980 Housing Act, the drop in the availability of public sector housing is manifest.

There were two main reasons for the fall-off in local authority house building. Firstly, Central Government restrictions on local authorities' use of capital receipts (i.e. income from the sale of council houses and flats) had increased − from 1984 they could use only 20% of income instead of the previous 40% − and the Government had curtailed its Housing Investment Programme allocations to councils. The HIP for 1985/6 stood, at £1.65 billion − an all-time low in real terms.

Secondly, a high proportion of the nation's housing stock left, according to official data, much to be desired. In fact, the government's own assessment indicated that 11% was 'unfit' (9) and local authorities claimed that £18.8 billion was needed to repair and renovate the 84% of their properties which they said were suffering from faults ranging from minor defects to serious structural/condensation problems. (10) The SHAC report *Capital Decay: An Analysis of London's Housing*, published in October 1985, put things in a nutshell by stating:

"London is sitting on a time bomb" (11)

The Government did not, however, warm to the views expressed by Tony Banks. Indeed, it was proud of the achievements of its 'Home-owning Democracy' policy which had contributed much to the advance of private ownership shown in Table 3. This policy gave tax relief on mortgage interest payments (up to a stipulated ceiling) to private home buyers − a factor of primordial significance − and maintained consistent legislative pressure on local authorities to sell off their stock at a discount. (12)

1. Liverpool's ethnic minorities make up 10% of the population of the city. Less than 300 of the council's 31,000 staff are black as are only 30 of the 6,000 staff employed by the Merseyside Metropolitan Authority.

2. A survey carried out by the Commission for Racial Equality in 1983 in the huge St. John's shopping centre in Liverpool found that only 12 of the 3,000 staff were black. Similar results were found in a 1985 CRE survey on the Beaumont Leys Shopping Centre in Leicester.

3. Black people in Liverpool are concentrated predominantly in the 8 electoral wards around Liverpool 8. "Once you cross the boundary" commented John Reilly (inhabitant of Toxteth with a white mother and a black father) "you're fucked. Even my white friends get pressure in the wrong clubs if they are with me. A friend of mine got 58 stitches when he went to the club without the trilby hat he usually wears. He's got very light skin. Without the hat, they could see his hair."

EXHIBIT 1 :   **THE VIEW FROM THE GHETTO**

Sources: 'When a Scouse Accent fails to affect discrimination'. David Rose. *Guardian*, 27.12.85. Quoted verbatim.
'Inside the limits of Liverpool's Multi-Racial Ghetto'. David Rose, *Guardian*, 28.12.85. Quoted verbatim.

Another facet entirely of the housing picture was presented in Professor Greve's investigation into homelessness in London. (13) This revealed that:

- a record number of 27,500 families was accepted as homeless in 1985 by London Boroughs. Another 20,000 single people not covered by the Homeless Persons Act were being forced to stay in hostels or live rough.

- two thirds of the homeless families were allocated temporary housing, often at the expense of those on council waiting lists, and the remainder were sent to bed and breakfast accommodation. This latter was seen by critics as the most expensive and least socially-desirable solution.

Yet another dimension of the problem was the fact that, at the end of 1985, London's council tenants were collectively behind with their rent to the tune of £125 m.! In Camden 54% of tenants were in arrears

Region	% of the workforce unemployed in December 1985
Northern Ireland	21.6
North	18.1
Wales	16.2
North West	15.7
Scotland	15.0
West Midlands	14.9
York & Humberside	14.7
East Midlands	12.3
South West	11.8
East Anglia	10.7
South East	9.7

TABLE 4 :   **REGIONAL UNEMPLOYMENT (d)**

Source: Financial Times, 10.1.86

and owed £6.9 m. In Brent the situation was even worse — £10.4 m. was owed by 71% of tenants. (14)

Not that the Conservative Government was unmindful of the qualitative problems posed by the nature of some of the council building over the 20 years up to 1986. This was made plain in Kenneth Baker's response to Labour's attack during the Commons debate on the Housing Crisis and Urban Deprivation which took place on 11 December 1985. He referred to

> "These Socialist councils" which "had built those appalling estates in the 1960's and 1970's. Social engineers and planners have sold the country a whole lot of quack remedies" (15)

In his speech he also criticised the Church of England's "Marxist" *Faith in the City* report for not distinguishing between "absolute" and "relative" poverty — "not being as well off as one's neighbour is put in the same category as destitution" — and rejected the arguments advanced by Labour's spokesman, Dr. John Cunningham, who had stated the Opposition's position in the following forthright terms:

> "We certainly agree that throwing money at problems is an inefficient use of previous public resources but taking money away from the inner cities, the under-privileged and the poor and ladling it into the hands of the high income earners is an obscenity. There must be a

longer-term strategy which brings resources to the inner cities. But Central Government action must not be an excuse to undermine or by-pass democratically-elected local councils. Central to a new strategy should be a commitment to full employment. In combatting poverty they must also address the problems of black people." (16)

The Conservative Government's position by contrast rested firmly, according to Kenneth Baker, on its overall control of public expenditure and its targetting spending to the areas of greatest need. "Injudicious public expenditure" had, he averred, often been a cause of the problem rather than a solution. He asked:

"What good would more money do for Councillor Stringer in Manchester, Councillor Grant in Haringey, Councillor Knight in Lambeth and Councillor Hatton in Liverpool?" (e)

The Government was even interested in a break-up in the management and ownership of large council estates. That was why, he claimed in the debate:

"In our Housing Bill this session we will be increasing the discount for tenants of council flats by 10% across the board." (17)

Loud Labour protests were made as Conservative Party Chairman Norman Tebbit wound up the debate. The opposition was angered at his allusions to the Militant Tendency and their use of inner city areas as "fertile ground for revolution or confrontation with Government in order to bring about radical change in society." (18)

Going To The Dogs

Labour's criticism of the Government's approach as expressed in the December debate was muted and decorous compared with the reactions of some of the Councillors named by Kenneth Baker. Take, for example, the views of Ted Knight, Leader of Lambeth Council and a stalwart in the 1985 "Rates Rebellion" (as a consequence of which he was disqualified from holding public office for 5 years in March 1986). In a letter to the *Guardian* (19), he accused the Government of maintaining the "pretence" of aiding inner city authorities and of giving a false impression "that millions of pounds of additional grant" were being "continually" spent on the problem. By way of evidence, he cited the case of his own authority:

"In 1978 Lambeth Council received just over £5m. in Urban Aid Grant. In 1985 it received £10.3m., which, after inflation is taken into

"What has most astonished (and depressed) us has been a widespread feeling . . . in the Urban Priority Areas that 'nothing can be done' about unemployment. We wonder whether some politicians really understand the despair that has become so widespread in many areas of the country.

It is not a simple story of economic decline and physical decay in the inner city. It is a more complex story of mismatch between people, skills, housing and jobs which planning has failed to overcome and the economic recessions of the later '70's exposed and exacerbated.

More alarming, the migration of people and the movement of capital, employment opportunities, private enterprise and voluntary effort is increasingly away from the urban districts. The process is one of deprived people being left as the successful move out to Middle Britain.

It is by their outcomes that macro-economic policies must be judged. We are united in the view that the costs of present policies, with the continuing growth in unemployment, are unacceptable in their effect on whole communities and generations. A degree of hardship may be needed to attain longer-term objectives but it is unacceptable that the costs of transition should fall hardest on those least able to bear them . . . We must not fall into the trap of letting economics suffocate morality by taking the decisions for us . . . The main assumption on which present economic policies are based is that prosperity can be restored if individuals are set free to pursue their own economic salvation . . . We believe that, at present, too much emphasis is being given to individualism and not enough to collective obligation . . . There is no guarantee that the pursuit of innumerable self-interests will add up to an improvement in the common good.

The urban policy of Government . . . is open to the charge of being inadequate and superficial . . . It is an inadequate response to say that throwing money at the problem is not the answer. It is part of the answer . . . It must be for the Government, first and foremost, to demonstrate this confidence through a sustained programme of public investment on both current and capital account, as has happened in the docklands . . . To create new jobs by increasing public expenditure may require tax increases or higher rates of borrowing. We believe that the present situation may well necessitate such a response."

EXHIBIT 2 :   **GOD OR MAMMON?**

Source: Faith in the City, the report of the Church of England Commission of Inquiry (Chairman: Sir Richard O'Brien, former Chairman of the Manpower Services Commission), Church House Publishing, December 1985.

account, is worth £6m. at 1979 prices . . . It has also lost out in terms of Rate Support Grant and Housing Investment Programme funding. Since 1980 Lambeth's RSG has declined from £45m. to £37m. in cash terms and by 50% in real terms."

Unemployment in the inner city was focussed on in a letter to the Guardian by Manchester's leader, Graham Stringer. (21) He wrote:

"We know we are up against a Government whose policies are de-industrialising the North-West and our inner city area in particular . . . that Manchester is losing 20 jobs a day and that many are the jobs of women and members of ethnic minorities who suffer most during a recession."

His reaction to the Urban Programme? "Pathetic!"

One of many inner city examples of Graham Stringer's key concern was that of the Isle of Dogs in London's East End. Here the mighty £1.5 billion Canary Wharf Development, consisting of office blocks and housing, was one of the largest such schemes in Western Europe. Its original aim was the creation of 40,000 jobs under the aegis of the London Docklands Development Corporation.

"The poverty trap still operates. For a married couple with 4 dependent children, an increase in earnings from £60 to £135/week would not materially affect their spending power because of the increase in income tax and withdrawal of means-tested benefit."

"Black economy's share of GDP? . . . when the Inland Revenue last put its finger to the wind, it came up with a figure of about 7.50%. That's about £25 billion of undeclared income . . . or over 3p off the basic rate (of direct tax) for the rest of the country." (20)

SHADES OF THE BLACK ECONOMY

The Isle of Dogs was once a vital part of Britain's main trade artery, the port of London. It was here, in a shipyard off the West Ferry Road, that Isambard Kingdom Brunel built his famed steamship, *The Great Eastern*. In late 1985, however, in an area once noted for the skills and sense of community of its inhabitants and now dock-less, youth unemployment had reached over 50% and more than half the population was receiving rate relief under the Housing Benefit Scheme. Little wonder "islander" Ted Johns, who ran the local Youth Training Scheme/Small Business facilities "Resource Centre", felt somewhat aggrieved as he surveyed the £100,000/house building development taking place around him. And as he considered the fact that, out of the 1400 new jobs so far created, only 33 had apparently gone to local people. (22)

Gobbledegook?

The signals from Central Government in the run-up to its policy announcement seemed a trifle confusing.

Tight, by now traditionally-tight, control of local authorities was much in evidence as the Local Government Bill, aimed at curbing local authorities' ability to fund political propaganda "on the rates", began its passage through the House of Lords. (f) So was the desire to maintain tight control of public expenditure in spite of considerable pressure. Witness the following examples:

(1)   In October 1985 the Government suffered a set-back at the hands of the Commons All-Party Statutory Instruments Committee. This strangely-named body of MP's stated that any attempt by Government to impose new regulations which limited Board and Lodging payments to homeless claimants would be deemed *ultra vires*. The rules which the Government was seeking to apply covered first-time claimants under the age of 26 and stipulated residential qualifications as a basis for benefits entitlement. This aimed at cutting down on what was seen as a major scandal – the Costa del Dole – perpetrated by claimants who spent the summer drawing their benefit by the coast rather than at home.

(2)   The failed attempt by the Government to maintain its approach in another social security field: payments to help most pensioners' extra fuel bills in the winter. An important defeat since February 1986 was the second coldest of the century!

Here it was the highest Social Security appeals body (the Tribunal of Commissioners) that found against the Government in the case of a Kent woman who had appealed against a benefit assessment. The key element in the Tribunal's ruling was that the DHSS' method of calculating "exceptionally severe weather payments" on the basis of average Meteorological Office data for pre-selected locations was illegal. To compound the felony, the Tribunal recorded that the defence's star witness, Dr. W. H. Moores, Head of the Meteorological Office's Land Climatology

"Isn't it time we interred the dog-eared Marxist tracts alongside Marx himself? Isn't it time we made up our minds to be less like Albania and more like America?"

Norman Tebbitt, Conservative Party Chairman

"What will the service industry be servicing when there is no hardware, when no wealth is actually being produced? We will supply the Changing of the Guard, the Beefeaters in the Tower."

Lord Weinstock, GEC Chairman

"In the ordinary working of the economy we are practically bankrupt, save for oil. We are the Abu Dhabi of today." The way forward? . . . "not by scrimping and saving here and there, not by selling off national assets — Georgian silver, furniture, Canalettos — here and there, but by creating wealth." "If Britain tries to resist technological change, she will slowly go back and sink like a great galleon . . . . living on past glory."

Lord Stockton, formerly Conservative Prime Minister, Harold Macmillan

"We do need a sense of urgency in the regeneration of industry . . . otherwise we're going to finish up a fourth-rate country."

HRH Prince Charles

"I do believe that if we are to move out of present economic and capital market conditions, and we most certainly must, it is better for us to move towards the stable Japanese direction than to slip towards the fragile American condition."

Neil Kinnock, Labour Party Leader

EXHIBIT 3: **GOING WEST (OR IS IT EAST)?**

Sources: Norman Tebbitt's speech at the Young Conservatives Conference, *Times*, 10/2/86
Lord Weinstock's evidence to the Lord's Select Committee on Overseas Trade, *Times*, 15/10/85
Lord Stockton's speech to the Tory Reform Group, *Times*, 8/11/85
Lord Stockton's speech on Technology in the House of Lords, *Times*, 14/11/85
HRH Prince Charles' speech at a Scottish 'Business in the Community' symposium, *Times*, 28/11/85
Neil Kinnock's speech to the Industrial Society, 20/1/86 (g)

Division, was "plainly critical" (23) of the use to which his department's statistics were put.

On 18 December 1985, however, there came an ostensible switch in the Government's policy direction with the announcement by Kenneth Baker, in his Rate Support Grant statement, that £227m. extra was to be channelled to the towns and cities.

"Birmingham appears to be the capital of racial discrimination in Britain . . . If real changes are not forthcoming, this rebellion is perceived as a beginning, not as an end . . . Black people's grievances are many. The extent of social deprivation and racial disadvantage make life intolerable. Harsh policing – by an ill-disciplined and brutal force which has manipulated and abused its powers in dealings with the black community over a long period of time – on top of all this provides the chemistry for violent reaction . . . Violent resistance is now permanently on the agenda while the oppression and the denial of rights and resources continue . . . In 1986 black people in Birmingham are saying that they are not alien, they are not part of an undesirable chunk of surplus labour to be eradicated. They are not a problem, as depicted by the Government and the media, and they will not accept anything less than equal treatment, justice and control of their own destiny . . . The combustible atmosphere has not been removed. Handsworth is one of the most deprived parts of Britain. Many black people in the area have no confidence in the social agencies or the local authority that they will be treated fairly or get jobs on their merits and qualities . . . The local authorities must get together to work out imaginative, alternative strategies and the best way to inspire confidence is to give local people a say in where the money goes."

These comments are taken from *A Different Reality*, a report into the September 1985 Handsworth riot which resulted in 2 deaths and £16m. of damage, compiled by a panel chaired by Herman Ouseley, Assistant Chief Executive of Lambeth Borough and sponsored by the West Midlands County Council. It was issued on 20/2/86. (i)

EXHIBIT 4 : A DIFFERENT REALITY

Notes:

(1) The Chief Constable of the West Midlands, Geoffrey Dear, had blamed, on apparently sound evidence, 'drug barons' for inciting the rioting.

(2) His subsequent request to the Labour-controlled West Midlands Police Committee for his police force to be issued with riot-control plastic bullets (like the thirteen forces that have already been so equipped) was turned down.

(3) On 1 April 1986 the West Midlands County Council was scheduled for dissolution in the Local Government re-organisation. Its Police Committee role would be taken over by the Conservative-controlled West Midlands Police Authority.

(4) On 20 February 1986 West Midlands Police announced a £60,000 ethnic minority recruitment programme. Of the 6,650 officers in this force at the time only 95 were from ethnic minority backgrounds. (24)

(5) It was reported by the *Guardian* on 14 January that Mrs. Michelle Ahmed and her sister Miss Claudette Ensor admitted handling stolen goods from shops and premises razed to the ground in the riot. They were sentenced to 3 months imprisonment, suspended for two years. Michelle told Birmingham Crown Court that looters had threatened to burn down her home if she refused to hide the stolen clothes and electrical equipment. Police had later thwarted the attempt by a Rastafarian to retrieve the goods.

Warmth was, however, positively the last word that could be used to describe the Opposition's reception of this news. Instead, they rounded on the Government with a 3-pronged onslaught:

- that the difference between what local authorities needed to maintain the existing level of community services and the RSG settlement was £1.25 billion.

- that the 47% coverage of local authority by Central Government compared unfavourably and unacceptably with the level inherited by the Conservatives from Labour when they won the 1979 election — 62%.

- that there was nothing in the statement which addressed the "deepening problems of our inner city communities".

Kenneth Baker firmly rejected these accusations and reaffirmed the Government's view that Labour was "the spokesman" for high levels of public spending. (h) "They would give in" he declared "to every single demand for spending from the Town Halls." Not so the Conservatives . . .

> "If I had given in to the Town Halls, it would have meant either higher rates or higher taxes. The thrust of this settlement is that, if authorities can make economies and savings, then rates will come down. It is really up to the councils to find the savings." (25)

What was worse, from Kenneth Baker's position, was the attack mounted by his own back-bench MP's

This he rebutted, with some difficulty, by referring not so much to the decreases in RSG to the shire counties so much as to the increases that would occur if they made appropriate economies. A fuller picture of the complicated logic involved is given in Appendix 2.

Kenneth Baker's sweet reasonableness availed little with two of his Party colleagues either. Whilst Midlands MP Patrick Cormack (South Staffs) remarked acidly that "gobbledegook and incomprehensibility are rarely the hallmarks of good government" (26), fellow-Parliamentarian Robin Maxwell-Hyslop went for the jugular:

> "How" he queried "does the Secretary of State acquit himself of the charge of sheer political cowardice in reducing the percentage of Central Government Grant instead of reforming the basis of Local Government taxation to which this party, to which he is alleged to belong, has been committed for many years?

Can he deny that he is deliberately fiddling the GREA formula to transfer funds from the rural areas to the towns? How can he deny that he has fiddled the GREA formula this year to transfer money in support of the abolition of the Metropolitan Authorities?"

Labouring Long

The Government's long-awaited statement on Inner City Aid was made in the Commons on 6 February 1986. Against a backcloth of Opposition laughter and jeers, Paymaster-General Kenneth Clarke announced that £8m. was to be spent on new approaches to providing training, employment and self-employment opportunities in the 8 inner city areas of Notting Hill and North Peckham (London), Chapeltown (Leeds), North Central Middlesbrough, Highfields (Leicester), Moss Side (Manchester), St. Paul's (Bristol) — scene of major public disorder at the time of the Toxteth (Liverpool) riots in 1981 — and Handsworth. Of the £8m., £3m. was to come out of the Department of the Environment's existing provision.

"You cannot be a Tory convinced of the need to set the strong free, to create the wealth upon which society depends, then blame the weak when the strong fail — it is not foot soldiers who lose wars . . . For those who can compete the race must be free and fair, but fairness means compassion for those to whom a free concept of competition is a race they do not even qualify to enter." Unemployment costs £7 billion a year but "that is the money cost, the smaller cost, the short-term cost. The real cost is higher, not just in lost income. The cost is in attitudes . . . that spread as the numbers spread, that harden as frustration and bitterness grow; attitudes that succumb to the cancerous villainy of the drug pedlar, the criminal boss, the violence, the inner city crime and the vested interests behind it."

EXHIBIT 5 :   **"CARING CAPITALISM"**

Source: Speech by ex-Defence Secretary Michael Heseltine at the Young Conservatives Conference, Blackpool, 9/2/86

The sum in question was certainly in stark contrast to that mentioned in the Commons All-Party Employment Committee's report *Special Unemployment Measures and the Long-Term Unemployed*, issued on 18 December 1985. This called for the spending of £3.3 billion, admittedly not on inner city projects but on job-creation schemes for the nation's 770,000 long-term unemployed. (j)

The work was to be carried out, said Kenneth Clarke, by "Task Forces" of civil servants (à la CAT Model) who would work with local authorities and local community/voluntary organisations to try to saturate areas with all available Urban Aid and MSC funding. The total population affected was 300,000.

> "One purpose of the project" he explained "will be to take much more advantage of the Race Relations Act's provisions . . . to channel training specifically to racial minorities which are disadvantaged."

"A mouse of a statement" was the view of the Opposition's Chief Spokesman on Employment, John Prescott. "A con trick" the reaction of other Labour members.

On the very same day the Association of District Councils published a report entitled *The Rural Economy at the Crossroads*. This pointed out that the "ignored" problems of the "forgotten" rural areas — chronic unemployment, low income, poor housing and environmental problems — were leading to "rural decay". (27)

APPENDIX 1

MRS. THATCHER'S DIARY

(1)	"Manufacturing productivity has risen at an average annual rate of 6% for the last 5 years, higher than France or Germany." "Company profitability is at its highest for two decades."
(2)	"The rate of inflation is almost half the level the Government inherited, with further falls in prospect."
(3)	"The United Kingdom is in its 5th successive year of growth, with gross domestic product at an all-time high. Output is expected to have grown faster in 1985 than all other European Community countries and the USA."
(4)	Employment rising, with around 700,000 more people in work since March 1983.
(5)	Income Tax thresholds raised by about 20% in real terms. (k)
(6)	Twelve leading state-owned companies (including British Petroleum: £819m., British Aerospace: £389m., Cable & Wireless: £1025m., Britoil: £1058m., and British Telecom: £2156m.) privatised and with a target of 40% of the state-owned industrial sector to be privatised by the end of the Parliament.
(7)	Pay, price and dividend controls abolished along with controls on foreign exchange, bank lending, hire purchase, industrial and office development. (l)
(8)	Productivity per person in agriculture improved by more than 40%.
(9)	Retirement pension at a record level in real terms.
(10)	Total manpower in the police force in Great Britain up by 17,000 and expenditure in England and Wales up by one third in real terms.
(11)	Spending on the NHS up by 21% in real terms.
(12)	The highest % in Europe of young people owning their own home.

Source: Commons Written Reply by the Prime Minister on a Question regarding her achievements since 1979. Quoted in 'UK outpacing Germany', Anthony Bevins, *Times*, 25/2/86.

Notes: State-owned companies slated for future privatisation include British Gas, Royal Ordnance, National Bus Company and British Airways.

APPENDIX 2

THE RATE-SUPPORT GRANT SETTLEMENT FOR 1986/7

For all but a handful of authorities, he said, "more spending will result in less grant and less spending will result in more grant": the aim was to bring local authority current spending down to a level the economy could afford. The main feature of the settlement was, he explained, the abolition of expenditure targets and the associated grant penalties.

"The aggregate of Exchequer grant will be the same cash sum – £11,764m. – as the figure originally supplied for this year. But it is about £400m. more than the amount of grant now being paid for the year, because local authorities are (this year) forfeiting £400m. through holdback . . . Provision for local authority current expenditure has been set at £22.25 billion."

"I announced provisional Grant-Related Expenditure Assessments, GREAS, on October 28th. These incorporated various technical adjustments. The cities will benefit from changes in the concessionary fares and social work GREAS. The remote shires will gain from changes in the Education GREA . . . As in past years, the pressure will become more severe if the authority's expenditure exceeds a threshold set at an average of 10% above GREA."

"I now turn to rate limitation. In July, my predecessor (Patrick Jenkin) announced the list of 12 authorities selected for rate limitation in 1986/7, together with (their permissible) expenditure levels. In most cases these represented a cash freeze on 1985/6 budgets. Seven of the 12 authorities have now applied to me for a redetermination of their expenditure level – Camden, Greenwich, Hackney, Lewisham, Lambeth, Liverpool and Newcastle. I have considered their applications carefully and, in each case, I have increased their expenditure level somewhat, though overall by substantially less than they themselves had thought (necessary). I am today proposing rate limits for these authorities."

"My proposals for 1986/7 represent a major advance. I have abolished targets. I have improved GREAS. I have established a clearer relationship between what councils get and what they spend. And I have built on the success of rate limitation in 1985/6."

Source: Kenneth Baker's speech in the Commons 18/12/85. 'Rates Grant Settlement irks County MPs', *Times*, 19/12/85.

Note: A GREA is a statement of the level of spending on services Central Government thinks a local authority ought to incur and a basis for the Government's calculation of how much Grant the authority ought to receive.

APPENDIX 3

THE GOVERNMENT'S PUBLIC EXPENDITURE PLANS 1986-9

Departments £000,000	Est. Outturn 1985-86	Plans for 1986-87	Plans for 1987-88	Plans for 1988-89
Ministry of Defence	18,200	18,520	18,820	18,990
EEC	800	800	1,150	950
CAP expenditure	1,900	1,550	1,640	1,670
Domestic Agriculture	880	830	820	830
Forestry Commission	50	50	50	60
Department of Trade	1,650	1,300	1,080	940
Export Credits Guarantee	340	280	170	100
Department of Energy	1,000	110	- 550	- 290
Department of Employment	3,300	3,760	3,810	3,990
Department of Transport	4,500	4,810	4,840	4,830
DOE − Housing	2,700	2,750	2,830	2,880
DOE − Property Services	- 110	- 90	- 110	- 110
DOE − Other Environment	3,950	3,620	3,530	3,560
Home Office	4,750	4,960	5,010	5,040
Lord Chancellor's Dept.	540	590	650	700
Department of Education	14,400	14,320	14,400	14,480
Office of Arts and Libraries	700	730	750	760
DHSS − Health	16,700	17,720	18,450	19,140
DHSS − Social Security	41,200	42,900	44,400	45,900
Civil Superannuation	1,050	1,180	1,310	1,400
Scotland	7,400	7,540	7,390	7,420
Wales	2,800	2,910	2,940	3,000
Northern Ireland	4,300	4,520	4,690	4,820
Chancellor's Departments	1,800	2,010	2,050	2,070
Other Departments	350	450	460	470
Reserve	0	4,500	6,250	8,000
Special sales of assets	- 2,500(4)	- 4,750	- 4,750	- 4,750
Adjustments	- 300	- 650	- 250	- 260
PLANNING TOTAL:	134,200	139,100	143,900	148,700

Source: Guardian, 13.11.85.

APPENDIX 4
INNER CITY JOBLESS AID – 1986/7

Authority	Total Nos. Unemployed	Urban Aid 1985-86 (£m)	Urban Aid 1986-87 (£m)	% Cut In Real Terms
PARTNERSHIP AUTHORITIES				
Birmingham	91,181	24.5	24.5	4.5
Hackney	20,650	12.0	11.6	8.0
Islington	16,642	10.4	10.0	8.0
Lambeth	26,141	13.5	13.1	7.5
Liverpool	56,476	24.1	22.8	10.0
Manchester/	44,689	24.5	23.8	7.5
Salford	19,074			
Newcastle/	25,603	18.0	17.2	9.0
Gateshead	16,816			
PROGRAMME AUTHORITIES				
Blackburn*	18,779	3.6	3.6	4.5
Bolton*	28,512	3.59	3.59	4.5
Bradford*	31,082	4.58	4.58	4.5
Brent	16,391	4.5	4.5	4.5
Coventry*	36,908	4.3	4.3	4.5
Hammersmith/Fulham	12,311	5.63	5.63	4.5
Hull	30,660	4.47	4.47	4.5
Knowsley	20,038	3.7	3.7	4.5
Leeds*	41,572	4.13	4.13	4.5
Leicester*	27,008	5.43	5.43	4.5
Middlesbrough*	30,439	4.62	4.62	4.5
Nottingham*	44,039	4.85	4.85	4.5
Oldham	12,994	3.66	3.66	4.5
Rochdale*	10,509	3.6	3.6	4.5
Sandwell	25,864	4.5	4.5	4.5
Sheffield*	45,179	4.01	4.01	4.5
Sunderland*	37,853	3.17	3.17	4.5
Tower Hamlets	16,006	4.5	4.5	4.5
North Tyneside	14,595	3.12	3.12	4.5
South Tyneside	15,366	3.93	3.93	4.5
Wandsworth	16,601	4.5	4.5	4.5
Wirral*	39,317	3.67	3.67	4.5
Wolverhampton*	25,738	4.84	4.84	4.5
TOTAL	915,032	223.9	219.9	6.3

*Travel-to-work areas.

Source: Financial Times, 7.2.86 (Announced 28.1.86)

NOTES

(a) It was in Bradford, in December 1985, that headmaster Ray Honeyford resigned after a campaign waged by the mainly Asian parents of children at his school over his published views on "multi-racial" education. His attitudes were not regarded as racialist by his profession and he reached a substantial financial accommodation with the Local Education Authority over his untimely departure.

Note that John Carlisle's topic would have included, it was thought, references to South Africa and apartheid.

(b) In 1983 a policy change meant that unemployed men over 60 could claim unemployment benefit without having to "sign on" at unemployment offices. This was also the year in which the Government's Youth Training Scheme was launched.

This guaranteed a YTS place — involving education/training and planned work experience — for all unemployed school-leavers, 17 year olds and some older young people with special needs. The target YTS "employed" coverage for 1985/6 was 379,000 young people.

The MSC's expanded Community Programme, started in 1985, was aimed at providing training/work experience opportunities for 230,000 adults. These also are not listed as unemployed during their participation in the Programme.

(c) According to the *Sunday Telegraph* of 2 March 1986, the Scotland Yard report on the Tottenham riots was to remain secret. It was understood that the report, compiled by Chief Supt. David Williams, was highly critical of some aspects of the police's operations. Training for such riot situations was carried out in simulated conditions at the Metropolitan Police's Public Order Training Centre in Albert Street, Hounslow.

(d) At the end of February 1986 UK unemployment stood at an all-time high of 3.2m. or 14% of the workforce. Within this total inner city youth unemployment ranged from 21.5% in Notting Hill to 56% in Handsworth.

The Government's Regional Policy directed aid (in the form of grants for plant, machinery and job-creation) to companies in Development and Intermediate Areas. Aid was also claimable from the EEC's Regional Development Fund. A Cambridge University study on behalf of the DTI reported in February 1986 that Regional Policy over the period 1960-81 had created a total of 450,000 jobs at an average cost/job of £40,000. The most costly jobs were in metal manufacturing: an average of £367,000.(28) Note also the Development Corporation Model established by Michael Heseltine for the Merseyside and London Docklands.

(e)   Councillor Hatton was one of those named in the Labour Party's 3-month inquiry into the Militant Tendency in Liverpool as being a member of "an unconstitutional organisation" and apparently earmarked for expulsion from the Labour Party. He, like Ted Knight, had been a long-time leader of the "rebellion" against the Government's policy on the control of local authority expenditure. This policy was made up of the 1980 Local Government Planning and Land Act (which set up the GREA system), the 1982 Local Government Finance Act (made legal "expenditure capping") and the 1984 Rates Act (empowered "rate capping").

(f)   Note, however, the Home Secretary's announcement on 11 February 1986:

"In view of the increasing demands on the police service, particularly the need to counter drug abuse, public disorder and terrorism, I intend to increase the proportion of police expenditure met by Central Government through Police Grant from 50% to 51% in 1986/7. (29)

This was backed up by the issue, on 7 March 1986, of the Government's White Paper on Criminal Justice. This proposed life sentences for carrying fire arms in the furtherance of crime, more power for courts to confiscate criminals' assets and changes to the jury system (including abolition of jury trial for some offences).

(g)   The geographical exhortations of Messrs. Tebbitt and Kinnock are interesting in view of the following points:

1.   President Reagan's 1985 deficit-budget economic management approach had — despite disclaimers to the contrary — the air of a classic Keynesian model, albeit defence-spending led and accompanied by an extremely tight credit policy. It is noteworthy that the USA sustained a record trade deficit of $17.65 billion for the month of December 1985.

2.   The call by the Keidranen (Japan's prestigious Federation of Economic Organisations) for "freer" trade made in February 1986. This took the form of a recommendation for consideration of the need for Japan to reduce the level of tariff protection it enjoyed in the light of the long-run change in $/yen parity and the country's enormous trading surplus with the USA. (30)

(h)   According to John Macgregor, Chief Secretary to the Treasury, the cost of Labour's published programme would amount to £24 billion in a single year. He estimated that employment measures would account for approximately 27% of this sum, social security changes for 27% and housing, Urban Programme and sewerage schemes for £4 billion. The figure was rejected by Roy Hattersley, Shadow Chancellor, as an "invention". What was not in dispute was a statement by Neil Kinnock on Tyne Tees Television that he would impose £3 billion extra tax on the country's richest 1m. tax payers. Conversely, it was generally held that the Conservative Chancellor would have less freedom to implement tax cuts — a long-cherished and fundamental policy aim — in his forthcoming budget in March 1986 due to adverse movements in the price of Britain's North Sea Oil. Brent crude for delivery in April fell below $15 on the 27 February.

The London Stock Market shrugged off previous bad oil price news and the fact that the UK's January 1986 trade in manufactures was in deficit to the tune of £266m. to break through the 1200 level (FT 30-share index) and close at an all-time high on 12 February. Take-over bidding was in spate.

(i) The Independent Inquiry into the Handsworth Disturbances of 1985, commissioned by the City of Birmingham and conducted by ex-MP Julius Silverman, was published one week later. Its findings were that mass unemployment and alienation among the tightly-knit ethnic minority communities in Handsworth were major elements behind the riots. Among a host of practical suggestions were the needs for more Afro-Caribbean teachers (rastafarians were reported to have accompanied the police on patrol after the riots), for more pre-school play groups, for more youth clubs and for more police training.

(j) It was reported (31) that a local Job Centre Manager told the Commons Select Committee during its visit to the Broadwater Estate that he had never been required to read the Commission for Racial Equality's Code of Practice. This despite the not unusual level of 50% concentration of ethnic minority residents in the area.

An interesting addendum . . . Gerald Howarth, Conservative MP for Cannock and Burntwood, called on 1 March for the return of conscription. "I believe" he said, "that there is a latent demand . . . I understand the reluctance of the services . . . but we are virtually alone among our European allies in holding out. There is a military need. But it would also instill a sense of discipline and respect." (32)

(k) Note also that, according to *Social Trends 16* (HMSO): the wealthiest 10% of Britain's population owned 54% of the nation's marketable wealth in 1983, burglaries increased by 21% between 1981 and 1983, firearms were reported to have been used in 8% of the robberies reported in 1984 and that children of partly-skilled and unskilled manual parentage took 7.2% of university places in 1984, as opposed to 5.2% in 1981.

(l) Total Government spending as a % of GDP moved from 43% in 1978/9 to 46.5% in 1982/3 and back to a projected 43% in 1986/7. It was thought that the Government expenditure for 1986/7 would amount to £158 billion, inclusive of £18 billion interest on debt. It was forecast to be met through Tax revenue of £149 billion and a Public Sector Borrowing Requirement of £9 billion. (33)

References:

1. Robin Young, 'Campus Fracas MP Used to Violence', *Times*, 15/2/86.
2. Tenth Report from the Committee of Public Accounts, Session 1985/6, *The Urban Programme*.
3. *Hansard*, 2/12/68.
4. 'Brixton Outlook: One Law for Black, One Law for Blue', *Guardian*, 11/11/85
5. David Simpson, 'Riots Prompt Review of Inner City Aid', *Guardian*, 6/11/85.
6. As 4.
7. *Times*, 9/10/85.
8. 'Parliament', *Times*, 21/12/85.
9. Geoff Andrews, 'Extra £200m. to meet £19 billion Housing Repairs', *Guardian*, 13/11/85.
10. As 9.
11. SHAC = Shelter Housing Aid Centre.
12. From the 1980 Housing Act to the 1986 Housing Bill.
13. Seamus Milne, 'London Homeless up to 700% in 15 years Says Report', *Guardian*, 25/11/85.
14. Colin Hughes, 'London Council Rent Arrears Top £125m.', *Times*, 21/12/85.
15. 'Parliament' — 'Tebbitt Attack on Extremism Howled Down', *Times*, 11/12/85.
16. As 15.
17. As 15
18. As 15.
19. *Guardian*, 12/11/85.
20. Robin Young, 'Britons Better Off, Better Educated and a Better Class of Person', *Times*, 9/1/86: Andrew Rawnsley, 'Well-met by Moonlight', *Guardian*, 27/11/85.
21. As 19.
22. 'Canary Row', *Guardian*, 12/11/85.
23. David Hencke, 'Pensioner Wins Fuel Cash in New Blow to DHSS', *Guardian*, 12/11/85.
24. Paul Hoyland, 'Handsworth Report Blames Apartheid System', *Guardian*, 21/2/86.
25. 'Parliament' — 'Rates Grant settlement irks county MP's', *Times*, 19/12/85.
26. As 24.
27. 'Vanishing Villages Crisis Brings Call for £20m. Cash Rescue', *Daily Telegraph*, 7/2/86.
28. David Smith, 'CBI Calls for £1 billion Action after Jobless Hits Peak', *Times*, 28/2/85.

29. Peter Evans, 'Ministries Give Police an Extra £52m. to Boost Forces to Fight Crime', *Times*, 12/2/86.
30. 'Japan Business Chiefs Call for Freer Trade', *Financial Times*, 28/2/86.
31. Patricia Clough, 'MPs look at Ethnic Job Plight', *Times*, 25/2/86.
32. John Lewis, 'Tory MPs Demand Return of National Service', *Sunday Telegraph*, 2/3/86.
33. Christopher Huhne, 'Asset Sales Disguise Treasury Concession', *Guardian*, 13/11/85.

CASE NO. 10
D-DAY ON THE BUSES

Free-For-All

Howard Hoptrough was not amused. In fact, truth-to-tell, he was in a vitriolic mood about the Conservative Government's "Buses" White Paper which was published on 12 July 1984. Writing from St. Just in the fastnesses of Cornwall he poured out a stream of acrimony to the Editor of the *Guardian*:

> "Sir — As usual the Maggie Government is putting forward its nonsensensical and extreme partisan views as a practical policy. The nonsense is in the word "competition". The last thing it (deregulation of the buses) does is to make the service or industry more efficient; the first thing it does is to encourage the 'quick-buck merchant' to move in, with no moral, welfare, social or safety responsibility to the society or group it is supposed to be serving.
>
> Competition in trade is an euphemism for 'cut-throat commercial war'. It has always been so, the only difference today being that the so-called social conscience has less influence and greed is greater and more widespread." (1)

His was not the only voice raised in violent criticism of plans to radically change the public bus transport system in Britain. Indeed the chorus of antagonism comprised contributions from bodies as ideologically diverse as the Labour-dominated Association of Metropolitan Authorities (AMA) and the Conservative-dominated Association of District Councils (ADC), the Bus & Coach Council and the Womens Institute.

The proposals in the White Paper which were generating such a heated response concerned in part the notion of allowing anyone with a bus to operate for gain where desired, subject only to meeting requisite safety standards and registering the route and timetable with the local authority. This entailed the abolition outside London of the system of road service licensing and service regulation which had ruled local bus operations for a half-century. Clearly, a major strategic shift.

Not that uneconomic but still socially-essential public transport services would cease in the brave new competitive world foreseen by the White Paper. Local authorities would still continue to subsidise such routes as in the past but they would have to put them out to tender.

Another significant worry for a high proportion of the bus-using population was dealt with by the White Paper's guarantee of the continuation of concessionary fare schemes. Any other changeover difficulties were to be handled, it said, within the context of the Special Innovation and the Transitional Grants.

Average Take-Home Pay: (£ per week at constant 1986 prices)	1979		1986	
	Richest 10%	Poorest 10%	Richest 10%	Poorest 10%
Single Man	174.28	79.32	215.14	82.09
Single Woman	115.34	58.96	143.10	64.41
Married Man with Two Children	195.52	100.56	236.50	103.45

TABLE 1:   **RELATIVE DEPRIVATION?**

Source: Relative Values – The New Poor: not starving, just missing out, Tim Rayment, *Sunday Times*, 7/12/86.

Mrs. Thatcher's Government saw its suggestions as a bold but needful step to counteract the consistent, seemingly inexorable decline in bus travel in Britain from 42% of all travel in 1953 to only 8% in 1983. They were also seen as an inescapable antidote to the run-away rise in revenue support for bus transport which had taken government subsidies from £10m. in 1972 to £530m. in 1986. The White Paper stated:

> "Britain needs good bus services. We must get away from the idea that the only future for bus services is to contract painfully at large cost to taxpayers and ratepayers as well as travellers." (2)

It promised a mixture of blessings which included an overall saving of £200m. and a combination of cheaper fares and better services based on alternative transport vehicles, like minibuses or shared taxis, where appropriate. A pleasant vista for the Conservative Government which did not view an annual tax cost for public bus travel of well-nigh £1b. (£150m. central rebates on fuel duty + £290m. for concessionary fares + £530m. subsidies) with equanimity.

Secretary of State Nicholas Ridley, chief protagonist of the deregulation policy, held the view that the existing pattern of services reflected the needs of "a different age" and inspired an operational philosophy which was "defensive and inward-looking". (3) Speaking on this theme at the Bus & Coach Council's annual conference at Blackpool on 26 September 1984, he declared:

"People do want buses, but their demands are changing. And, if they do not get what they want they won't be stoical. They'll take the car, or walk, or not bother to make the trip."

Few sympathised with the Minister's stance. Indeed his speech was interrupted on occasion with shouts from some of the more vociferous delegates of "absolute rubbish" and "nonsense". (4) A politer reaction on the other hand, was expressed by a local authority representative, Councillor Alec Waugh of the South Yorkshire Metropolitan Council:

"You know damn well your policy is getting little support from anybody. You have got it wrong and you are going to destroy the major service in this country. If the government was confident in its proposals it would have included London in the planned deregulation. But they would not dare do it in the capital because of the chaos that would ensue." (5)

One of the chief elements in the "chaos" that was prophesied was the spectacle of buses again "hunting in packs" for custom as in pre-regulation days.

This awesome vision simply compounded other pessimistic views taken by bus producers of the state of their market place. According to speaker David Hargreaves, Managing Director of bus manufacturers Hestair Dennis, his company's output had dropped from 3,700 buses in 1979 to 1,100 in 1984.

Of all those protesting against the plans for change, the strongest public outcry came from a body entitled The Public Transport Campaign Group. It had been formed specifically to orchestrate such opposition by the soon-to-be-abolished Metropolitan Authorities (GLC and the County Councils of Greater Manchester, Merseyside, South Yorkshire, Tyne and Wear, West Midlands and West Yorkshire), the Transport and General Workers' Union and interest groups such as Friends of the Earth, Capital and Transport 2000. Its media advertising pulled no punches:

"What Mr. Ridley sees as toys, the rest of us can see as a vital national asset built up over generations. The words are "deregulation" and "privatisation" and "cutting public expenditure". The reality will be reduced services, higher fares, lower standards.

Cut back public transport in a country where nearly 40% of households have no car at all and you restrict the mobility of a large part of the population." (6)

Its conviction that "a successful, reasonably-subsidised public transport system is good for efficiency and good for the economy" was buttressed by statements of the subsidies enjoyed by Amsterdam (79% of costs), Denver (70%) and 30 other major cities in Europe, North America and Australasia (over 50%).

Spokespersons on behalf of the rural lobby also worked hard to make their protests felt, faced as they were with the perceived threat of a reduction in services. Take Linda Hart of the WI, for example:

> "Only a monopoly service can afford to commit itself to running buses on isolated routes. It is an absurd, doctrinaire policy that will cause enormous hardship" . . . What is required is "a coherent, integrated policy of transport planning. If councils are no longer responsible for overall planning, it is unlikely that operators will coordinate services with each other or with rail services — so the passenger will lose out again." (7)

Or Susan Hoyle, Executive Director of Transport 2000 — itself an interest group whose backers included The Civic Trust, The Conservative Ecology Group and The Council for National Parks. She complained:

> "It is inevitable that private operators will cream off the busy routes. Many unprofitable country services which provide a life-line will simply disappear. Government philosophy seems underpinned by the fallacy that the bus industry is full of thrusting young executives who will risk bailing out uneconomic routes on . . . meagre subsidies." (8) "What will happen to our countryside? the trains have already gone and now the buses are under threat of the axe. Are rural areas to be abandoned to those rich and healthy enough to have cars?" (9)

Or David Clark, Secretary of Rural Voice.

This pressure group certainly deserved the Minister's attention. If not for its pronouncements, then for the particular establishment bodies it represented. These included the National Farmers' Union, the Country Landowners' Association, the Council for the Protection of Rural England and the National Federation of Womens Institutes.

It, too, in David Clark's words, was apprehensive:

> "We are not opposed to competition" but "we believe that the Government's proposals for competitive tendering route-by-route without some form of regulation could lead to the loss of rural routes and instability in the services that survive." (10)

Penny Numbers

Deregulation was not the only significant proposal in the White Paper. It also advocated wholesale changes in the organisation of bus transport provision and in the ownership of the major operator in this field. If enacted, these changes would mean the certain fragmentation and potential privatisation of the main mass-market bus transport provider in Britain, the National Bus Company, and disaggregation of the metropolitan counties-based Passenger Transport Executives. Some of the PTEs in fact used NBC subsidiaries as their carriers by agreement under Section 24 of the Transport Act 1968. The White Paper foresaw an ending to such agreements. It also proposed the breaking up of the PTEs that did run their own fleets into smaller companies, possibly independent, possibly local authority-owned.

Name of Subsidiary	Net Revenue £m.	Turn-over £m.	Net Assets £m.
London Country	1.9	60.3	11.5
Midland Red	1.2	50.5	9.4
Northern General	2.5	46.8	19.4
United Automobile	2.0	42.9	23.0
Ribble Motor	1.9	42.4	22.8
Total : Top Five	9.7	243.0	86.2
City of Oxford	.5	11.3	2.3
East Yorkshire	.3	7.9	3.9
Lincolnshire Road	.05	7.7	1.3
Cumberland Motor	.16	6.7	3.5
Southern Vectis	.4	4.7	3.0
Total : Bottom Five	1.43	38.4	14.1

TABLE 2: **NBC'S PERFORMANCE – 1984**

Notes: 1) All data are rounded
2) Net Revenue is after interest and taxation and calculated on an historical accounting basis
3) Support Payments were – Top Five: £23.3m.; Bottom Five: £2.7m.

Data Source: NBC Annual Report

There was considerable and widespread concern at the possible results that the break-up of NBC would bring. As Table 2 indicates, the company spanned the nation in its provision of local bus services or stage carriage operations as they are known in the industry. Additionally, NBC had subordinate but still important interests in the fields of long-distance travel (National Express) and in holiday transport (National Holidays). NBC as a whole recorded an operating profit (before interest payable and tax) of £45.9m. on an operating income of £764m. (of which £604m. was stage carriage) in 1984. The total capital employed was £442m. Employing 50,000 people and owning over 14,000 buses, NBC was a major service provider. It earned in 1984 no less than 78% of its turnover from its passengers.

The Hereford Trial Area was one of three such areas where road service licensing provisions were removed for a period as an experiment under the provisions of the 1980 Transport Act. The influx of new competitors who wished to take on the incumbent Midland Red West on lucrative city services included Stretton Coaches, Buchanan's, Primrose and Flash. When the last named fell foul of the Traffic Commissioners, its licence was revoked with the words "It is just as well that those who travelled in your vehicles did not know how much their health and safety were at risk." It was at the outset an undignified leap-frogging exercise with buses racing each other to get to the next stop first. At the end it was recognised that bus traffic had risen by 50% and fares had fallen by 30% and that Midland Red users were in a strong position with all competitors eliminated save one.

"Chaos" was the PTCG word for the Hereford Trial.

As part of the West Country Trial, Harry Blundred of Devon General successfully replaced 9 conventional buses with 38 Ford Transits and increased service frequency to some city housing estates in Exeter. It meant some new and welcome jobs for those on the dole but also some changes in attitudes as national union conditions did not apply to these minibuses.

EXHIBIT 1:   **TESTING, TESTING**

NBC management were much concerned at the message of the White Paper. Lord Shepherd, NBC Chairman, fired off a pre-emptive metaphorical shot across the Government's bows when he announced the company's results for 1983 on 13 June 1984. He said that any change would have to be carried out in a "thoughtful and informed way" if profits were not to be cut and services were not to be damaged. These principles were more fully covered in NBC's Annual Report for 1984 by Lord Shepherd's successor, Robert Brook. (11) He discussed the particular nature of NBC's market-place — "highly sensitive to the overall economic climate" — and spoke plainly of the possibly deleterious effect of removal of subsidy:

> "NBC agrees that financial support for local bus services needs to be carefully controlled and that the long-established principle of cross-subsidy between services can produce unwelcome social effects. However it remains gravely concerned about the effects of a sudden removal of the support available through cross-subsidy which must inevitably follow deregulation. This is because on the busy, profitable route sections it is likely that, as the Government intends, competition will increase the number of buses and cause fares to fall, at least in the first instance. However, this in turn will reduce the existing operator's ability to cross-subsidise services from within their own means."

A clearly anxious NBC Chairman also laid stress on what he saw as the need to achieve fair play in the market-place:

> "If competition is expected to bring the expected benefits to the local bus business, NBC believes it essential that the legislation provides throughout for fair competition, with the same ground rules for all parties involved . . . small operators competing with larger ones . . . established operators competing with newcomers . . . between types of operator (NBC companies, local authority and PTE undertakings and independent operators) and between modes (taxi, minibus, conventional bus, rail)."

This was a decorous approach to what was, in organisational terms at least, a delicate matter for any head of a nationalised undertaking. Others could be, and were, more forceful. Larry Smith of the TUC's Transport Committee, for instance, made a statement on behalf of the TUC and AMA which condemned the possible privatisation of NBC. It would not nothing, he averred, other than "feed the vultures waiting to pick off profitable elements of public industry." (12)

Others were fairly sure that privatisation of NBC was a reasonable thing to do. One such, Digby Anderson — Director of The Social Affairs Unit — explained his position as follows:

> "The central objections to the break-up of NBC — that we do not know precisely what will happen and it might be an unplanned mess —

are risks that have to be taken. Anyway, unplanned messes are to be preferred to planned ones and often turn out to be messes only from the theorist's or bureaucrat's view." (13)

Whatever the worries that concerned interested parties as a result of the White Paper, they lost some of their moment when, at the end of January 1985, Nicholas Ridley announced new guidelines for Metropolitan CCs' transport subsidies amounting to a 10% cut. And when the Transport Bill started its parliamentary passage.

. . . Like Grim Death

The publication of the Transport Bill coincided with the Minister's announcement of the cut guidelines. Known universally by opponents as "The Cowboys Charter", it attracted immediate and enduring pressure group hostility throughout its legislative journey.

To start with there were adverse comments from those with perhaps the greatest vested interest of all – the Bus & Coach Council – to the effect that "The Bill is too theoretical and will do as much harm as good". Furthermore, as its Director-General Dennis Quinn pointed out:

> "The bus industry has recently accepted the call for increased competition, high safety standards and relaxation of bus licensing but has tried to temper the Government's proposals to make them workable. This advice appears to have been rejected." (14)

As were the representations of Transport 2000, at least according to Director Susan Hoyle (15), and, ostensibly, those of the AMA. The latter went so far as to call the pre-Bill consultation "a sham". (16)

Then there was the almost unprecedented picture of local politicians, left and right, united in antipathy.

1) Abolition of road service licensing, except in London. Clause 84 states that local authorities shall "so conduct themselves as not to inhibit competition between persons providing or seeking to provide public passenger transport services in their area".
2) Allowing public transport services to be operated by non-bus vehicles.
3) Privatisation of NBC.
4) Councils to put non-commercially-viable services out to tender.

TRANSPORT BILL: MAIN POINTS

Nicholas Ridley cannot but have had some qualms at the prospect facing him in the light of such apparent extra-parliamentary hostility. If so, any such worries can only have been greatly increased by the rough handling the Bill received in both Houses. In the Commons it was fought against tooth and claw, hammer and tongs.

The Second Reading debate set the tone. Labour's Mrs. Gwyneth Dunwoody led the attack with the claims that the Bill was about saving money and not improving services, that its content reflected ignorance of the transport industry rather than real knowledge and that it had been introduced in a hurried and incompetent fashion. "Total anarchy", she declared, would ensue. (17) Nicholas Ridley, by contrast, saw in the Bill "a full-scale rescue plan for the bus industry" which would alter the basis of subsidisation to those passengers who really needed help and which would make sure the country got the best value-for-money it could. (18)

The Conservatives obtained a relatively low majority of 83 when the Bill was given a Second Reading. At the heart of this lay the disquiet of some Conservatives over the Bill itself and the annoyance of others that the debate had taken place before the Commons Select Committee on Transport had produced its awaited report on the bus industry. Any possibility of a serious back-bench revolt was avoided by an undertaking by Transport Minister David Mitchell that the Government would defer the Committee Stage on the Bill to allow the Select Committee time to report. This news was welcomed by the 43 members of the Standing Committee (26 Conservatives, 15 Labour and 2 Liberals).

Exchanges in the Commons on 25 February did nothing to sweeten the discussion. Nicholas Ridley announced that NBC was to be asked to provide a statement of restructuring options and that discussions on privatisation would follow "soon", with the Government's preference leaning towards employee buy-outs. Conservative Jonathan Sayeed (Bristol East) chipped in with the comment that in Avon bus subsidies had risen in the last 10 years from £66,000 to £4.5m. An acid question came from Peter Pike (Burnley, Labour):

> "As the Bill lays down that, when inviting tenders it is not possible to lay down conditions of employment, is it the Secretary of State's intention that benefit to consumers shall be achieved on the backs of workers in the industry, with low pay and bad conditions?" (19)

It was met with a dead-bat reply. Having stressed that the Government was in no way seeking to privatise municipal undertakings, the Secretary of State responded:

"Local authority associations asked for, and we were happy to agree, that there should be greater flexibility in the rules for tendering. This is allowed in the Bill. The Midland Red Bus Co. in Hereford and Worcester achieved a 25% increase in productivity without any of the scare stories he is peddling." (20)

Mrs. Elaine Kellett-Bowman (Lancaster, Conservative) took up this last theme:

"I have been besieged with protests from my ratepayers who have received throught their doors — as every single ratepayer in Lancashire has — an expensive, glossy leaflet trying to mislead the public. Many of my rural constituents are greatly looking forward to the day when they get more flexible bus services and do not have 72-seater buses running around country areas with one or two people on them." (21)

Such were very small beer however, compared with what happened on 1 April. Grossly dissatisfied with the Bill's progress, the Government put forward a guillotine motion to strictly timetable, and thus curb, further debate. This was passed 277 to 189. Explained John Biffen, Leader of the House, "After 94 hours of debate, only 11 clauses and two schedules have been completed". No more opposition filibustering would be permitted was his message. "An outrage" countered Mrs. Gwyneth Dunwoody (22), especially concerned at the Commons Transport Committee's expressed viewpoint that it was possible that "each operator will seek to maximise his share of the traffic by running as closely as possible in front of his rivals". (23)

One of the largest bones of contention was quarrelled over during the Report Stage. Namely, how, on the one hand, to ensure competition among rivals on a given route and, on the other, to get the rivals to dovetail their services with each other in order to produce a viable service for that route. The Government dealt with this by passing a new clause which ended the current exemption enjoyed by bus and coach operators from the Restrictive Trade Practices Act 1976 and which made all fares-coverage-service frequency deals among rivals on a given route registerable with the Office of Fair Trading.

Exchanges on this subject and the NBC privatisation issue drew stinging comments from Mrs. Dunwoody that:

- the Bill reflected the prejudices of a Secretary of State who had "probably never been on a bus in his life" (24) and
- that, in his handling of policy, he had given "a passable imitation of Pontius Pilate" (25) and
- that he had decided "in the most arbitrary and insensitive way that the total transport system should be thrown into chaos and disaster". (26)

Nicholas Ridley was not having any. He enjoined the House to support "a radical, imaginative and well-constructed package of measures to revitalise an ailing industry . . . overwhelmingly in the interests of the travelling public". (27)

The Ermine View

The Government's Third Reading Debate victory by 246-170 took the Bill into the House of Lords. Here their Lordships had an ideological field-day without the bitterness of some of the Commons exchanges.

In the Lords' Second Reading Debate Lord McIntosh of Haringey (Labour) claimed that the Bill came from "the sleep of reason which, as the painter Goya said, gave rise to monsters". (28) His colleague Lord Carmichael of Kelvingrove deployed a less aesthetic argument. He pointed out to the Government spokesman, Lord Brabazon of Tara, that in Hereford only 25% of the population lacked a car whereas the comparative figure for Merseyside and Strathclyde was 75%. To this he added, somewhat archly. that the Bill seemed to be aimed at encouraging small businessmen. But, if so, he said:

> "A bus bought by someone using his redundancy money would be secondhand and pretty well clapped-out. How long such a bus would last and how safe it would be could be guessed from some of the results in the trial areas . . . The Government was embarking on a high-risk approach to unknown territory." (29)

In the Committee Stage Debate Lord McIntosh returned prosaically to the attack with reference to the inadequacy of the "unsatisfactory" trials that had been carried out. This was a view shared by his Labour colleague and former NBC Chairman, Lord Shepherd who declared that the Government:

> "Was going against all the trends, resting its case on the experience of two third world countries and three unconnected experiments." (30)

The Government found this legislative stage in the passage of the Bill in some ways more worrisome than the processes which had led to the imposition of the guillotine in the Commons. The rejection of a Government amendment on rural bus grants by 115 votes to 114 on 29 July could have led to more embarrassment had the position not been retrieved by success with yet another amendment on Innovation Grants. It had been a case where detailed appreciation of the specific needs of some sectors of the industry had been necessary. Not easy in a field consisting, in the words of commentator Stephen Aris, of:

> "a labyrinth of routes and networks, rural and urban, whose economics have over the years become inextricably intertwined in a cat's cradle of cross-subsidisation." (31)

Not easy also in terms of some calculations (32) that a cut in the Government's Transport Supplementary Grant to a particular local authority could conceivably increase the costs incurred by that authority by a large amount, since:

(a) a reduction in the subsidy given by the local authority (as a result of the TSG cut) would result either in fare increases or, perhaps more likely, service cuts and

(b) any service cuts would necessitate higher-cost extra transport provision to meet the authority's statutory education and social service needs.

Indeed, it was the case that in October 1985 all the metropolitan authorities were forecasting horrifying combinations of service cuts (<10%) and fare rises (approx. 20%), sufficient to provoke Cyril Bateman (Ex-head of West Midlands PTE) into the comment:

> "Government policies are shocking. The Transport Bill is the worst legislation we have ever had. I don't know how they can do it." (33)

Notwithstanding, the Bill continued its far-from-lordly progress. Until mid-October that is, when Bill Morris, Deputy General-Secretary designate of the Transport and General Workers Union announced that a series of rolling strikes was to take place in protest at the Transport Bill. Speaking at a rally in Sheffield, he claimed that the Government had refused to give adequate protection to the index-linked pensions of the NBC employees who would be affected by privatisation. The Government's suggestion was that the £450m in the NBC Pension Fund be invested in private insurance. He said:

"This union will not shrink from using its industrial strength to prevent the £450m. of workers' money in the Pension Fund being handed over to the fat cats in the City at our pensioners' cost." (34)

> "The competition has resulted in a dramatic increase in the number of bus vehicles present in the limited confines of the city centre. It has created major environmental problems with little or no opportunity to limit or control the problems created. Public reaction has not welcomed the increase in the city centre and complaints have been long and generally justified . . . in Hereford the experiment has been a trial in a good many respects."

EXHIBIT 2: THE HEREFORD CITY SURVEYOR'S TALE (35)

The 24-hour, 63,000 -worker strike which took place on 29 October over this matter was described by Nicholas Ridley as "extraordinary" and "misguided". (36) His statement reflected also on the assertion (disputed by the union) that no national strike ballot had been held, as required by the 1984 Trade Union Act. The strike itself was patchily felt and the North suffered most from the 40% stoppage.

Year	Turn-over £m.	Net Revenue £m.	Fixed Assets £m.	Employees '000
1980	581.9	(11.4)	213.9	58.4
1981	621.6	5.4	209.9	53.1
1982	677.0	16.5	207.6	51.9
1983	723.9	25.4	289.2	51.0
1984	772.0	22.1	310.0	50.0

TABLE 3: NBC RESULTS

Note: Net revenue is after tax and total interest
Source: NBC 1984 Report.

Deliberately timed by the TGWU to coincide with the day the Bus Bill finished its ultimate stage, after transfer from the Lords, in the Commons (37), it achieved its purpose in the TGWU's eyes in safeguarding NBC employees' pension conditions.

Thinning Pains

The prospect of the Thai order had really encouraged the managers and workforce of Leyland Buses to believe that better times lay ahead. The hope it gave was very much needed since the domestic market for conventional buses had halved over the period 1983-5 and Leyland, the industry leader, had been obliged to shut its factories in Bristol and Leeds with the loss of 1,000 jobs.Won against severe competition from Motor & Leasing (Singapore), a Van Hool (Belgium)-Volvo(Sweden) consortium, Renault (France) and Pegaso (Spain), the order represented a commercial triumph of high order for Leyland and its partners The National Bus Company and the MVA Consultancy. It had taken no less than 22 months to set up the deal — at £380m. one of Britain's biggest-ever export orders — which was underpinned by an attractive Government finance package. This consisted of £20m. grant plus ECGD-guaranteed 85% finance at a "soft" loan interest rate of 9%.

Year	Balance of Payment £b.	
	Deficit on Manufactures	Surplus on Oil
1983	2.4	6.8
1984	3.8	7.1
1985	2.0	4.2

TABLE 4:   **THE STATE OF PLAY**

Source: Report of the House of Lords Select Committee on Overseas Trade, October 1985.

It was an exciting undertaking for all concerned. No less than 4,000 new buses to be manufactured for the Bangkok Mass Transport Authority — almost two years work for the Leyland plants at 1984 output rates — and the wholescale refurbishment of the operations of the ageing and debt-ridden BMTA.

It will be easily understood that the attention of many in the industry was concentrated more on these happy vistas than it was on the contentious implications of the Transport Act. Imagine, therefore, the widespread and deep disappointment that followed the announcement on 15 October 1985 of the cancellation of the order by the Thai Government. The statement issued by the Thai Prime Minister, General

Prem Tinsulanonda said:

> "The Thai Government's financial standing . . . does not warrant a project which will create heavy foreign debt."

Despite rumours that had been circulating about new austerity measures to be taken by the Thais to curb overseas debt, the cancellation came as a surprise. Not least in the light of Mrs. Thatcher's discussions of the potential deal with General Prem in London two weeks previously and in view of the presence in Bangkok on the day of the announcement of Trade Minister Paul Channon. He was attending a long-scheduled round of EEC-Association of South-East Asian Nations talks.

It was a massive blow to Leyland's 3,500 workforce at their factories in Leyland, Workington and Lowestoft. Worse was to follow.

At the end of November 1985 Optare of Leeds (formerly Charles Roe Ltd, part of the Leyland Bus Group) declared their intention of marketing a new 25-seater bus based on a Volkswagen chassis and engine. To be called the "Optare City-Pacer 25", it would have a £27,000 price tag.

Optare had been re-opened with financial backing from the West Yorkshire Enterprise board and the West Yorkshire Council. Seven months later Peugeot's UK subsidiary announced that it too was going to commence assembly of a Minibus. But not, according to Peter Snelling, its Light Commercial Vehicle Manager, in the 12-15 seater sector already dominated by Ford, General Motor, Bedford and BL's Freightrover. His view was that there was a wide-open market for 20-seaters for use in built-up areas on commuter-type services, despite the presence of Mercedes and Freightrover (Sherpa) in this slot. (38)

EXHIBIT 3:   **SEEKING THE GAP**

The disclosure of the Government's thinking on the possibility of the break-up and sale of the constituent parts of the state-owned British Leyland Group provoked a considerable parliamentary furore. The notion that Austin-Rover could be taken on by Ford, and Leyland Vehicles by General Motor incensed the Opposition, despite assurances that the talks (with General Motors at least) were proceeding with the full support and approval of the BL Board. Witness the Commons questions to the Prime Minister put down by Neil Kinnock on 4 February 1986:

"When British money has rightly gone into British Leyland, what possible reason can there be for serving it up, gift-wrapped, to a foreign competitor? . . . Security of work, of technology and orders for BL and its component suppliers should command a higher priority. How does the Prime Minister think any objective of security could be achieved by ensuring that a further act of colonisation takes place in the British economy?" (39)

Mrs. Thatcher countered by arguing that the Government's commitment to British Leyland could not be doubted and spoke of the funds that had already been put into BL, namely £2b. in grants plus £1.5b. in guarantees. She said also that aid on this scale could not be continued.

"We are determined to create an internationally competitive British Leyland. That is what the discussions now underway are aimed to achieve — to protect jobs long-term. I note that Mr. Kinnock seems to be against inward investment, although many regions in Wales are competing for inward investment, particularly from motor companies." (40)

SDP Leader David Owen got similarly short shrift when he ventured to ask:

"If British Helicopters go to Sikorsky, if airborne early warning goes to Boeing and Land Rovers (a highly successful part of British Leyland Vehicles) go to General Motors and 44.5% of the British car market goes to Ford, would the Prime Minister, at the very least, give an assurance that she would refer it to the Monopolies and Mergers Commission?" (41)

"That" replied the Prime Minister "is a matter for the Secretary of State for Trade and Industry . . .

"This country also invests extensively overseas. There have been many years when our direct investment in the States had exceeded the States' investment here. That investment gives us enormous advantage and invisible returns which help the balance of trade every year." (42)

By 20 February the situation was much clearer: "indicative" bids for the acquisition of parts of BL had to be in by 6 March.

Within days senior executives at British Leyland had announced that they too were interested in a management buy-out of Leyland Buses and that a plan for this was to be put forward by LB's Managing Director, Ian McKinnon.

EXHIBIT 4:   **WHYS AND WHEREFORES**

Source: Commons exchanges 25/2/86, *Times*, Parliament, 26/2/86.

This plan was one of three that the "invitation to tender" for Leyland Buses had attracted. The others were from Leyland's biggest rival, the Laird Group, and from the Aveling Barford, itself a former British Leyland subsidiary bought out by its management. The Government's preference was thought to lie in the Laird camp by virtue of the fact that amalgamation of LB and Laird's Metro-Cammell Weymann (LB's biggest competitor) would, so it was said, produce a welcome restructuring of the industry and ultimately greater competitiveness. Those keen on such a development must have welcomed the statement by John Gardiner, Laird's Chief Executive that his Group's proposals were "ruthless and brutal but the only way of bringing the British bus industry back to life". (43) Conversely, it was well known that management buy-outs were particularly well regarded as a privatisation mechanism by the Government.

In fact, the Laird plan, which was conditional on the closure of LB's Workington and Lowestoft plants, did not succeed and it was the McKinnon-led management buy-out which was accepted by the Government on 24 July. Not that it was not harsh. Effective steps to counteract any continuation of the situation which had caused LB a 1985 pre-tax loss of £33.2m. had to be taken. And indeed they were, with 480 job losses announced at the end of July and a further 757 in mid-August. The Lowestoft plant was to be closed.

The buy-out cost £11.7m. Once the redundancy difficulties had been settled — the redundancy payments being met by British Leyland it-

"The Committee takes the view that, together, these prospects (contracting manufacturing base, an adverse balance of payments necessitating deflationary measures and a stagnating unemployment-ridden economy pressured by inflation) constitute a grave threat to the standard of living of the British people. Failure to recognise these dangers now could have a devastating effect on the future economic and political stability of the nation"... Steps must be taken, says the Report, to enlarge the declining manufacturing base to combat the imminent fall in North Seal oil revenue.

"All members agree that there is an urgency about the position of manufacturing industry which needs tackling by the whole nation at once. It is neither exaggeration nor irresponsible to say that the present situation undoubtedly contains the seeds of a major political and economic crisis in the foreseeable future. Yet the nation at large appears to be unaware of the seriousness of the predicament."

EXHIBIT 5: **AND NOW THE GOOD NEWS**

Source: Report from the House of Lords Select Committee on Overseas Trade, October 1985.

Note: Chaired by Lord Aldington (Chairman of Sun Alliance), the Committee included such industrial notables as Lord Boardman (Westminster Bank Chairman), Lord Ezra (Ex NCB Chairman), Lord Kearton (Ex-Chairman of Courtaulds and BNOC) and Lord Beswick (Ex-Chairman of British Aerospace).

self — the company began its counter-attack. Firstly it made known its intention of reducing capacity from the 1985 output level of 1,500 buses to 1,000 per annum. Secondly it publicised a new £2m. programme to double the productivity of the 1,400 employees who would constitute the eventual workforce. Improving skills in using computer-aided design and flexible manufacturing techniques would be heavily accented. The main part of the funding for the training would come, it was thought, from the EEC's European Social Fund and Lancashire Enterprises, a job-creation company funded by the Lancashire County Council.

Talking Turkey

The employees of Leyland Bus were not the only members of the bus industry to receive a surprise from the Government. At the end of November 1985 it had been the turn of the staff of the National Bus Company.

They were informed on 29 November that the Government was inviting worker-takeovers for 60 of the NBC's subsidiaries, but not within the time-scale anticipated by both senior management and the media. Indeed summer 1986 was being spoken of by them as an operative date for some transfers of ownership. The NBC Chairman Robert Brook welcomed the Government's urgent call:

> "Our Group has suffered too long from uncertainty. The important
> thing is for us to get along the privatisation road." (44)

He also struck a cautionary note, however, by stating that the programme would have to be an "orderly" one.

There was no shortage of positive and speedy responses to Nicholas Ridley's proposal to advance the breaking-up of NBC by up to two years. Some of the subsidiaries looked especially exciting commercial prospects, for example the Bristol and Hants & Dorset Groups whose aggregate 1984 result of a post-tax profit on net assets of 100% was outstanding. Others were well worth investigation even though three — The Welsh National Group, The South Wales Transport Group and the National Welsh Omnibus Services — had by no means sparkled in 1984, having achieved a 7.8% loss on net assets despite support payments of £6.9m. Indeed, by the turn of the year, some 20 expressions of interest from subsidiary managements had been received.

This was considered by some to be a little premature given the Government's view that subsidiaries should be sold off as individual independent units and not, as NBC's top management preferred, in groups. It is noteworthy that this condition ran counter to the regionalisation policy the NBC had begun at the end of 1985 and which covered subsidiaries operated under United Counties Omnibus (Midlands), Southdown Motor (Sussex) and Alder Valley (around Reading). Nicholas Ridley also wanted the disaggregation of such established NBC Groups as Ribble Motor (N.E. England), Crosville (North Wales) and London Country on the grounds of promoting competition.

The process gained much impetus when the Secretary of State announced in early April that purchase proposals needed to be made by mid-May in time for as many sales as possible to be completed by 26 October 1986, the day on which deregulation of the industry was to start. Robert Brook took early retirement in disagreement over some aspects of these plans and was replaced as Chairman by Rodney Lund whose job specification seemed, in fact, to revolve around ensuring his own redundancy!

Of those interested in buy-outs, four consortia were now front runners. Each could claim £50,000 from NBC as assistance towards creating a bid and obtaining further buyout finance did not look to be a significant problem as a complete financing package was on offer from Bankers Trust, the US merchant bank, for such purposes.

Year	Company	% Sold
1979	BP	5
1981	British Aerospace	51.6
	Cable & Wireless	49.3
1982	Amersham International	100
	Britoil	51
	National Freight	100
1983	Associated British Ports	51.5
	BP	7
	Cable & Wireless	22
1984	Associated British Ports	48.5
	British Telecom	50.2
	Enterprise Oil	100
	Jaguar	100
	Sealink	100
	Wytch Farm Oilfield	100

TABLE 5:   **PRIVATISATIONS 1979–84**

Notes: (1) The total amount received by the Government for the sales of these companies exceeded £7b.

(2) The sale of Wytch Farm refers to the BGC holding.

The publication in Mid-May of NBC's 1985 results caused something of a hiccough. They were considered poor by comparison with 1984's and particular attention was paid to two aspects. Firstly, the fact that, despite an increase in turnover of 7%, operating profit had fallen by some £10m. to £35.8m. And, secondly, the cost of "clearing the decks" prior to privatisation which was put at no less than £103m. These "extraordinary" charges included a large deferred tax provision and produced a record net loss of £85m. compared with 1984's net profit of £22m. Such factors naturally focussed the minds of NBC analysts on such disquieting operating detail as the extent of its cross-subsidisation of routes (£62m. received in 1985 in local authority grants, £65m. spent on subsidising unprofitable routes) and the value of the company as a whole. Whilst NBC had a book value of about £155m. it was thought unlikely that, in the light of a more rigorous depreciation approach, more than around £100m. was obtainable. And then there was also the question of the £79.4m. still owed to the Department of Transport. Some of this debt stretched back to NBC's foundation by Harold Wilson's Labour Government in 1968.

"It is already clear to me who mainly prospers through privatisation. The shareholders of the companies we have sold prosper, the employees prosper, and most of all, the customers and the whole nation prospers."

John Moore, Transport Secretary and former Treasury minister responsible for privatisation.

EXHIBIT 6:   PROSPERING THROUGH PRIVATISATION

Source: Privatisation in the UK, John Moore, *Aims of Industry*, June 1986.

Note: John Moore was made Transport Secretary in May 1986.

Rodney Lund was not discouraged, though. He attributed the poor post-tax showing to "setting the stall out for privatisation" and declared buoyantly that:

"We are beginning to talk turkey on a dozen or so and we should make our first sale in around a month." (45)

He was as good as his word. In July National Holidays was sold to the Pleasurama Group for £2.5m. Their offer was apparently considerably in excess of the ex-management's offer which would have been accepted by NBC (in the light of Government guidelines) had it been within 5% of the competitive bid.

Devon General was the first management buy-out, its bid having been master-minded by its Chairman and Managing Director, Harry Blundred, who had started work in the industry in 1962 as a bus conductor. He it was who had brought the company back to profits in 1985, after several years of losses, with success in pioneering Britain's first large-scale Minibus project as part of the Deregulation Trials. No less than 200 of these had been used to provide "hail and stop" services in Torbay and Exeter. The price tag was thought to be £3m.

Cock o' the North

> "By Government order, we have been told 'To hell with the public service — you'll have to survive in a capitalist jungle or to to the wall'. That flies in the face of what is happening in the rest of the world where it is recognised that this is the one industry that cannot be left to market forces." (46)

This was the way in which Albert Booth, Technical Director of the South Yorkshire PTE, greeted the news that subsidies for the coming year for his 1,000-bus transport network were not to be the £80m. considered necessary, but £59m. As Labour's former Shadow Transport Secretary (until the 1983 General Election), he could not but react with some hostility to this Governmental curtailment of support, especially as it came on top of the dramatic changes to the PTE which would take place on de-regulation day. Namely, that the PTE would be re-named South Yorkshire's Transport (SYT) and that it would have to operate on a strictly commercial basis as a separate company. The legislation would also have displaced the Metropolitan County Transport Committee as transport policy arbiter for the region, an important point but one whose significance was wholly overshadowed by the fact that the South Yorkshire Metropolitan Authority — known to its left-wing supporters as "The Independent People's Republic of South Yorkshire" — was itself due to be abolished anyway on 1 April 1986.

Dire predictions abounded — of a drop in bus usage as a result of enforced fare rises of up to 250% and consequent reductions in bus services and employment. Albert Booth was in the van with his view that:

> "I don't know of any business that could survive after being forced to charge its customers such an increase. It's a nightmare because we don't know yet whether there will be any further increases later this year." (47)

Perhaps the worst consequence of all in terms of the PTE itself was the prophecy of the job cuts which were thought unavoidable: 10% of the 5,400 workforce before October and a further 1,600 afterwards, as a result of slashing route mileage by a fifth to achieve strictly commercial targets.

There were similar outspoken reactions from other senior PTE executives in other Metropolitan Authorities. One such, clearly embroiled in immense operational difficulties stemming from the changes, was Tyne and Wear's Director General, David Howard. Having created a wholly integrated Metro-bus transport facility for the region, based on coordination of timetable and fare structure and the building of special Metro-bus interchange stations, his PTE foresaw a post-deregulation situation in which the buses had to compete with the Metro!

> "We are being told to turn our business round into a profitable concern at every level in a matter of months. I ask you, what other company could cope?
>
> It might please the people in the Adam Smith Institute but, in terms of what the rest of the world does it's all very odd. The human problems of this cut very deep. It sounds soft, but if you sat back and thought about all this you'd cry." (48)

Another was Leslie Latter, Merseyside PTE's Director-General. He had spear-headed the implementation in his region of a similar low-fare policy to that pioneered in South Yorkshire. A past success in hoisting the use of public transport by a claimed 24% over 5 years was compared by him to the uncertainties of the future with not a little bitterness. Similar feelings were shared by senior executives in the Greater Manchester PTE, who found themselves faced in January 1987 with selling off 534 surplus buses.

"Many, many of the complaints we get are from people saying we don't want big buses on our country lanes. By bringing in new contractors we hope to have different sorts of buses, such as 8-seater minibuses, which will match the needs of communities better.

It is an opportunity to make the whole thing more cost-effective and efficient."

Group-Captain Douglas Longley, Chairman of Bucks CC's Public Transport Sub-Committee.

EXHIBIT 7:   **A MATTER OF PERSPECTIVE**

Source: 'All Change on the Buses', Jacki Davis, *Bucks Advertiser*, 11/6/86

It was, however, in the Sheffield-Rotherham-Doncaster-Barnsley area — once one of the mightiest of the nation's industrial power-houses — that the most acrimony was expressed. After all, it was in South Yorkshire that the average bus fare on 31 March 1986 was 10p and the maximum 25p. Here it was also the case that fares had remained frozen since the mid-70s and that transport subsidies per head of South Yorkshire's 1.3m. population amounted to £60 per year — as opposed to £2/head in Oxfordshire. As David Blunkett, Leader of Sheffield City Council explained:

> "On Tuesday, 1 April, a defiant piece of municipal socialism was struck a grievous blow by the power of central government. . . The experiment in cheap travel, begun years before the GLC popularised it, was at an end . . . But this is not simply a story of local determination and commitment succeeding against the power of the central state. It is a tale of local democracy in action, an alternative to market economics . . . It was in fact the community collective at its best — popular, successful and an ideological as well as practical threat to its political opponents . . . Cheap transport has been a boon for everyone. No need for the massive public expenditure on inner city motorways, for bigger and better car parks . . . As (bus) ridership collapsed across the country, bus travel in South Yorkshire increased. People with cars left them at home for many journeys and families and individuals who would normally face isolation . . . could escape. The impact on the health of the community has been incalculable and the social and economic pressure can only have been helped by what in effect became a lubricant to prevent the friction so obvious in other city areas . . . For the low paid and part-time workers the change in transport costs can be crucial . . . " (49)

It was quite apparent that wholehearted acceptance of many facets of David Blunkett's viewpoint lay behind the pledge, given by Labour's Shadow Spokesman on Transport, Robert Hughes, on 20 October 1986 that Labour would repeal the Transport Act 1985 and return to a "sensible system" of licensing services and cross-subsidisation of routes. (50)

Nor could the Labour leadership have been unmindful of the already obvious impact that the forthcoming deregulation was having on the domestic demand for new traditional single- and double-decker buses. Their annual registrations were, in fact, expected to fall from over 3,000 in 1984 to little more than 300 in 1987. Conversely, Ford were forecasting minibus sales of approximately 20,000 over the coming 4 years in the 15-20 seat bracket alone. The big bus producers — MCW, Hestair Dennis and the post-buyout Leyland Buses — had every reason to worry. Dennis Quinn of the Bus & Coach Council was deeply concerned:

"The time will come when we will desperately need our conventional buses and, if in the meantime suppliers have been killed off, we will be in a horrendous position." (51)

What was definitely an ill wind for Dennis Quinn did not look like being so for Freight Rover. In mid-October they announced they had orders in hand for no less than 1,000 minibus chassis based on the Sherpa design.

You're in the Fast Lane Now

The deregulation timetable laid down by the Government specified that all those who wished to compete on routes deemed commercially-viable had to make their intentions known to the relevant County Council authorities by 12 March. Once applications (which involved firm undertakings to provide specified services at stated prices initially for 3 months) had been received, these bodies would be in a position to put out to tender routes which were seen to require subsidisation. Bids for the latter were to be made by the end of June and would then be adjudicated by counties' Public Transport Sub-committees in the light of budgets earmarked for the purpose. "Highly encouraging" was the Minister of Transport's description of the registrations received by 12 March. Others were not so sure. Indeed, when details of the bids by NBC subsidiaries were announced in early May some aspects emerged which, if true of the country as a whole, were rather disturbing. As Table 6 indicates the route mileages on services bid for by NBC were substantially down (relative to previous mileages achieved) in respect of rural, off-peak urban and Sunday services.

According to Cliff Twort, The Transport & General Workers' Passenger Services National Secretary, the cuts in services implied by NBC's reduced bids were "massive" and amounted to an overall 17% pull-out. (52)

Not that this necessarily meant the ceasing of non-viable route servicing since these would be tendered for in Stage II of the bidding. But there were considerable anxieties in the minds especially of those living in remote areas who, though relatively few in number, were inescapably dependent on the public bus. Journalists consequently spent some healthy hours probing the impact of deregulation on rural transport economics and societal workings in such far-flung and inaccessible spots as Duggleby (Malton 7 miles). Longridge (Blackburn 7 miles)

	Proposed Mileage Changes %
Type of Carrier:	
Minibus	+ 237
Traditional Bus	- 17
Geographical Cover:	
Urban	- 8.5
Rural	- 35.4
Service Times:	
Weekdays Early Morning	- 37
Weekdays Late Evening	- 43
Sunday Services	- 52

TABLE 6:   **NBC PROPOSALS**

Source: 'Sharp Cuts Feared in the Costlier Services, Michael
      Baily, *Times*, 6/5/86.

and Llandyssul (said to be 12 miles from Carmarthen). (53)

The Ministry would also have drawn encouragement from the volume of Taxi-Bus Operator licenses applied for — no less than 200 issued for the October start. Firms like Mercury Taxi Service of Brighton evidently saw good opportunities in regular late night, town centre-outlying estate services at fixed prices.

Bus Type (average)	Capital Cost (£000)	Life (Years)	Seating Capacity	Viable Service Frequency (Mins)
Traditional	80	20	75	20
Minibus	20	4	20	5

TABLE 7:   **CARRIER COMPARISON**

Source: 'Minibus — The Fruit of Deregulation', Michael Baily,
      Times, 7/5/86.
Note: Three Star Coaches of Luton has been operating a fleet of six
      such minibuses for the past two years on town centre-estate
      routes. Owner Bob Dudley reckons on clearing about £1,000
      net profit per week. (54) Marketing men had already labelled
      minibuses with such names as "Hoppers", "Shoppers" and
      "Poppers". Their operational characteristics and economics
      differed considerably from those of the traditional bus.

The final tally of registrations, given that the central thrust of the Transport Act 1985 was to encourage competition, must have been something of a disappointment to the Conservative Government. Proposals had been received from 1,500 of Britain's 5,000 private bus and coach operators but no less than 1,300 of these had already been operating stage carriage services. Not so, however, the forecast of claimed savings on subsidy. With examples to contemplate like Lancashire (£5m.) and Avon (£1m.), Berkshire (£350,000) and Surrey (£2m.) the Government cannot have been displeased. (55)

Neil Kinnock, Leader of the Opposition stated that there had to be a long-term industrial policy for the recovery of manufacturing industry with extra investment on the same basis and with the same institutional support as that of the main competitor economies.

"Unless we follow that long-term course for strengthening our industrial base" he said "we shall continue to decline as a productive nation" . . . Since 1979, there had been, he continued, a growth of poverty through unemployment, low pay and disability unparalleled since the war. In 1979 there were six million people at or below the supplementary benefit level of income. The figure now, in 1986, was nine million. "In the families of those who are poor, there are no less than two million children . . . who face again a jumble sale Christmas."

Mrs. Thatcher, Prime Minister, rejected Mr. Kinnock's criticism of the UK's manufacturing performance. In fact, she declared, manufacturing output had risen 10% overall since the 1983 election and was still going up . . . Manufacturing productivity had increased each year since 1979 at an average rate of 3.5% a year. Manufacturing export volume was at a record level and manufacturing profitability was at its highest level since 1978. Since 1981 Britain's economy had grown faster than that of France and Italy and a little faster than W. Germany's.

The investment of N. Sea oil revenues? He did not seem to appreciate, she said, that overseas assets had gone up from £12b. in 1979 to £80b. now.

The Opposition's formula for success — expanding the powers of the State, increasing Government control over people's lives and putting penal taxation back on the shoulders of those who led the way to growth and jobs — she also rejected.

EXHIBIT 8: FROM THE DEBATE ON THE QUEEN'S SPEECH

Source: Kinnock Attacks Poverty Scandal, Parliament 12/11/86, *Times*, 13/11/86.

Minister David Mitchell certainly did not seem so when he replied to a furious Opposition attack in a Commons debate on 26 November. With strong support from Richard Caborn (Sheffield Central) and Edward Loyden (Liverpool, Garston), Labour's spokesman Robert Hughes attempted to lambast the Government for what he called the "abject failure" of deregulation. He catalogued the miseries:

> "Those who depended on public transport for mobility . . . sacrificed in pursuit of profit . . . The Office of Fair Trading had already had 50 complaints of unfair competition . . . In Lancashire there had been 12,000 phone calls of complaint . . . In Tyne & Wear the Bus Watch monitoring group had been inundated with letters of complaint . . . Bus fares up . . . 9,000 jobs lost with the PTEs and 9,000 with the NBC . . . Those remaining having to accept wage cuts . . ."

Moving an amendment calling for the repeal of the Act and condemning the loss of essential services to the public, he said that all the sacrifices would produce "at best, transitory savings and at worst, illusory ones". (56)

John Moore, Transport Secretary, had pleasure, by contrast, in moving an amendment which congratulated the Government on its radical measures to arrest decline in the bus industry. His Minister, David Mitchell, added that it was already clear that many of the problems that had prompted the debate were already fading away.

Whether their view would still be proved correct on 26 January 1987 remained, however, an open question. On this date, under the Transport Act 1985, anyone with an operator's licence would have to give only 42 days' notice to start or stop a service. That would be the real D-Day for the buses.

APPENDIX 1

THE FALL IN THE NUMBER OF PEOPLE WITH JOBS OVER THE PERIOD 1971 - 1981	
Category	**%**
Total	4
Manufacturing Employment	24
Manufacturing Employment in London, Birmingham and Manchester	40
Source: Census Guide 3: Britain's Workforce, Office of Population Censuses and Surveys.	

APPENDIX 2

INDICATIVE NBC OPERATING DETAILS			
Company	**% of passenger journeys**	**% of grant support**	**% of vehicle mileage**
Yorkshire Traction	5.1	—	2.6
Northern General	9.8	1.3	5.4
West Riding	4.2	.1	3.8
Thames Valley	2.1	5.1	2.9
National Welsh	2.5	3.6	3.5
Source: NBC Annual Report 1984.			

APPENDIX 3

REGIONAL DIFFERENCES

UK Region	GDP per Head (UK Average = 100)		Job Losses/Gains ('000)	
	1975	1985	June 1979-83	June 1983-86
Northern Ireland	80.1	74.1		
Scotland	97.1	97.4	- 204	- 12
North	93.6	92.9	- 191	+ 20
North West	96.2	96.0	- 374	- 41
Yorkshire & Humberside	94.1	91.8	- 240	+ 5
East Midlands	96.1	95.7	- 132	+ 91
West Midlands	100	92.3	- 298	+ 78
East Anglia	92.8	100.7	- 15	+ 74
Wales	88.7	88.9	- 298	+ 78
South West	90.3	93.9	- 84	+ 54
South East:			- 391	+269
● Greater London	125.9	125.7		
● Rest of South East	103.6	107.7		
TOTAL			- 2071	+500

Sources: *Economic Trends* (HMSO, November 1986) and *Employment Census Data* (HMSO, January 1987)

APPENDIX 4

ONE LAST FLING

Neil Kinnock, Leader of the Opposition:

"Will she tell us whether she is prepared to accept the demand from the CBI that, unless the Government takes the initiative now on capital projects, the UK will lose the chance and will slip further behind in the competitive league?

If she will not listen to demands from North and South, from this side of the house and many others, will she accept the demands of the CBI?"

Mrs. Thatcher, Prime Minister:

"May I say exactly what has happened on road spending *(protests)*. They do not want to hear the facts.

On roads, capital spending on motorways and trunk roads increased by 25 per cent in real terms to £900m. . . since 1979 and has increased to £2.5 billion on railways . . . capital spending on housing renovation is up by 54% in real terms. Which of the figures does he say is wrong?"

Source: Parliament 21/10/86, *Times,* 22/10/86 — 'Prime Minister using jobless as a weapon' says Kinnock.

APPENDIX 5

A FRESH START NEEDED

"The committee's inquiry has disclosed the gravity of the UK's prospects in R & D. To remedy this the committee has recommended a high profile for science and technology, dynamic leadership at the centre and a new approach to funding R & D.

These all matter greatly. But what matters most is the determination of both the public and private sectors to create new confidence and to restore the UK's prosperity and its international position in science and industry. The country needs a fresh start and the optimism to make its talents work."

Source: House of Lords Select Committee on Science and Technology: Civil Research and Development (HMSO)

References:

1. 'Let the buses compete, but they need a conductor', Letter to the *Guardian*, 17/7/84.
2. *Buses*, Department of Transport, CMND 9300, July 1984.
3. Michael Baily, 'Government aims to abolish licensing and increase bus routes'. *Times*, 13/7/84.
4. Geoff Andrews, 'Ridley is jeered at by bus industry leaders', *Guardian*, 27/9/84.
5. As 4.
6. The advertisement appeared in the *Times* on 26 November 1984.
7. David Rosenberg, 'The villages that are missing the bus', *Sunday Telegraph*, 11/11/84.
8. As 7.
9. As 3.
10. 'Tory concern in shires may force Minister to change Bus Bill', *Daily Telegraph*, 4/2/85.
11. NBC Annual Report 1984.
12. As 3.
13. Digby Anderson, 'Let the buses pull out all the stops', *Times*, 25/7/84.
14. As 10.
15. As 10.
16. As 10.
17. Parliament 12/2/85, *Times*, 13/2/85.
18. As 17.
19. Parliament 25/2/85, *Times*, 26/2/85.
20. As 19.
21. As 19.
22. Parliament 1/4/85, *Times*, 2/4/85.
23. Jock Bruce-Gardyne, 'More fun on the buses', *Sunday Telegraph*, 10/3/85.
24. Parliament 21/5/85, *Times*, 22/5/85.
25. Parliament 22/5/85, *Financial Times*, 23/5/85.
26. As 24.
27. As 24.
28. Parliament 11/6/85, *Times*, 12/6/85.
29. As 28.
30. Parliament 8/7/85, *Times*, 9/7/85.
31. Stephen Aris, 'The skids under Ridley's Bill', *Times*, 21/2/85.
32. Geoff Andrews, 'Bus privatisation studies show runaway costs', *Guardian*, 3/12/84.
33. Michael Baily, 'Fears of huge bus fare rises', *Times*, 14/10/85.
34. Phillip Bennett, 'Bus staff plan series of strikes over Bill', *Financial Times*, 14/10/ 85.

35. As 31.
36. Stephen Ward, 'Buses halted in strike over pension', *Daily Telegraph*, 30/10/85.
37. Jane Mcloughlin and Alan Travis, 'Bill passed after 63,000 stage day's strike', *Guardian*, 30/10/85.
38. Arthur Smith, 'Peugeot Talbot to make small buses', *Financial Times*, 27/6/86.
39. Parliament 4/2/86, *Times*, 5/2/86.
40. As 39.
41. As 39.
42. As 39.
43. Kenneth Gooding, 'Leyland Bus attracts 3 bids', *Financial Times*, 19/5/86.
44. John Petty, 'Speed up order on state bus privatisation', *Daily Telegraph*, 30/11/85.
45. Tony Jackson, 'National Bus buyouts encouraged', 22/5/86.
46. Peter Hetherington, 'Buses run into free market forces', *Guardian*, 31/3/86.
47. As 46.
48. As 46.
49. David Blunkett, 'A Free-for-All that missed the bus', *Guardian*, 11/4/86.
50. Rodney Cowton, 'Doubts on whether small firms can be competitive', *Times*, 21/10/86.
51. Kevin Brown, 'Demand for big buses devastated by deregulation', *Financial Times*, 27/10/86.
52. 'Bus services to be cut in October, TGWU says', *Financial Times*, 6/5/86.
53. Peter Hetherington, 'Ryedale waits for buses to stop', *Guardian*, 1/5/86: Jonathan Foster, 'Rural bus reaches the end of the road', *Observer*, 11/5/86: Geoff Andrews, 'Ticket to catch the hoppers', *Guardian*, 23/10/86.
54. Philip Beresford, 'Fast lane for buses', *Sunday Times*, 13/4/86.
55. Mark Ellis, '£40m. saving in subsidy when buses deregulated', *Times*, 25/10/86.
56. Parliament 26/11/86, *Times*, 27/11/86.

SUPPLEMENTARY NOTE 1

CASE EPILOGUES

Introduction

The intention behind the inclusion of the following case "epilogues" is not to draw conclusions in respect of the original cases but to allow the reader to note some of the important, relevant events that have since occurred. In short, to bring them up to date (December 1986). Naturally enough, the material included is highly selective and general but not to the point of bias or tendentiousness.

1. THE FALKLAND ISLANDS BUSINESS

The problems posed by the dispute over the Falkland Islands between Britain and Argentina have in no way moderated since Britain's military victory. Indeed, in the eyes of many observers, they have become much more intractable.

Three particular issues (out of many) are seen as paramount in the debate. These are:

- *Argentina's Diplomatic Fightback*

    The replacement of the military junta by the civilian regime under President Alfonsin has led to no slackening in Argentina's desire to "regain" the Malvinas. Indeed the nation's democratisation — and the long-term imprisonment of its military ex-leaders — General Galtieri included — has, if anything, strengthened its will. It has certainly increased the appeal of Argentina's case in the eyes of the international community. Since the heady days of massive UNO support for Britain on the grounds of Argentine aggression, the position has changed to one where Britain is effectively diplomatically isolated not only in the OAS but also in the UN. In both 1985 and 1986 Britain suffered humiliating defeats in the latter forum over motions that she should negotiate with Argentina over the dispute. In 1985 support for the British stance was given, for example, only Belize, Oman and the Solomon Islands. Argentina has warned that there will be no formal end to hostilities until after such negotiations.

- *The Military Defensibility of the Falklands*

    This has been improved out of all recognition by the completion of the Mount Pleasant airport at a cost of £309m. On the other hand, questions have been repeatedly raised about Britain's logistic capabilities in terms of British-registered mercantile shipping which could be impressed into military service in case of further hostilities. Such worries were indeed not without foundation given that:

    (a)   over the period 1979-1986 Britain's registered mercantile marine fleet had declined in number from 1200 to 600 vessels and its seafarers from 80,000 to 40,000. They had, in Mrs. Thatcher's view "priced themselves out of being employed in shipping".(1) Notably BP's fleet had by 1986 been "flagged out" to sail under the Bermudan flag with Filipino crews.

(b) in late 1986 the EEC Commission warned that, for Europe to stay competitive as an international shipbuilding power in the face of massive world-wide over-supply, it would have to shed one third of capacity by late 1988. In Britain, employment in shipbuilding had already fallen from 35,000 in 1978 to about 8,000 in 1986 and the state-owned British Shipbuilders had lost £430m. in 1985.

The opinion of a former Conservative Party Chairman, Sir Edward duCann, was significant. Namely, that without urgent Government action to save the fleet, it would be impossible to mount another Falklands-type operation.(2)

- *Parliamentary Opposition to Conservative Policy*

Successive announcements of the cost of Operation Corporate (the military campaign) and its aftermath only fuelled the view of Government opponents that a policy change was necessary. Particularly the statement that the cost had, by the end of the financial year 1985/6, reached £2.6 billion. Labour MPs like Dale Campbell Savours, Michael Meadowcroft and William McKelvey who harassed the Government on the cost of the Falklands/need for an honourable settlement theme were, in fact, forming part of a rising, seemingly anti-militarist, undeniably anti-nuclear tide within Labour ranks.

Imagine, therefore, the mixture of anger, consternation and disbelief on the part of the Government's opponents — domestic and international alike — that greeted the announcement at the end of October 1986 of the establishment of "The Falkland Islands Interim Conservation and Management Zone" (FICZ). This licence-only fishing zone applied to the entire area 150 miles round the Falklands and was intended to conserve fish stocks in the face of the enormous growth in factory fishing around the Islands since 1984. It was a palpable British affront to Argentina which had already signed a deal with the USSR *giving it rights to fish within a 200-mile area around the Islands*. It also, in the view of Shadow Foreign Secretary Dennis Healey, embroiled Government still more deeply in what he called "the quagmire of the Falklands commitment".(3)

Why had it been imposed? So far as the Conservative Government was concerned, the position was straightforward. Normalisation of relations with Argentina was eagerly desired (and had been strenuously pressed for) but there would be no question of sovereignty discussions for as long as the islanders wished to remain under the protection of the Crown. In an unofficial referendum carried out for the UK-Falkland Islands Committee in March 1986, no less than 95% of the 1900-odd inhabitants had voted for this. As the £31m. development cash already allocated to the Islands was not bearing much fruit, action to preserve the "Kelpers" natural riches and to contribute to the cost of maintaining the garrison was inescapable.

2. BRITISH LEYLAND

The challenges which faced State-owned British Leyland from 1984 onwards were of truly Homeric proportions. They not only resulted in the
company's fourth change of name (to "Rover Group") since its creation in
1968 but in something far more awesome: its dismemberment. Jaguar was
the first part to go – privatised in 1984. The ailing Bus Division, caught up
in the maelstrom of Europe-wide industrial over-capacity and the economic knock-on effects of the 1985 Transport Act, went next. That was sold
off to a banker-management consortium in 1986. And then it was the turn
of the Leyland Truck and Freight Rover Divisions. The merger of these two
with the Dutch truck maker DAF was called for in the Rover Group's 1986
Corporate Plan and accepted, to the consternation of Labour opposition,
with alacrity by the Government. Even though the merger would mean the
loss of 2,300 jobs, the alternative might have been even more drastic surgery, especially on the BL Truck Division. This had run up an accumulated
loss over the 5 years to 1986 of £300m.

Year	UK Car Industry (a)			BL (b)	
	Output Volume Index (1980 = 100)	Employment ('000s)	Productivity Index (units/man) (1980 = 100)	Operating profit be-fore inter-est and tax (£m)	Employees weekly average ('000s)
1980	100	415	100	(535)	N/A
1981	82,9	359	95.8	(244)	126
1982	79.6	321	103	(126)	108
1983	83.9	307	113.4	4.1	103
1984	81.3	292	115.6	(11.7)	96

TABLE 1:   **PER ARDUA *AD HONDA?***

Sources: (a) Society of Motor Manufacturers and Traders.
          (b) BL Annual Report 1985.

The Plan did not foresee any merger of the Austin-Rover (mass car)
Division, not surprisingly, perhaps, in view of the Parliamentary furore
that had erupted when it had become known that previous BL-Ford talks
had explored merger possibilities.

Whilst the amputation of some of the Group's arthritic limbs might have reduced the range of the worries of Rover Group's new Chairman, Graham Day, brought in in late '86 after the spectacular reduction in British Shipbuildings' losses during his tenure there as Chairman, it had not necessarily reduced their scale. There were still anxieties a-plenty in respect of the car element. How much more Government subsidy would be forthcoming? Given that cooperation with Honda over the Rover 200 and 800 series, based on the Honda Ballade and Legend respectively, had worked well so far, how much further should it be taken beyond the already scheduled launch of the AR8 in 1989? And, more significantly, would Austin-Rover/Honda mutuality be the best way of dealing with the threat posed by the already-announced expansion of Nissan's brand-new Washington plant towards output capacity of 100,000 cars? And just how trying would the union response actually be to the disclosure of Rover Group's plan to make redundant 1,265 out of its 10,500 white-collar work-force? Would the ASTMS National Officer, Paul Talbot, prove as difficult as his comment on the required redundancies suggested:

> "Our members feel very angry with the company (over the announced redundancies). They feel they are paying the price for successive failures by top management. Making people redundant doesn't help to sell more cars." (1)

What urgent action could be taken to lift the company's UK market share from the parlous under-16% notched up in December 1986?

Some of their past difficulties related to British Leyland's attempt to come to terms with the union-dominated industrial relations context of the late '70s and to deal specifically with the aftermath of the sacking of Longbridge convenor Derek "Red Robbo" Robinson in 1979 and the pay and productivity disputes of the early '80s. But by the mid-'80s such affairs seemed ancient history. The problems of that era related, by contrast, to the strategic issue of how to match the competition in creating contented consumers. If misguided nationalistic pride was in evidence in approaching this matter, then, said the *Times*, it should be appreciated that:

> "To be part of an Anglo-Japanese partnership is a greater asset in the market-place than pretending, with ever less credibility, that Austin-Rover cars are wholly British." (2)

The old orders had clearly changed . . .

3. CONFLICT OVER COAL

Conflict indeed! The events that took place in the UK mining industry after the unofficial 1981 union action made that action seem wholly inconsequential. No less than £2.5 billion has been estimated to have been the cost to the nation of the year-long Miners' Strike that began on the 5th March 1984.

This arose out of a variety of causes. Most notably and immediately from the NCB's re-imposition of its pit closure programme, in general, and its announcement of the closure of certain named pits, like Polmaise (Scotland), Cortonwood and Bulcliffe (Yorks), Herrington (Durham) and Snowdown (Kent), in particular. The total cut-back programme,

---

NUM National Executive's Demands:
14th June 1984

1. Complete withdrawal of pit closure programme
2. Re-affirmation by the NCB and the Government of the expansionary 1974 Plan for Coal
3. Development of 40 tonnes of new capacity from new pits
4. New investment to extend the life-span of every British colliery
5. 4-day working week
6. Early retirement at 55
7. "Substantially increased wages"

NCB Stipulations: 14th September 1984

1. The minimum size of the industry to be 100m. tonnes
2. No compulsory redundancies. All personnel affected by closure would get another job and not suffer. Voluntary redundancy and early retirement terms generous.
3. The pay rise was to be 5.2% backdated to 1st November 1983.
4. There would be continued high investment in the coal industry.

EXHIBIT 1: A MEETING OF MINDS?

announced on the 6th March 1984, foresaw a time-scaled reduction in the output of deep-mined coal from 101.4m. tonnes to 97.4 and manpower cuts of approximately 20,000. This was by no means out-of-step with the

1983 Monopolies and Mergers Commission Report which had indicated that a 10% capacity reduction would produce savings for the NCB of £300m. per annum.

The Strike was the first in the industry since 1981 (with the exception of the reaction to the announcement of the closure of Ty Mawr—Lewis Merthyr in February 1983) and it was unexpectedly long-lasting and ferocious. Especially when it is borne in mind that ballots of union members in 1981 and 1982 had shown acceptance of pay rises which were much smaller than pay claims and that a further secret ballot on the 10th March 1983 had, in fact, rejected an NUM Executive recommendation relating to the use of industrial action over pit closures by 118,954 votes to 76,540.

Notwithstanding such apparent signs of some membership hesitancy over strike action, the Area Councils of Yorkshire and Scotland had no compunction in calling for, and effecting, a total stoppage on hearing of the threat to the particular pits in their areas. This call (5/3/84) was echoed at the NUM National Executive meeting held on the 8th March. The meeting approved by 21 votes to 3 the action that had been taken in Yorkshire and Scotland and endorsed in advance the actions of any Area which might follow their example. It was noted at the time that this procedure of legitimising individual and piecemeal Area action avoided what would otherwise have been absolutely required by the NUM's own rule book — a secret national ballot.

Had such a ballot been held, a 55% "yes" would have been needed to proceed with a national strike. One Area — Leicestershire — did, in fact, call for such a ballot but the ruling by Arthur Scargill, who had been elected President-for-life of the NUM in succession to Joe Gormley on the 8th December 1981, was that the proposal was "out-of-order". This ruling was later upheld by the National Executive by 13 votes to 8, with 3 abstentions. A Special Delegate Conference called for the 19th April also backed the ruling and went further. By 69 votes to 54, delegates adopted a motion calling for strike action throughout Britain and lowering the ceiling for a "Yes" vote on a strike call in a national ballot to 50%.

As the strike progressed, picketing having stopped work at 140 of the NCB's 170 pits from the 15th March, the dispute was played out under the sometimes more-than-lurid spotlight of the media, with abortive NUM-NCB talks interspersed with confrontations between flying pickets and police detachments centrally organised from The National Reporting Centre, the latter reaching a crescendo with violent demonstrations at BSC's Orgreave coking plant near Rotherham on 29-30 May 1984.

Labour Motion

"That this House strongly condemns the Government for its mishandling of the coal dispute and the way in which severe hardship has been inflicted on miners, mining families and communities and for its abandonment of the principles and objectives of the *Plan for Coal*; calls for the withdrawal of the plan to lose 20,000 jobs and close 20 pits in the coming year, which was a unilateral decision of the NCB."

Government Amendment

"That this House confirms that the future of the coal industry will depend on the industry's success in deploying its assets so as to keep coal competitive with other fuels; welcomes the action of the Government in providing more capital investment for the industry than any previous government . . . noting that the investment of £3,900m. has substantially exceeded the scale of investment envisaged in the *Plan for Coal*; welcomes the steps taken by the NCB to ensure that, in areas where a reduction in uneconomic capacity is being considered, miners affected will be treated more generously and with greater understanding than in the past."

EXHIBIT 2: COMMONS DEBATE ON COAL INDUSTRY POLICY 7 JUNE 1984

Result: Government victory 273 - 178

When it was becoming clear that such tactics alone were not likely to bear the requisite fruit, even with immense symbolic backing anticipated and obtained from the TUC at its Annual Conference in September and with Labour's furious Commons onslaughts on the Government's doctrinal position and its handling of the strike, the NUM sought to tighten the screw by blockading power stations and BSC's steel works, Ravenscraig in Scotland being earmarked for special treatment. Old alliances were also reactivated. The NUM sought and got aid from railwaymen, transport workers and seamen. But to no ultimate avail since support was not forthcoming from steel or power workers. The latter's antipathy towards the strike, coupled with the abundance of coal in power station yards, formed an insuperable obstacle to the NUM. The position was plainly identified by Eric Hammond, General Secretary-Elect of the Electricians, Electronic, Telecommunications and Plumbing Union (EETPU) on the 15th May 1984 when he declared that his union would not be used as "yet another domino" in Arthur Scargill's "attempt to bring down the Government". This in riposte to a speech in Mansfield by the Miners' President in which Arthur Scargill had stated that the dispute:

> "would roll back the years of Thatcherism . . . turn economic ruin into economic recovery . . . above all pave the way for a general election to elect a Labour Government."(1)

Eric Hammond's uncompromising stance was backed in a secret ballot of his members who voted on the 19th October by 20,642 to 3,864 not to support the miners.

Not only was this crucial support not forthcoming but the NUM Executive was persistently hamstrung by the fact that three Areas had resolved at the outset, despite enormous pressure, not to join in the strike but to carry on producing and that a new, and potentially dangerous, rival – the Union of Democratic Mineworkers (UDM) – had been formed from their ranks, ironically as a direct result of the strike. It was also shackled by a much worse fact of life – the legal actions brought by various litigants, including the NCB and the UDM, which ultimately led to the sequestration of the NUM's assets and their seizure despite the union's attempts to circumvent it.

A brave face initially accompanied high hopes. Delegate Conferences on the 11/12 July and the 10th August were unanimous in seeking a continuation of the strike. Rousing speeches of support were heard at the Labour Party and TUC Conferences. But the drift back to work started in some areas with the onset of the October cold. It was hastened by NCB and Government action, respectively involving the payment of some back pay plus a Christmas bonus for those returning to work by mid-November and tighter application of restrictive benefit clauses in the 1980 Social Security Act for those not doing so. It was also accelerated by the publicity effect of televised scenes from South Wales showing the extent of the dangerous hatreds that could and did develop in mining communities between those returning to work and those who remained solid.

Here, severe injuries were feared: manslaughter occurred.

The new year brought little, if any, respite as the miners' leaders twisted and turned in the legal snares set for them. March brought for many a hugely-welcome relief from inordinate hardship as a Special Delegate Conference voted to legitimise what was already happening in many areas: a return to work. This took place symbolically on 5th March 1985.

The strike had seen the sacking of 460 miners for criminal/disciplinary

> "Congress records its total support for the NUM and its campaign to save pits, jobs and mining communities — a campaign which has inspired the Labour movement, both at home and around the world . . . Congress condemns the police-state tactics deployed against striking miners and their families . . . Congress, recalling its total opposition to the 1980 and 1982 Employment Acts . . . demands the immediate repeal of all anti-union legislation and agrees that, to that end, all affiliated unions be called upon to join the mightiest mobilisation of the power and strength of the movement at all levels."

EXHIBIT 3: **Resolution moved by Arthur Scargill at TUC Congress 3/9/84 and overwhelmingly supported**

activity and the bringing of 10,372 charges. It does not seem to have deterred British Coal (as the Board was re-named) from implementing (subject to review by the newly-established Independent Review Body) its closure plan.

By the end of 1986 there were 110 collieries left. Cortonwood (nicknamed by its doughty defenders "The Alamo"), Polmaise, Hucknall, Cadeby, Yorks Main, Comrie, Bates, Nantgarw, Cwm, Tilmanstone, Barony, Maerdy (the last of the Rhondda pits) . . . all gone, as were many others. The closure of Cadeby in November 1986, in particular, stung Arthur Scargill to fury:

> "It is becoming obvious", he declared, "that, with an employer who will not listen to logic or common-sense, the only way to save jobs, pits and communities is to take some form of industrial action." (2)

Not if the NUM's financial situation had been accurately reported by MP Spencer Baptiste during the Third Reading of the Coal Industry Bill on the 15th January 1987. In this he referred to a financial report, issued by the NUM's Finance and General Purposes Sub-Committee after its meeting on the 13th November 1986, which stated that unless action was taken the union's superannuation scheme could be in serious difficulties. The report stated:

> "The extent of the projected deficit is horrendous and the national union is rapidly heading towards a disastrous situation." (3)

In fact, the deficit was thought to be of the order of £2m. A very great cost for the NUM to bear in the light of the 46,732 fall in pit manpower since the end of the strike (to 125,631). (4)

Not that the future looks bleak for British Coal and its residual work-force. New pits are scheduled to come on stream, like Castlebridge in Scotland, Margam in Wales (where Welsh miners unilaterally agreed, against Arthur Scargill's wishes, previously unheard of productivity concessions) and the open-cast development of Douglas Valley in Lancashire. Trials of MIDAS, the automatic coal cutting system, are now well under way at Wath Colliery and are promising. Hopefully, BC is now well over what Secretary of State for Industry, Peter Walker called "the most tragic year in the industry's history". (5)

4. BRITISH STEEL

"I am pleased" wrote British Steel's Chairman Bob Scholey, "to announce that the Corporation continues its steady recovery by achieving . . . a bottom-line profit of £38m. . . . The result was better than the financial objective for the year (1985/6) set by the Government." (1)

This result represented the culmination of a colossal turnaround for BSC. It was the first profit to be earned since 1974/5 and came after 9 successive years of bottom line losses amounting in all to a staggering £5.8b. It was furthermore remarkable as it was achieved in the wake of the Miners' Strike of 1984/5 which had cost BSC an estimated £174m.

	Year			
	1976/77	1979/80	1982/83	1985/86
Total Sales (£m)	3059	3105	3231	3735
Cost of Sales (£m.): materials	1286	1582	1640	1877
employ- ment	992	1081	948	889
Liquid steel production (m. tonnes)	19.7	14.1	11.7	14.0
Employees at year end ('000)	207.9	166.4	81.1	54.2
Bottom-line profit/loss (£m.)	(117)	(1784)	(869)	38

TABLE 2:   THE BSC TURNAROUND

Source: *BSC Annual Report 1985/6*

The cost of achieving this turnaround, as reference to Table 2 shows, had been very high in terms of job losses. In 1985/6 the number of BSC employees was 32.5% of the level in 1978/9 and only 26% of that in 1976/7. A key element in the process of restructuring the Corporation and so improving productivity — 65.8 tonnes delivered/man in 1976 as against 197.4 in 1985/6 — was the EEC's thrust towards reducing European steel output and capacity. This had culminated in the imposition in 1982 of the Crisis Regime.

How bright were the prospects for a continuation of the '85/86 success? Very bright, according to Bob Scholey, provided that BSC could cope with the pressures arising from:

- the EEC Commission's Decision (31/12/85) that all financial aid to European steel producers given by their respective governments be discontinued.

  This meant that any future BSC debt finance requirement would carry market-rate interest as opposed to its being interest-free (under Section 18(1) of the Iron and Steel Act 1982).

- the US Government's restrictions on the importation of European steel.

  Whilst the arrangement specifying types and volumes of permissible imports was re-negotiated in October 1985 — and whilst BSC had mitigated its effect somewhat by shipping slabs to be finished in the USA by the Corporation's Alabama associate, Tuscaloosa Steel — the issue continued to worry the industry. No more so than in 1986 when there was increasing anxiety over the possibility of the outbreak of a EEC-USA trade war. Admittedly not primarily over steel (the cause, in fact, was Spain's accession to the EEC and the consequential cessation of some of the USA's grain shipments to that country) but problematic insofar as steel, like gin, was unlikely to escape the imposition of punitive US measures.

- the EEC's own Voluntary Restraint Arrangement deal with some Third World countries.

  The fact of a world-wide excess of supply over demand and the comparatively low cost of entry to the industry of new high-technology, low-cost producers was causing great worry to all European producers. Indications were that the giant integrated steel producing complexes of the '60s and

'70s were not necessarily the most cost-effective way forward.

Very bright also, provided BSC reached its "next immediate objective" – "financial self-sufficiency". As Bob Scholey pointed out:

"Simply making a small profit is not enough." (2)

5. FARES FAIR

Two of the lead players in the Fares Fair drama were the London Transport Executive and the Greater London Council. They are now part of the metropolis' long history since they were abolished on the 29th June 1984 and April Fools' Day 1986, respectively, as a result of two quite fundamental pieces of legislation — The London Regional Transport Act 1984 and the Local Government Act 1985. Whereas, however, the former was reborn as London Regional Transport, the latter (given the enmity it aroused in Government ranks by what was perceived to be political and financial recklessness) is unlikely ever to be exhumed.

	1985/6	1983	1981
Total traffic income (£m)	293.4	267	211.7
Cost of traffic operations (£m)	437.6	433.4	382.3
Net loss on services (£m)	140.2	164.5	169.3
Passenger miles (m)	2597	2440	2510
Bus miles (m): One-person operated bus	104	85	84
Bus crew	58	78	90
Total staff ('ooo)	24.7	27.0	28.4
Average fare per passenger mile (p)	11.3	10.8	11.5
Passenger journeys (m)	1146	1090	1080

TABLE 3:   BUS TRANSPORT IN LONDON

Source: Annual Report 1985/6

The change in the management and funding of London's transport which was achieved by these two Acts was politically, if not operationally, climactic. Whereas LTE had been since 1970 under the overall financial and policy control of the GLC (and, therefore, deeply involved not only in the original Fares Fair action but also its legally-contested fares-reduced/ fares-frozen policy sequels of 1983 and early 1984) from mid-1984 it became directly responsible to the Department of Transport. The system of support was also affected. Instead of the GLC's precepting the London Boroughs, the Government would do it in future.

As can be imagined the replacement of the heavily-Socialistic GLC by the money-conscious Conservative Government of Mrs. Thatcher as transport policy arbiters for the capital provoked much concern. Would subsidies fall? Just how much of the subsidies would be footed by London's rate-payers? Two-thirds, as allowed for by law, or less? A foretaste of what possibly lay in store was provided in the objective laid down for LRT by the Secretary of State, namely to break-even on services other than those natural loss-makers which would be covered by grant.

On the part of the Government's political opponents the concern manifested itself in the form of non-stop outrage at the destruction of one layer of London government and the removal of associated democratic rights. The outrage, and the advertising campaign, failed to halt the legislative process. Interestingly only 3000 staff out of the GLC's total workforce of 24,000 were made redundant, the remainder were absorbed predominantly among what the GLC's anti-Government advertisements listed as its heirs — "32 Boroughs, 19 Joint Boards and Committees, 7 County Councils, ILEA, City of London, 7 Assorted Quangos, a Couple of Whitehall Mandarins and a Brace of Trusts".

Has it been as bad as opponents expected? The answer depends on your viewpoint on LRT's results as evidenced, for instance, in Table 3. In interpreting these, you should bear in mind, however, that the Government has maintained the range of concessionary fares which existed under the GLC and that London ratepayers might conceivably be content with the Government's thrust towards subsidy reduction and LRT's increasing productivity.

6. FLEXIBLE ROSTERING

On the railways the union passions cooled. In 1983 British Rail — under a new chairman, Sir Robert Reid — began to pursue again, just as ardently as Sir Peter Parker had done, the el dorado of productivity targets. The unions, particularly the NUR with Jimmy Knapp by this time in the van, were equally hostile to the particular productivity advance sought: driver-only trains (DOT). But the longer the management-union dispute dragged on, the more apparent it seemed this time that the fire which had driven ASLEF over Flexible Rostering was going out in the unions' boilers. For a start, the unions' wage demands specified pay increases in excess of 30% (and a 35-hour week) in 1984 and in 1985. In complete contrast, the management responses were pay rise offers of 5.1% and 5% respectively. These were accepted by union members without any great demur. Another factor was the vote against industrial action over the introduction of DOT in 1985 by BR's guards, a vote against union executive policy hardly anticipated by the NUR leadership.

Perhaps this nascent acquiescence was not surprising if one bears in mind the Conservative Government's stringent approach to BR's External Financing Limit and the PSO. The 1986 PSO award looked forward to a 25% reduction over the coming three years almost in counterpoint to the 25% cut that had occurred in the 3 years to 1986. As Transport Secretary John Moore pointed out in the Commons on the 22nd October 1986:

> "We must get away from the idea that the only way to improve the railway is to throw more taxpayers money at it."

A further element in this tight money approach was the privatisation of BR's hotels (from 1983 onwards) and its Sealink operation (1984).

Given such a regime and, of course, the savage impact on BR's fortunes of the 1984/5 Miners' Strike, major action to save money was not unexpected. When it came, the surgery was dramatic. Huge cuts in BREL's activities affecting works at Swindon, Doncaster, Eastleigh, Wolverhampton and Springburn, resulting in the loss of no less than 7650 jobs! Even on this matter BR engineers were unwilling to take strike action.

There was indeed light at the end of the tunnel, however, as BR did win what Sir Peter Parker had called "the prize paramount". On the

28th July 1984 the Government announced its approval for the £240m electrification of the whole of the London-Edinburgh East Coast line. By the time work on this was under way in May 1985, a further £224m of electrification was being carried out elsewhere in the system.

7. DE LOREAN

The Public Accounts Committee Report published on the 18th July 1984 described the De Lorean episode as "one of the gravest cases of the misuse of public resources for many years". The evidence, stated the report, revealed "a shocking misappropriation of public and private money", "misplaced optimism" and "ineffective supervision". Whilst the major culprit is seen to be John de Lorean himself, "hardly any of those who dealt with him on behalf of the British taxpayer at a high level can escape substantial blame or criticism for their failure to prevent a major waste . . . ".

Spending Category	1980/1 outturn £m.	1985/6 est. £m.
Law, order and protective services	308	435
Industry, energy, trade and employment	338	417
Education and science	458	628
Social Security	716	1282
Total	2882	4270

TABLE 4: PUBLIC SPENDING IN N. IRELAND

This acid, but withal reasoned, judgement was one of the factors underlying the Government's decision to take legal action to try to recover some of the £79m. invested and lost by the Northern Ireland Office. The writ alleged that the company had misled the British Government and had acted "fraudulently and with gross incompetence".

It was not a judgement with which all agreed, however. The Labour Government Minister most involved, Roy Mason, for instance. He indicated in a debate in the Commons on May Day 1985 that he still believed the company could have been saved had not the successor Government's approach been so "lackadaisical". (1) He also pointed out the interesting fact that his Labour colleague Robert Sheldon, chairman of the Commons Accounts Committee which had issued the damning report, had himself been a Treasury Minister at the time of the initial negotiations in 1978!

Roy Mason's was an increasingly lonely voice, however. More commonplace was the view expressed by Down South MP Enoch Powell:

> "Ministers, civil servants and cabinets entertained a proposition which was positively hair-raising. They were confronted by a personality who, to the most ordinary psychologist, would have been recognisable as a manifest shark." (2)

"Manifest shark" or no, John de Lorean was acquitted of an $8.5m. fraud and racketeering charge stemming from his US operations in December 1986. "Praise God", he said on hearing the verdict, "I still know an awful lot about the automobile business. I'd like to devote part of my life to trying to help America become competitive again."(3) It is unlikely that such a task will be able to claim too much of his attention in 1987 as it is then that bankruptcy proceedings are due to start, with civil claims amounting to some $100m.

What of the situation in the province which had spawned the De Lorean affair? Despite the most valiant economic efforts, it was ranked by the EEC in 1986 as the second most impoverished of the Community's 139 regions with an unemployment level approaching 22%. Moreover, N. Ireland's obvious dependence on public expenditure is nowhere more evident than in its major State-owned employers – Harland & Wolff and Short Bros. The first runs one of the most technologically-advanced yards in Europe but is heavily reliant on a continuation of Government orders for Auxiliary Oil Replacement vessels. The second produces the Tucano trainer for the RAF, the Sherpa freighter for the USAF and has just won a valuable contract for the production of the Starstreak supersonic defence missile. It is very much the case, as Michael Smyth Economics Lecturer at the University of Ulster pointed out, that "Public spending keeps this place together". (4)

Economics notwithstanding, it is also very much the case that neither Harland & Wolff nor Short Bros. has been free from some of the province's cankerous sectarian and political difficulties which resulted in 1986 in a petition to the Queen to abrogate the Anglo-Irish Accord and which had, in 1978, brought American John deLorean to the shores of Northern Ireland.

8. GCHQ

The European Court of Human Rights' verdict could not have come as a worse shock to the civil service trade unions. They, with TUC backing, had taken their case against the Conservative Government's de-unionisation of the GCHQ to the highest judiciary in Europe and had fully anticipated vindication of their stand. Not only, however, did they have to listen to the Court's exoneration of the British Government but also to its findings that the unions' case was "manifestly ill-founded". Well might speakers at the unions' 1987 ban-commemoration rally in Cheltenham rail at what they saw as the "shameful", "incredible" and "disgraceful" injustice of the decision.(1) The die, at least until the next election, was cast. But there was still hope. Then, said John Prescott, Labour's Employment spokesman, his party would:

> "as one of the first pieces of legislation, restore the rights of
> GCHQ workers immediately on the return of a Labour
> Government." (2)

More difficult to accomplish than to promise, perhaps, given that 99% of GCHQ staff had already accepted the de-unionised working system which involved, inter alia, a brand-new civil service grade peculiar to GCHQ – the "Communication, Science and Technology Officer" – and a 25% rise in pay. Those who had refused to leave their union at the time of the ban and those who had since rejoined had certainly not enjoyed the latter. Indeed, they had suffered disciplinary threats and loss of increments and promotion prospects. But none of them had been dismissed.

Had Mrs Thatcher's Government been in any way deterred from pursuing its policy on the unions, as evidenced in the 1980, 1982 and 1984 legislation, by its experience over GCHQ? Or, for that matter, by the 1984/5 Miners' strike? Not at all, it seemed, if the thrust of the Green Paper "Trade Unions and Their Members" was anything to go by. Published in February 1987, this document foresaw that, if the Conservatives were re-elected, trade unionists would have the right to work in spite of a strike call by their union and that any industrial action taken to establish a closed shop would not have legal immunity. On top of the far-reaching proposals in the Green Paper, the Government also stated its intention to extend the Trade Union Act 1984 to oblige all union leaders, even those with life presidencies like Arthur Scargill of the NUM, to face the ballot box every 5 years.

The right to work in spite of a strike call? "An essential freedom" said Kenneth Clarke, introducing the Green Paper in the Commons. Labour's John Prescott thought differently. It was, he proclaimed, "a blackleg's charter".

9. INNER CITY TIME BOMB?

Mrs Thatcher's Government was clearly not unmindful of the problems − social, economic and political − of the inner cities. Despite the emphasis it had placed, loudly and continuously, on its 'get value for money', 'no irresponsible spending' (1), 'direct the money to where the problems really are' approach to public spending, it did vary the melody somewhat at the start of 1987. Public spending was to be raised in 1987/88 by £4.7 billion. "The lady" declared a somewhat tart editorial in the *Sunday Times* "turned after all." (2)

What was particularly noticeable about this increase was that the provision for local government spending in general had been upped by £4.4 billion in general − a 'realistic' and 'generous' rise said Secretary of State Nicholas Ridley (3) − and that more aid was to be targeted specifically to areas suffering from deprivation and dereliction. On top of a 9% increase in Rate Support Grant and a windfall grant of £385m. (4), there was planned spending of:

- £640m. of new money to set up new Urban Development Corporations in Trafford Park, Teeside, The Black Country and Tyne & Wear.

- £272.3m. on the 1986/7 Urban Programme allocation, representing a greater-than-inflation increase on 1986/7 of 9%.

  There was, however, a change in the basis of apportionment in favour of those of the 57 inner city areas which had, in the past, demonstrated efficient management of Urban Programme projects. Thus some would get more (e.g. Middlesborough and Birmingham) and others less (e.g. Brent, Hackney and Lambeth).

Critical of the extent to which such policy shifts had more to do with electioneering spadework than inner city improvements, the Labour opposition counter-attacked by harassing the Government over unemployment, perceived low pay and the Government's public housing privatisation policy. On the first, Labour put forward its "Real Needs − Local Jobs" programme for taking 1m. off the unemployment register in 2 years, partly by expanding the number of service-based jobs in local government. On the second, the TUC approved without demur the notion of a statutory minimum wage.

But the political ground on which Labour was fighting seemed to be getting weaker, especially after the publication on the 28th January 1987 of the Audit Commission's Report *The Management of London's Authorities: Preventing the Breakdown of Services*. This horrifyingly-titled document, issued by the Government's local government value-for-money watchdog, showed that, if the Conservative Government were open to the charge of parsimony in its inner city policies, then some inner city local authorities were equally open to charges of profligacy and 'amateurish' political management (as opposed to professional administration).

World Sales ($b) : Top Ten					
(a) Integrated Circuit Manufacturers (1985)			(b) Computer Companies (1986)		
Company	Sales	Nationality	Company	Sales	Nationality
IBM	3.2	USA	IBM	48.5	USA
Nippon Electric	2.2	Japan	Burroughs & Sperry	9.4	USA
NEC	2.2	Japan	DEC	7.0	USA
Texas Instruments	1.9	USA	Fujitsu	4.3	Japan
Hitachi	1.9	USA	NCR	3.8	USA
Fujitsu	1.5	Japan	NEC	3.7	Japan
Motorola	1.4	USA	CDC	3.6	USA
Toshiba	1.3	Japan	Hewlett-Packard	3.6	USA
Intel	1.0	USA	Siemens	3.2	W.Germany
Natnl Semi-Conductors	.9	USA	Hitachi	2.8	USA

TABLE 5 :   **THE CUTTING EDGE**

Sources: (a) *Financial Times* 29/10/85
        (b) *Financial Times* 25/9/86

The Government did not hesitate in rounding on what came to be known in the media as the 'loony left' councils whose 'totalitarian' and 'anti-democratic' stances on some issues were reminiscent of Poland and E. Germany.(5) And it wasn't just the Government. Labour leader Neil Kinnock could hardly have been ecstatic over an article in the *Sunday Times* of the 1st March 1987 by Michael Cocks, former Labour Chief Whip. Written after Labour's débâcle defeat in the Greenwich by-election and entitled 'Alibis Won't Do', the article outspokenly attacked Labour's MP reselection process, claiming that it did not allow for adequate 'middle-of-the-road' Labour rank-and-file representation in such an important decision. Michael Cocks did not, however, stop there:

> "It has to be faced" he wrote, "that the London Labour Party has done great damage to the Labour movement throughout the country. The London party seems to have an obsession. It appears to believe that, if only enough minorities can be persuaded to support Labour, a majority can be constructed from that.

> This is an unsound strategy. The majority of people do not belong to minorities or pressure groups. What can one say on the doorstep to parents who say they are doing their best to bring up a family but all the Labour Party seems interested in are gays and lesbians." (6)

That there was more than enough ammunition in the Audit Commission's Report for this kind and level of attack was beyond doubt. The facts were that 8 London authorities – labelled 'Group A' – significantly deviated from a comparative norm on a wide range of criteria, such as staffing, productivity, expenditure per household, etc. and that these authorities (Brent, Camden, Hackney, Haringay, Islington, Lambeth, Lewisham and Southwark) would have a gap between income and expenditure of £400m. in 1987/8.

> "Large parts of London" it concluded, "appear set on precisely a course which will lead to financial and management breakdown. In the Commission's view *the problems facing some London boroughs are not due solely to social and economic factors over which they have no control.*"

To rebut such a conclusion, based on such an accumulation of comparative evidence (the study covered inner city boroughs in the provinces as well as in London), was hard. The Association of London Authorities tried, calling the Report "simplistic". The Labour Party drew attention to the Report's conclusion that some London boroughs were short of grant and to the November 1986 Report of the Commons Public Account Committee which stated that the Government's spending controls were "seriously flawed".(7) But the Commission's Report remained a powerful illuminator of what Nicholas Ridley called "gross inefficiency" and a severe warning of the possibility – unless changes were made – of the spawning of a new "Urban Underclass". It was, in fact, high-quality grist to the Conservatives' mill:

> "The most damning indictment of Labour rule that I have ever read"
> said Nicholas Ridley. "It is ridiculous to try and distance oneself from
> the fact that they (the Group A Labour councils) are run by Labour
> idealogues." The origin of their problems? "It is because they have
> interfered with management and have put the trade unions before
> management in importance." (8)

The issue of 'twin tracking', dealt with in the Widdicombe Report of
1985, was seen as an especial bugbear. Under existing rules this meant
that a serving officer in one borough could be a political member in
another. Like Bernie Grant, for example, a Housing Officer in
Newham and Council Leader in Haringey. Forthcoming legislation was
intended to cope with this.

Meanwhile, the problems of the inner cities persisted. One man, Lord
Scarman, had seen them all before and was still anxious. His words are
well worth study by all of us:

> "Those suffering these disadvantages (social, housing, educational), a
> suffering greatly enhanced by the existence in our inner cities of racial
> disadvantage and prejudice, are in danger of being alienated from the
> mainstream of British society.
>
> If we allow that alienation to develop so as to become a sturdy weed
> in our Society, I fear for the future of our country." (9)

10. D-DAY ON THE BUSES

D-Day? Hardly, at least in the first few months following the second stage of deregulation. More like "All Quiet on All Fronts"! Save for the fare increases in the metropolitan areas like S. Yorkshire, where low fares had long been an article of political faith, the price impact had been minimal. So also the increase in competition. In fact the *Times* noted that by mid-February 1987 there was commercial rivalry on only 3% of routes. So also the change in the level of services.

One trend that was making itself increasingly felt was, however, the shift from traditional buses to "midis" and "minis". Much impetus was added to rising flexibility in transport services provision, which these new "buses" symbolised, by the rate at which National Bus subsidiaries were being privatised through management buy-outs. Experienced hands could see the economic value of the new modes of product and were not slow to follow Devon General's lead. By the 5th February 1987 no less than 18 NB companies were in the private sector.

The Labour party continued its opposition to the Conservative policy on bus transport. *Fresh Directions*, a policy document issued on the 12th February 1987, again pledged the repeal of the 1985 Transport Act. Buses, it stated, would be brought under local authority control by a future Labour Government and transport would be provided at fares "people can afford". By this time loss-making Leyland Buses itself had been sold off to a joint management-bank consortium.

References:

1. The Falklands Business

1. Parliament, 23 October 1986.
2. Rodney Cowton, 'Decline in merchant fleet "catastrophic" ', *Times*, 15 December 1986.
3. Hella Pick, 'Britain imposes Falklands fish zone', *Guardian*, 30 October 1986.

2. British Leyland

1. *Times*, 31 January 1987.
2. *Times*, 20 February 1987.

3. Conflict Over Coal

1. *Keesing's Contemporary Archives.*
2. *Times*, 8 November 1986.
3. *Financial Times*, 13 October 1986.
4. David Hunt, Commons, 27 October 1986.
5. Parliament, *Times*, 2 May 1986.

4. British Steel

1. BSC Annual Report 1985/6.
2. As 1.

7. De Lorean

1. Parliament, 1 May 1985.
2. As 1.
3. *Times*, 19 December 1985.
4. *Financial Times*, 30 October 1986.

8. GCHQ

1. Philip Bassett, 'Massed marchers demonstrate against GCHQ's union ban', *Financial Times*, 26 January 1987.
2. As 1.
3. Tim Jones, 'Government throws down new challenge to power of unions', *Times*, 25 February 1987.

9. Inner City Time Bomb?

1. Nigel Lawson's speech at the Conservative Conference, 10 October 1986.
2. *Sunday Times*, 9 November 1986.
3. Debate on the Queen's Speech, 17 November 1986.
4. This was grant that had been withheld 2 years previously because of alleged local government overspending.
5. As 3.
6. Michael Cocks, 'Alibis won't do', *Sunday Times*, 1 March 1987.

7. Geoff Andrews, 'Spending controls seriously flawed, say MPs', *Guardian*, 21 November 1986. This is a reference to the ways in which councils have used "creative accounting", in particular deferred purchase schemes, to circumvent Government controls.
8. *Times*, 30 January 1987.
9. House of Lords. Inner City Debate. 2 February 1987.

SUPPLEMENTARY NOTE 2

THE ANALYSIS OF POLITICAL COMMUNICATIONS

Introduction

The art of politics is first and foremost the art of communication. It is through its processes that voters are enjoined to enter a political party, that the party faithful are inspired and that the political enemy is cast down. In a democracy it is only through the skilful communication of well-crafted argument that commitment through conviction can be said to be achieved.

Politicians seeking power as a means of implementing the ideology they espouse must inevitably seek to master all appropriate skills needed for delivering the written and the spoken word. They must shine in the prepared speech, the cut-and-thrust of debate, the media interview and on the hustings. They must be as capable of stimulating the uninterested as they are of converting the sceptics and outparleying their opponents.

An inference is said to be soundly drawn from a set of arguments if:

(a)   the premises on which the conclusion is based are empirically true (i.e. provable) and

(b)   the conclusion follows logically (i.e. in a correctly-argued fashion) from them and is itself empirically true.

Example No.1

All men are mortal. Napoleon was a man. Therefore, Napoleon was mortal.

In this syllogism the minor premise is true as is the major premise, that "All men are mortal". The conclusion is empirically true and follows logically. It thus represents a validly drawn inference.

Example No.2

Some men are Protestants. Some Protestants smoke cigars. Therefore, some men smoke cigars.

Premises true! Conclusion true! The inference (Therefore . . .) is invalid, however, since the Protestants who smoke the cigars need not necessarily be men. They could conceivably be women. In other words, each part of this chain of reasoning makes sense on its own but the argued linkage of the parts does not.

EXHIBIT 1:   **VALID INFERENCES**

In this required mastery lies, however, part of the reason for which politicians tend to be unfavourably regarded by some. On the one hand they must be credibility and trustworthiness personified yet, on the other, they are known to walk in the corridors of power and to inhabit a value-driven, highly-unpredictable world in which the future is the only time dimension of any real importance. They are obliged to persist in trying to sell their version of 'certainty' to 'don't knows' on trust. Without the benefit of any proof (at least in the sense of the physical sciences) that their stratagems and tactics will work! Their concern, in willing us to share their ideological economic and societal visions, is with prophecy and promise. Actuality comes later. A clearly-experienced Shakespeare described the worst case scenario (*King Lear*, Act IV, Scene VI):

> "Get thee glass eyes;
> And, like a scurvy politician, seem
> To see the things thou dost not."

The model of the politician as a plausible, self-seeking, dissimulating rogue is necessarily far from the truth, at least in our democratic system. Nevertheless it must be accepted that an ability to verbally duck and weave, twist and turn, stonewall or counter-attack in the face of hostile probing (say from the media whose stock in trade is the cunning, 'catch-'em-out' question) is at a premium. Handling questions is a prime political art. Lessons well-learned in the hard-knock school of political dialectics are rehearsed daily in the media and in Parliament. Examples are commonplace:

- "Always give a positive answer to a negative question" and

- "If the question put is impossible to answer (it's too 'loaded'; it's an invitation to commit political suicide, etc), then simply devise one of your own that you can" and

- "Never descend without due cause from the Olympian heights of principle to the marshy plains of practicality" and

- the oldest military precept of all — "Never hand your enemy a weapon, particularly a propaganda weapon, if you can avoid it".

Note well that this comment does not signify any implied criticism whatsoever of the principles behind democratic political creeds nor of their proponents.

Instances of the artistry the politician requires in dealing with unpalatable questioning are not far to seek. What of the Labour Govern-

Deduction: The act of reasoning from the general to the particular . . . of inferring a matter of practice from a principle. "Since it's summer, that bird must be a swallow" is such a commonly-drawn (but not necessarily correct) inference. If it is the case that the premises are all known to be unquestionably true, then an *a priori* (no further proof is needed) conclusion may be logically 'deducted' without reference to the premises. Sometimes, however, 'sweeping' conclusions (i.e. invalid inferences) are erroneously drawn on the basis that premises which are assumed *a priori* to be true are, in fact, either false or not wholly true.

Induction: The act of reasoning from the particular to the general . . . from a piece of evidence to a principle – "If that bird's a swallow, it must be summer". Again, a not necessarily valid inference. "Every swan I have ever seen has been white, therefore all swans are white" was a perfectly arguable proposition. Until the discovery of Australia, that is!

Note: 'Illogical' means that a propostion has not been argued correctly. It does not necessarily mean that the propostion is 'irrational'. This latter signifies that, however well-argued the proposition, it does not necessarily accord with the speaker's view of reason.

EXHIBIT 2: TWO-WAY REASONING

ment's enforced borrowing of IMF money in 1976, the Conservative Government's handling of the British unemployment statistics since 1983, the USSR's handling of Chernobyl and the White House's Watergate cover-up in the USA? It was not easy to put a constructive gloss on, or to escape censure in some part, for such matters but, in obedience to the assumed first law of politics ('survive!'), it was attempted. No-one would wish, of course, to suggest that politicians lie: merely that they are very careful with the truth.

Of course, public information/disinformation systems dealing with propaganda and news suppression have a considerable importance in their own right. Our concern here is less grand.

It will be readily appreciated that the task of the policy analyst does not reside solely in the assessment of the genesis and viability of policies adopted in the political system. He/she must also be concerned with how politicians communicate with their audiences, their supporters and opponents. Not just in terms of systematic policy presentation – blamed instantly and sometimes irrationally by party leaders when the policies themselves are disliked by the electorate – but in terms of the comments made by politicians in public. Did a particular statement or answer to a question sound agreeably straightforward or was there a devious tone to it, however slight? Was the case plainly made or was the 'pudding overegged' by exaggeration of the virtues of the speaker's case and/or denigration of the opponent's? What is the basis on which the case was being argued — emotion or fact or a mixture thereof — and did it appear cogent and convincing as opposed to merely plausible? Was what was said so biased, tendentious and slanted as to amount to a travesty of the truth? Did it improperly dismiss contentious problems, claiming they didn't exist or that they were overplayed or that they were simply a challenge in disguise? Was a claim of frankness, honesty and plain dealing being made because the speaker was, in fact, open and sincere or because he/she had been forced into a situation where there was no alternative but to disclose the truth? Was a virtue being made out of a necessity?

The Natures of Political Utterances

A useful starting point in creating a platform for basic analysis is some familiarity with the different natures of political utterances. They can be labelled as:

- Factual and objective. "Inflation, as measured by the Retail Price Index, rose by 1% in September" is a specific, detailed and verifiable statement. A categorical statement is such a statement of fact, plain and unadorned.

- Normative. These are based on value-judgements or subjective, non-verifiable viewpoints relating to the 'oughts' and 'shoulds' of policy-making, e.g. "Inflation is the main scourge of industry", "This piece of Labour Law is draconian" and "Corporal punishment should be used in schools".

- Negative (in respect of your opponent's argument) and positive (with regard to your own). Note, however, oratorical techniques used in outflanking an adversary's arguments such as "damning with faint praise" and "the Aunt Sally". In the latter A tries to pre-empt B's attack by (a) listing what are seen to be B's major arguments and (b) presenting them in the weakest possible way and/or exposing them to ridicule. In this way B's fire is drawn. Irony is also a powerful tool. This is a satirical way of speaking in which the words said are used with an intention exactly contrary to their meaning.

- Complex/simple. Does the material itself, and the delivery of it, match the audience's capacities?

- Conditional. Such statements are beloved of politicians because they contain an escape hatch which can be used if things go wrong. For example — "If we can bring inflation down to 3% and if the trade unions moderate their current pay demands, then we, for our part, will speedily implement those social commitments which have long been one of our key priorities". The statement, as can be seen, is long on "ifs" and remarkably unspecific on "thens".

Such a basic classification is helpful but it does not answer the key question of whether the content of what is being said makes sense in terms of the arguments used. Is it logical . . . does the conclusion follow inexorably from the evidence? The following questions can be used to form a very powerful checklist in this area:

(a) Is there any equivocation here? Some ambiguity in, or mid-argument re-definition of, the terms used? Some deliberate quibbling over a part of the issue which seems not to warrant much importance as a means of avoiding dealing properly with a part that does? An intention to mislead? Any hedging of the bets through the use of qualifications such as "perhaps" and "maybe"?

(b) Is the question being "evaded", i.e. is the point at issue (which should be being addressed) not being tackled because A is fearful of losing the argument to B if it is? Has A suddenly "changed the subject"? Or is it being "begged" by one side who has assumed that their version of what is at stake is so automatically correct that nothing else need be said?

(c) Are unwarrantable (*a priori*) assumptions being made and used as a basis for untenable conclusions? For example, is it sensible to assume that the life-style of the whole of the UK is similar to that of the South East? The logical fallacy of composition occurs when we do precisely that, i.e. assuming that what is true of the part is necessarily true of the whole. Its converse — the fallacy of division — is the assumption that what is true of the whole is true also of the parts, e.g. the assumption that, because Rotherham is a town noted for its consumption of black pudding, the same is true of the entire North Country.

A conclusion which does not follow logically from the premises used is called a *non sequitur*. A particular form of this, the fallacious argument that because A preceded B, A is necessarily the cause of B. This is referred to as *Post Hoc Ergo Propter Hoc* or the fallacy of false cause. For instance, it can be argued that the advent of the military junta in Argentina played a role in precipitating the Falklands War. It certainly preceded it. But can it logically be said, as some would have it, to be the sole cause of it?

(d)   Is the way in which the statements are being made somewhat rhetorical? An elegant style masking specious content? Some slanting of the material? A little too much "affirming" for comfort . . too many "undeniables" and "absolutelys"? An excessive amount of 'playing to the gallery'?

(e)   Is the argument being advanced or countered in an invalid way by the use of a false analogy. An example of the use of such a device would be the argument that "Productivity in the UK would necessarily be improved if Japanese working methods (admirably successful in Japan) were imported into Britain". Why is the analogy (or comparison) false? Because it's based on an unproven assertion rather than a fact. Agreed it might work, but would it "necessarily" do so? Just because the Japanese system works well in Japan does not automatically mean it will in the UK. And just because you happen to be convinced that your arguments are correct does not make them valid.

Logical Fallacies

There are very many devices that are employed, in the field of politics especially, to strengthen weak arguments. Some, of which the analyst needs to be only too aware, involve 'logical fallacies'. When listening to politicians it is advisable to check for these by ascertaining whether the assumptions they make are warranted and the conclusions capable of some substantiation. Examine, in this regard, the following techniques which can be deliberately used to manipulate argument:

(i)   A cannot defeat B's argument on logical grounds so A ceases attacking it and starts attacking B personally by impugning B's motives or slurring B's reputation, for instance. Logically, one's reasons for advancing a certain argument may have nothing to do with the validity or otherwise of the argument. (The *ad hominem* fallacy.)

A particular form of this fallacy – the *tu quoque* or 'you did the same' – is widely used. A is accused by B of some unspeakable outrage (e.g. failure to keep the money supply under control as pledged previously by A). A, not being able to deny guilt, defends the position by referring to B's inability to do this when last in office or some equally horrific sin of commission or omission.

(ii) "Everybody knows that you cannot defeat terrorism in Europe unless you integrate the data handling systems of all the national police forces" is an instance of an assertion that, because X is popularly believed to be true, it must be true. This is called the *argumentum ad populum* or 'popular belief' fallacy. Indeed, in this particular case, the premise that "Everyone knows X" is it-self unlikely to be true.

Note that, however strongly and/or sincerely an assertion is made, it remains an assertion — a statement of opinion — and not a fact, unless it is capable of empirical proof.

(iii) Two fallacies involve the speaker in calling on outside help to support the arguments he is using. The first — *argumentum ad verecundiam* or the 'argument from authority' — concerns specious reference to famous people and their thoughts/actions to simply add some weight to what might otherwise be, or seem to be, a weak argument. Either that or as an indication of the speaker's erudition which is calculated to overawe an opponent! It clearly does not automatically follow that, because the illus-trious X advocated Y 30 years ago, Y is naturally the solution to our difficulties. It may be, but the proof rests elsewhere than on its mere advocacy by X, however famous he may have been.

'The sympathy vote' or the *argumentum ad misericordiam* is a different version of the same thing. Here the speaker makes a deliberate attempt to achieve his purpose by playing on the emo-tions of his listeners. For example, "We must continue the struggle . . . We must never yield . . . To do so would betray all those who have sacrificed so much for so long". It possibly is the case that this is a cogent (powerful-looking) reason for action of the type recommended. It may, in fact, be a valid (arguably sound) reason. But does it automatically make "continuation of the struggle" the right (logically-sound and rational) thing to do? That may be a different matter.

(iv) Getting one's opponent to accept some restrictions on their free-dom of manoeuvre in debate is a favoured tactic. One form is the 'disjunctive' question in which A rhetorically narrows the choice (say, of actions) available to B to only a few options and then confronts B with the dilemma of stating which option should be accepted. If opponent B naively accepts this restriction (maybe he does not recognise the tactic used), he will find that A has marshalled more than enough ammunition to destroy the case for the only option which B could possibly have chosen out of the artificial range allowed.

Another version of this is 'the impossible alternative' fallacy or the *argumentum ad ignorantiam*. In this A gets the agreement of B to proceed with X rather than Y, not by proving the viability or appropriateness of X but by 'proving' the stupidity/impossibility of Y.

This listing of logical fallacies is by no means definitive but is adequate for basic communication analysis. It will be found to be an interesting adjunct to the use of other policy analysis tools.

Categorisation of Arguments

At the heart of all political discord lie ideological differences between the involved protagonists over the means and ends of political action. These differences manifest themselves in political debate in the arguments used by politicians to support their points of view. As we have already noted, these can be knowledgeable or uninformed, 'value-driven' or factual, positive or negative, weak or strong. Further categorisation is, however, needful.

Arguments can be, for example, couched in terms which are:

(a) Economic – Support for 'X' on grounds of efficiency, cost-effectiveness, profitability, value-for-money, better resource utilisation, opportunity cost. What's the financial pay-off?

(b) Political – Support for 'X' on the basis of the extent to which it contributes to or detracts from your portion of power and/or authority. How many votes are there in 'X'?

(c) Social – Support for 'X' on the basis that it helps with the achievement of welfare and/or social integration goals. Opposition on grounds of the encouragement of divisiveness.

(d) Technological — Support for 'X' on grounds of mechanical efficiency and technical modernity.

(e) Philosophical — Recognition of the symbolism involved in the particular problem being addressed. Adoption of an historical perspective on the industrial-state of Great Britain, for example.

(f) Moral — Ethically, 'X' is to be supported as the alternatives to it are all 'evil' or 'wrong'. Religious beliefs buttress this view.

(g) Expediency — Notwithstanding the 'rights and wrongs' of the debate, a practical (pragmatic, utilitarian) view suggests that 'Z' is more appropriate as a realistic solution to the problem than 'Y'. However socially desirable 'X' is, logistical (resource) problems make it impractical.

Opponents of this position may argue that 'Z' represents an 'amoral' (possibly 'immoral') or 'value-neutral' response which is lacking in 'principle' and which casts doubt on the 'moral integrity' of its backers.

Obviously this is not a complete typology but it does provide a basic framework for analysis. Note that these arguments can be presented negatively and positively through statements, questions, rhetorical questions, aspersions and asides.

A final note. It is of critical importance to relate the argument to the interests of the 'party' advocating it. Does it represent an individual, personal, party — political group, factional, sectional, regional or national interest? Is the interest clearly declared or can it be readily inferred. 'A plain unvarnished tale' or very special pleading?

And where does the 'crux' or major 'thrust' in the arguments used lie? And do they conflict in categorical terms to such a degree that no 'meeting of minds' is possible?

THE STRUCTURE AND ROLE OF THE EEC

The thrust towards international integration, cooperation and coordination

Universal problems — security, shortage of resources, economic development, regulation of trade — have led to the increasing integration of the world community and a recognition of the need for continuing administrative coordination. Political problems, particularly those of national sovereignty, arise in any inter-governmental attempt at achieving accords, whether by codes, conventions or agreements. There is a venerable history of moves towards world cooperation, e.g. Universal Postal Union 1874 and The League of Nations 1919 (of which the International Labour Organisation still stands).

Post-war moves resulted in the establishment of the United Nations and its inter-governmental organs, e.g. Food and Agriculture Organisation, Educational, Scientific and Cultural Organisation, International Monetary Fund, International Bank of Reconstruction and Development and the World Health Organisation. Each of such specialised bodies usually has an Assembly, Council and secretariat staff.

Apart from the development of friendly relations between nations, equal rights and self-determination for all mankind, the UNO symbolises cooperation in solving problems of an internationally economic, social, cultural and humanitarian character. The Head is the Secretary-General who is the Chief Executive and Chief Administrative Officer. Organs are the General Assembly (where all nations are represented equally), the Security Council, The Economic and Social Council, The International Court of Justice and the permanent administrative body — The Secretariat. The General Agreement on Tariffs and Trade was a looser form of organisation set up by multi-lateral agreement to induce internationally:

- a raised standard of living and economic development
- development of the world's resources and full employment
- and an expansion of the production and exchange of goods via liberalisation. Cartels such as OPEC fly in the face of such an organisation.

The United Nations Conference on Trade and Development, established in 1964, works hand-in-hand with GATT and is coordinated by an International Trade Centre. Under the Economic and Social Council of the UNO come the regional bodies which facilitate coordinated action:

- — ECE : The Economic Commission for Europe
- — ECLA : The Economic Commission for Latin America

The UNO has not been a conspicuous success, due to problems of financing and lack of Federal authority. The various organs lack sufficient power and authority to qualify as instrumentalities of government; most of their powers are advisory and recommendatory. The only authority to make decisions which are binding on all UN members is the Security Council, which can empower the Secretary General to take measures necessary for the maintenance of peace and in which a Veto can be used by member nations.

The historical development of the EEC

1)   The background of financial cooperation in Europe

- ■ The European Recovery Programme (Marshall Aid) led to the creation of a system of international economic institutions to coordinate the provision of aid. The Organisation for European Economic Cooperation later acted as a coordinator of the economic recovery of Europe, encouraging the liberalisation of trade and tariffs among its members.

- ■ The European Payments Union operated from 1950 to help achieve convertibility with the dollar. It died in 1959.

- ■ The Organisation for Economic Cooperation and Development replaced OEEC in 1961. Its tasks are to coordinate members' economic policies (annual review and mutual discussion of each member's economic situation), to coordinate aid to developing countries and to supply more specialised services to its members in various economic activities.

2)   The background of military cooperation

- ■ NATO is, in political structure, an assembly of scrupulously co-equal countries — an inter-governmental organisation not, like the EEC, a supranational one. The top body is the North Atlantic Council (National Ambassadors + Secretary-General + rotating Foreign Minister as President).

- ■ Behind the NATO ring is the curious political body called the Western European Union, set up in 1955 at Prime Minister

Eden's instigation as a kind of salvage operation from the ruins of the European Defence Community. It has a twice-yearly 'parliament'.

3) **Steps towards political union**

- The formation of Benelux (Belgium, Netherlands and Luxembourg) took place in 1948: this was a customs union with no internal tariffs and a common external tariff.

- The Council of Europe was set up in 1949 and has two organs — a Committee of Ministers (unanimous voting) and a Consultative Assembly of Representatives drawn from the Parliaments of each country, which has a recommendatory function. Its purpose was to achieve greater unity and economic progress. NATO also dates from 1949.

- The Treaty of Paris is directly concerned with achieving a balanced market and balanced production of coal and steel in six countries — Belgium, Netherlands, Luxembourg, France, Germany and Italy — via the mechanism of the European Coal and Steel Community. Britain declined to join in 1951 but became 'associated' in 1954. ECSC was a completely international governing and administering system in miniature with:
  - the High Authority
  - the Common Assembly
  - the Special Council of Ministers
  - the Court of Justice

  The High Authority was conceived as a truly executive organ by the six members who signed the EEC Treaty in 1957 which aims at:

  "A harmonious development of economic activities, a continued and balanced expansion, an increased stability, an accelerated raising of the standard of living and closer relations between the member states." (Rome Treaty, Article Two)

  The aim of the Rome Treaty is economic unity; there is no direct reference to political unity, but economics can hardly be divorced from politics.

- EFTA set up in 1959.

- The six signed a Treaty in 1965 (operational in 1967) providing for the merger of the executives of Euratom (1958), ECSC and the EEC into a single Council and Commission.
- Britain approached for membership in 1962, 1967 and 1970/2. It joined, post-referendum, in 1975.

The EEC now consists of most European countries.

The Organs of the EEC

Chief among the policy areas spanned by the EEC Organisation are the following: Agriculture, Commerce, Economics/Monetary Affairs, Industry, Regional Development, Foreign Affairs, Social Policy and Competition.

(a) The Commission

This permanent bureaucracy represents the 'supranational' element of the EEC. The Commission proposes; the Council disposes. If the Council cannot agree, the Commission comes back with another proposal. There have been successive crises between the Council and the Commission and bargains have sometimes been made from sheer exhaustion. Now the Commission consults member states before making major proposals.

The Commission is responsible for administering the Treaty of Rome. Its 5,000 Civil Servants are divided into departments, headed by Commissioners (appointed for a four-year renewable term), one of whom is President for two years at a stretch. Members are appointed by their governments and are sworn to independence of national interests. The Commission meets once per week and has the feel of a national cabinet about it. In drafting legislation its success depends on the quality of its staff, the political weight and skill of its members (who have to handle the Ministers of the member Governments) and the support it can win for its proposals. The Commission does have the following direct powers:

- Can ban or fine cartels
- Responsible for the day-to-day running of the common farm policy
- Can guide coal and steel industry investment
- Watchdog over the Rome Treaty and all Community rules
- Can and does take firms and governments to the European Court
- Has a mandate from the Council to represent the Community in trade talks with the rest of the world

Each Commissioner has a personal cabinet of 5/6 assistants of his choice. The post is often a stepping stone for national politicians who hope to gain experience and return home to further their political careers.

The Commission is therefore the recommendation-making/opinion-giving element of the EEC as well as being the Executive, ensuring enforcement of the Rules laid down by the Council.

(b)   The Council

This body takes the big decisions. It sits in session opposite the members of the Commission, who are poised to defend their proposals or to suggest compromises. Formally there is only one Council, but in practice each set of Ministers (finance, agriculture, etc.) constitutes a Council of its own. The cumbersome nature of the gathering and the sometimes intractable nature of the decisions, e.g. where there are political interests at stake, make for marathon sessions. Final solutions on big issues come when the Ministers go into conclave alone without their experts. The Council can decide on majority vote, but this rarely happens and never on an issue of vital importance to any one country. An ingenious voting system operates to prevent the outvoting of more than one big country and the steamrollering of the small ones.

(c)   The European Parliament

This has neither the power, nor the prestige of domestic Parliaments. Its role is 'advisory and supervisory', i.e. it is consulted but the Council of Ministers actually legislates. It is directly elected and sits about nine times per year. Virtually all proposals from the Commission to the Council are sent to the Parliament for its opinion and discussed in parliamentary committees meeting between sessions. The Commission, although appointed by Governments, is formally responsible to the Parliament and Commission members take part in debates explaining and defending their proposals. The Parliament has the power to censure or dismiss the Commission. This is, however, an empty power as the Parliament would have no say in the appointment of a successor.

(d)   The Court of Justice

This began life with the Coal and Steel Community and consists of 11 judges and 3 Advocates-General, who advise on points of law. Their task is to interpret texts which are intended to bring about change. It can rule on cases brought by the Commission against firms, governments and occasionally by firms against Commission or Council acts. It gives advice to national courts on how they should interpret Community law but has no means of enforcing its will except by imposing fines.

(e)   The Economic and Social Committee

A tri-partite Committee, representing the unions, employers and the general interest, is required to give its opinion before legislation goes through. All Commission proposals are sent here, too.

(f)   The Pressure Groups

The Commission has encouraged the industrial federations and the unions to get together at European level and both are consulted before proposals are made. UNICE, the Union of National Employers' Federations, has a permanent secretariat in Brussels. The farmers are strongly represented also through COPA – the Committee of National Farmers' Unions – a powerful pressure group campaigning for higher farm prices. Employers in most sectors have their European Coordinating Committees.

The Budget of the EEC

The Community is stuck at a half-way stage between straight national sovereignty and some future federal democratic state. Sources of its funds are:

- Part of the customs duties charged on imports
- Levies on food imports
- Direct national contributions
- Slice of revenue from VAT

The lion's share of spending is on farm support and export subsidies, the rest on the Social Funds, salaries and administration. Each year's estimates are drawn up by the Commission and debated by the Parliament and the Council, with the latter having the final word. As direct revenues are not subject to national parliamentary control, some say that the Strasbourg Parliament should be given greater budgetary powers.

Legislative Instruments

Based on the decisions of the Council the Commission can issue:

REGULATIONS   DIRECTIVES

Based on its own decisions the Commission can issue:

RECOMMENDATIONS   OPINIONS

Structure of the EEC

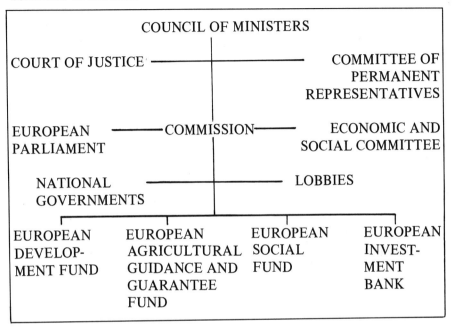

Elements of the EEC Social Policy

1) Free movement of labour:
   - Equal rights for all community members in applying for jobs in any EEC country
   - Equal treatment with local workers in respect of tax and social welfare systems, access to housing and the ownership of property.
2) Commitment to the ideal of equal pay for men and women for equal work.
3) Commitment to the concept of occupational training.
4) Major efforts on industrial health and safety.
5) Resettlements of redundant workers.
6) European Social Fund refunds to member Governments under certain conditions, half the cost of retraining workers.
7) Regional Development through assistance from the EEC Funds for:
   - regions lagging in development
   - regions whose main industries are in decline
   - regions with structural unemployment.

8) Working conditions.
9) No provision in the Rome Treaty for harmonisation of legislation in the field of industrial relations.
10) No harmonisation of social security systems.

Common Market Agricultural Policy

This consists of a detailed 'code' on agriculture. Different types of marketing arrangements exist, depending on the products involved, e.g.:

- Some imported products not directly competitive with Community production can be marketed with little intervention by the authorities

- Other products are subject to market management and protection against imports and, in some cases, direct price support.

The aims of the policy are to:

- Remove trade barriers and harmonise prices within the Community.
- To enable Community producers to compete in the market.
- To provide a guaranteed price for certain important products.

A common system of variable levies or custom duties bring the price of imports up to the Community market level, thus protecting Community farmers.

Price support, through the buying-in of certain products when prices fall below a fixed level, and the subsidising of exports of farm produce are financed by the European Agricultural Guidance and Guarantee Fund. The Fund gets its money from levies on imported produce and member states' contributions.

The Grain system — a good example of the working of the policy — has the following features:

- Main element is the COMMON TARGET PRICE. This is derived from that area of the Community which produces the lowest % of its own needs and where, therefore, prices will be the highest.

- Regional target prices are derived from this after allowing for transportation costs.

- The target price is not a guaranteed one but one that is calculated to give a fair return to the more efficient producer.

- The market price may fall below the target price, but if it falls as far as the intervention price (5-7% lower than the target price) the national farm support agencies must intervene to buy up supplies of home-produced grain to keep the price up. They are then reimbursed by the Agricultural Fund.

- The price the farmer receives is therefore between the target price and the intervention price.

A major current political problem is that of surpluses — the Milk and Wine Lakes and the Butter Mountain — directly attributable to over-production at the intervention price level. Moves in existence to curb production may be strengthened by the implementation of a 'set aside' policy in which farms are paid for not growing crops in oversupply i.e. the land is 'set aside'.

INDEX